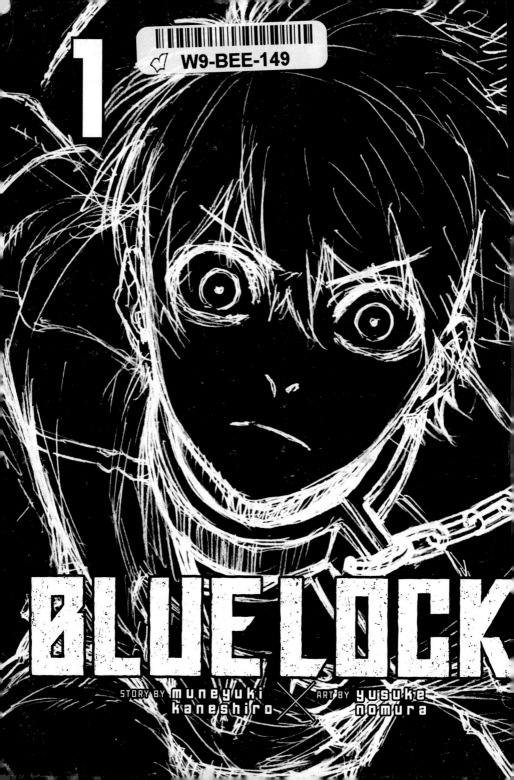

1

BLUE LOCK

STORY BY **MUNEYUKI KANESHIRO** ART BY **YUSUKE NOMURA**

CONTENTS

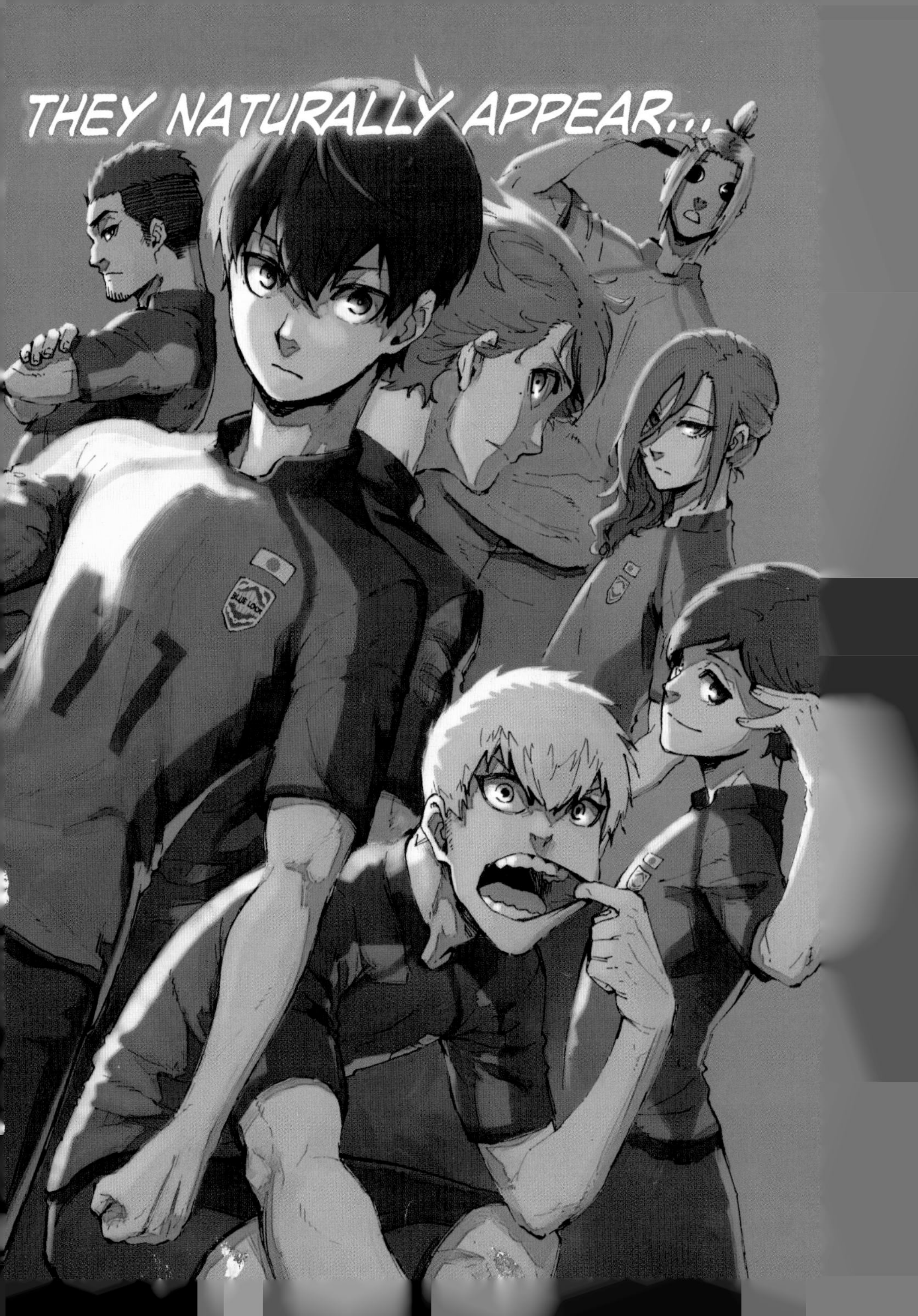
THEY NATURALLY APPEAR...

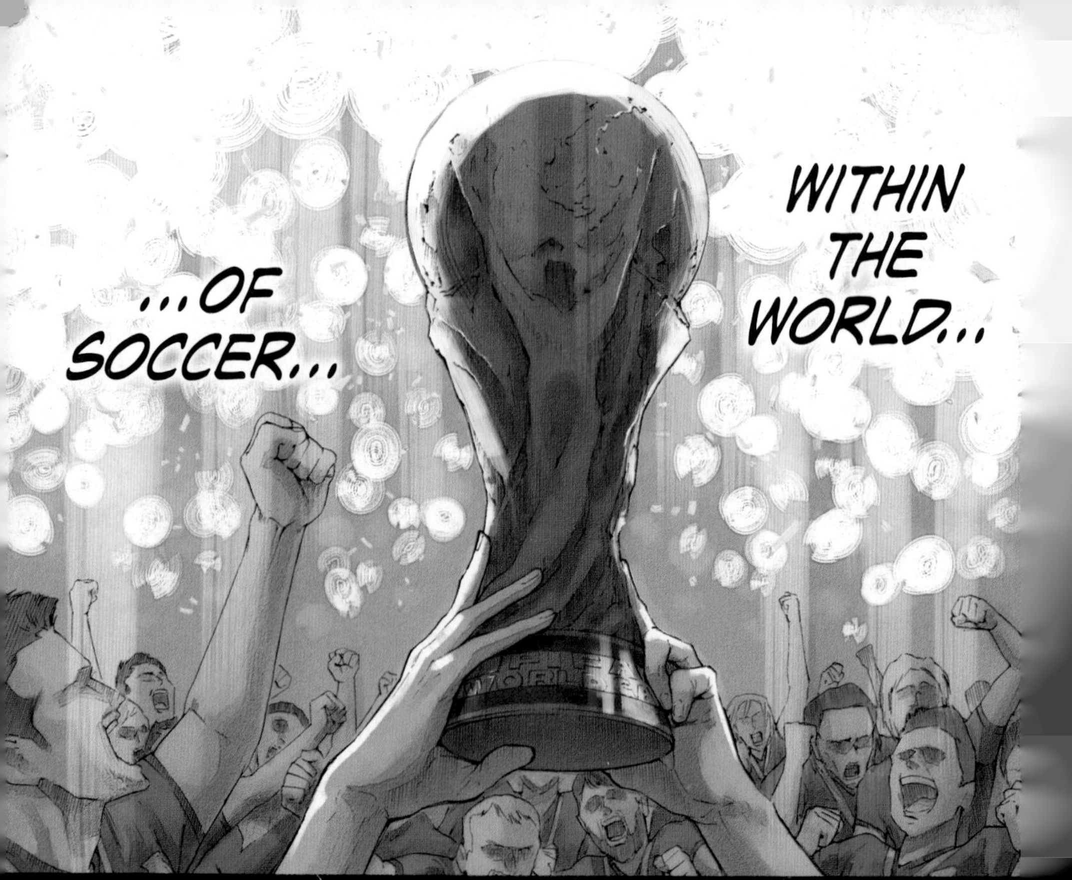
WITHIN THE WORLD...
...OF SOCCER...

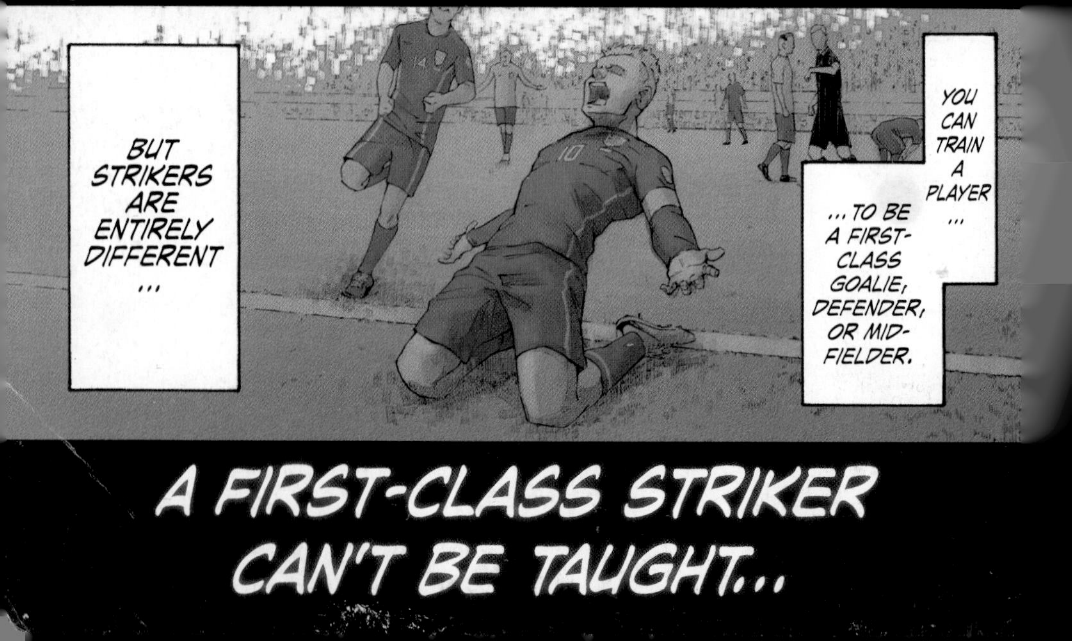
YOU CAN TRAIN A PLAYER...
...TO BE A FIRST-CLASS GOALIE, DEFENDER, OR MID-FIELDER.
BUT STRIKERS ARE ENTIRELY DIFFERENT...
A FIRST-CLASS STRIKER CAN'T BE TAUGHT...

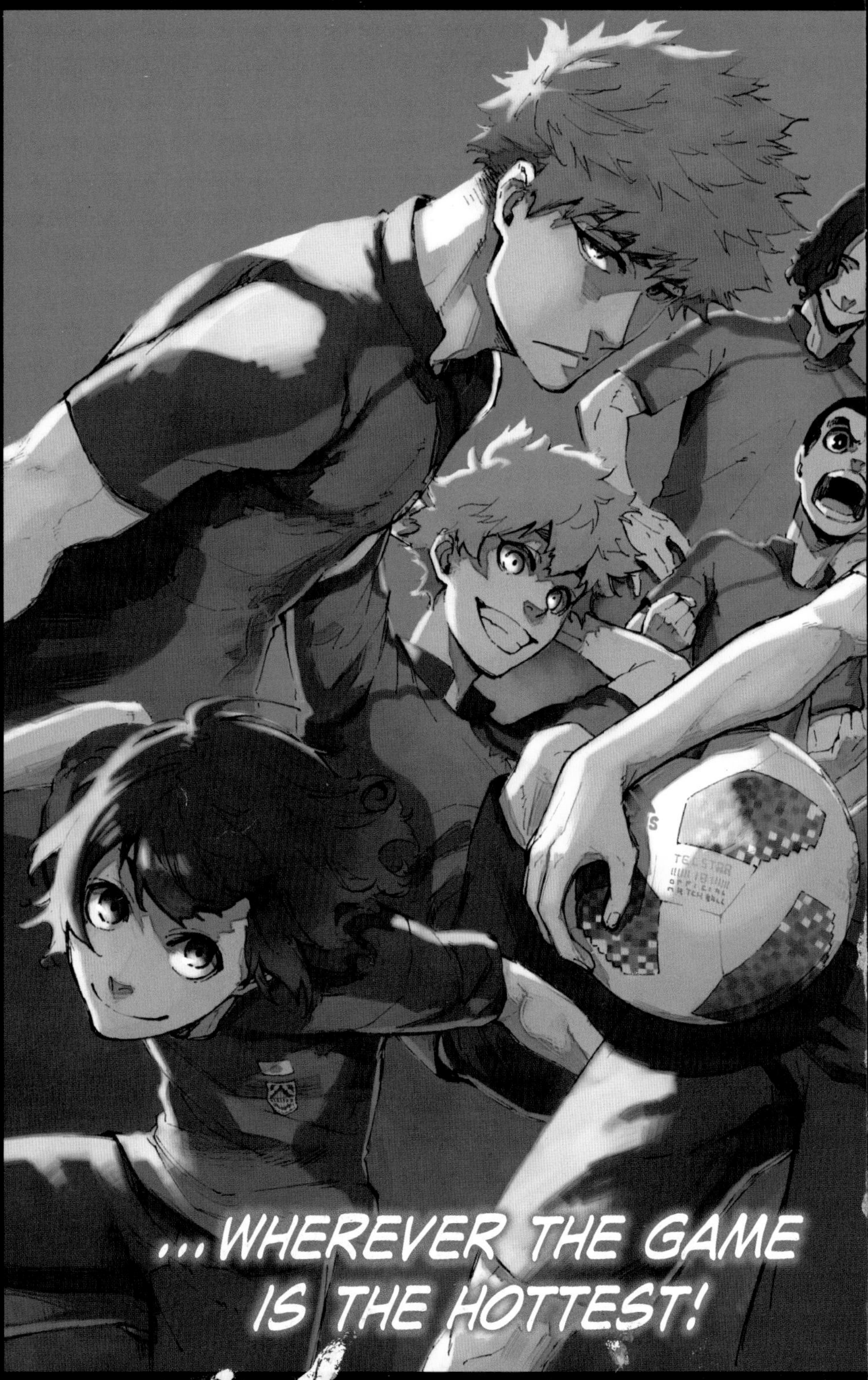
...WHEREVER THE GAME IS THE HOTTEST!

BLUELOCK

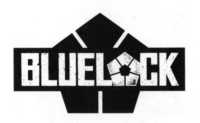

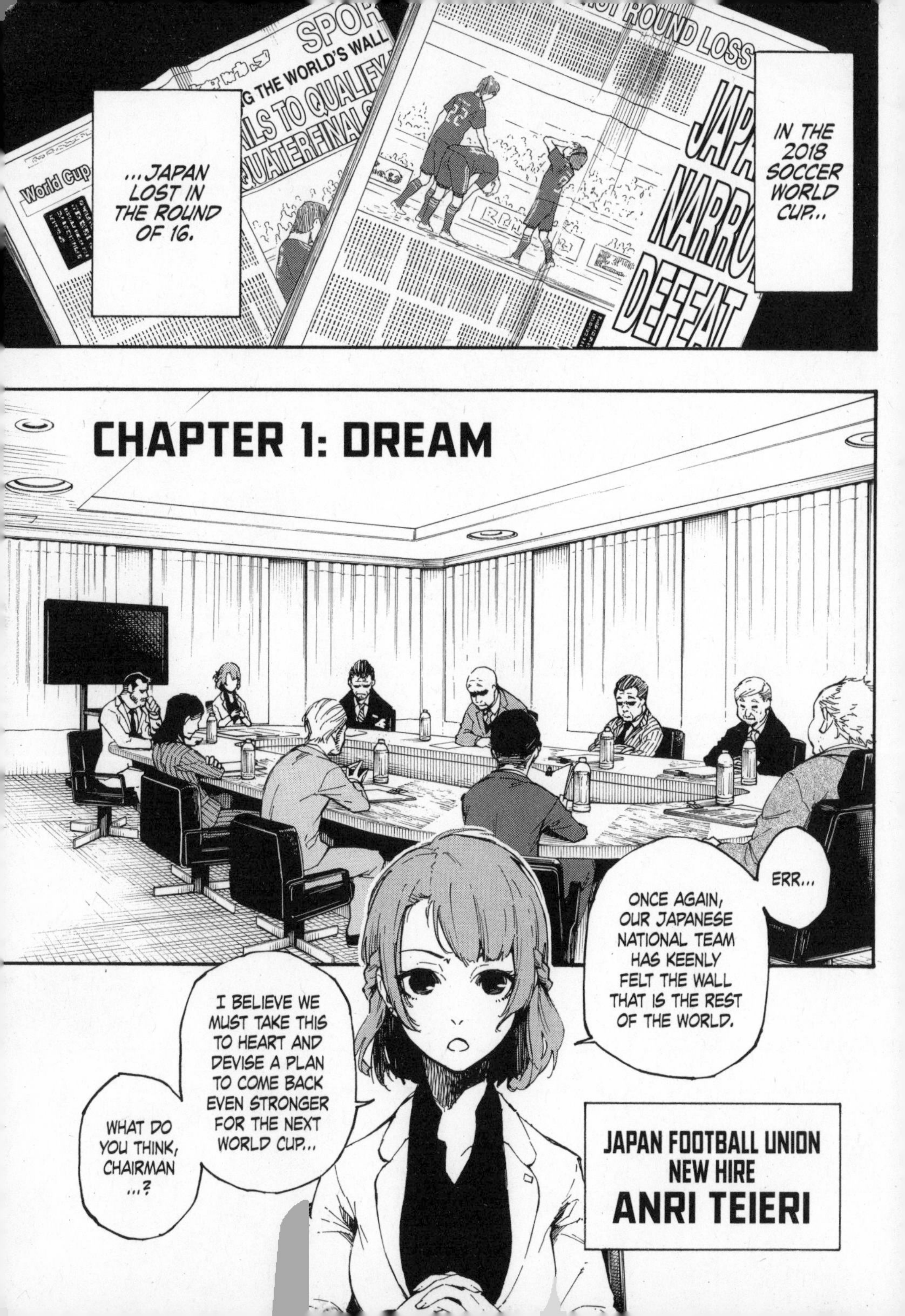

IN THE 2018 SOCCER WORLD CUP...
...JAPAN LOST IN THE ROUND OF 16.
DEFEAT
World Cup
CHAPTER 1: DREAM
ERR...
ONCE AGAIN, OUR JAPANESE NATIONAL TEAM HAS KEENLY FELT THE WALL THAT IS THE REST OF THE WORLD.
I BELIEVE WE MUST TAKE THIS TO HEART AND DEVISE A PLAN TO COME BACK EVEN STRONGER FOR THE NEXT WORLD CUP...
WHAT DO YOU THINK, CHAIRMAN ...?
JAPAN FOOTBALL UNION NEW HIRE ANRI TEIERI

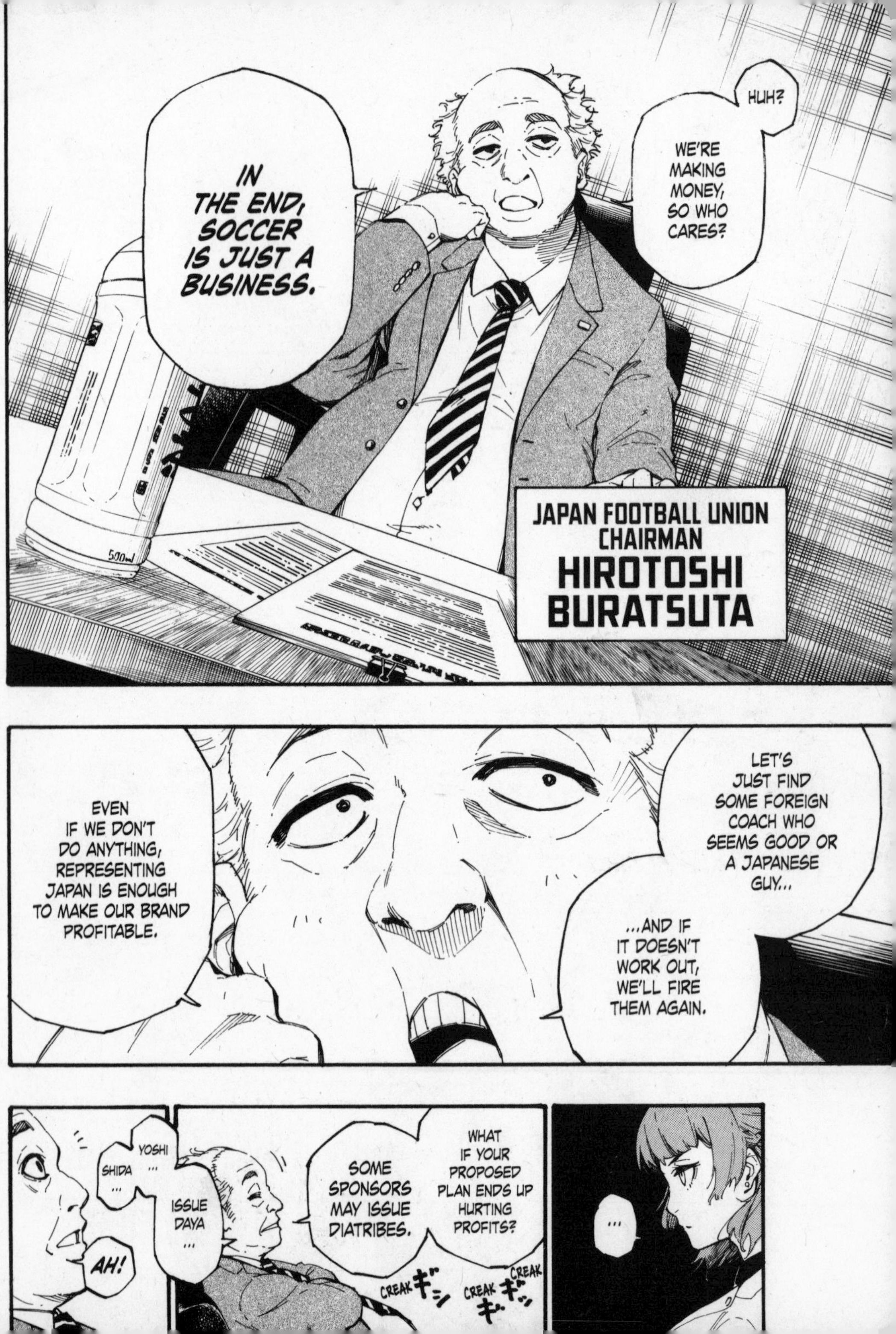
HUH?
WE'RE MAKING MONEY, SO WHO CARES?
IN THE END, SOCCER IS JUST A BUSINESS.
JAPAN FOOTBALL UNION CHAIRMAN HIROTOSHI BURATSUTA
LET'S JUST FIND SOME FOREIGN COACH WHO SEEMS GOOD OR A JAPANESE GUY...
...AND IF IT DOESN'T WORK OUT, WE'LL FIRE THEM AGAIN.
EVEN IF WE DON'T DO ANYTHING, REPRESENTING JAPAN IS ENOUGH TO MAKE OUR BRAND PROFITABLE.
...
WHAT IF YOUR PROPOSED PLAN ENDS UP HURTING PROFITS?
SOME SPONSORS MAY ISSUE DIATRIBES.
CREAK
CREAK
CREAK
ISSUE DAYA ...
YOSHI ...
SHIDA ...
AH!

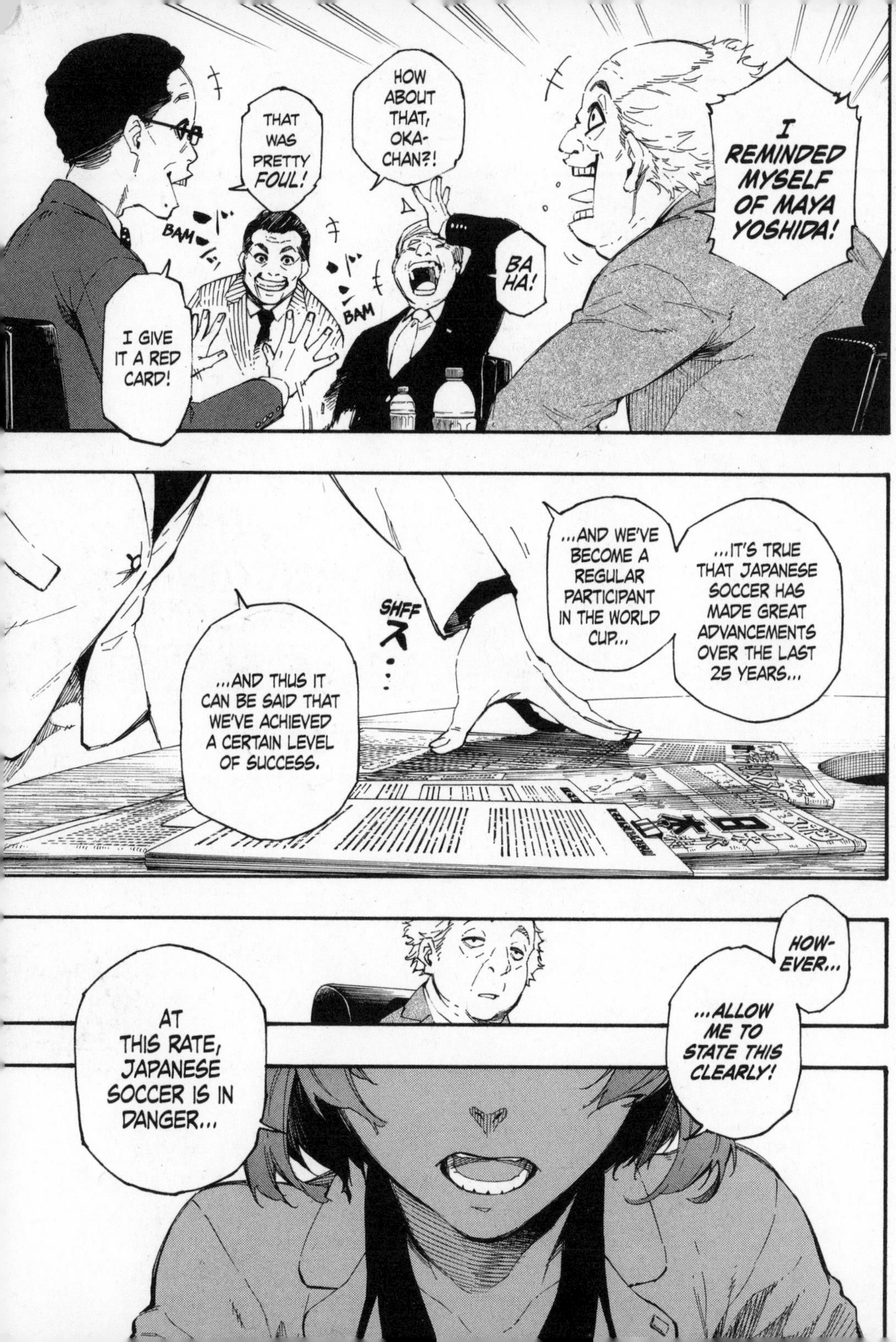
I REMINDED MYSELF OF MAYA YOSHIDA!
BA HA!
HOW ABOUT THAT, OKA-CHAN?!
THAT WAS PRETTY FOUL!
BAM
BAM
I GIVE IT A RED CARD!
...IT'S TRUE THAT JAPANESE SOCCER HAS MADE GREAT ADVANCEMENTS OVER THE LAST 25 YEARS...
...AND WE'VE BECOME A REGULAR PARTICIPANT IN THE WORLD CUP...
SHFF
ス...
...AND THUS IT CAN BE SAID THAT WE'VE ACHIEVED A CERTAIN LEVEL OF SUCCESS.
HOW-EVER...
...ALLOW ME TO STATE THIS CLEARLY!
AT THIS RATE, JAPANESE SOCCER IS IN DANGER...

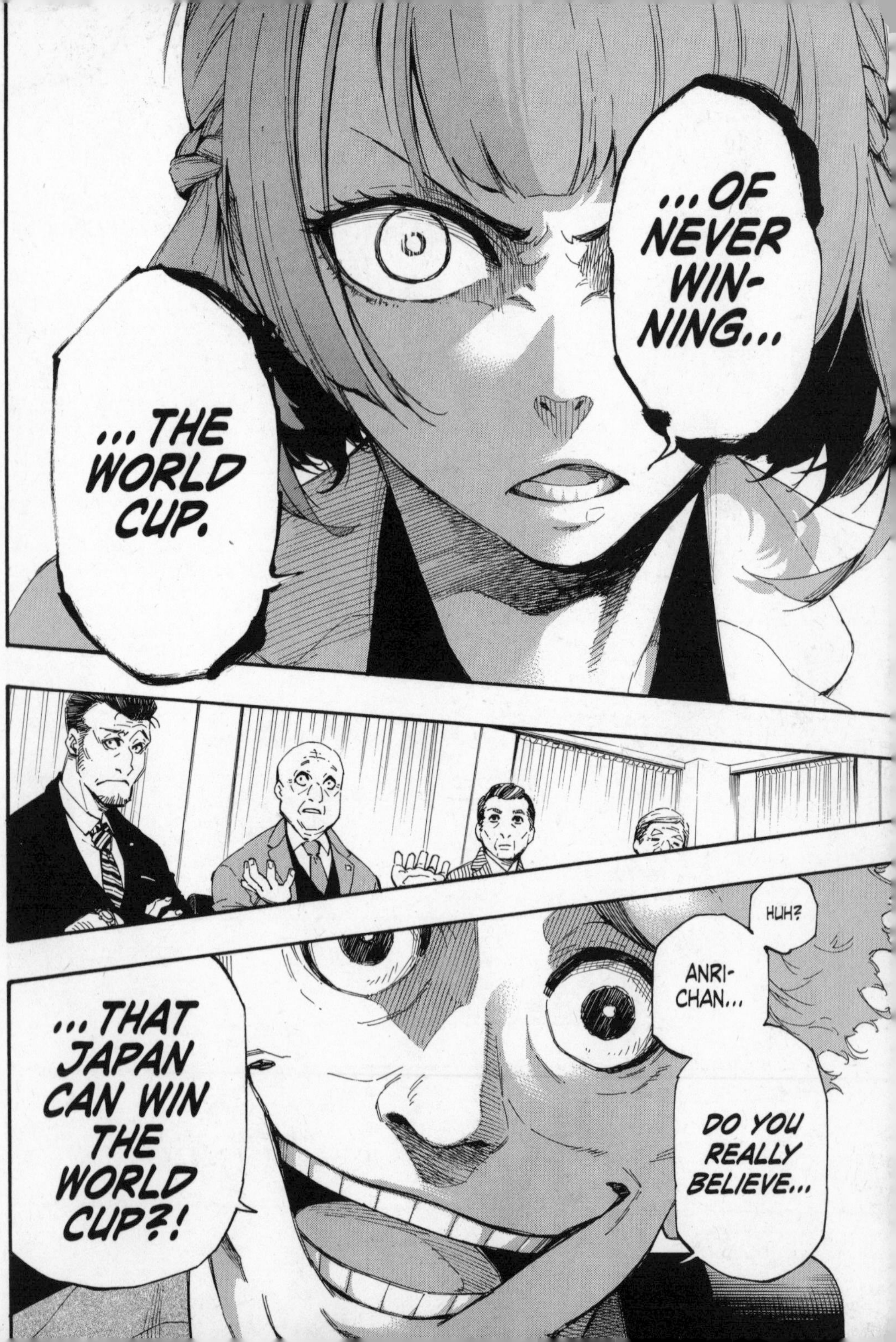
...OF NEVER WINNING...
...THE WORLD CUP.
HUH?
ANRI-CHAN...
DO YOU REALLY BELIEVE...
...THAT JAPAN CAN WIN THE WORLD CUP?!

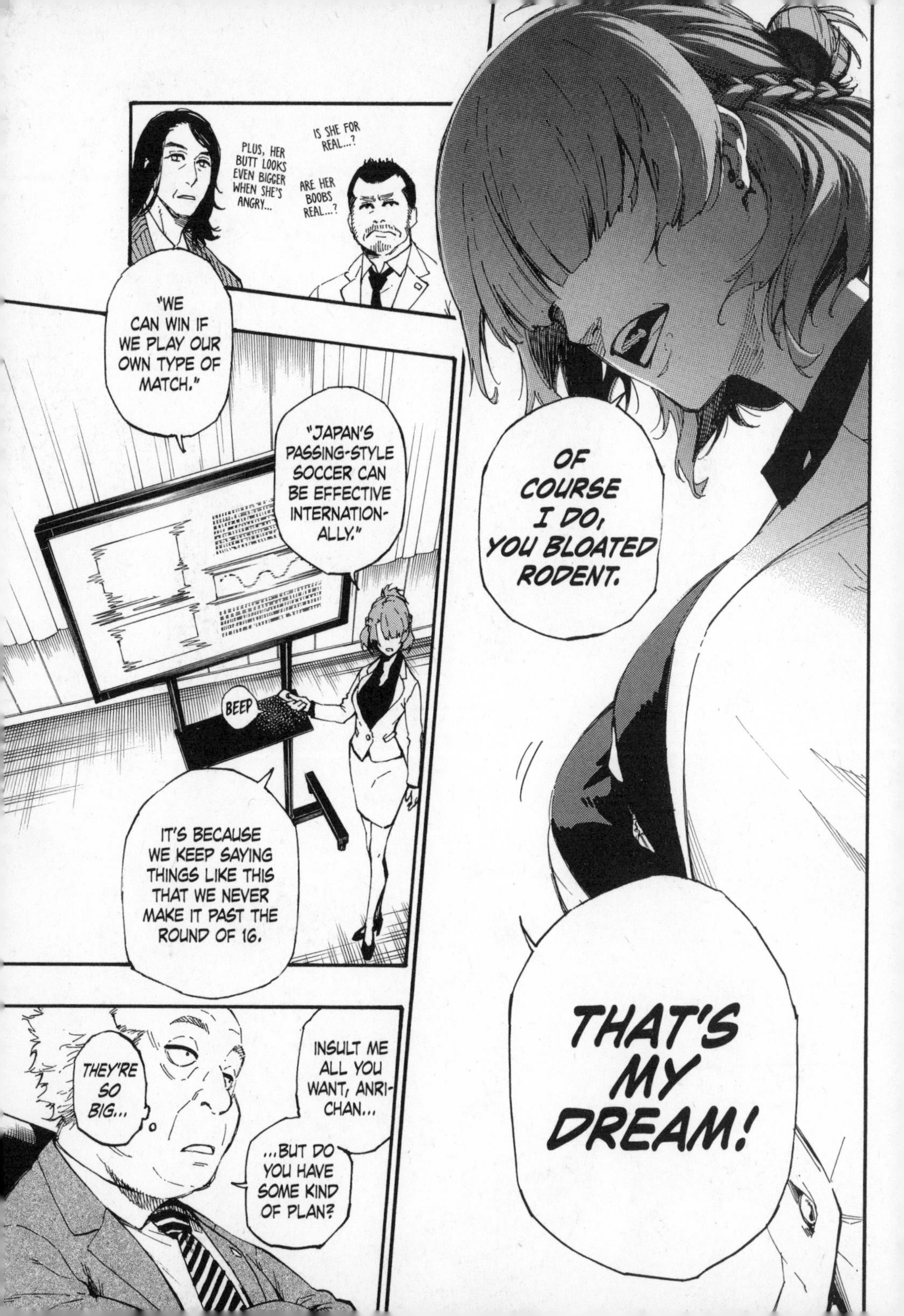
IS SHE FOR REAL...?
ARE HER BOOBS REAL...?
PLUS, HER BUTT LOOKS EVEN BIGGER WHEN SHE'S ANGRY...
"WE CAN WIN IF WE PLAY OUR OWN TYPE OF MATCH."
"JAPAN'S PASSING-STYLE SOCCER CAN BE EFFECTIVE INTERNATION-ALLY."
BEEP
IT'S BECAUSE WE KEEP SAYING THINGS LIKE THIS THAT WE NEVER MAKE IT PAST THE ROUND OF 16.
INSULT ME ALL YOU WANT, ANRI-CHAN...
THEY'RE SO BIG...
...BUT DO YOU HAVE SOME KIND OF PLAN?
OF COURSE I DO, YOU BLOATED RODENT.
THAT'S MY DREAM!

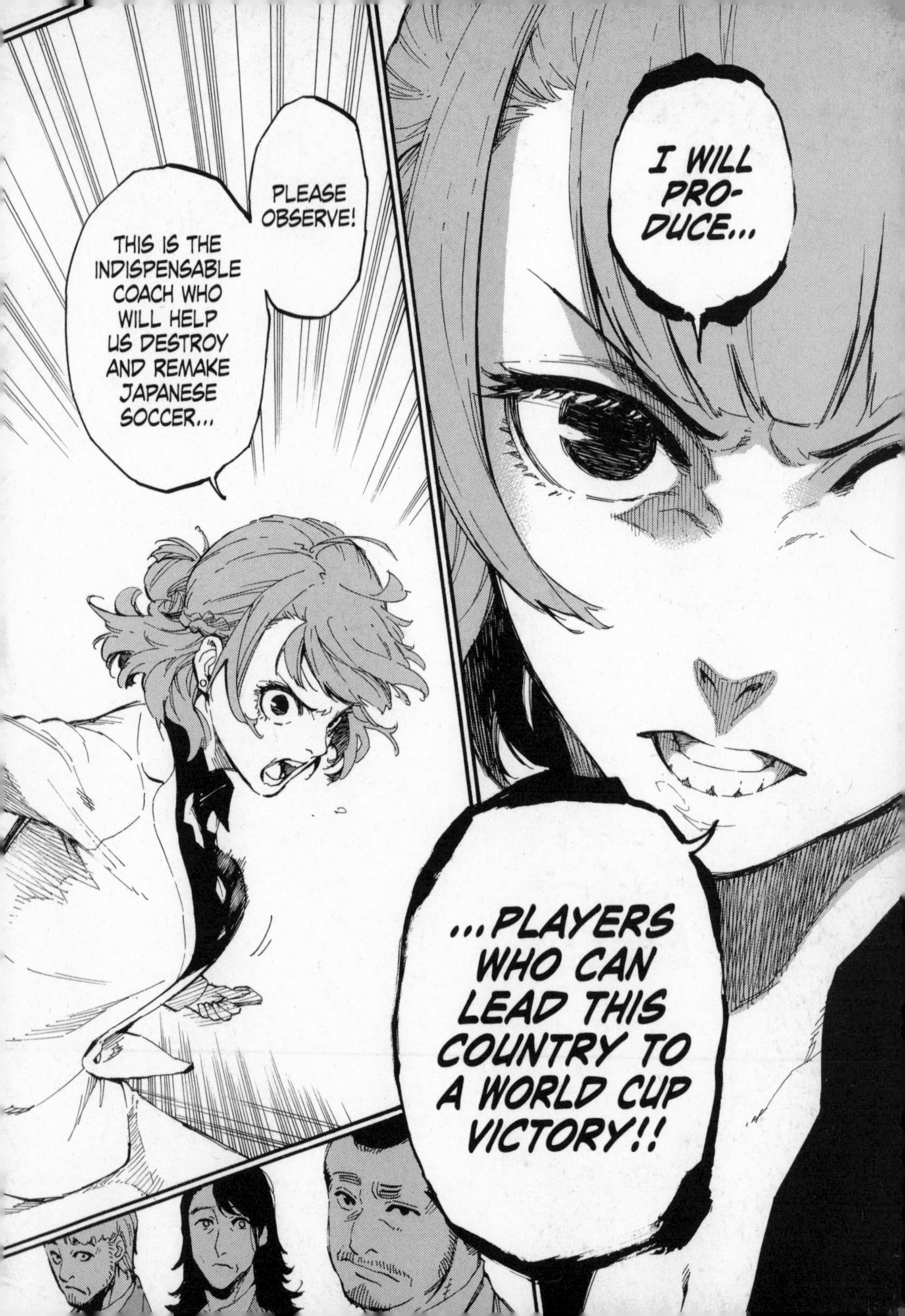
I WILL PRO-DUCE...
...PLAYERS WHO CAN LEAD THIS COUNTRY TO A WORLD CUP VICTORY!!
PLEASE OBSERVE!
THIS IS THE INDISPENSABLE COACH WHO WILL HELP US DESTROY AND REMAKE JAPANESE SOCCER...

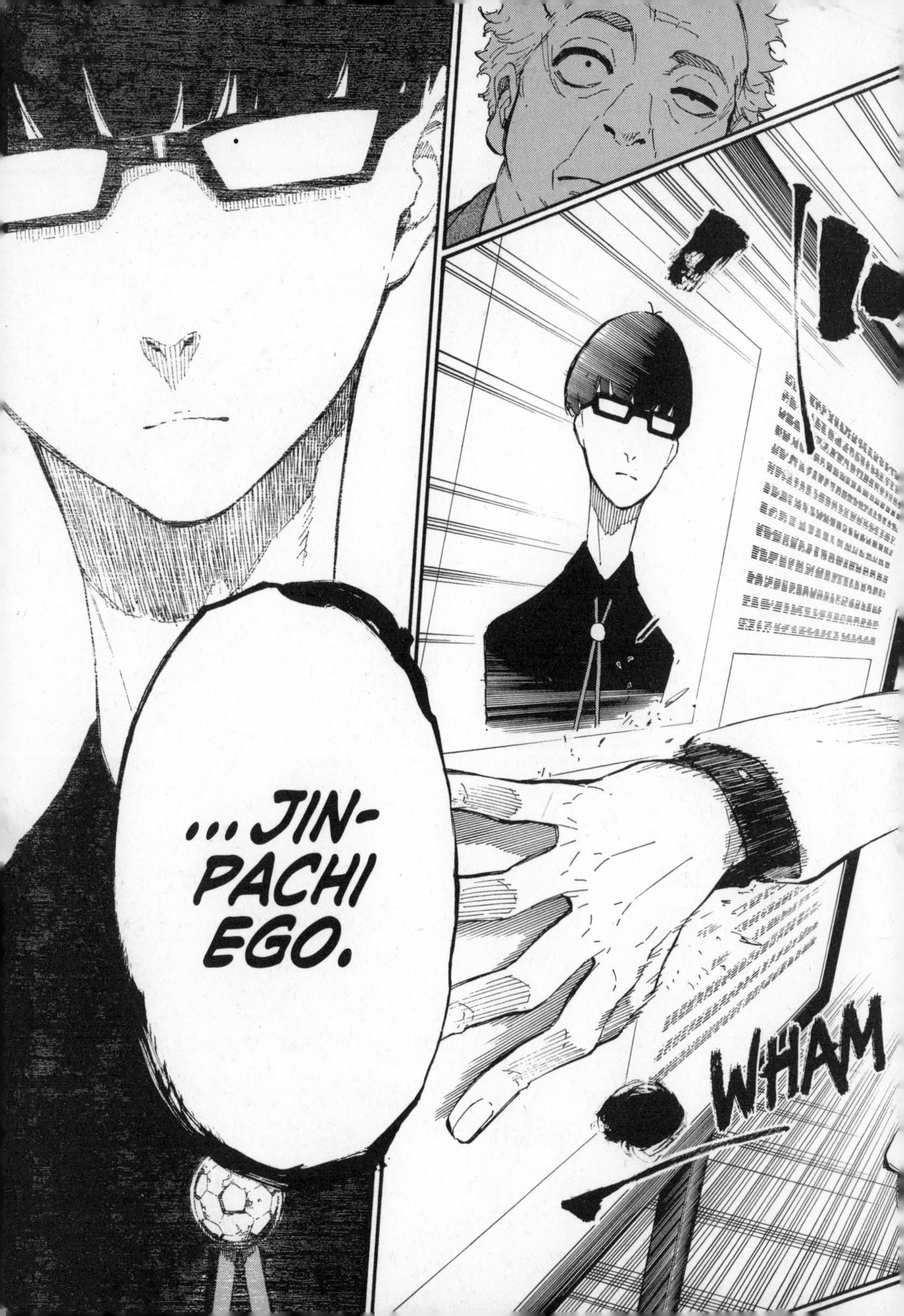
...JIN-PACHI EGO.
WHAM

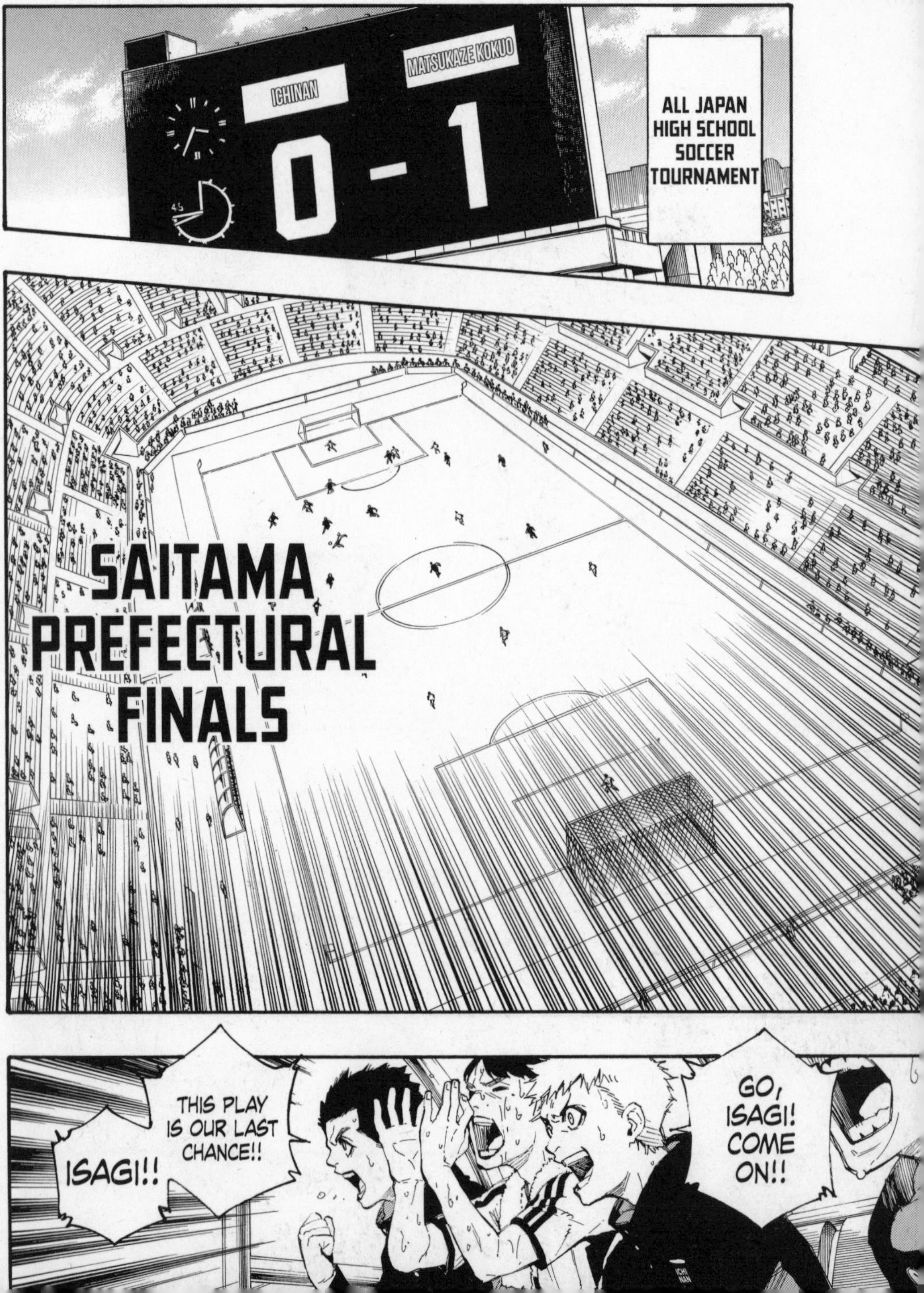
ALL JAPAN HIGH SCHOOL SOCCER TOURNAMENT
MATSUKAZE KOKUO
ICHINAN
0 - 1
SAITAMA PREFECTURAL FINALS
GO, ISAGI! COME ON!!
THIS PLAY IS OUR LAST CHANCE!!
ISAGI!!

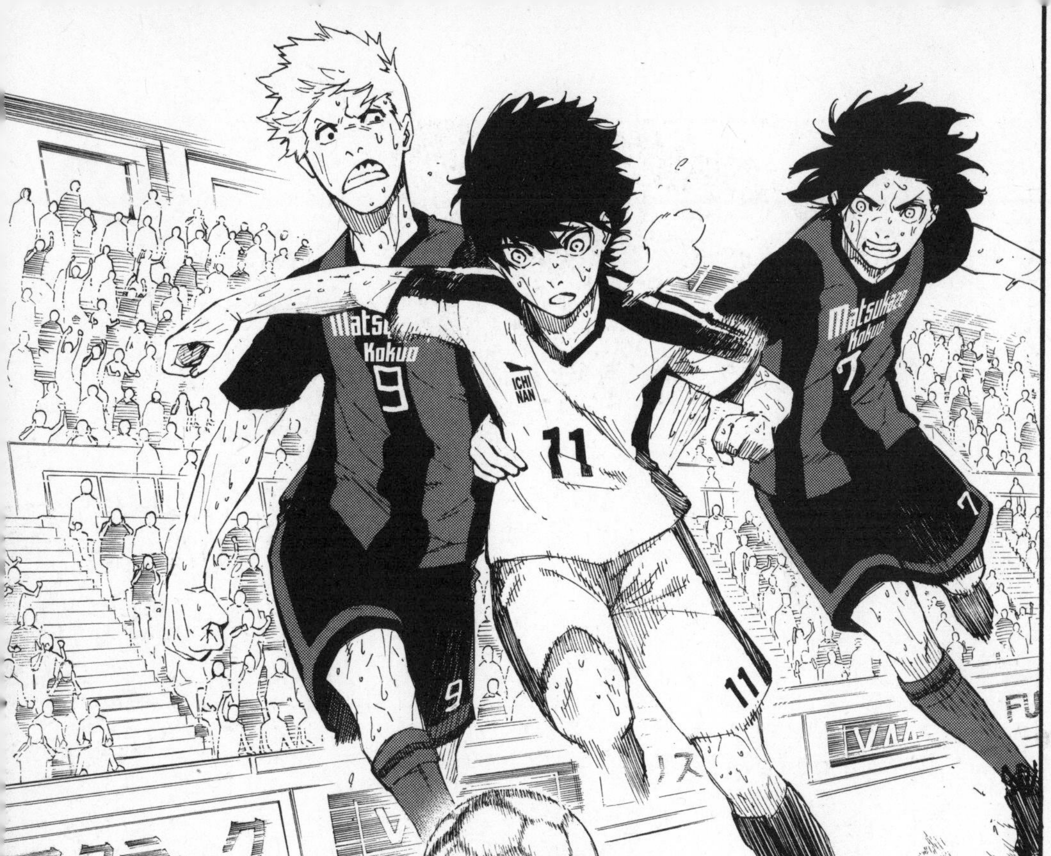
Matsukaze Kokuo
アクティック
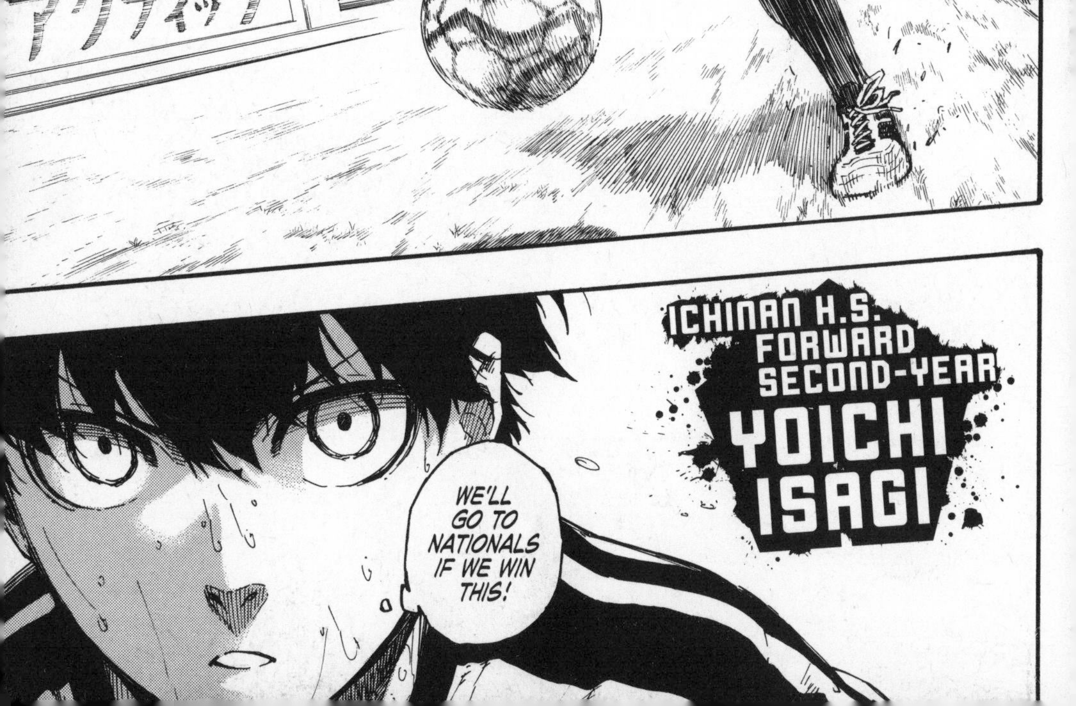
ICHINAN H.S. FORWARD SECOND-YEAR
YOICHI ISAGI
WE'LL GO TO NATIONALS IF WE WIN THIS!

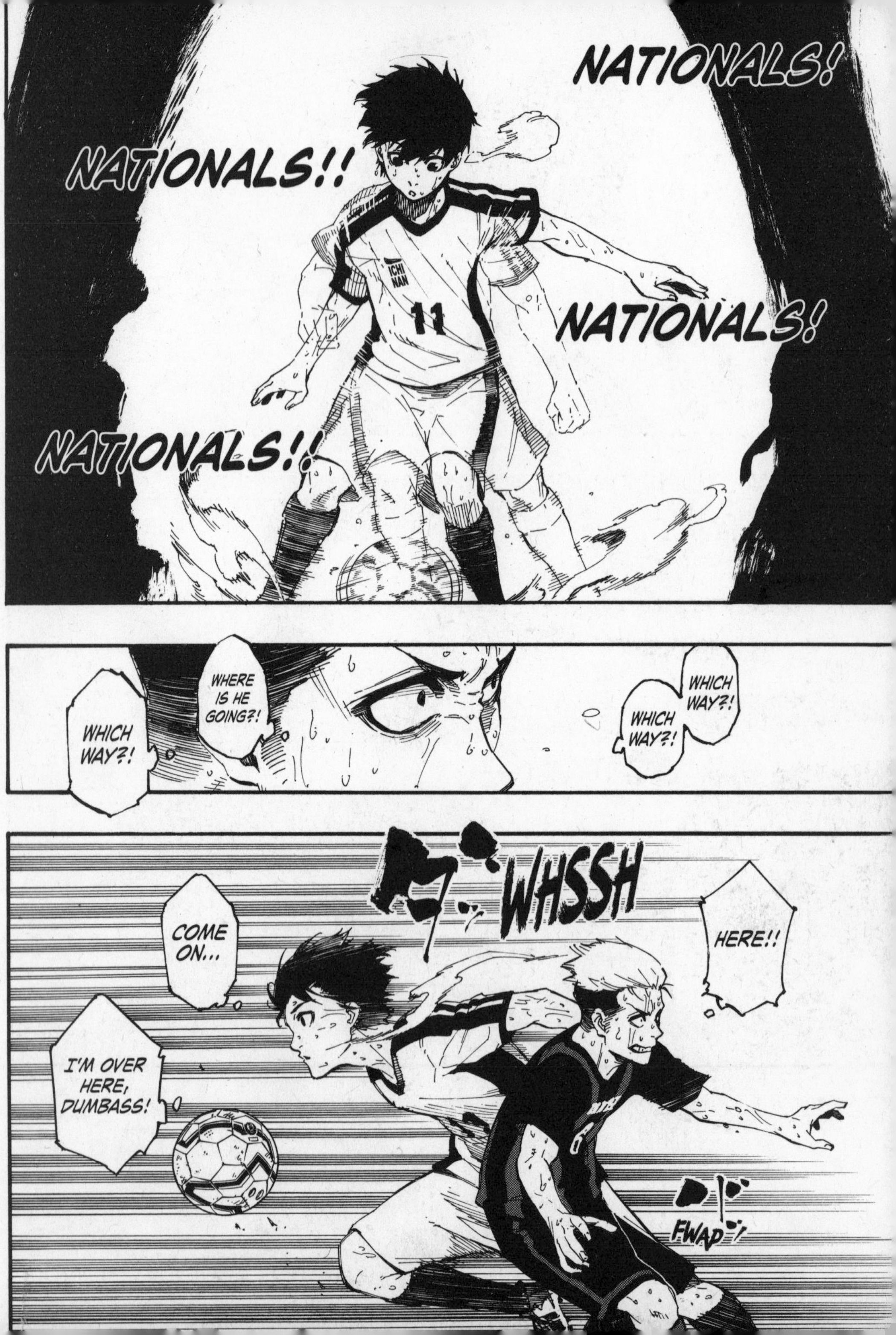
NATIONALS!
NATIONALS!!
NATIONALS!
NATIONALS!!
WHICH WAY?!
WHICH WAY?!
WHERE IS HE GOING?!
WHICH WAY?!
WHSSH
HERE!!
COME ON...
I'M OVER HERE, DUMBASS!
FWAP

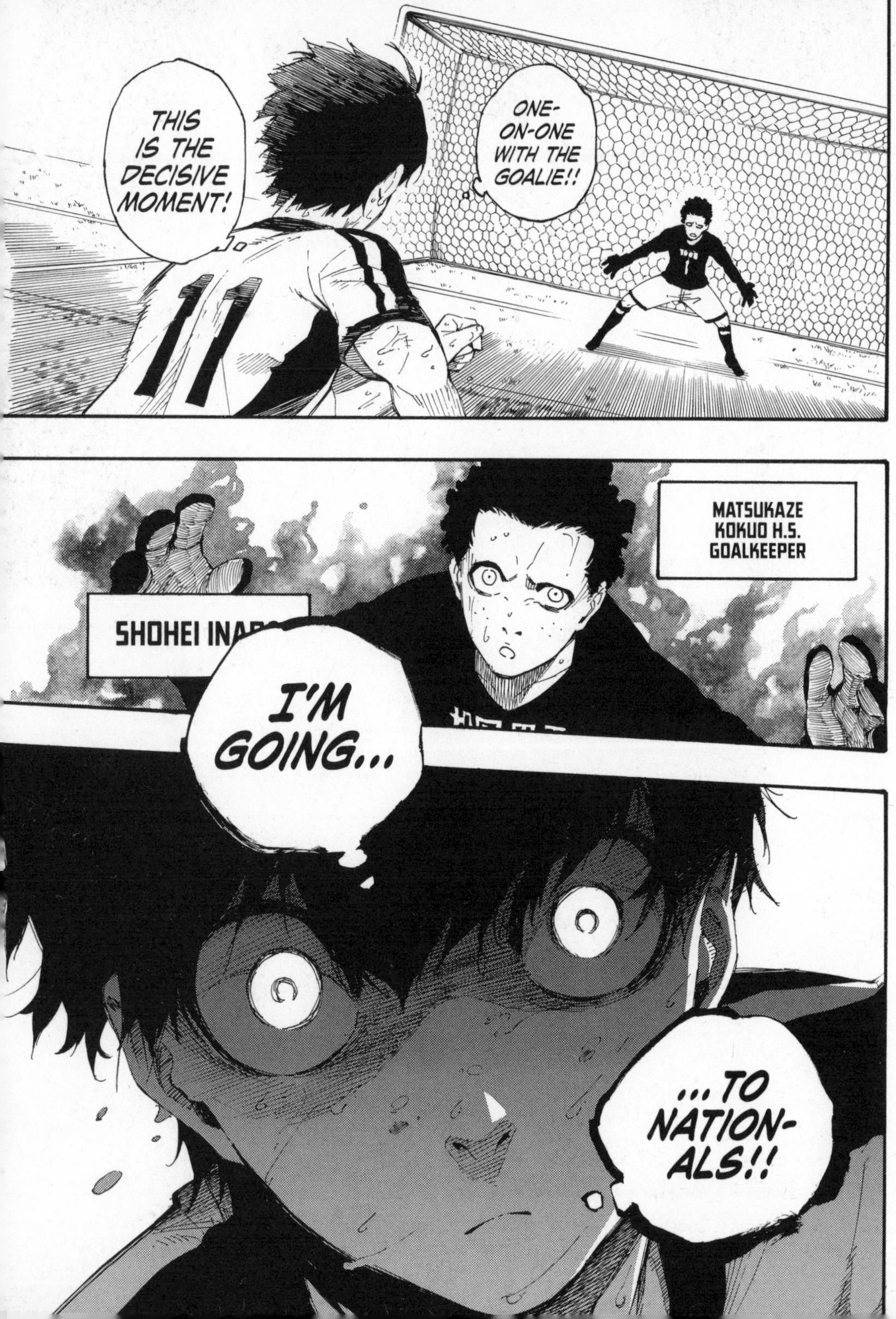
ONE-ON-ONE WITH THE GOALIE!!
THIS IS THE DECISIVE MOMENT!
MATSUKAZE KOKUO H.S. GOALKEEPER
SHOHEI INAB
I'M GOING...
...TO NATION-ALS!!

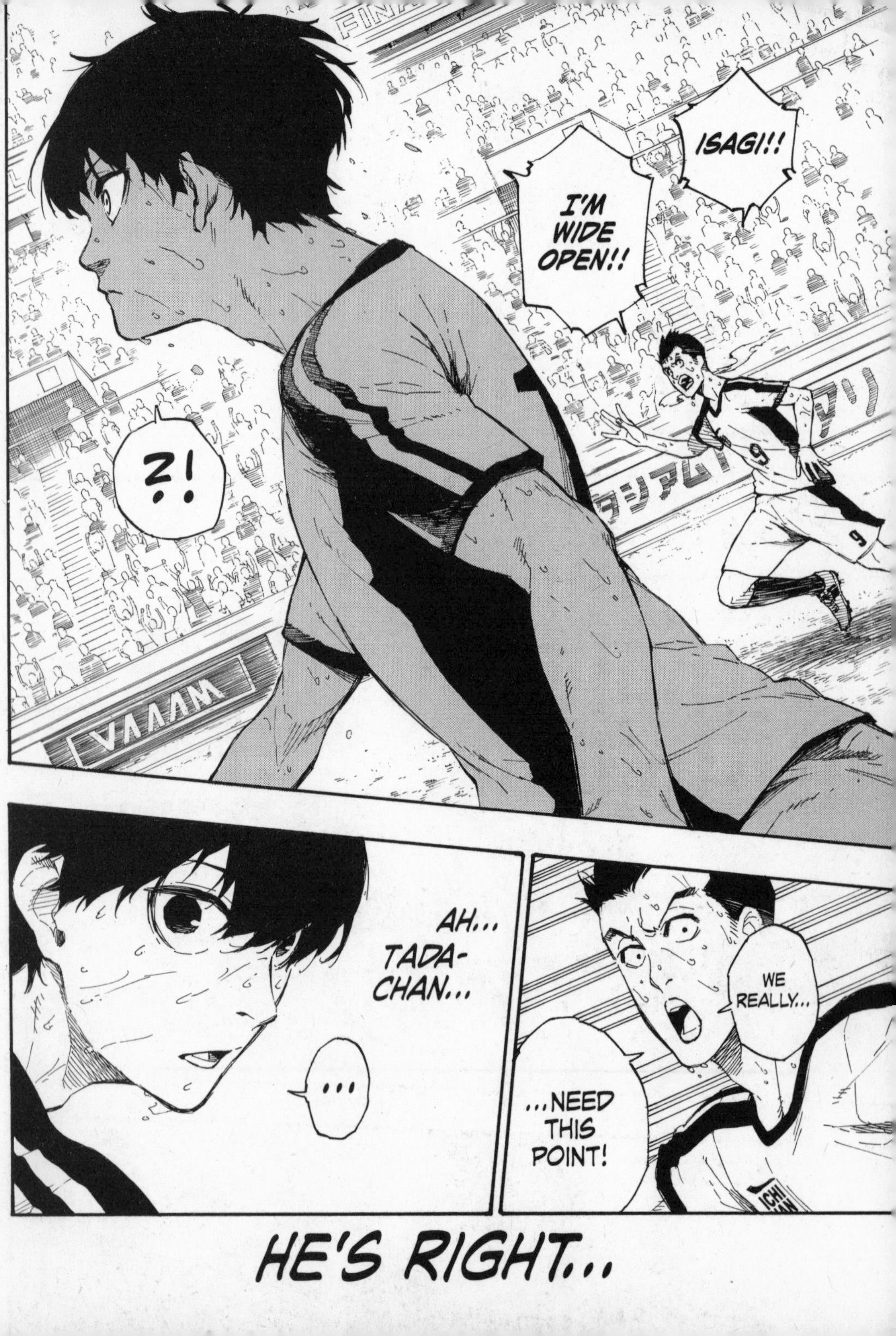
ISAGI!!
I'M WIDE OPEN!!
?!
WE REALLY...
...NEED THIS POINT!
AH... TADA-CHAN...
...
HE'S RIGHT...

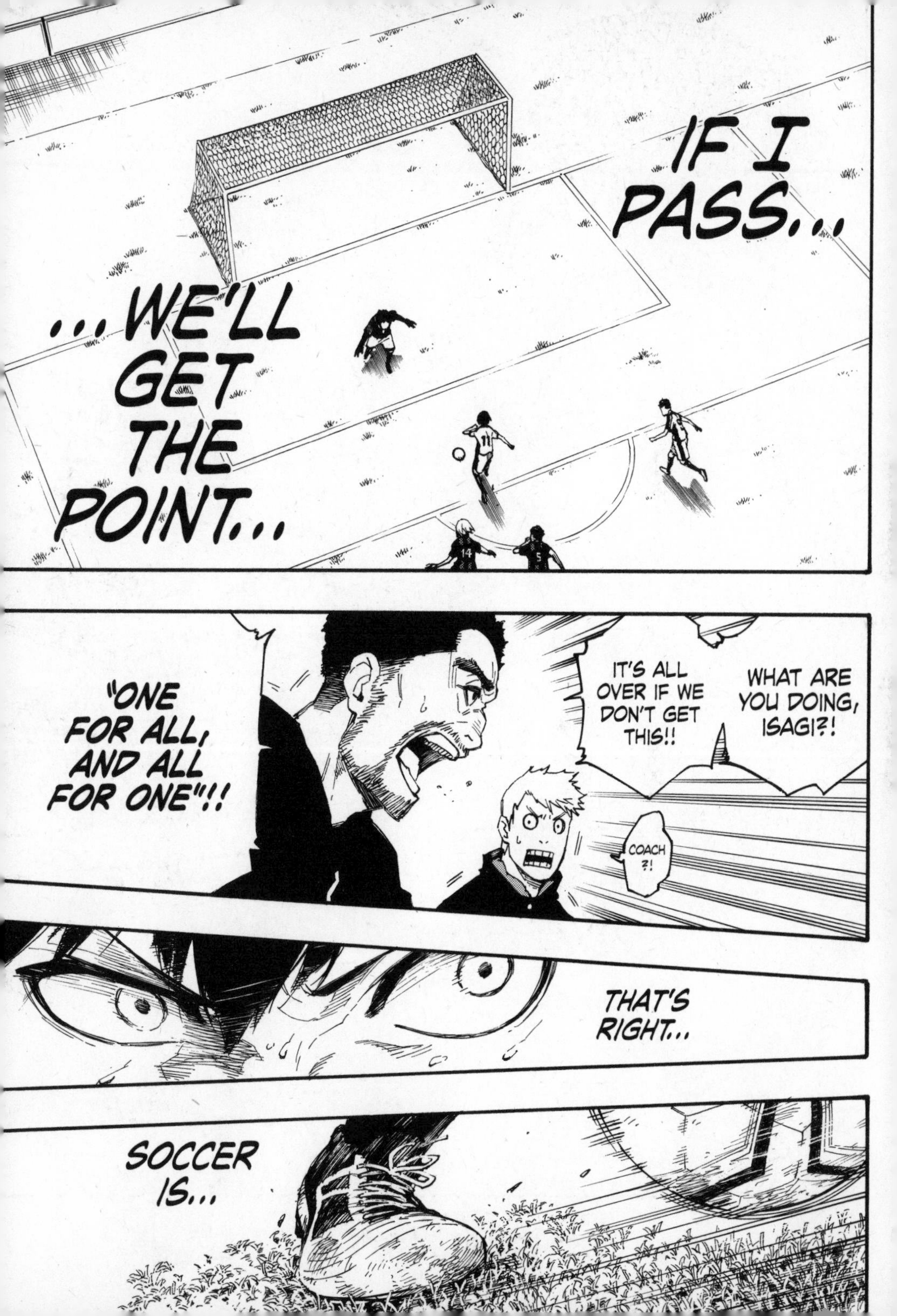
IF I PASS...
...WE'LL GET THE POINT...
WHAT ARE YOU DOING, ISAGI?!
IT'S ALL OVER IF WE DON'T GET THIS!!
COACH?!
"ONE FOR ALL, AND ALL FOR ONE"!!
THAT'S RIGHT...
SOCCER IS...

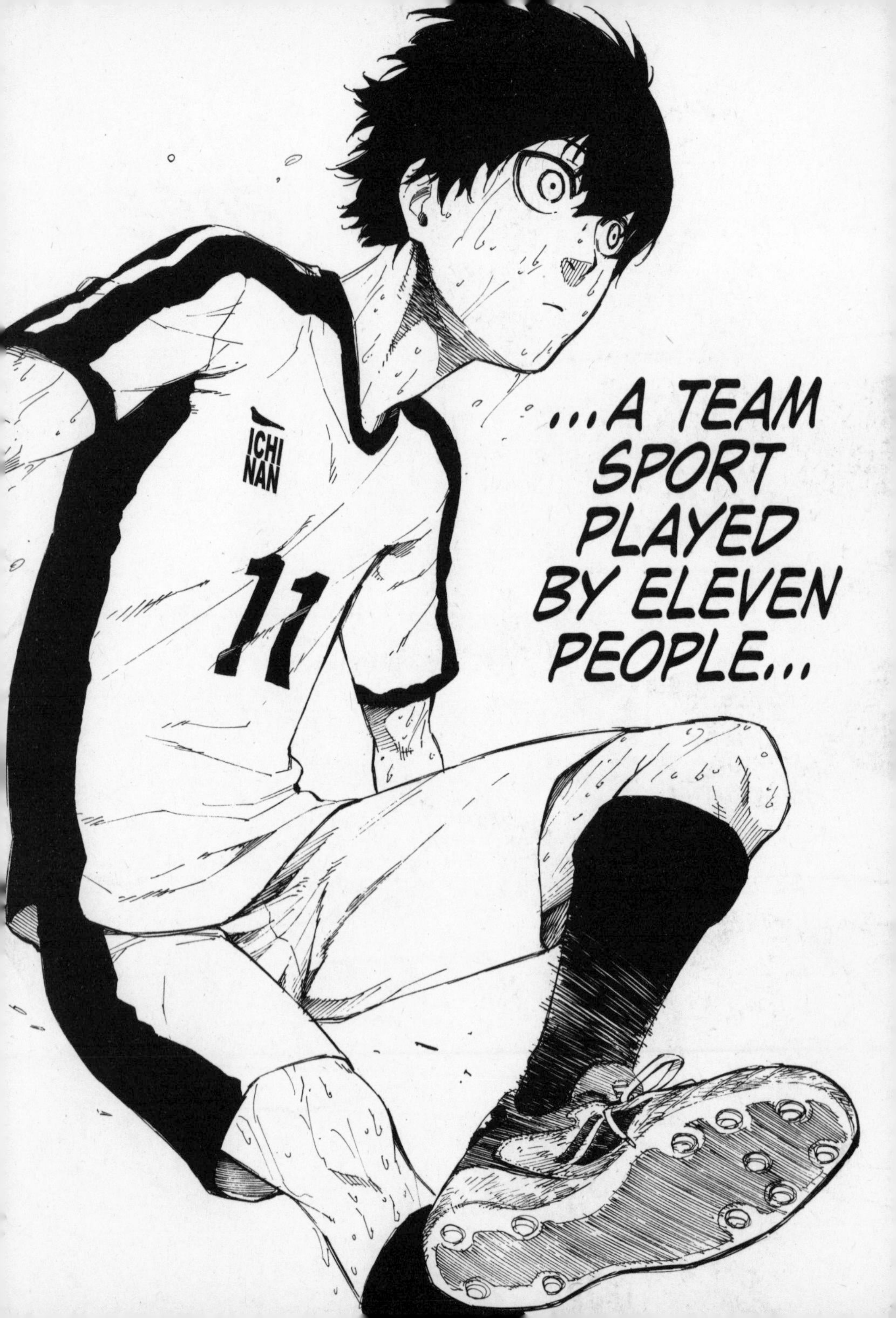
ICHI NAN
11
...A TEAM SPORT PLAYED BY ELEVEN PEOPLE...

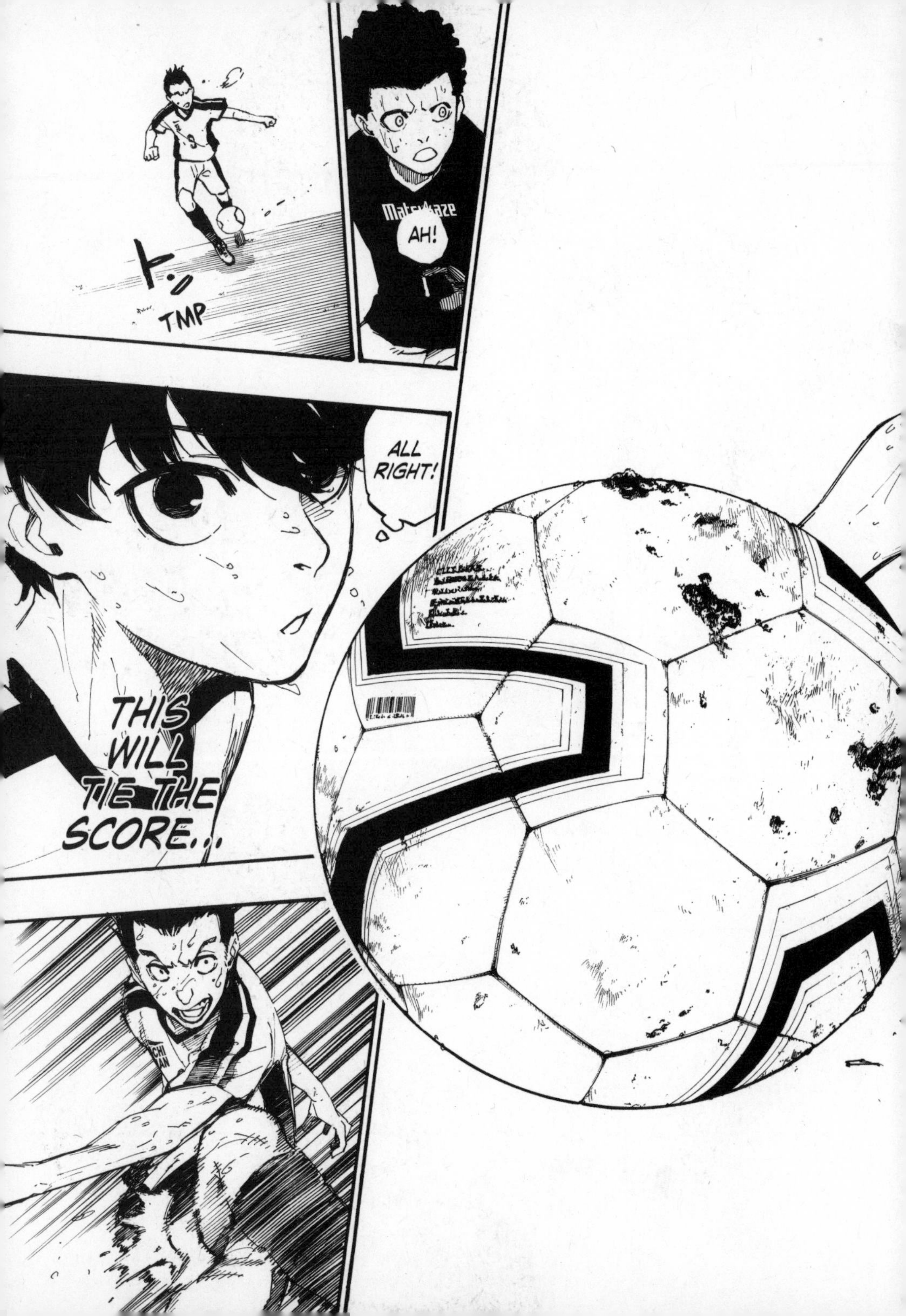
AH!
TMP
ALL RIGHT!
THIS WILL TIE THE SCORE...

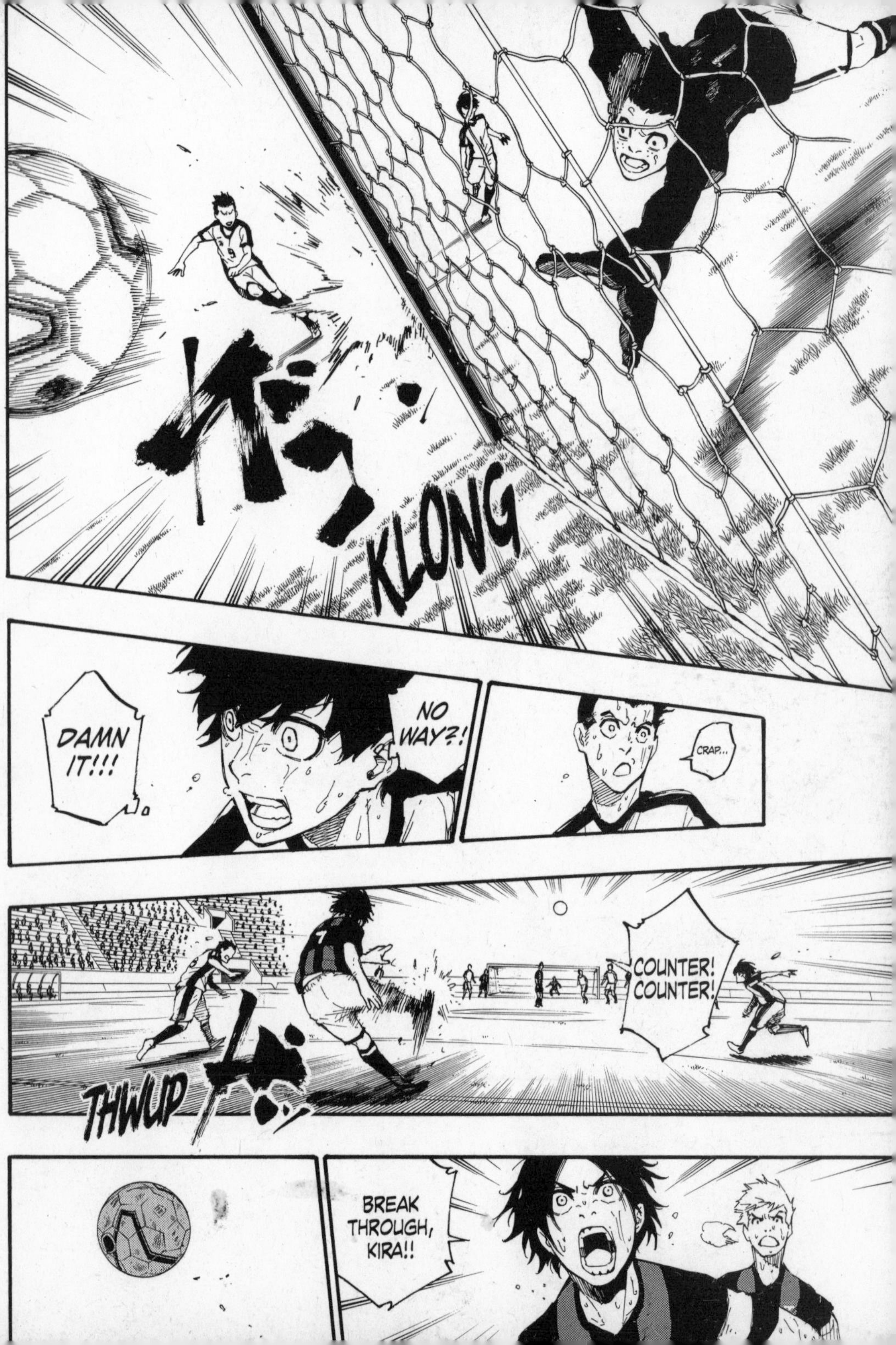
KLONG
CRAP...
NO WAY?!
DAMN IT!!!
COUNTER! COUNTER!
THWUP
BREAK THROUGH, KIRA!!

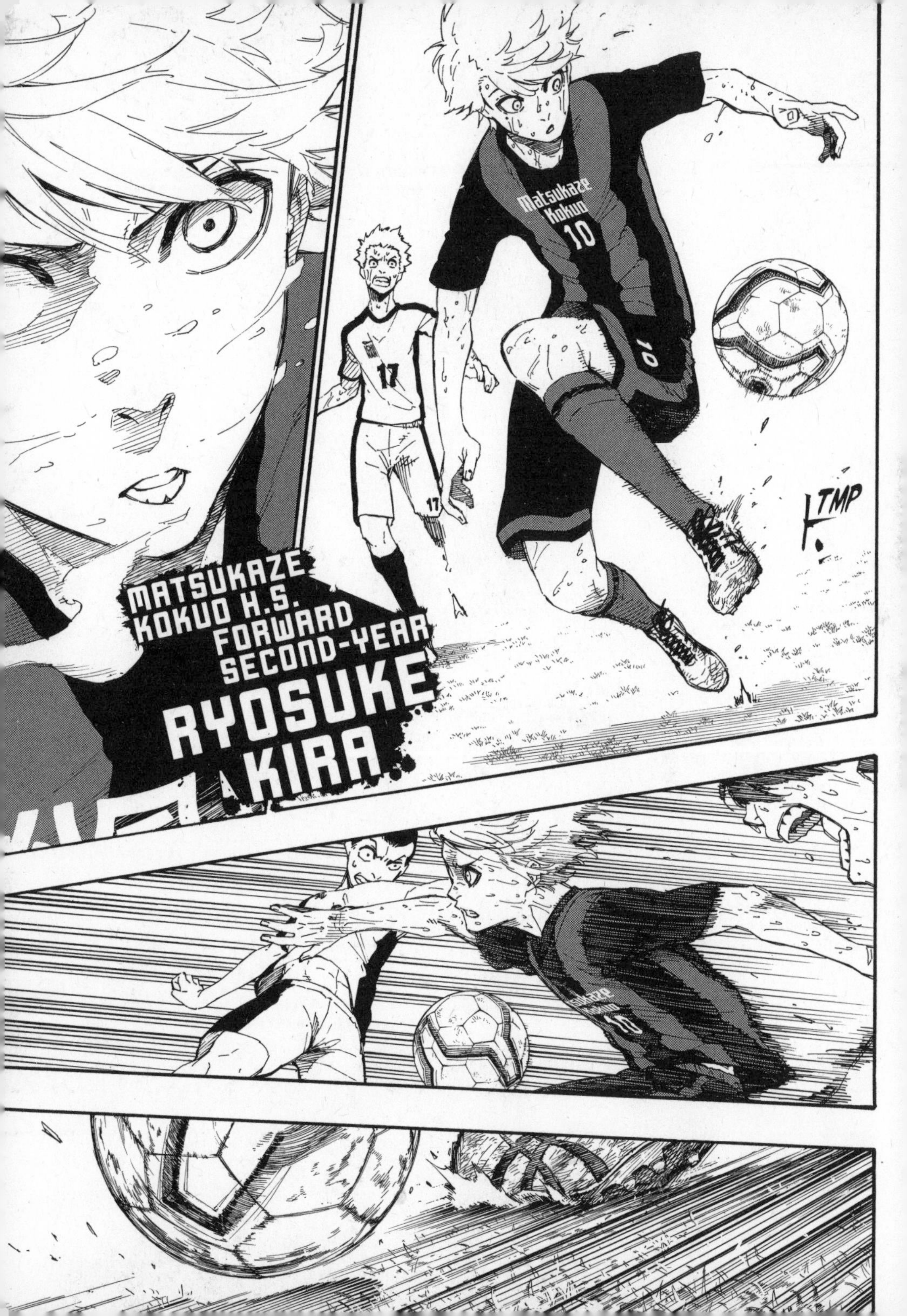

TMP
MATSUKAZE KOKUO H.S. FORWARD SECOND-YEAR
RYOSUKE KIRA

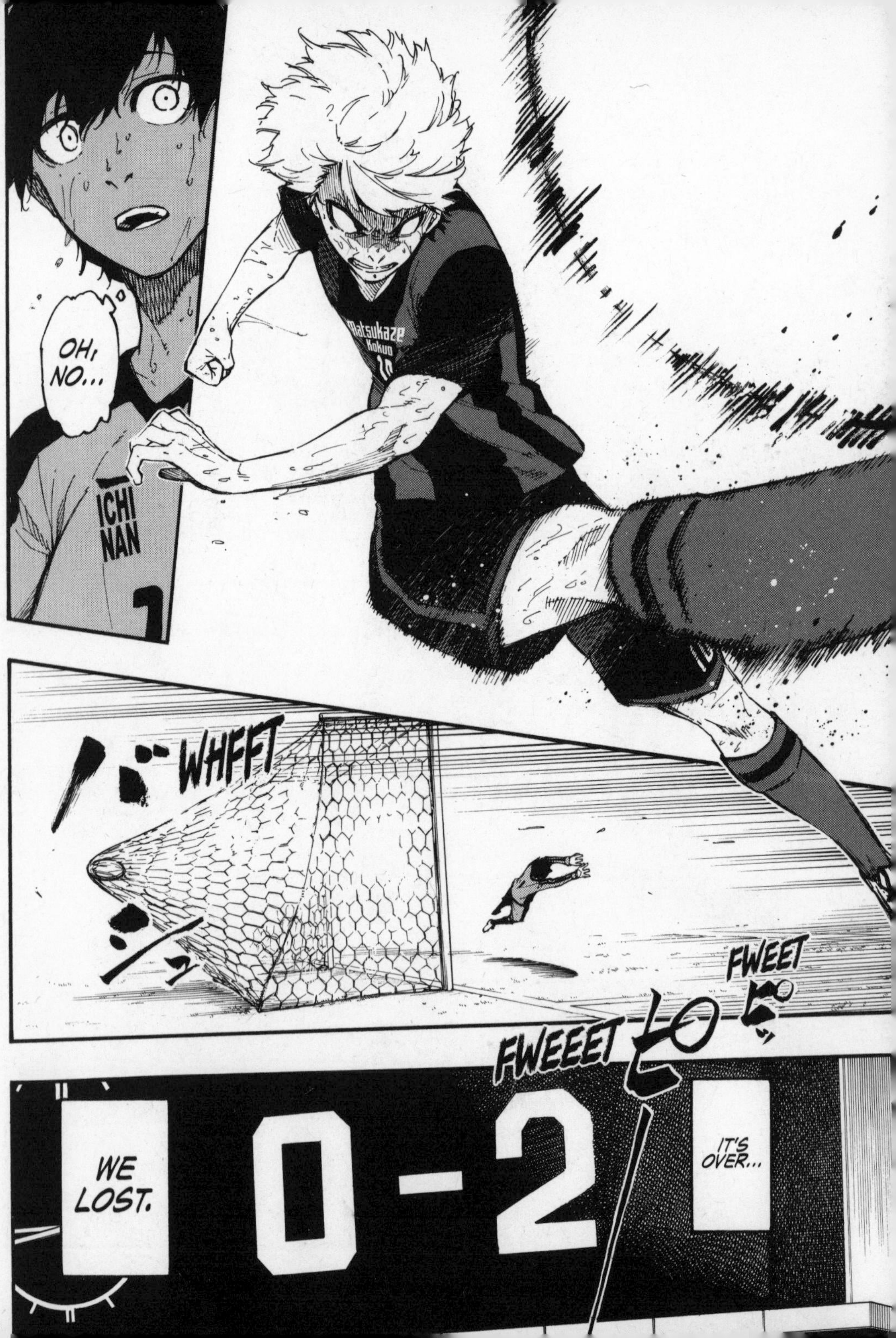
OH, NO...
ICHI NAN
WHFFT
FWEET
FWEEET
IT'S OVER...
0-2
WE LOST.

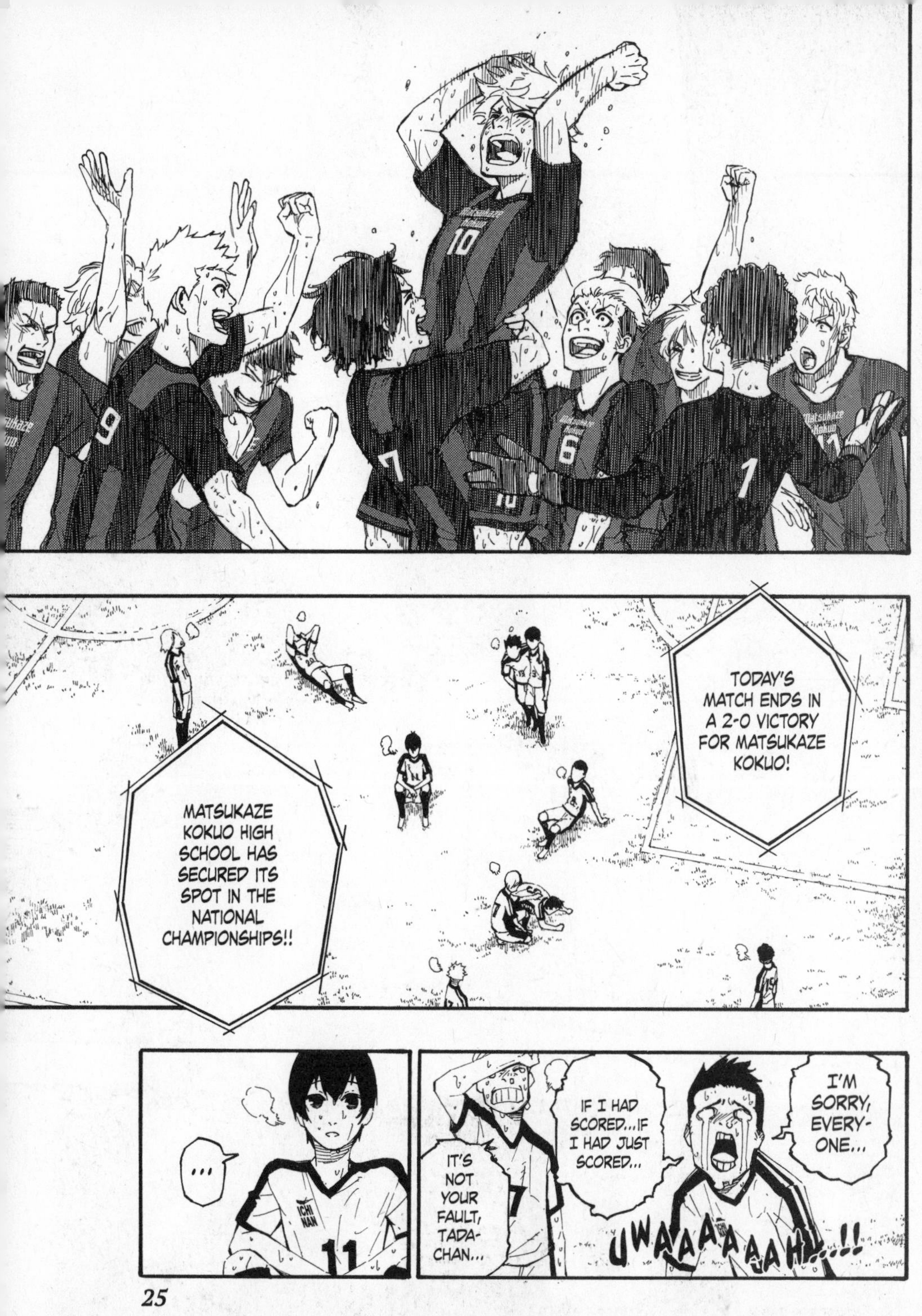
TODAY'S MATCH ENDS IN A 2-0 VICTORY FOR MATSUKAZE KOKUO!
MATSUKAZE KOKUO HIGH SCHOOL HAS SECURED ITS SPOT IN THE NATIONAL CHAMPIONSHIPS!!
I'M SORRY, EVERY-ONE...
IF I HAD SCORED...IF I HAD JUST SCORED...
IT'S NOT YOUR FAULT, TADA-CHAN...
UWAAAAAAAH...!!
...

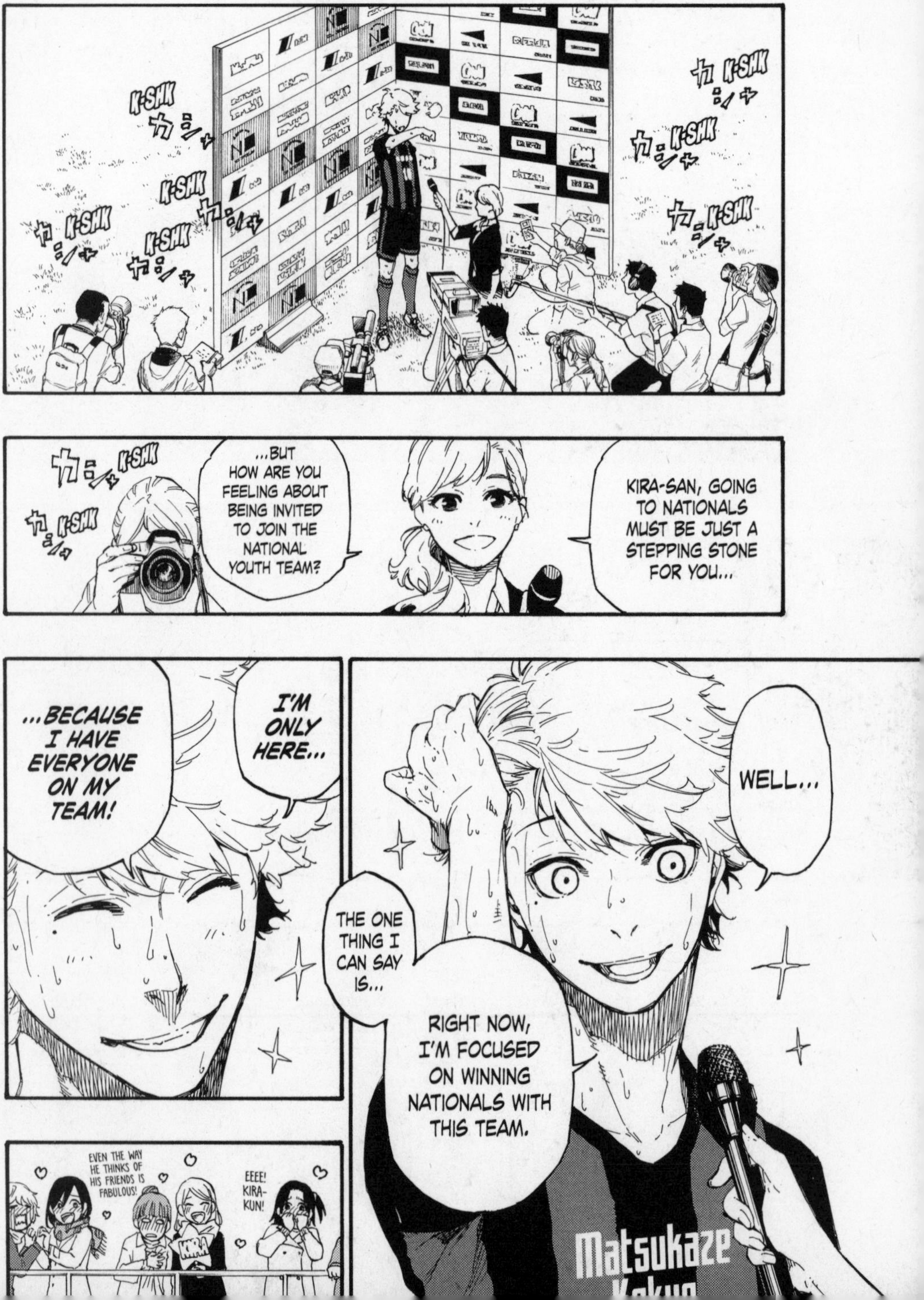
K-SHK
K-SHK
K-SHK
K-SHK
K-SHK
K-SHK
K-SHK
KIRA-SAN, GOING TO NATIONALS MUST BE JUST A STEPPING STONE FOR YOU...
...BUT HOW ARE YOU FEELING ABOUT BEING INVITED TO JOIN THE NATIONAL YOUTH TEAM?
K-SHK
K-SHK
WELL...
THE ONE THING I CAN SAY IS...
RIGHT NOW, I'M FOCUSED ON WINNING NATIONALS WITH THIS TEAM.
Matsukaze
I'M ONLY HERE...
...BECAUSE I HAVE EVERYONE ON MY TEAM!
EEEE! KIRA-KUN!
EVEN THE WAY HE THINKS OF HIS FRIENDS IS FABULOUS!
KIRA

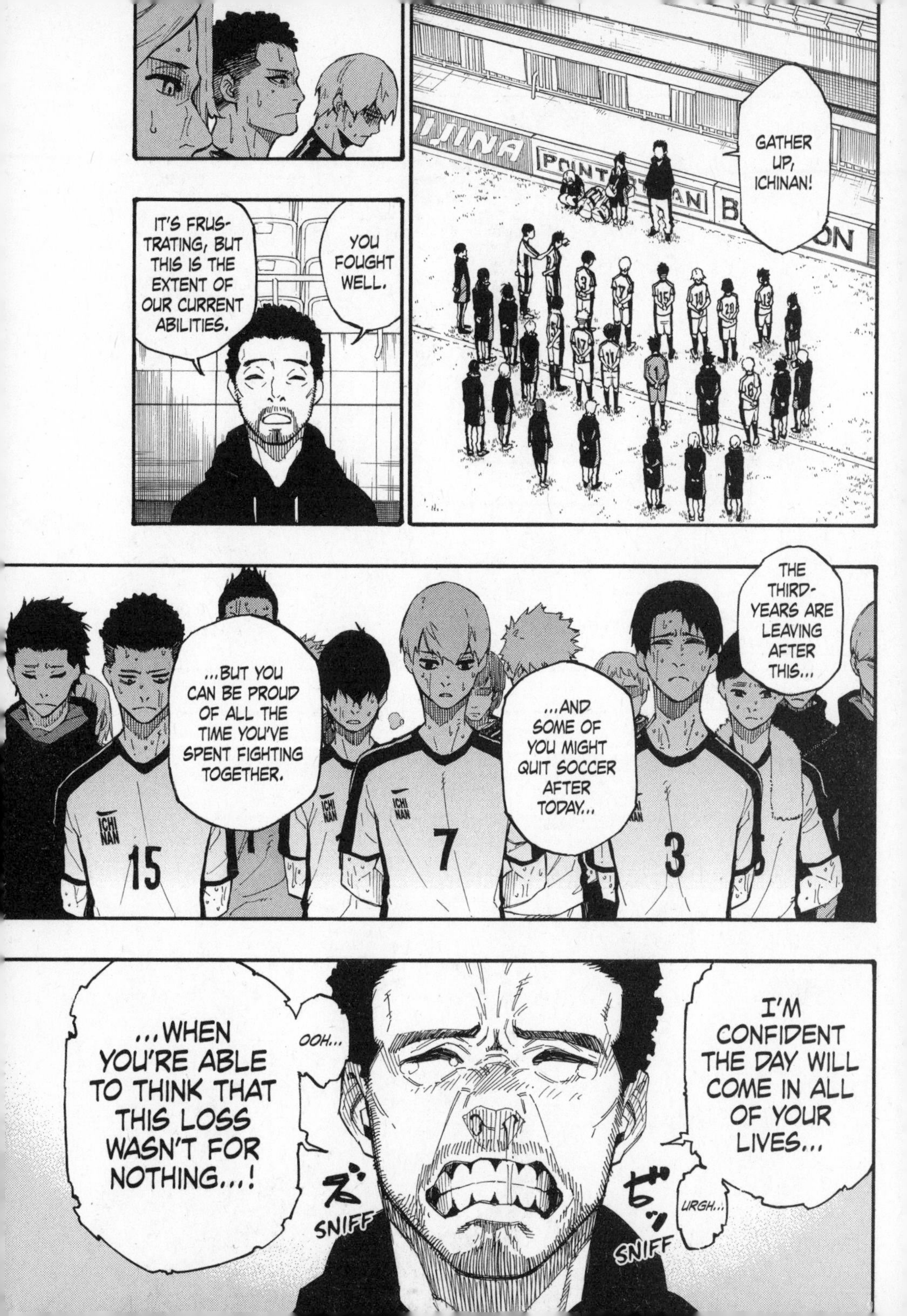
GATHER UP, ICHINAN!
YOU FOUGHT WELL.
IT'S FRUS-TRATING, BUT THIS IS THE EXTENT OF OUR CURRENT ABILITIES.
THE THIRD-YEARS ARE LEAVING AFTER THIS...
...AND SOME OF YOU MIGHT QUIT SOCCER AFTER TODAY...
...BUT YOU CAN BE PROUD OF ALL THE TIME YOU'VE SPENT FIGHTING TOGETHER.
I'M CONFIDENT THE DAY WILL COME IN ALL OF YOUR LIVES...
URGH...
SNIFF
SNIFF
OOH...
...WHEN YOU'RE ABLE TO THINK THAT THIS LOSS WASN'T FOR NOTHING...!

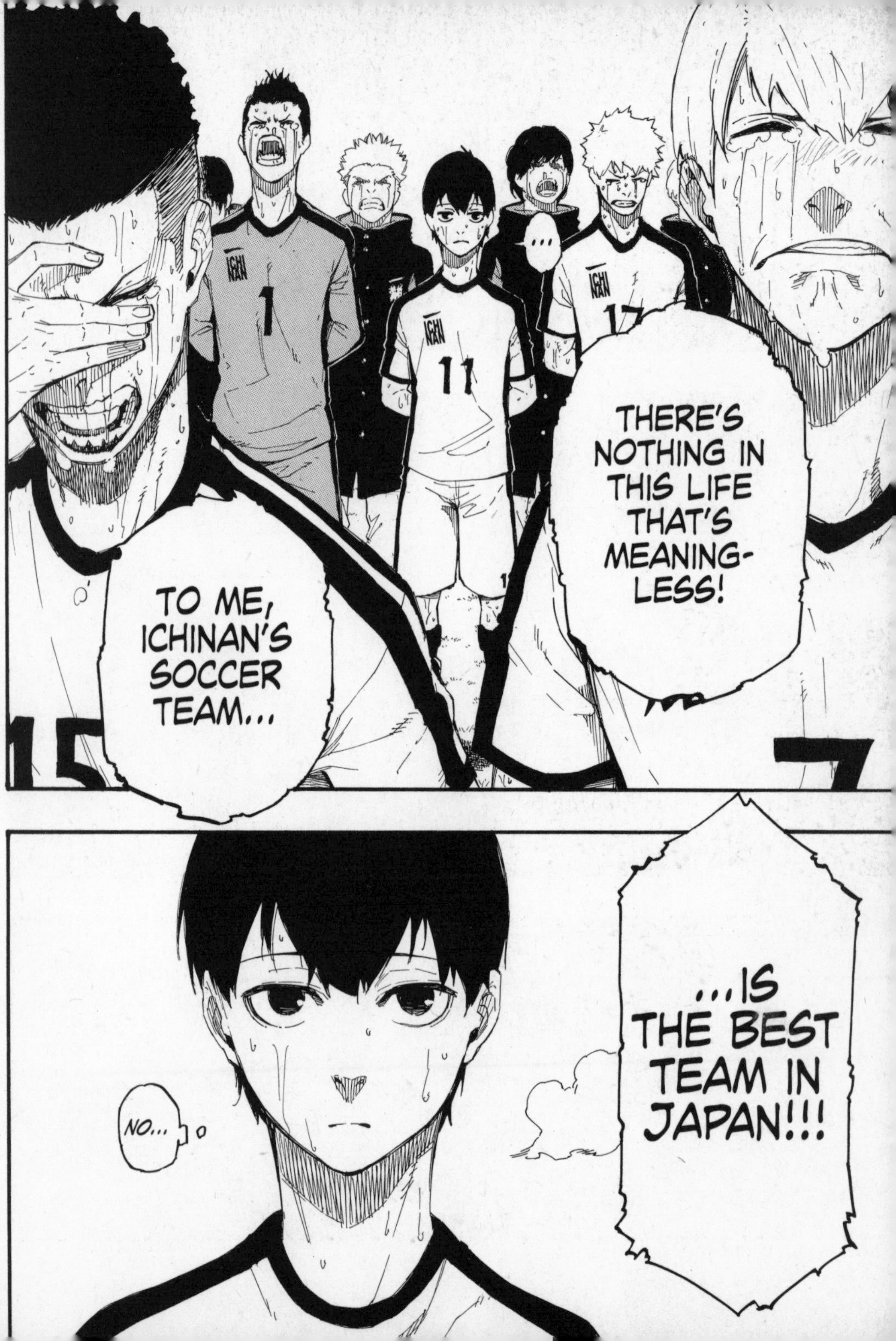
THERE'S NOTHING IN THIS LIFE THAT'S MEANING-LESS!
...
TO ME, ICHINAN'S SOCCER TEAM...
...IS THE BEST TEAM IN JAPAN!!!
NO...

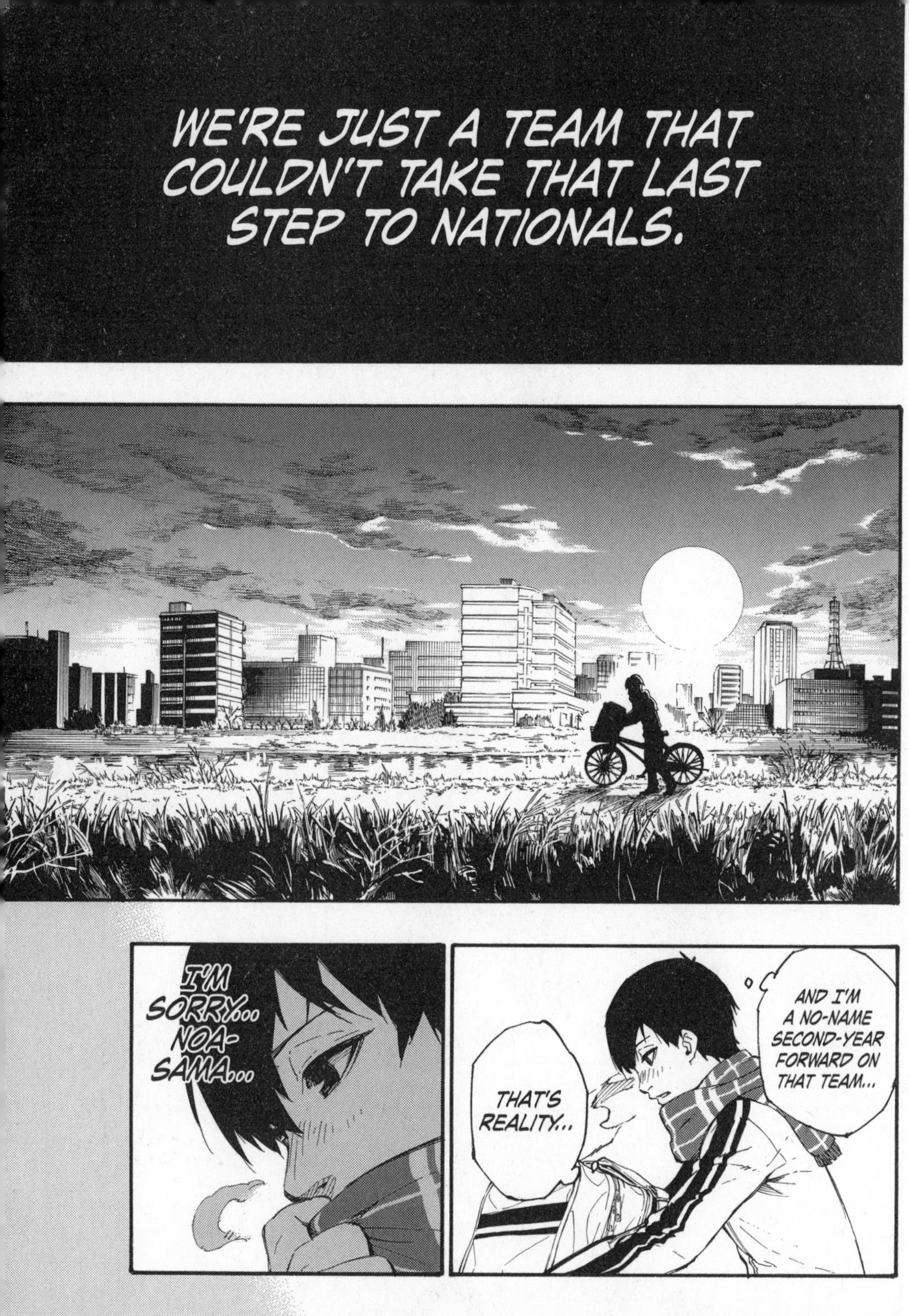
WE'RE JUST A TEAM THAT COULDN'T TAKE THAT LAST STEP TO NATIONALS.
AND I'M A NO-NAME SECOND-YEAR FORWARD ON THAT TEAM...
THAT'S REALITY...
I'M SORRY... NOA-SAMA...

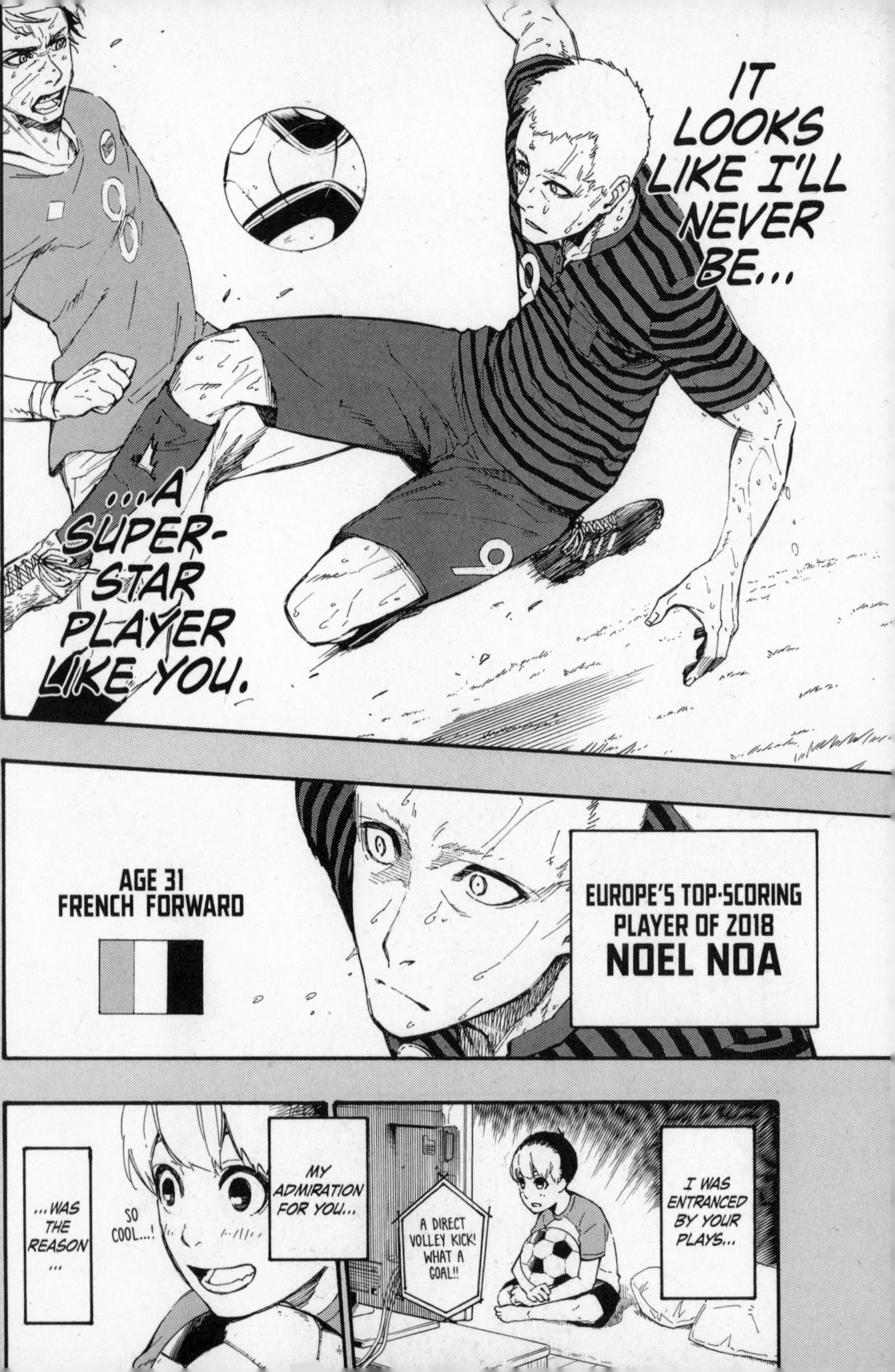
IT LOOKS LIKE I'LL NEVER BE...
...A SUPER-STAR PLAYER LIKE YOU.
EUROPE'S TOP-SCORING PLAYER OF 2018
NOEL NOA
AGE 31
FRENCH FORWARD
I WAS ENTRANCED BY YOUR PLAYS...
A DIRECT VOLLEY KICK! WHAT A GOAL!!
MY ADMIRATION FOR YOU...
SO COOL...!
...WAS THE REASON ...

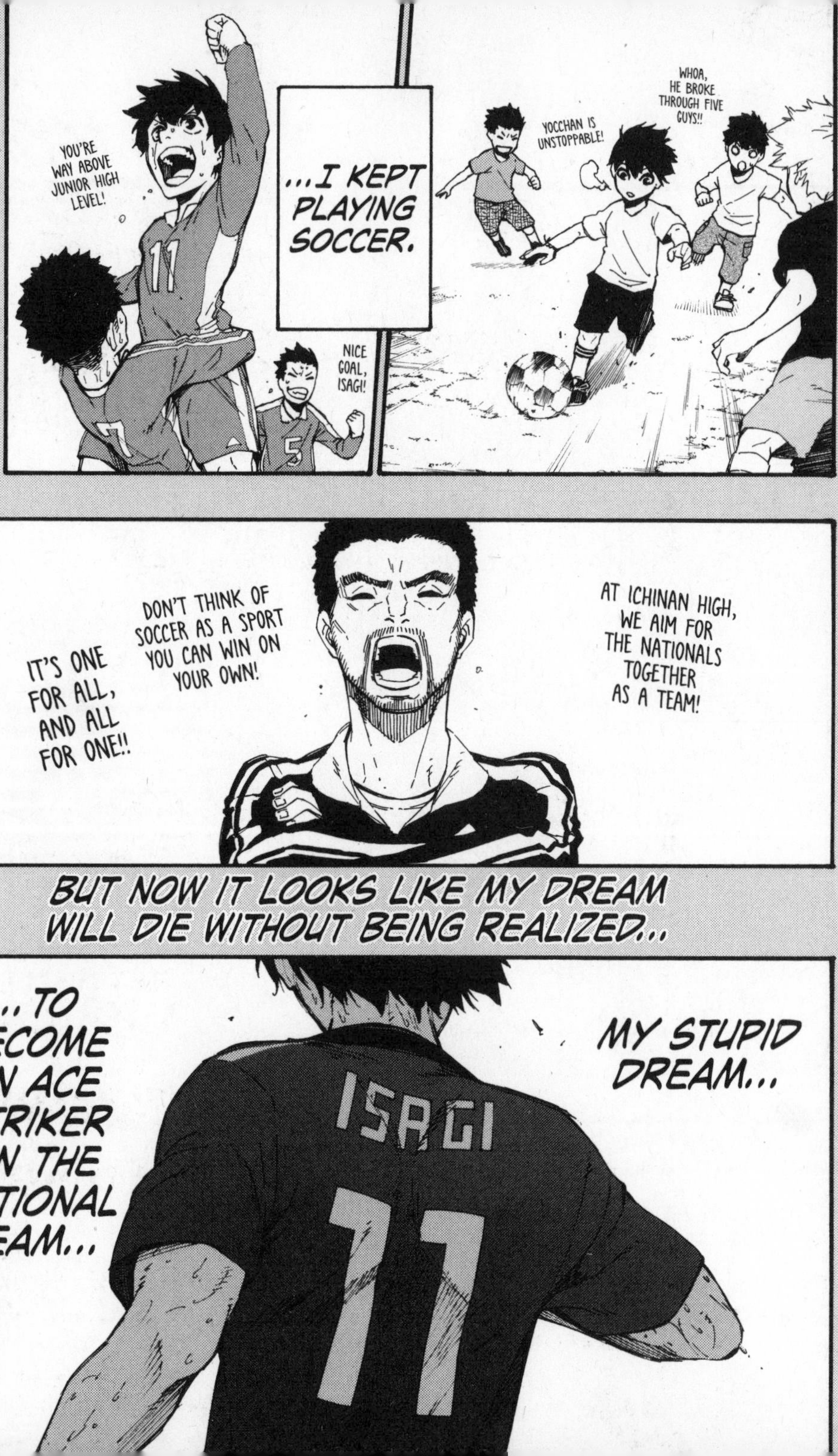
WHOA, HE BROKE THROUGH FIVE GUYS!!
YOCCHAN IS UNSTOPPABLE!
...I KEPT PLAYING SOCCER.
NICE GOAL, ISAGI!
YOU'RE WAY ABOVE JUNIOR HIGH LEVEL!
AT ICHINAN HIGH, WE AIM FOR THE NATIONALS TOGETHER AS A TEAM!
DON'T THINK OF SOCCER AS A SPORT YOU CAN WIN ON YOUR OWN!
IT'S ONE FOR ALL, AND ALL FOR ONE!!
BUT NOW IT LOOKS LIKE MY DREAM WILL DIE WITHOUT BEING REALIZED...
MY STUPID DREAM...
...TO BECOME AN ACE STRIKER ON THE NATIONAL TEAM...
ISAGI
11

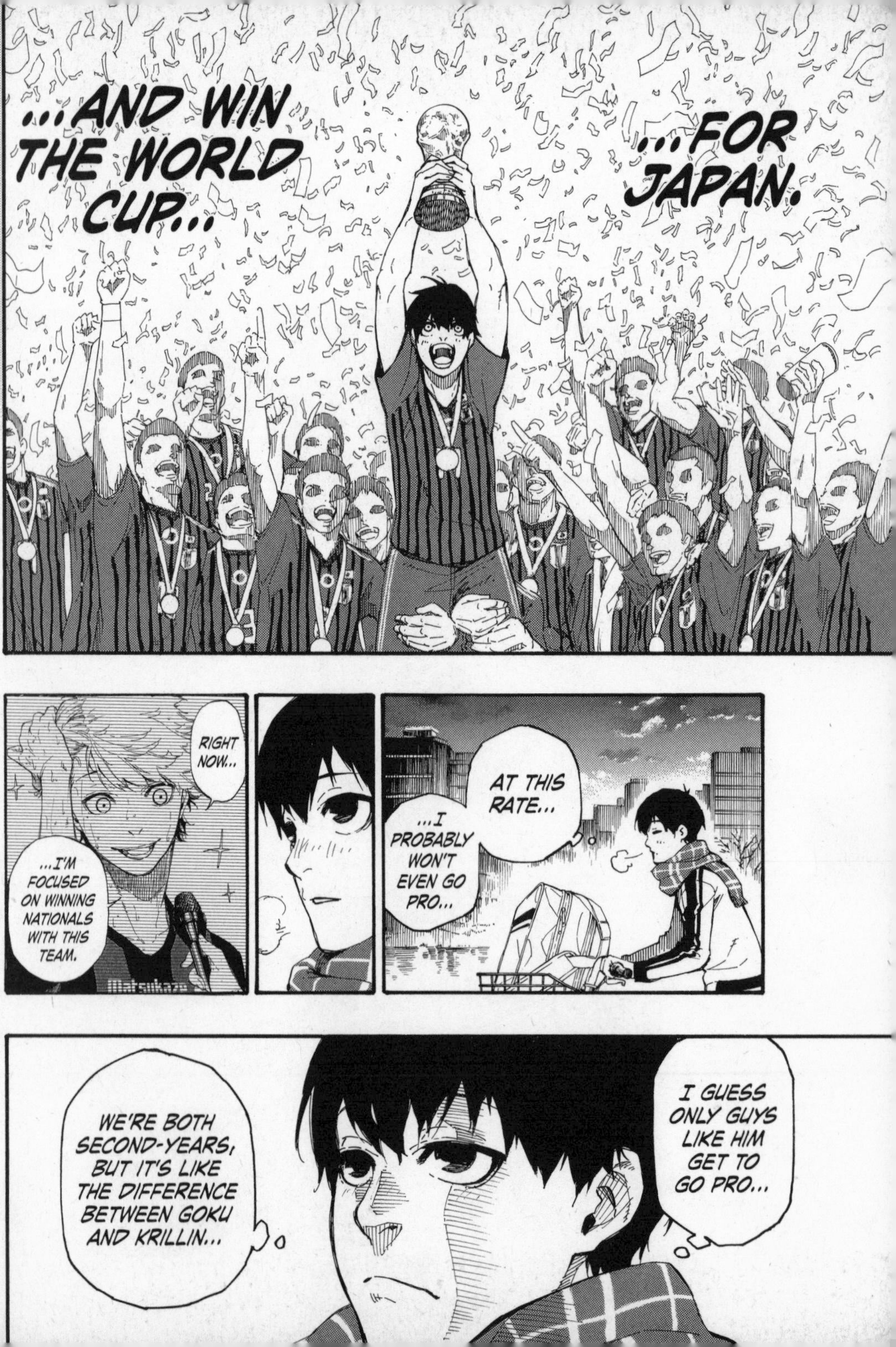
...AND WIN THE WORLD CUP...
...FOR JAPAN.
AT THIS RATE...
...I PROBABLY WON'T EVEN GO PRO...
RIGHT NOW...
...I'M FOCUSED ON WINNING NATIONALS WITH THIS TEAM.
Matsukaze
I GUESS ONLY GUYS LIKE HIM GET TO GO PRO...
WE'RE BOTH SECOND-YEARS, BUT IT'S LIKE THE DIFFERENCE BETWEEN GOKU AND KRILLIN...

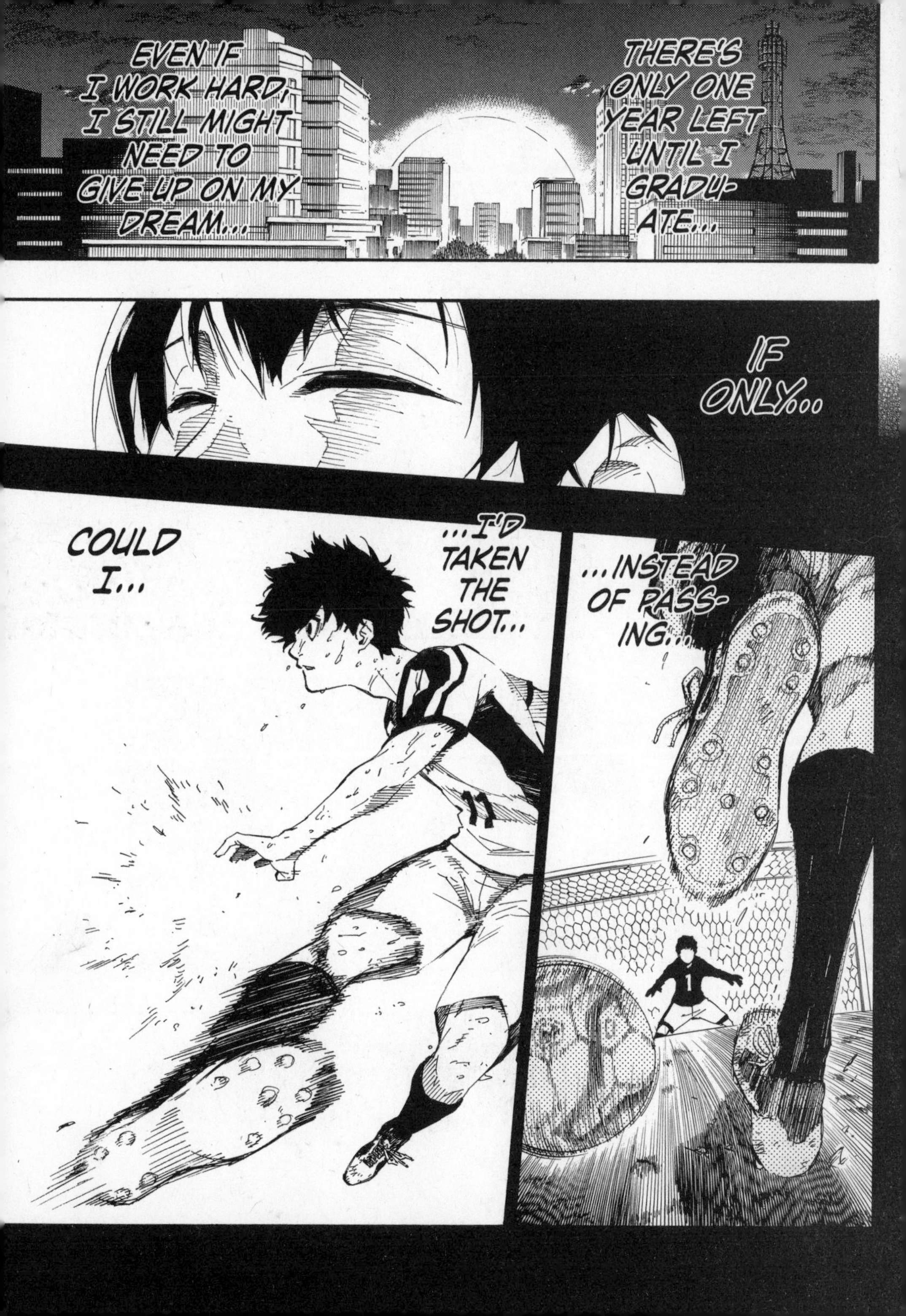
THERE'S ONLY ONE YEAR LEFT UNTIL I GRADU-ATE...
EVEN IF I WORK HARD, I STILL MIGHT NEED TO GIVE UP ON MY DREAM...
IF ONLY...
...INSTEAD OF PASS-ING...
...I'D TAKEN THE SHOT...
COULD I...

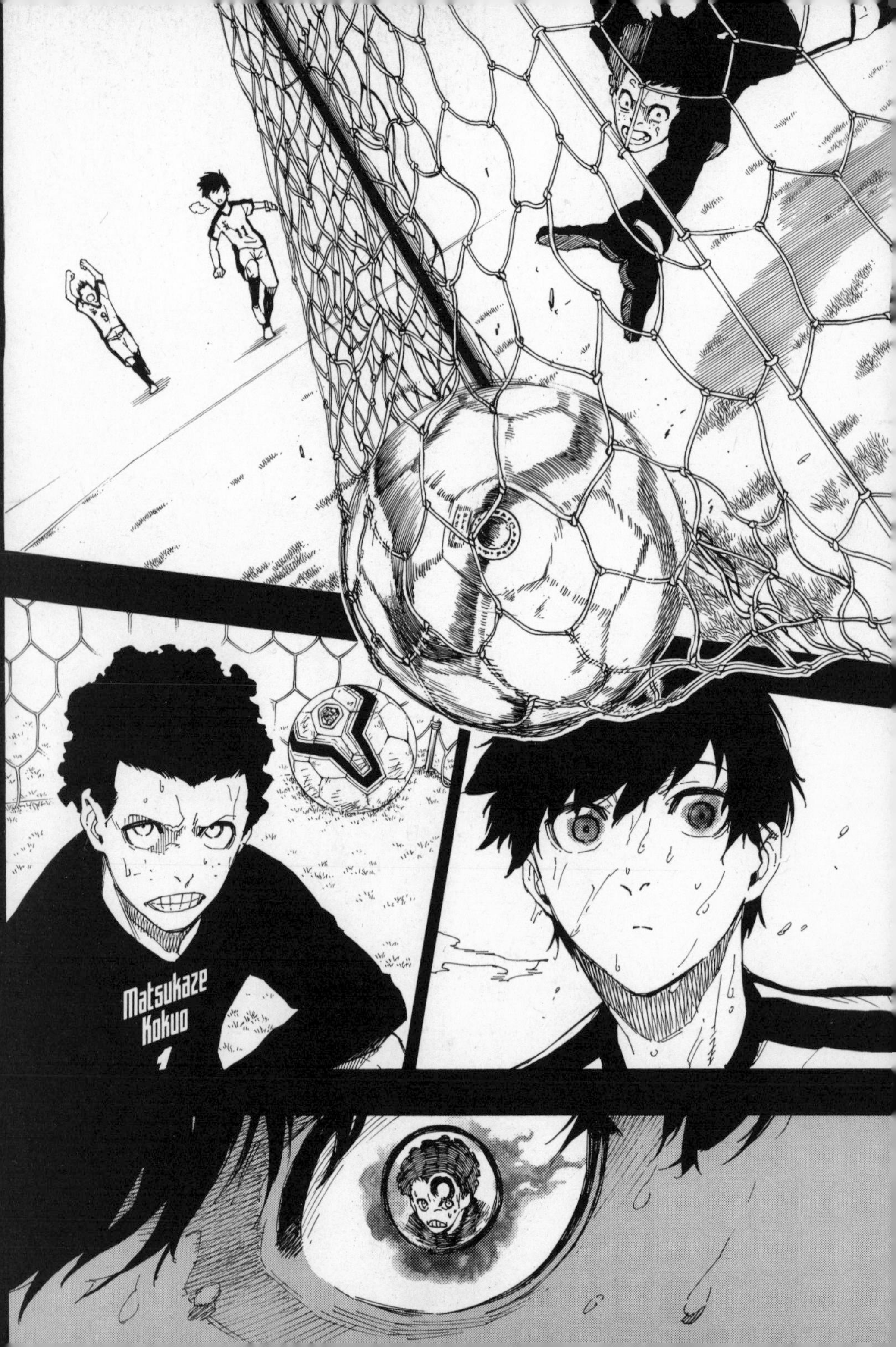
Matsukaze
Kokuo
1

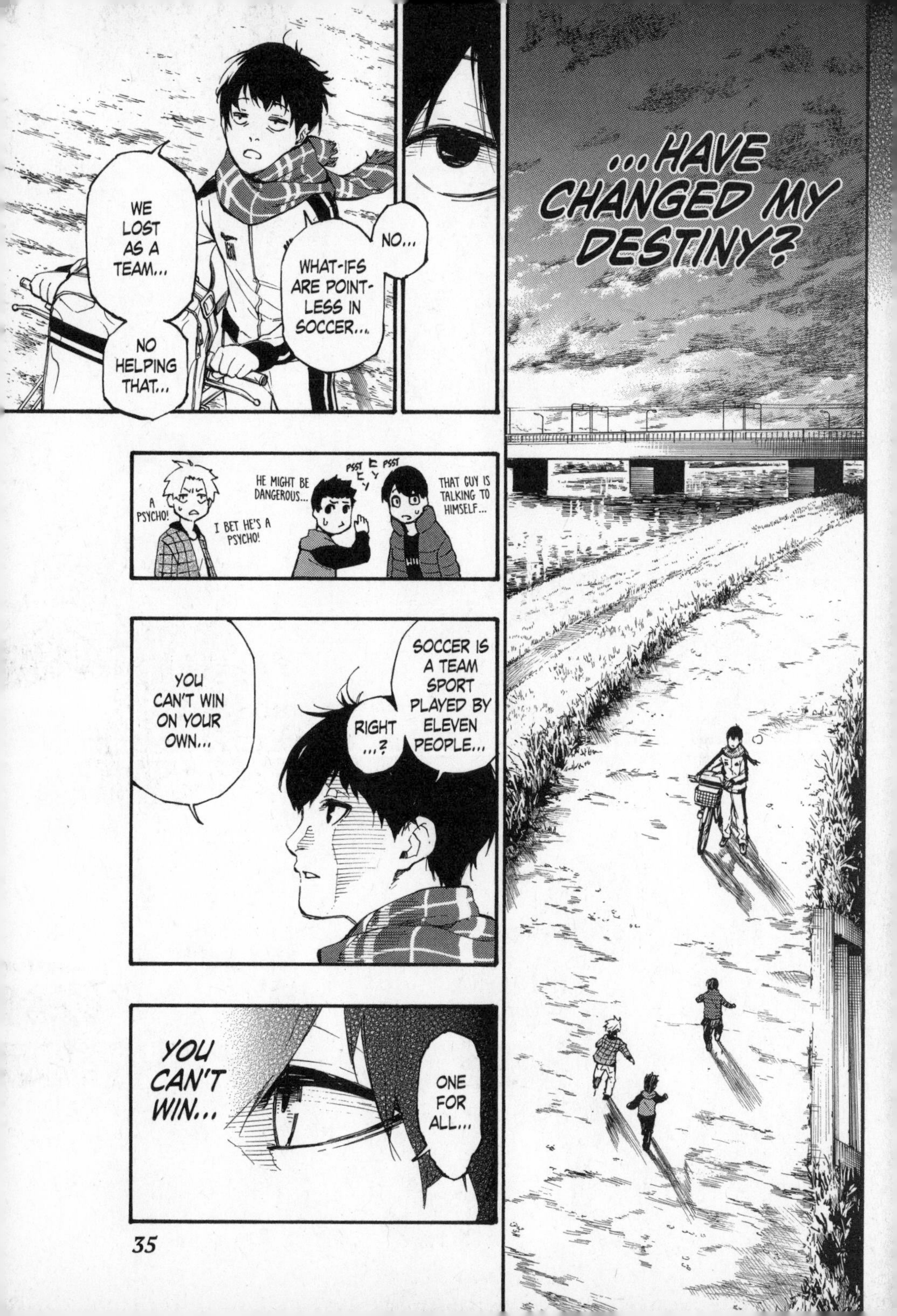
...HAVE CHANGED MY DESTINY?
NO...
WHAT-IFS ARE POINTLESS IN SOCCER...
WE LOST AS A TEAM...
NO HELPING THAT...
THAT GUY IS TALKING TO HIMSELF...
PSST
PSST
HE MIGHT BE DANGEROUS...
I BET HE'S A PSYCHO!
A PSYCHO!
SOCCER IS A TEAM SPORT PLAYED BY ELEVEN PEOPLE...
RIGHT...?
YOU CAN'T WIN ON YOUR OWN...
ONE FOR ALL...
YOU CAN'T WIN...

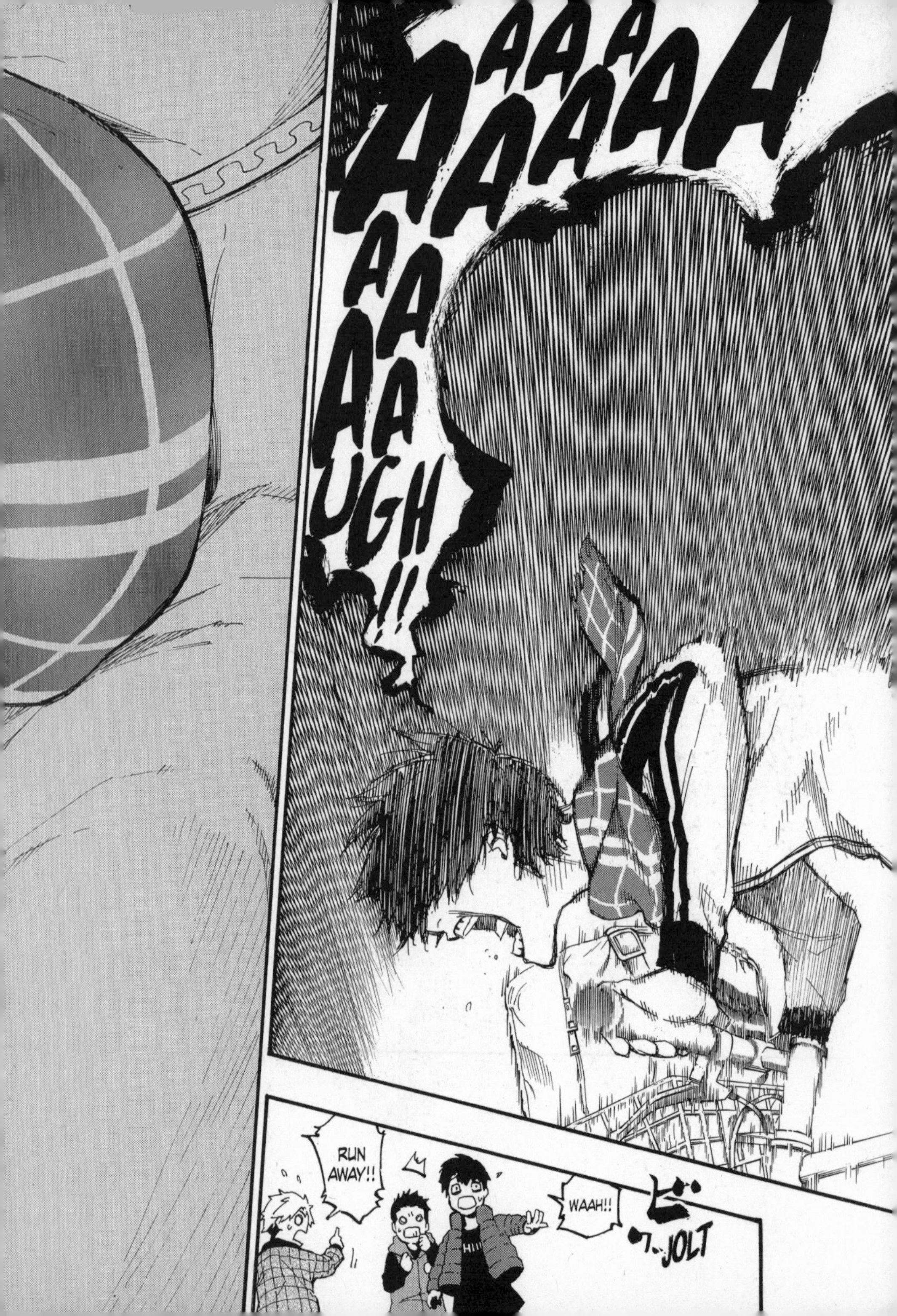
AAAAAAAAAAAAAUGH!!
RUN AWAY!!
WAAH!!
ビ
JOLT

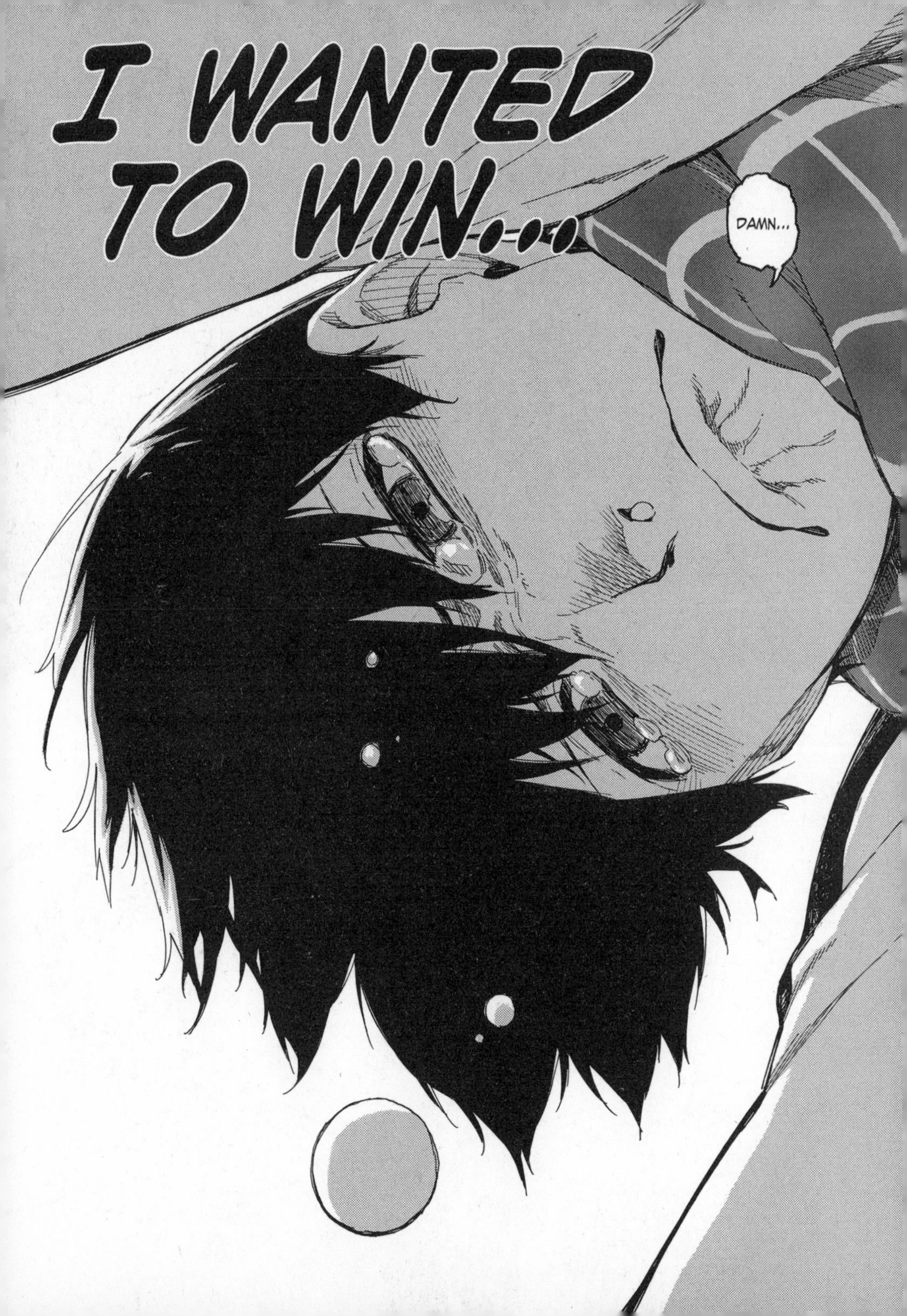
DAMN...
I WANTED TO WIN...

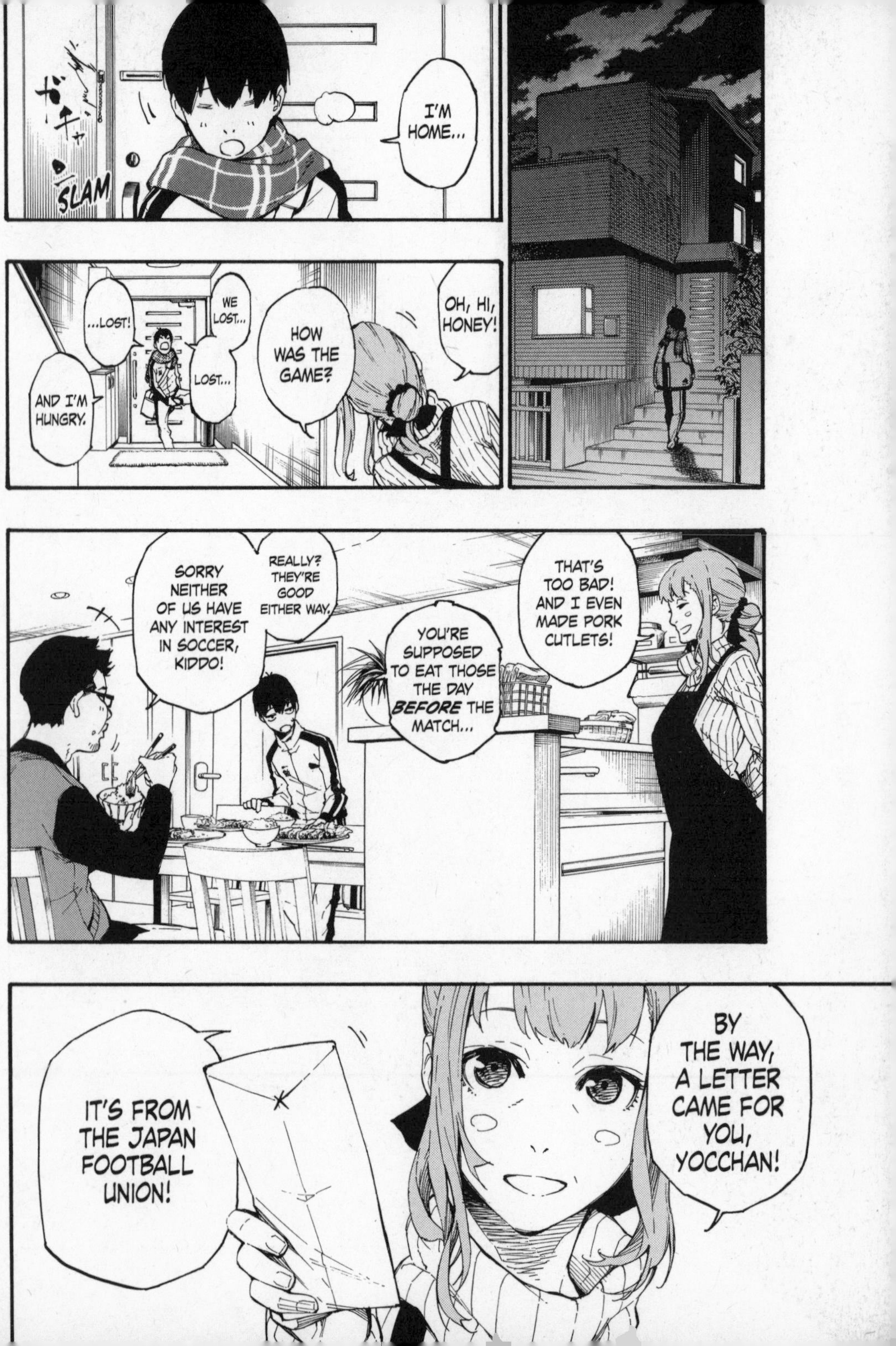
I'M HOME...
ガチャ
SLAM
OH, HI, HONEY!
HOW WAS THE GAME?
WE LOST...
LOST...
...LOST!
AND I'M HUNGRY.
THAT'S TOO BAD! AND I EVEN MADE PORK CUTLETS!
YOU'RE SUPPOSED TO EAT THOSE THE DAY *BEFORE* THE MATCH...
REALLY? THEY'RE GOOD EITHER WAY.
SORRY NEITHER OF US HAVE ANY INTEREST IN SOCCER, KIDDO!
BY THE WAY, A LETTER CAME FOR YOU, YOCCHAN!
IT'S FROM THE JAPAN FOOTBALL UNION!

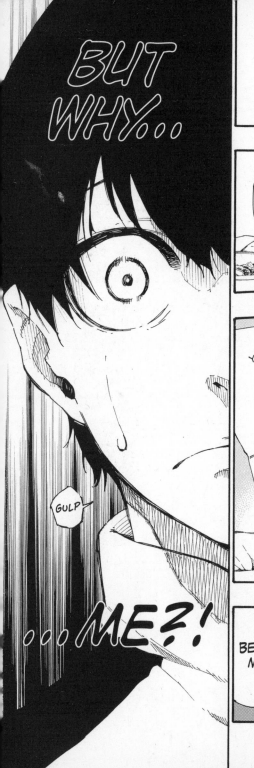

BUT WHY...

...ME?!

GULP

HUH...?

MUNCH MUNCH

HM? AN INVITATION?

WHAT'S IT SAY?

RUSTLE

...

YOICHI ISAGI-SAMA

YOU'VE BEEN SELECTED FOR A SPECIAL PLAYER TRAINING PROGRAM

SPECIAL PLAYER TRAINING?

BEATS ME!

...A GOOD THING?

I GUESS THAT'S...

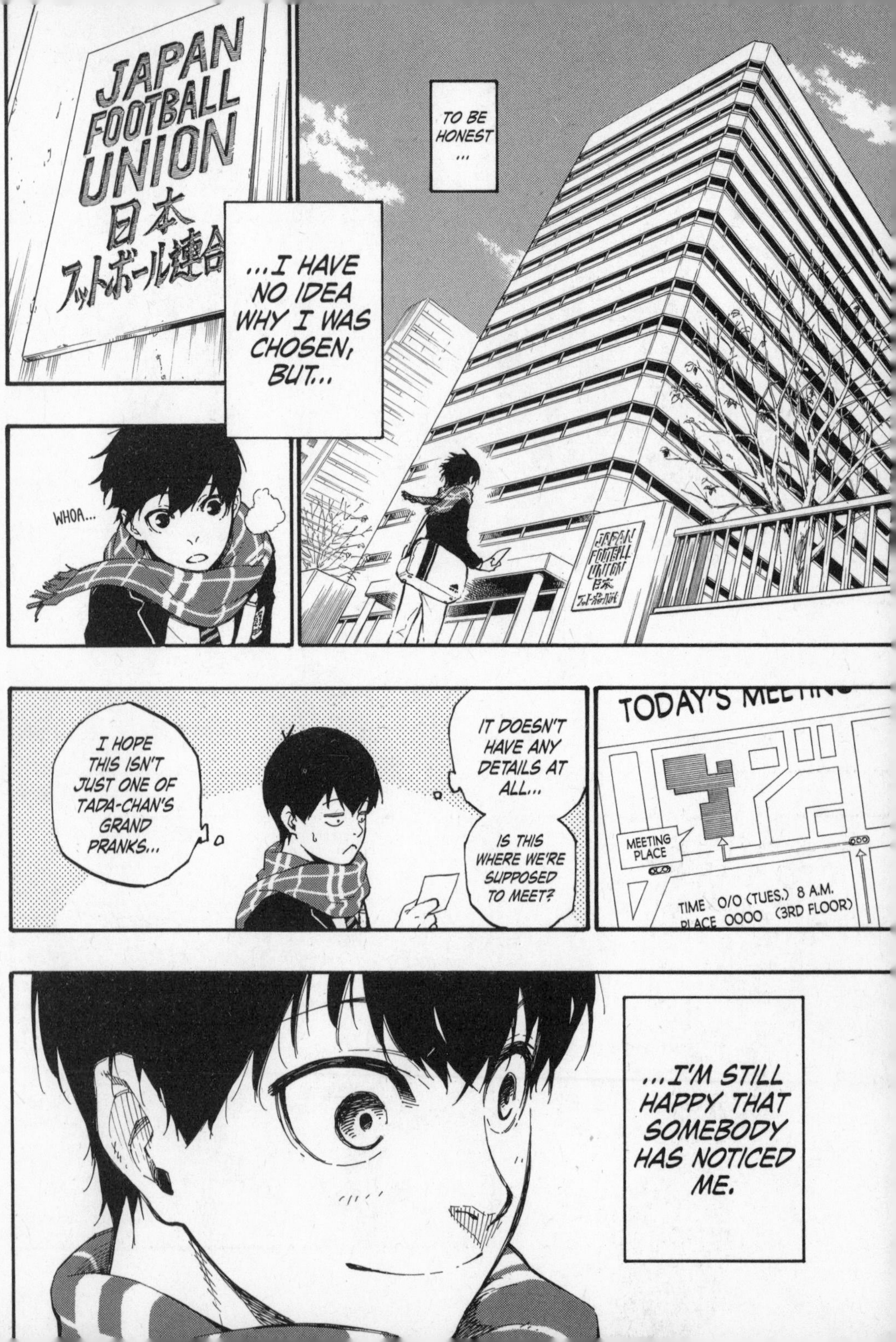
TO BE HONEST ...
...I HAVE NO IDEA WHY I WAS CHOSEN, BUT...
JAPAN FOOTBALL UNION
日本
フットボール連合
WHOA...
TODAY'S MEETI
MEETING PLACE
TIME 0/0 (TUES.) 8 A.M.
PLACE 0000 (3RD FLOOR)
IT DOESN'T HAVE ANY DETAILS AT ALL...
IS THIS WHERE WE'RE SUPPOSED TO MEET?
I HOPE THIS ISN'T JUST ONE OF TADA-CHAN'S GRAND PRANKS...
...I'M STILL HAPPY THAT SOMEBODY HAS NOTICED ME.

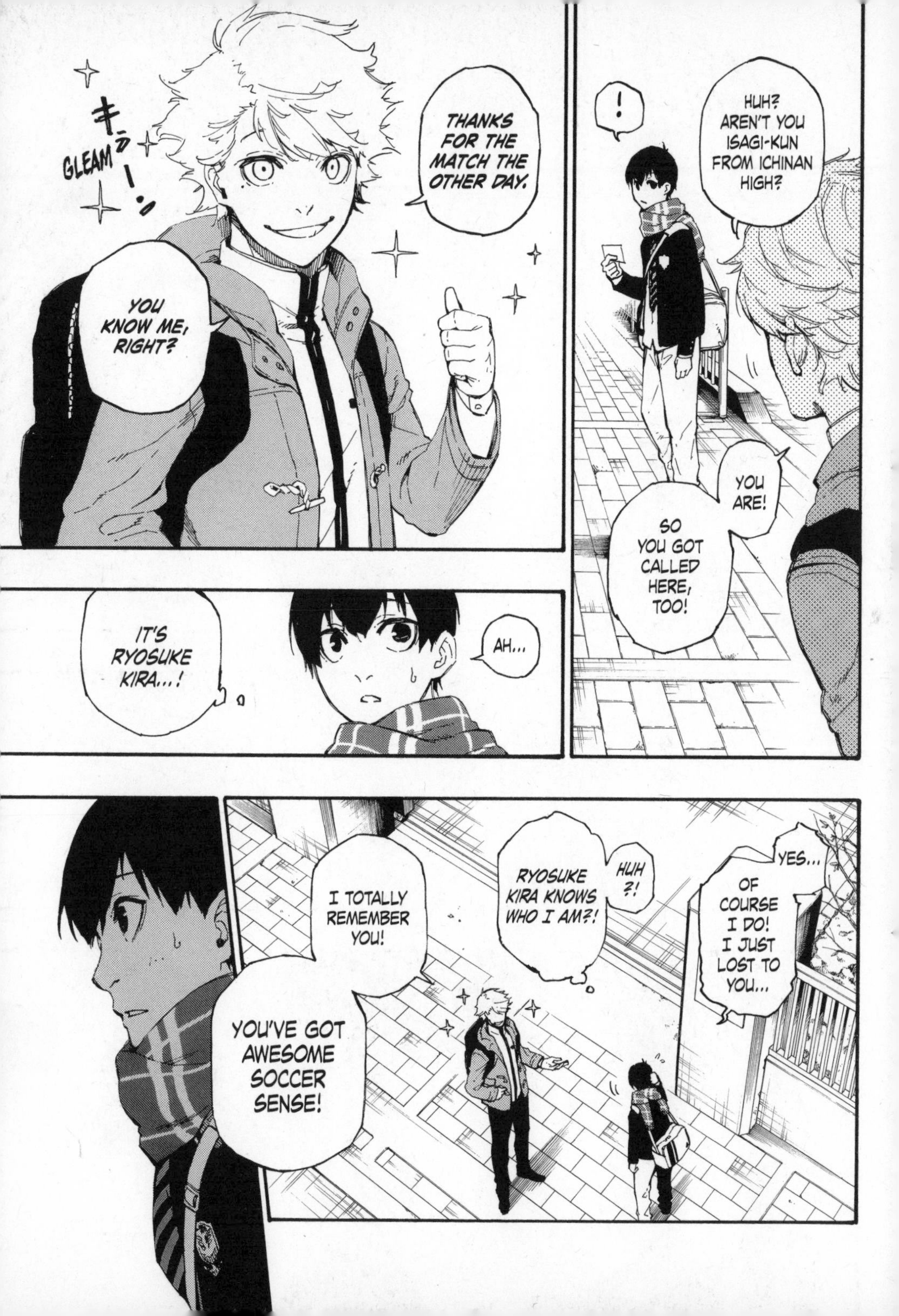
!
HUH? AREN'T YOU ISAGI-KUN FROM ICHINAN HIGH?
YOU ARE!
SO YOU GOT CALLED HERE, TOO!
GLEAM
THANKS FOR THE MATCH THE OTHER DAY.
YOU KNOW ME, RIGHT?
AH...
IT'S RYOSUKE KIRA...!
YES... OF COURSE I DO! I JUST LOST TO YOU...
HUH?!
RYOSUKE KIRA KNOWS WHO I AM?!
I TOTALLY REMEMBER YOU!
YOU'VE GOT AWESOME SOCCER SENSE!

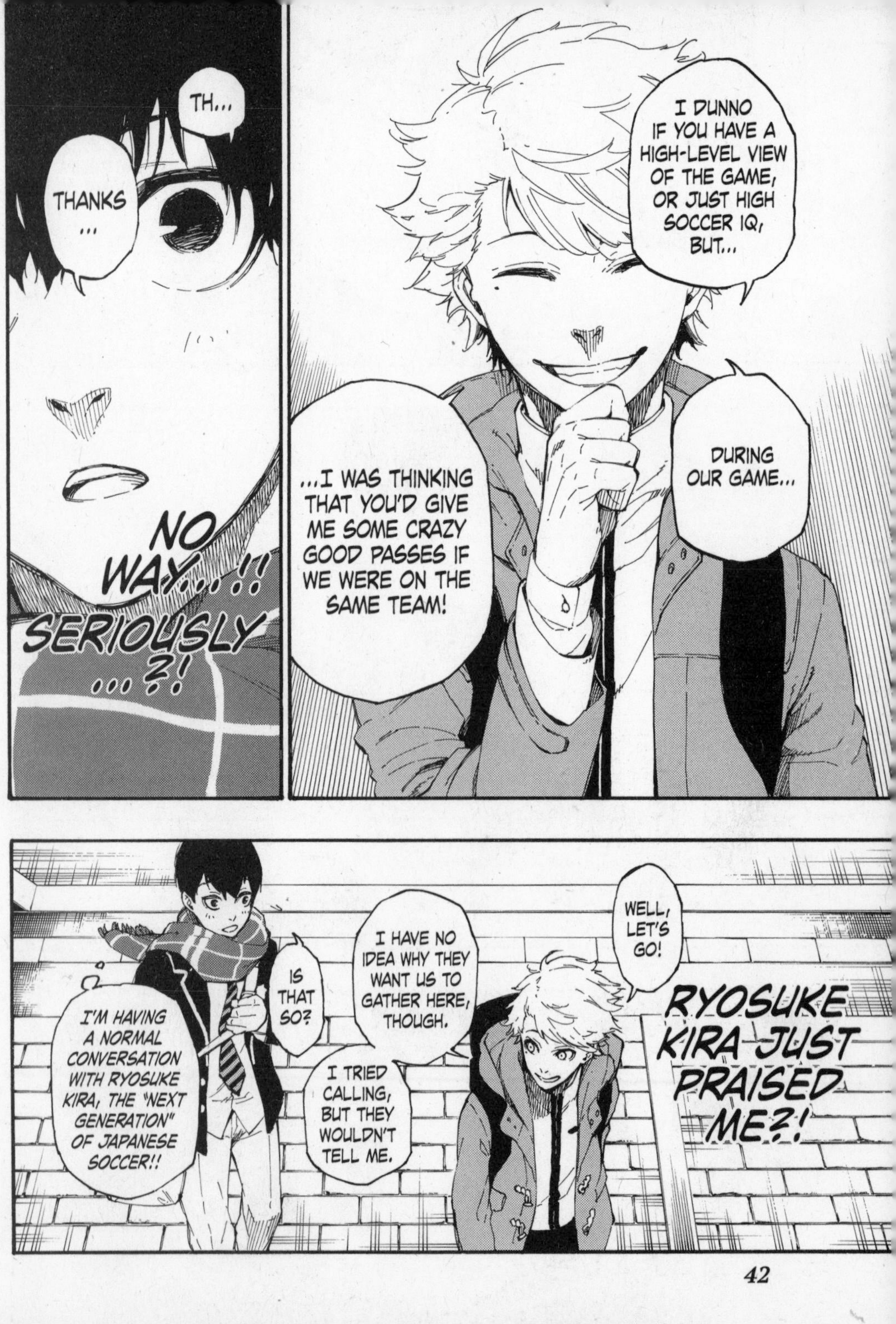
I DUNNO IF YOU HAVE A HIGH-LEVEL VIEW OF THE GAME, OR JUST HIGH SOCCER IQ, BUT...
DURING OUR GAME...
...I WAS THINKING THAT YOU'D GIVE ME SOME CRAZY GOOD PASSES IF WE WERE ON THE SAME TEAM!
TH...
THANKS ...
NO WAY...!! SERIOUSLY ...?!
WELL, LET'S GO!
RYOSUKE KIRA JUST PRAISED ME?!
I HAVE NO IDEA WHY THEY WANT US TO GATHER HERE, THOUGH.
I TRIED CALLING, BUT THEY WOULDN'T TELL ME.
IS THAT SO?
I'M HAVING A NORMAL CONVERSATION WITH RYOSUKE KIRA, THE "NEXT GENERATION" OF JAPANESE SOCCER!!

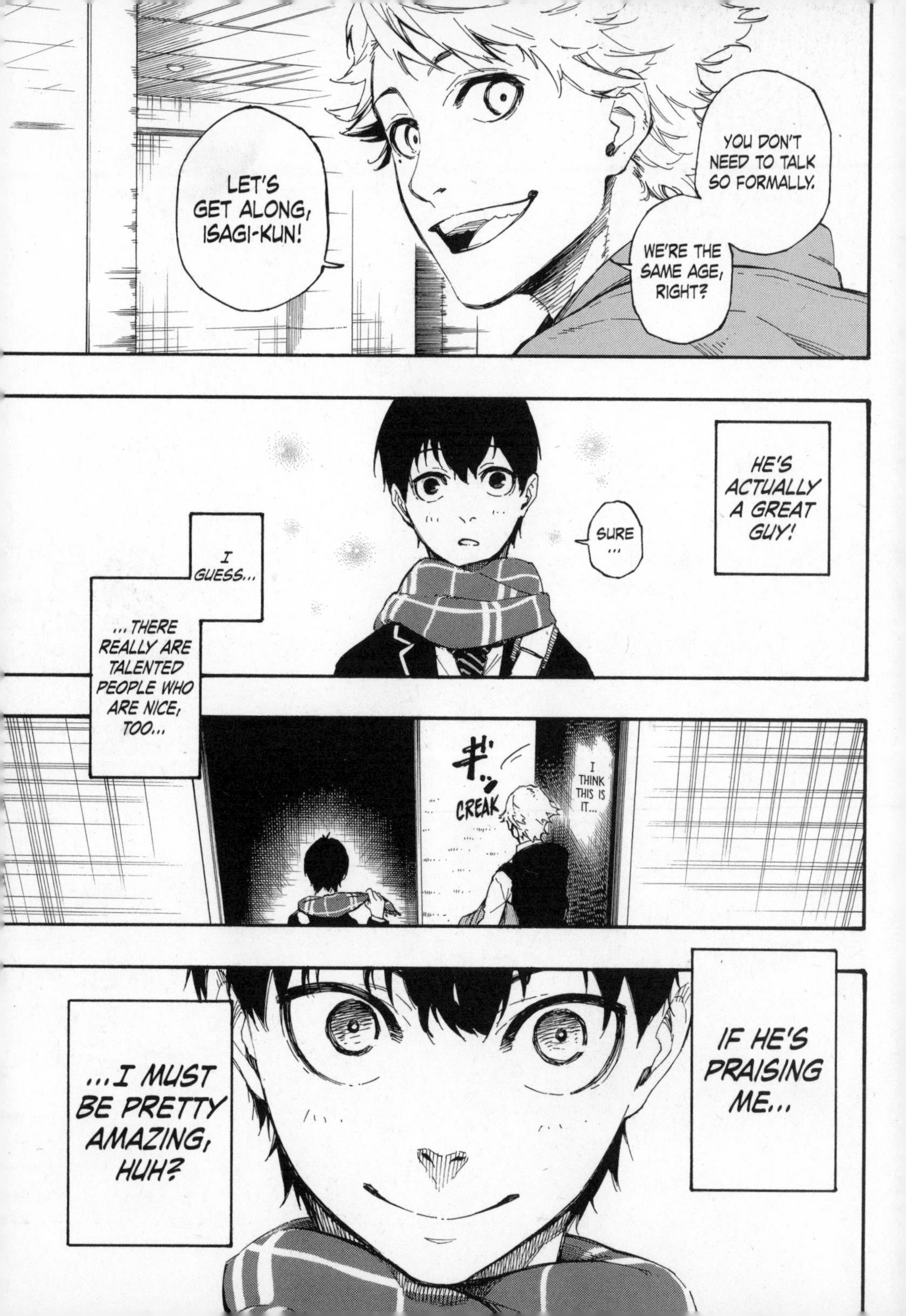
YOU DON'T NEED TO TALK SO FORMALLY.
WE'RE THE SAME AGE, RIGHT?
LET'S GET ALONG, ISAGI-KUN!
HE'S ACTUALLY A GREAT GUY!
SURE...
I GUESS...
...THERE REALLY ARE TALENTED PEOPLE WHO ARE NICE, TOO...
I THINK THIS IS IT...
ギッ
CREAK
IF HE'S PRAISING ME...
...I MUST BE PRETTY AMAZING, HUH?

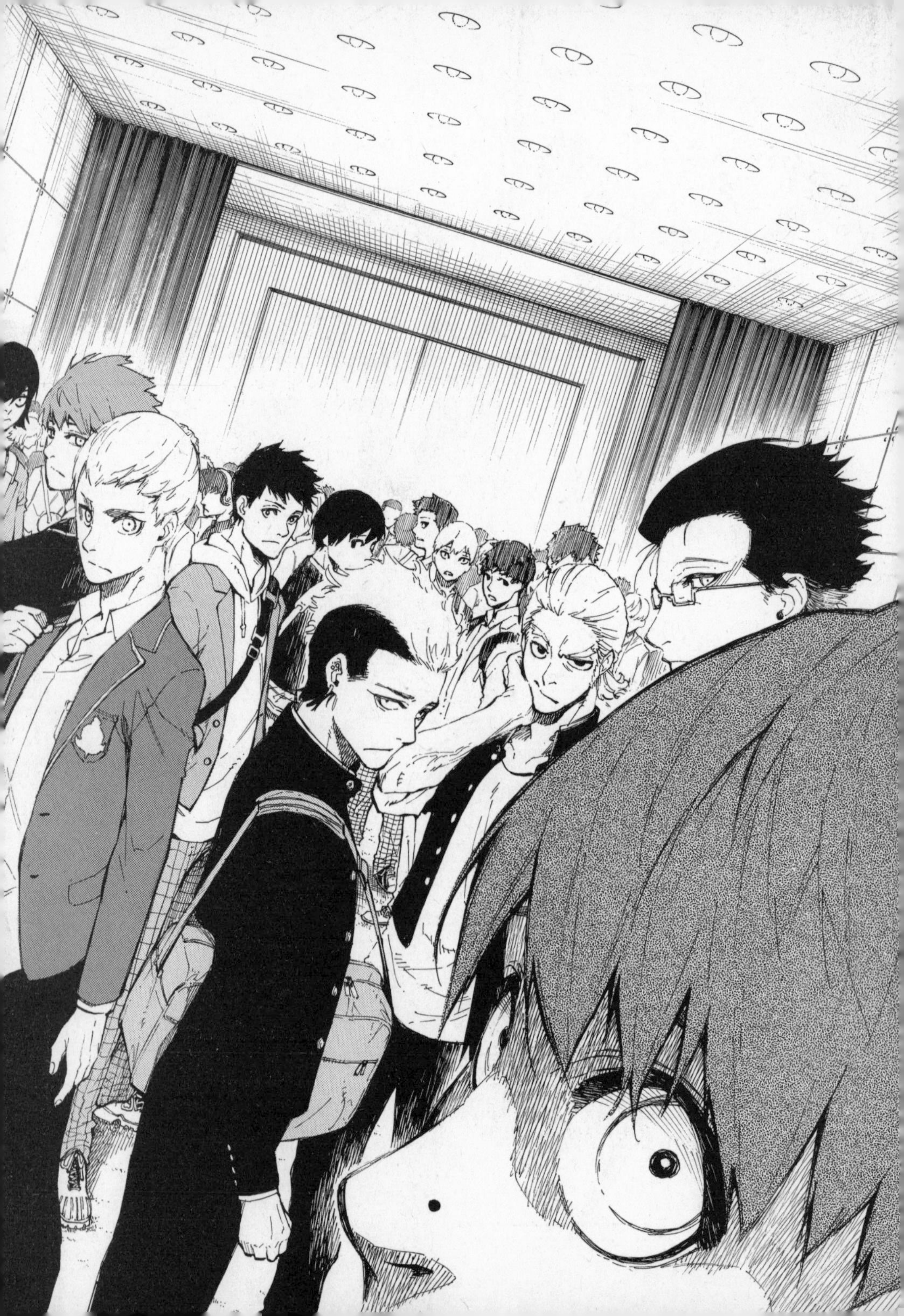

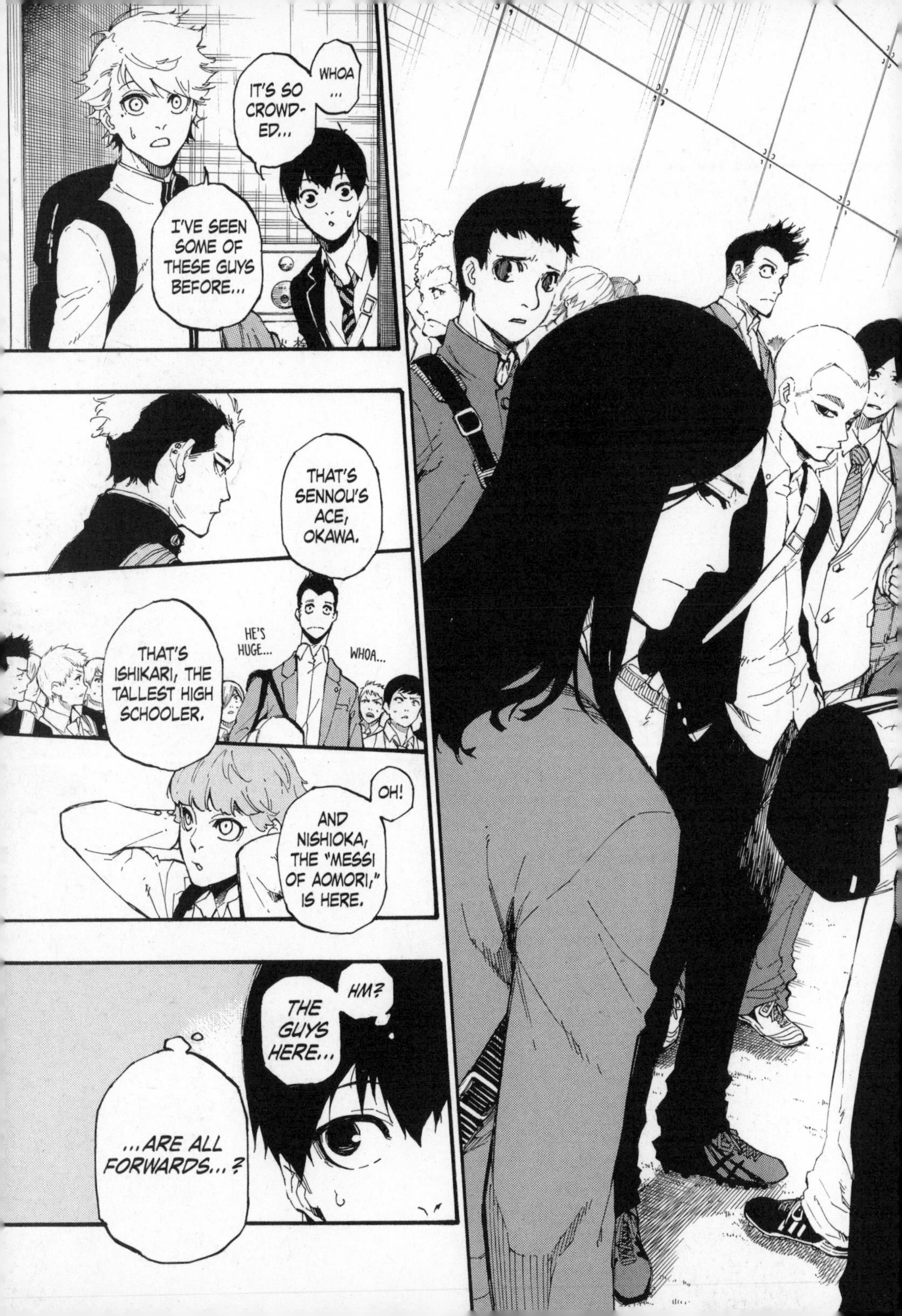
WHOA ...
IT'S SO CROWDED...
I'VE SEEN SOME OF THESE GUYS BEFORE...
THAT'S SENNOU'S ACE, OKAWA.
WHOA...
HE'S HUGE...
THAT'S ISHIKARI, THE TALLEST HIGH SCHOOLER.
OH!
AND NISHIOKA, THE "MESSI OF AOMORI," IS HERE.
HM?
THE GUYS HERE...
...ARE ALL FORWARDS...?

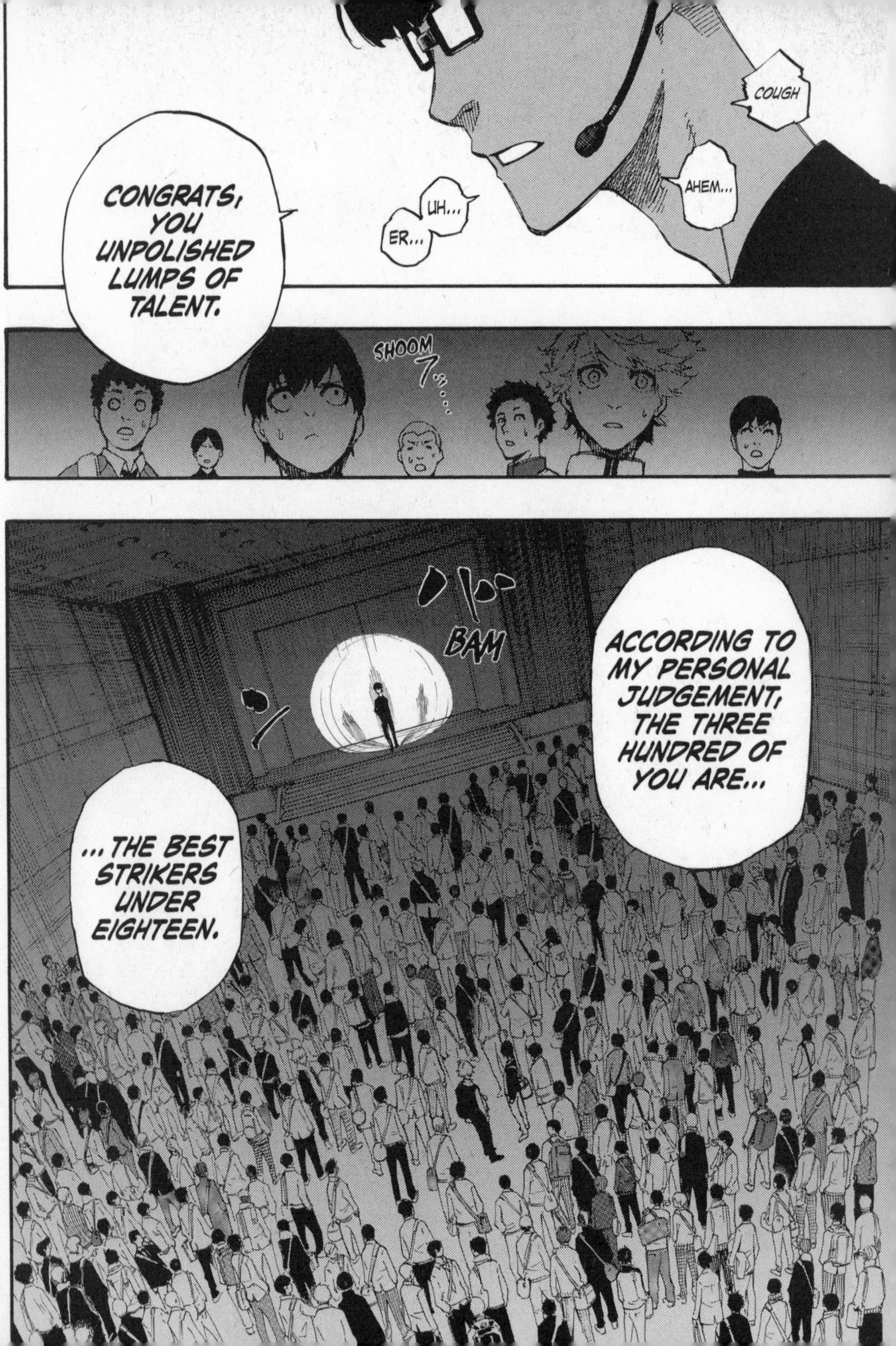
COUGH
AHEM...
UH...
ER...
CONGRATS, YOU UNPOLISHED LUMPS OF TALENT.
SHOOM
BAM
ACCORDING TO MY PERSONAL JUDGEMENT, THE THREE HUNDRED OF YOU ARE...
...THE BEST STRIKERS UNDER EIGHTEEN.

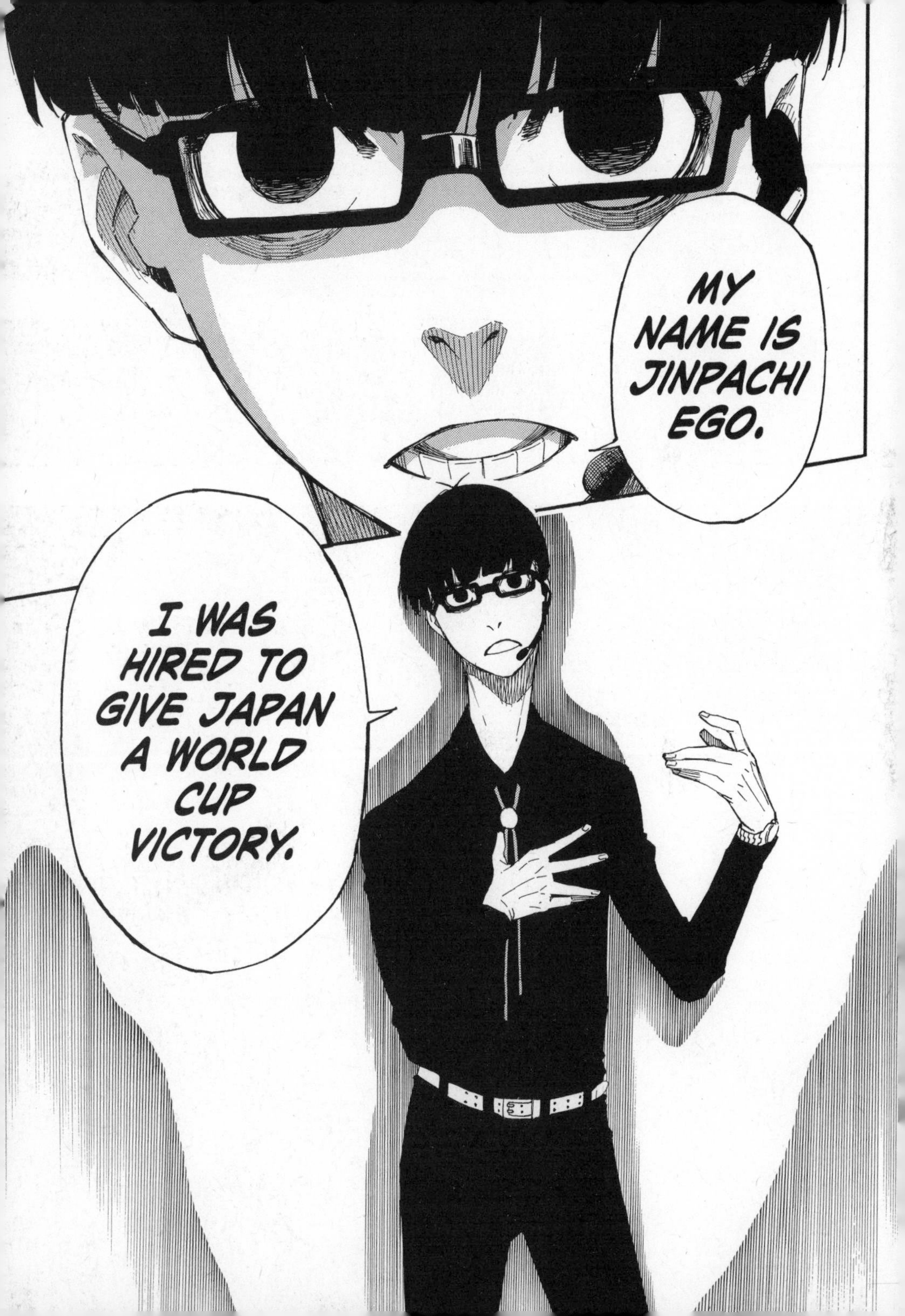
MY NAME IS JINPACHI EGO.
I WAS HIRED TO GIVE JAPAN A WORLD CUP VICTORY.

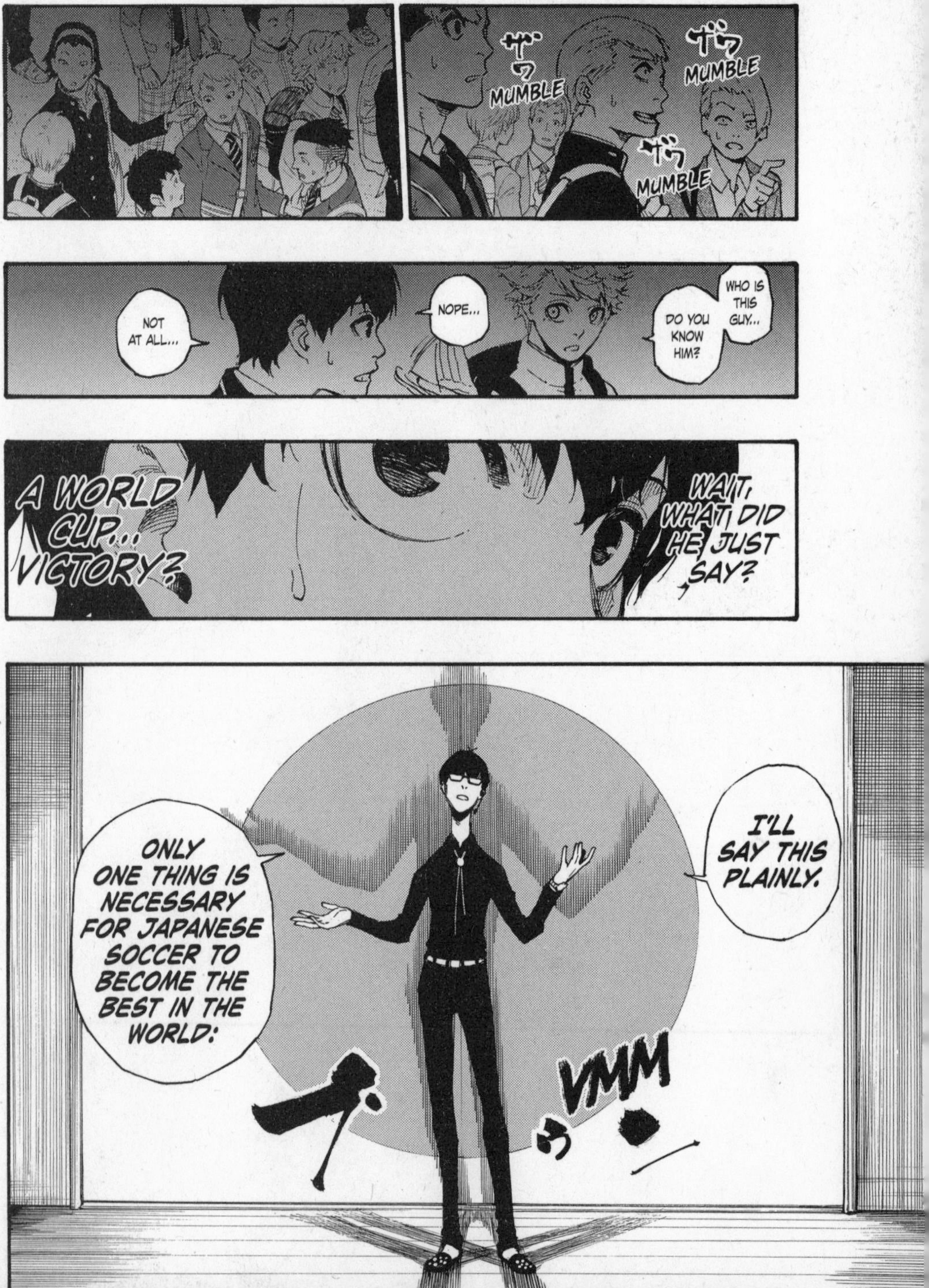
ザワ MUMBLE
ザワ MUMBLE
ザワ MUMBLE
WHO IS THIS GUY...
DO YOU KNOW HIM?
NOPE...
NOT AT ALL...
WAIT, WHAT DID HE JUST SAY?
A WORLD CUP... VICTORY?
I'LL SAY THIS PLAINLY.
ONLY ONE THING IS NECESSARY FOR JAPANESE SOCCER TO BECOME THE BEST IN THE WORLD:
VMM

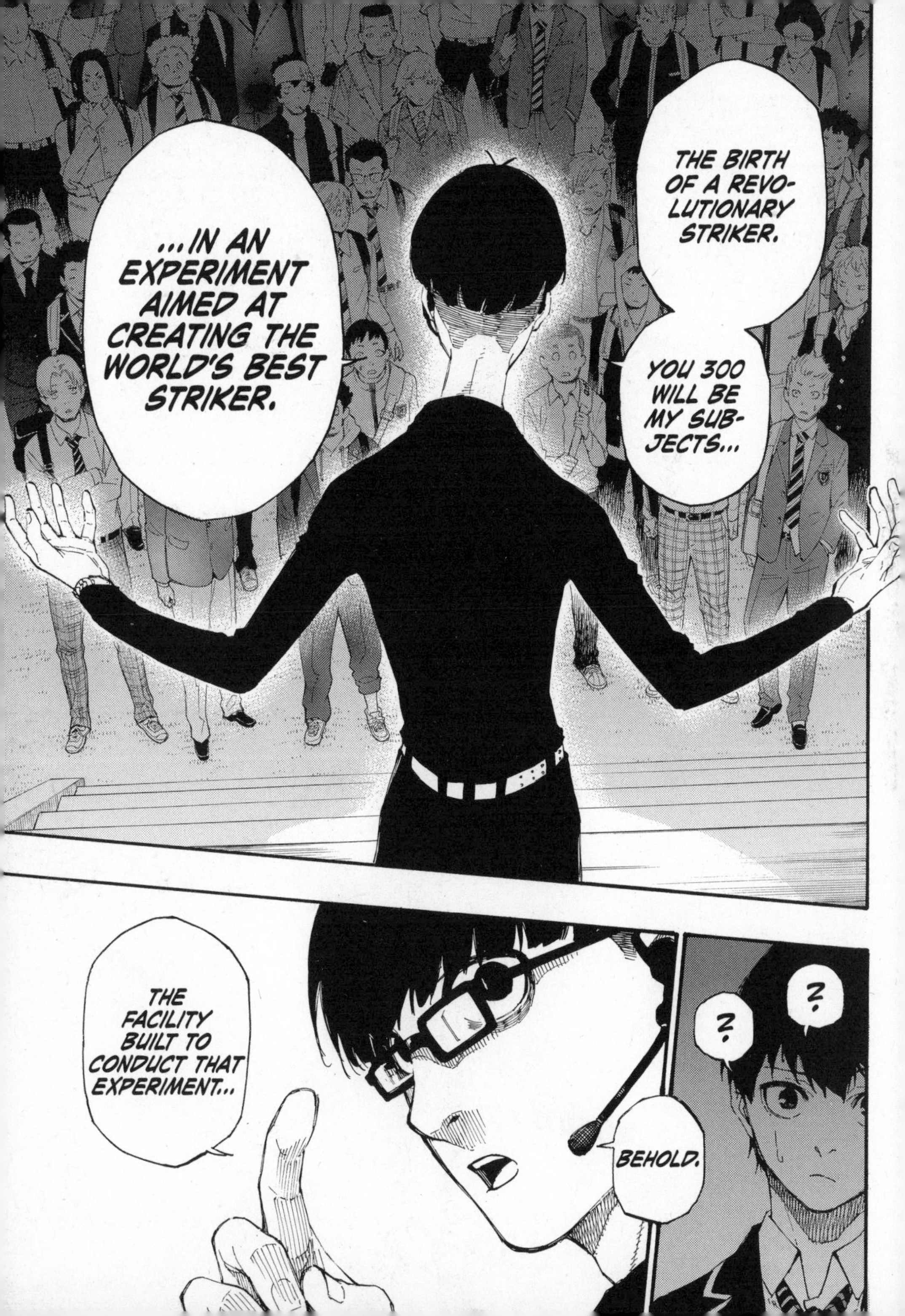
THE BIRTH OF A REVOLUTIONARY STRIKER.
YOU 300 WILL BE MY SUBJECTS...
...IN AN EXPERIMENT AIMED AT CREATING THE WORLD'S BEST STRIKER.
? ?
THE FACILITY BUILT TO CONDUCT THAT EXPERIMENT...
BEHOLD.

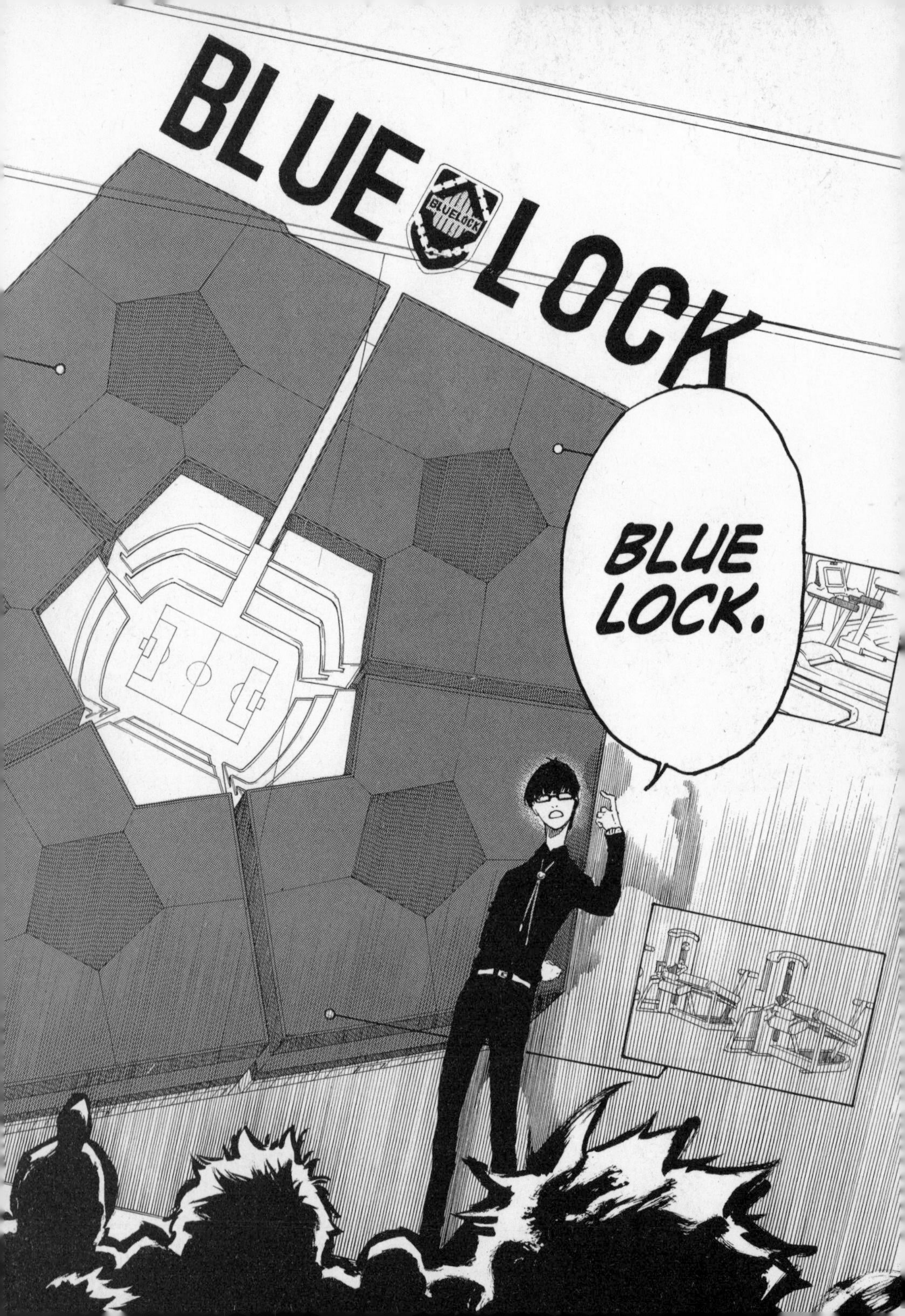
BLUE LOCK
BLUELOCK
BLUE LOCK.

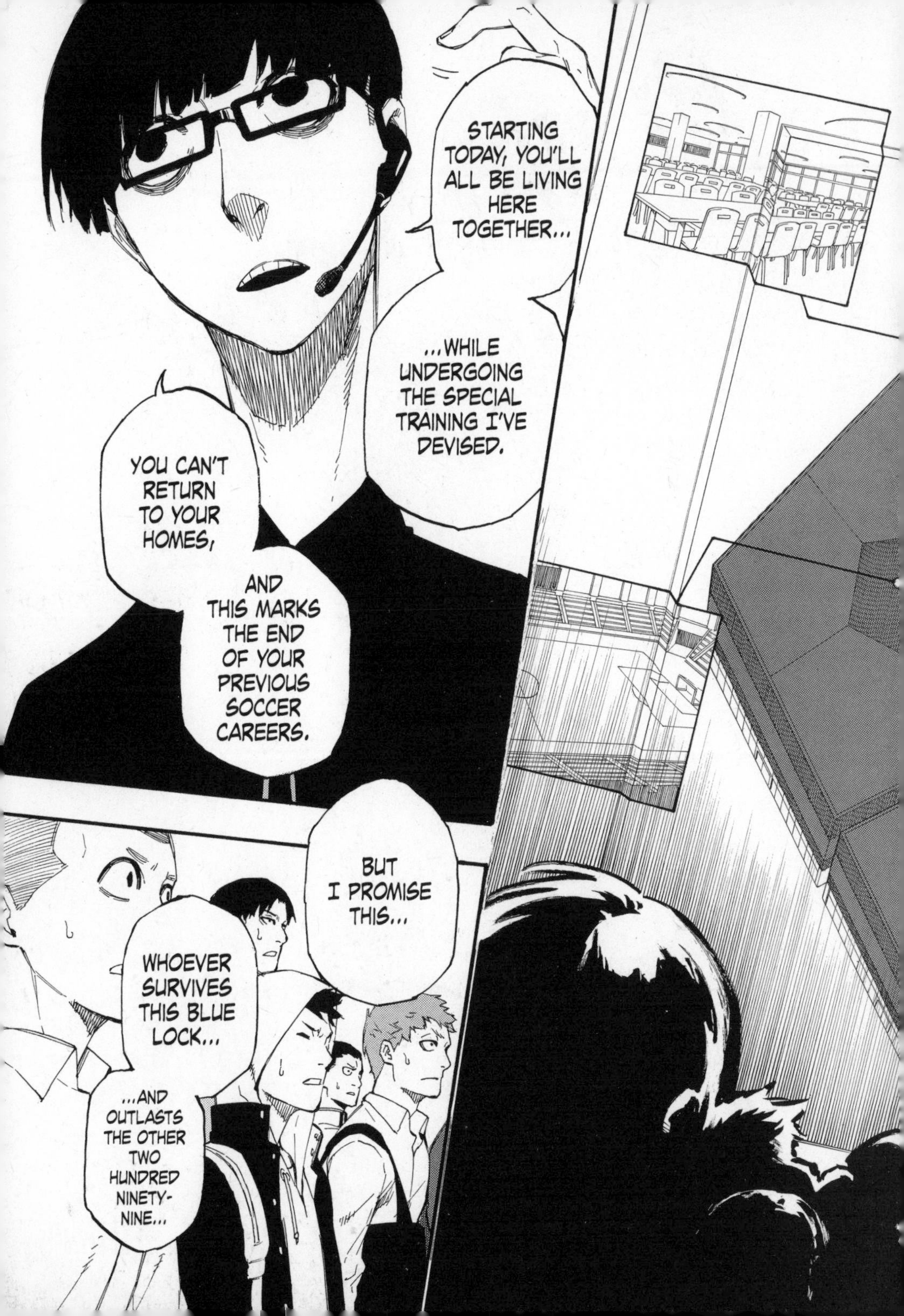
STARTING TODAY, YOU'LL ALL BE LIVING HERE TOGETHER...
...WHILE UNDERGOING THE SPECIAL TRAINING I'VE DEVISED.
YOU CAN'T RETURN TO YOUR HOMES,
AND THIS MARKS THE END OF YOUR PREVIOUS SOCCER CAREERS.
BUT I PROMISE THIS...
WHOEVER SURVIVES THIS BLUE LOCK...
...AND OUTLASTS THE OTHER TWO HUNDRED NINETY-NINE...

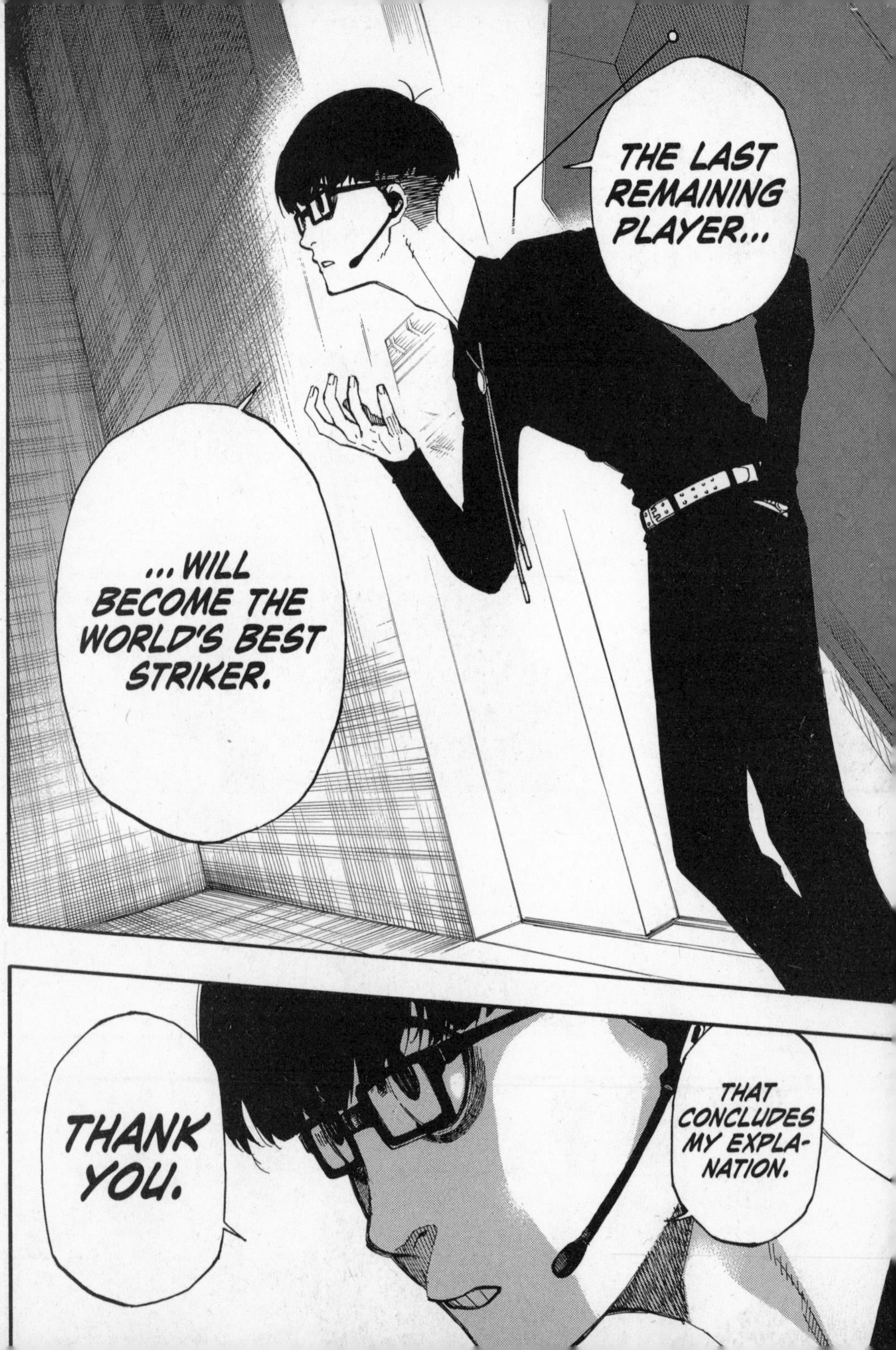
THE LAST REMAINING PLAYER...
...WILL BECOME THE WORLD'S BEST STRIKER.
THAT CONCLUDES MY EXPLA-NATION.
THANK YOU.

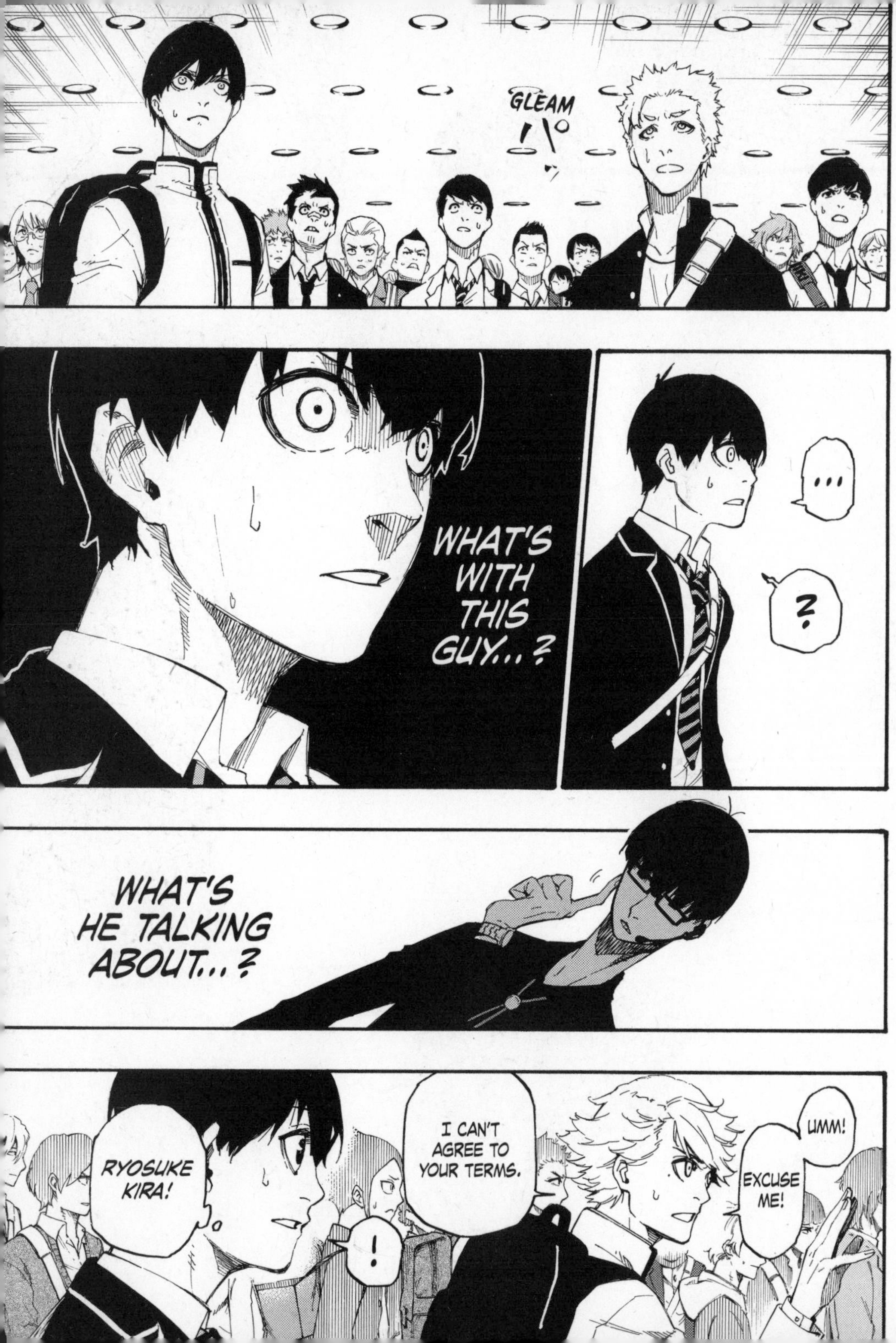
GLEAM
...
?
WHAT'S WITH THIS GUY...?
WHAT'S HE TALKING ABOUT...?
UMM!
EXCUSE ME!
I CAN'T AGREE TO YOUR TERMS.
RYOSUKE KIRA!
!

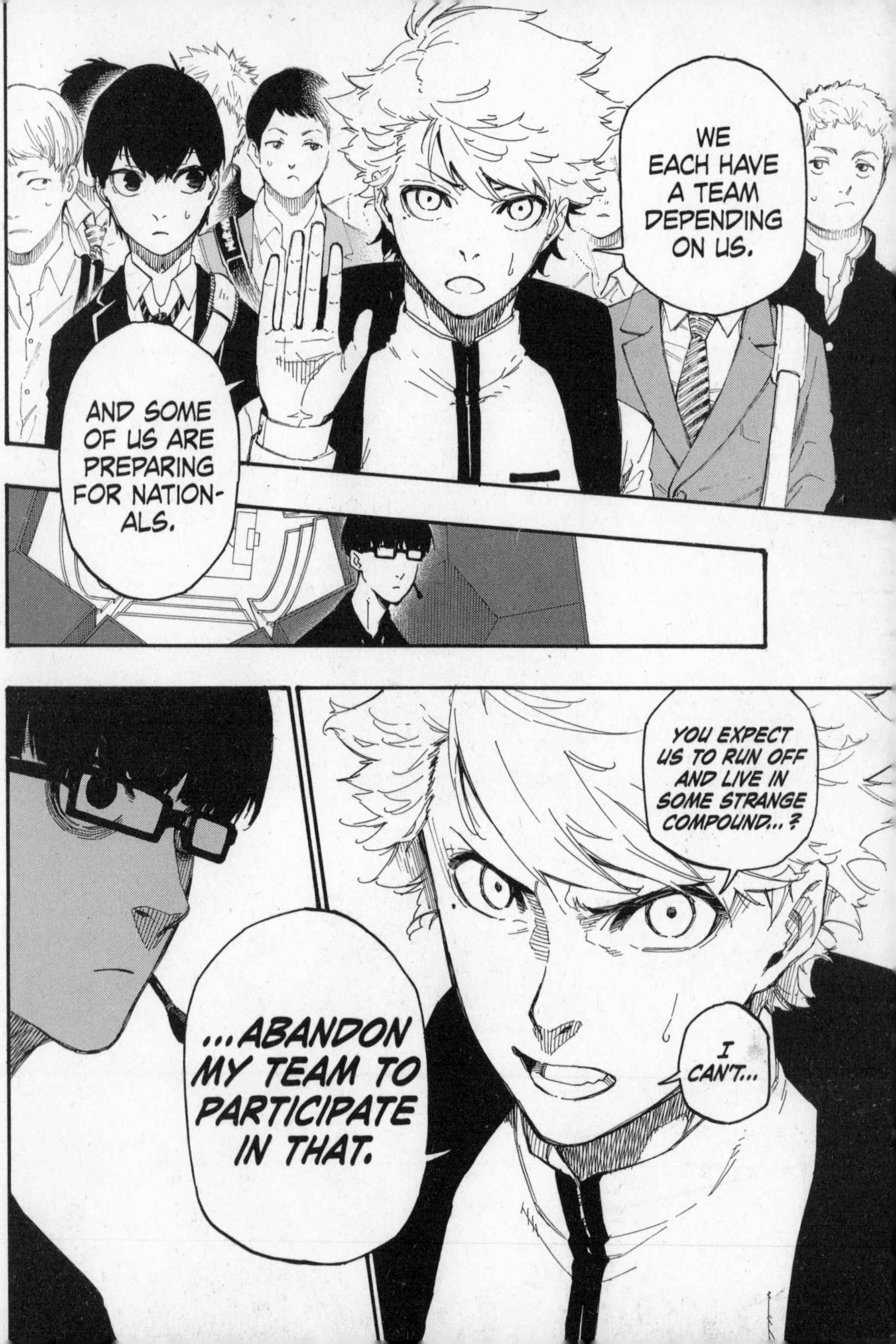
WE EACH HAVE A TEAM DEPENDING ON US.
AND SOME OF US ARE PREPARING FOR NATION-ALS.
YOU EXPECT US TO RUN OFF AND LIVE IN SOME STRANGE COMPOUND...?
I CAN'T...
...ABANDON MY TEAM TO PARTICIPATE IN THAT.

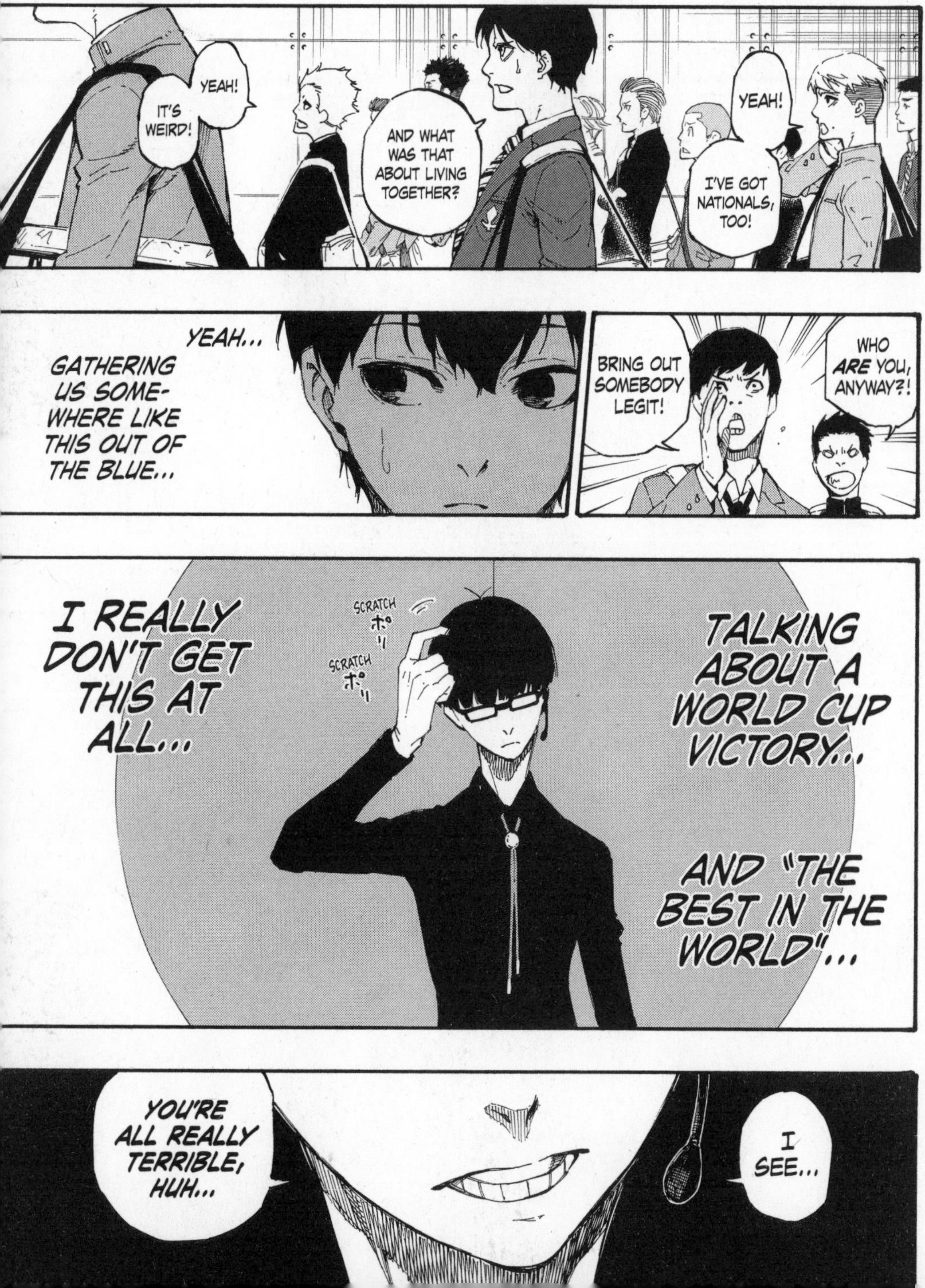
YEAH!
I'VE GOT NATIONALS, TOO!
AND WHAT WAS THAT ABOUT LIVING TOGETHER?
YEAH!
IT'S WEIRD!
WHO ARE YOU, ANYWAY?!
BRING OUT SOMEBODY LEGIT!
YEAH...
GATHERING US SOME-WHERE LIKE THIS OUT OF THE BLUE...
TALKING ABOUT A WORLD CUP VICTORY...
AND "THE BEST IN THE WORLD"...
SCRATCH ポリ
SCRATCH ポリ
I REALLY DON'T GET THIS AT ALL...
I SEE...
YOU'RE ALL REALLY TERRIBLE, HUH...

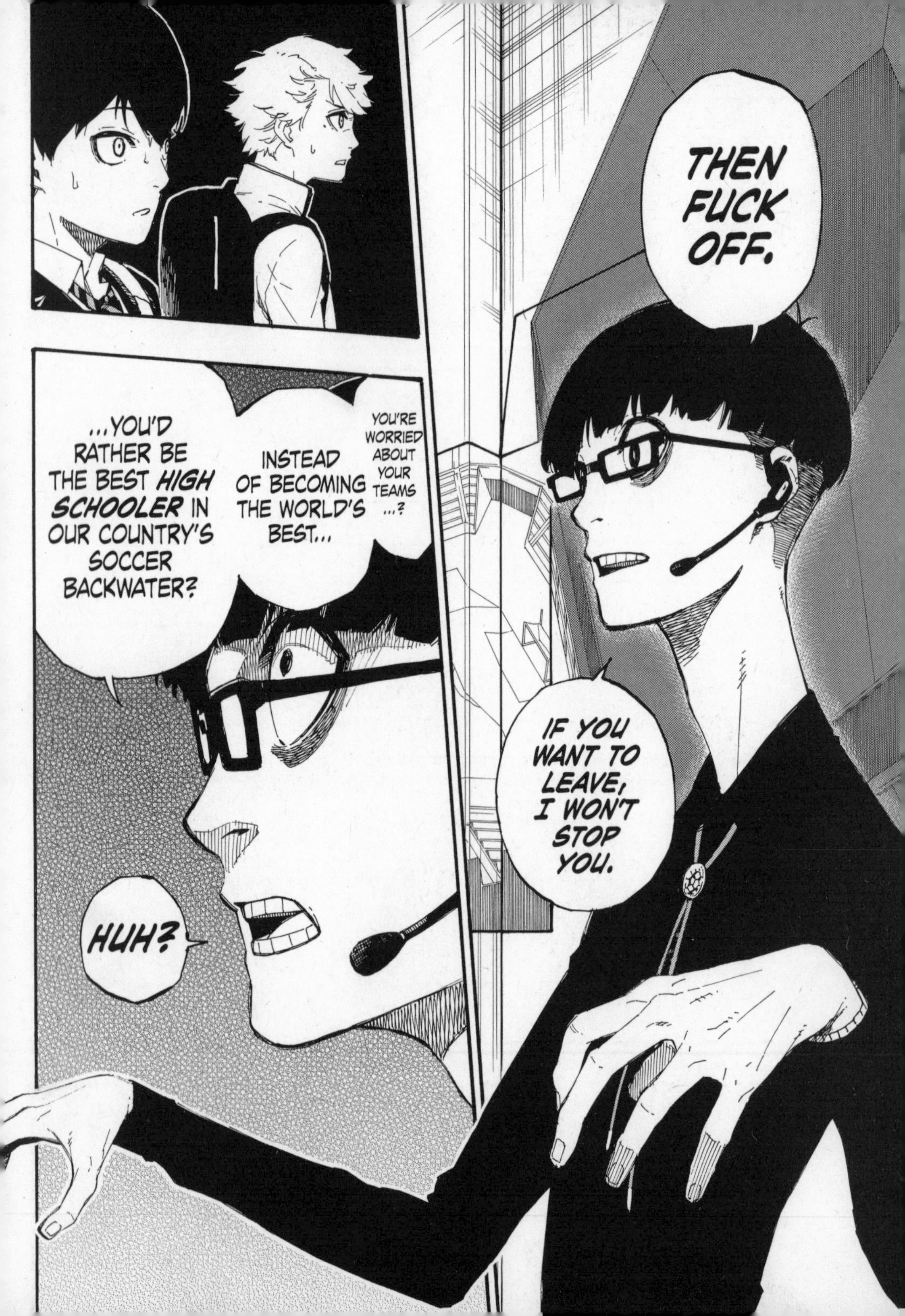
THEN FUCK OFF.
IF YOU WANT TO LEAVE, I WON'T STOP YOU.
YOU'RE WORRIED ABOUT YOUR TEAMS ...?
INSTEAD OF BECOMING THE WORLD'S BEST...
...YOU'D RATHER BE THE BEST HIGH SCHOOLER IN OUR COUNTRY'S SOCCER BACKWATER?
HUH?

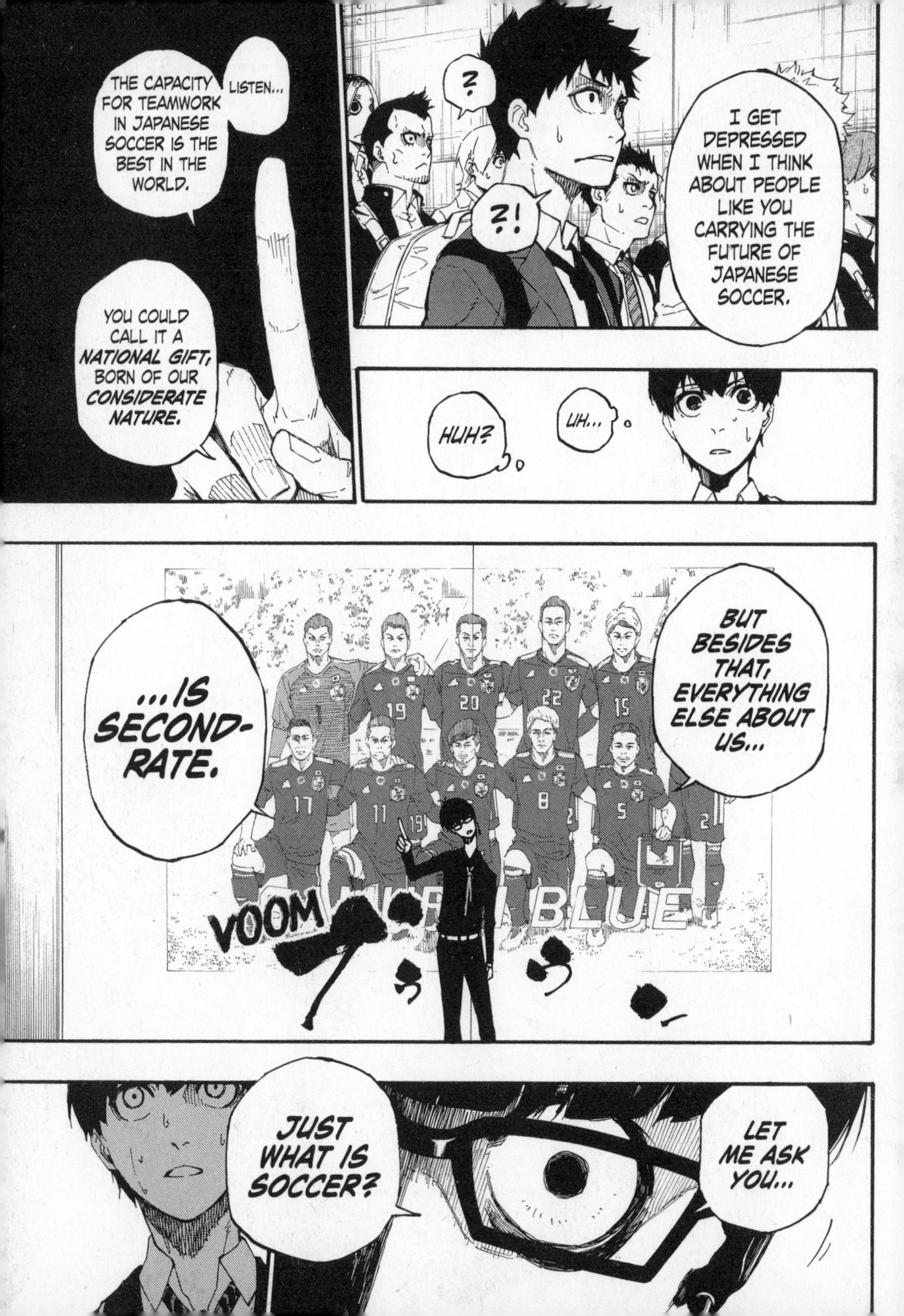
I GET DEPRESSED WHEN I THINK ABOUT PEOPLE LIKE YOU CARRYING THE FUTURE OF JAPANESE SOCCER.
?
?!
UH...
HUH?
LISTEN...
THE CAPACITY FOR TEAMWORK IN JAPANESE SOCCER IS THE BEST IN THE WORLD.
YOU COULD CALL IT A NATIONAL GIFT, BORN OF OUR CONSIDERATE NATURE.
BUT BESIDES THAT, EVERYTHING ELSE ABOUT US...
...IS SECOND-RATE.
VOOM
LET ME ASK YOU...
JUST WHAT IS SOCCER?

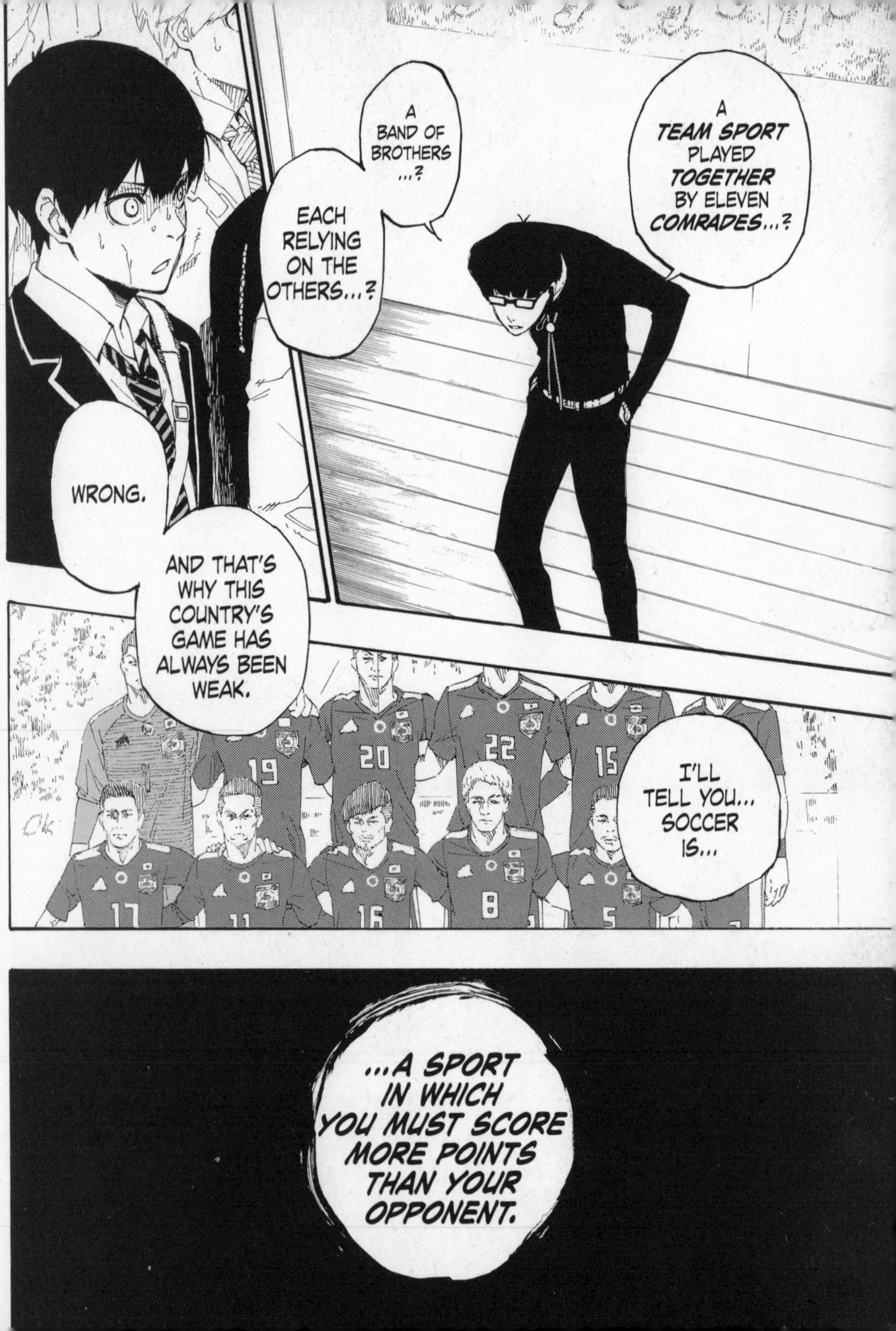
A TEAM SPORT PLAYED TOGETHER BY ELEVEN COMRADES...?
A BAND OF BROTHERS ...?
EACH RELYING ON THE OTHERS...?
WRONG.
AND THAT'S WHY THIS COUNTRY'S GAME HAS ALWAYS BEEN WEAK.
I'LL TELL YOU... SOCCER IS...
...A SPORT IN WHICH YOU MUST SCORE MORE POINTS THAN YOUR OPPONENT.

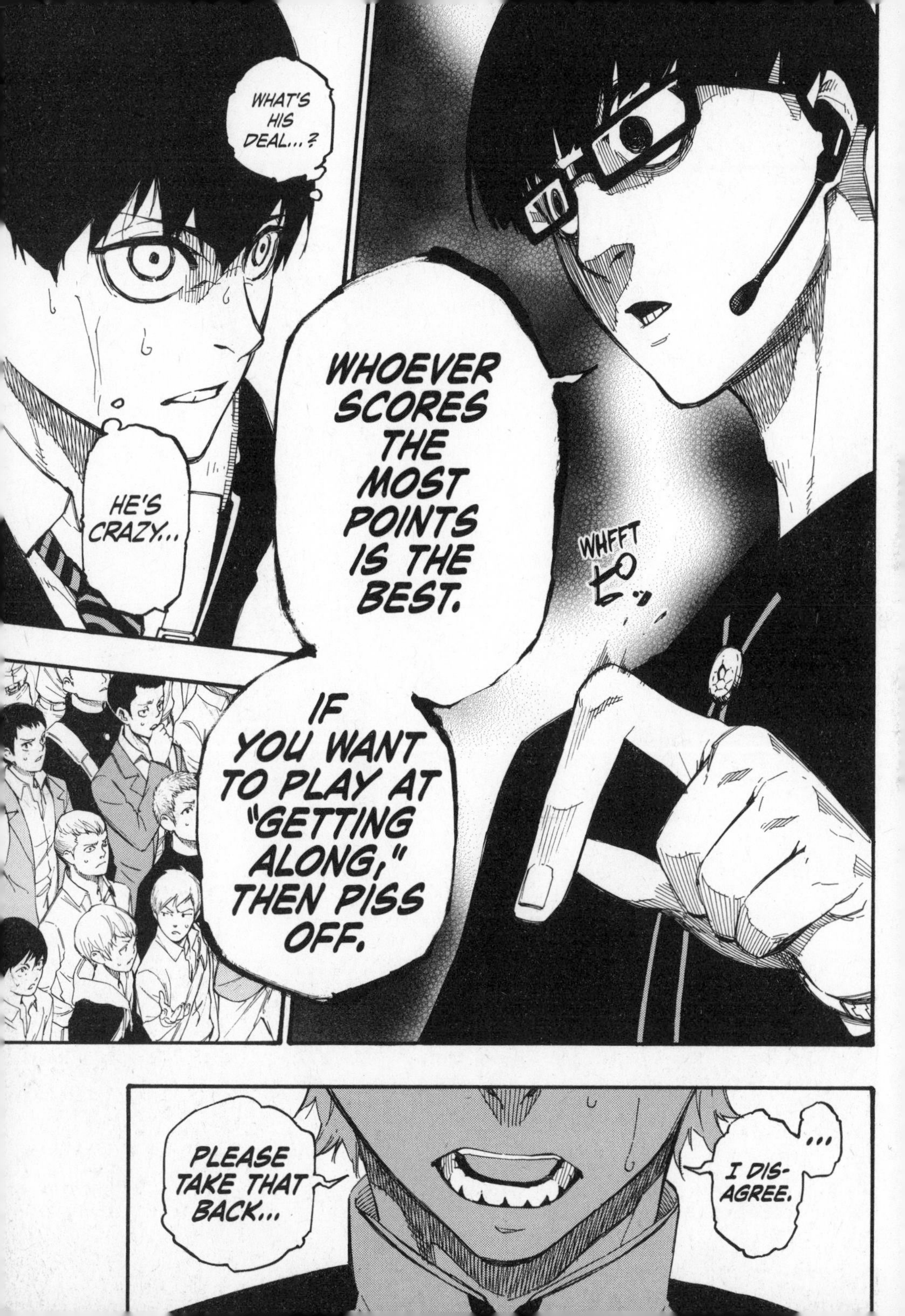
WHOEVER SCORES THE MOST POINTS IS THE BEST.
WHFFT
ピッ
IF YOU WANT TO PLAY AT "GETTING ALONG," THEN PISS OFF.
WHAT'S HIS DEAL...?
HE'S CRAZY...
... I DIS-AGREE.
PLEASE TAKE THAT BACK...

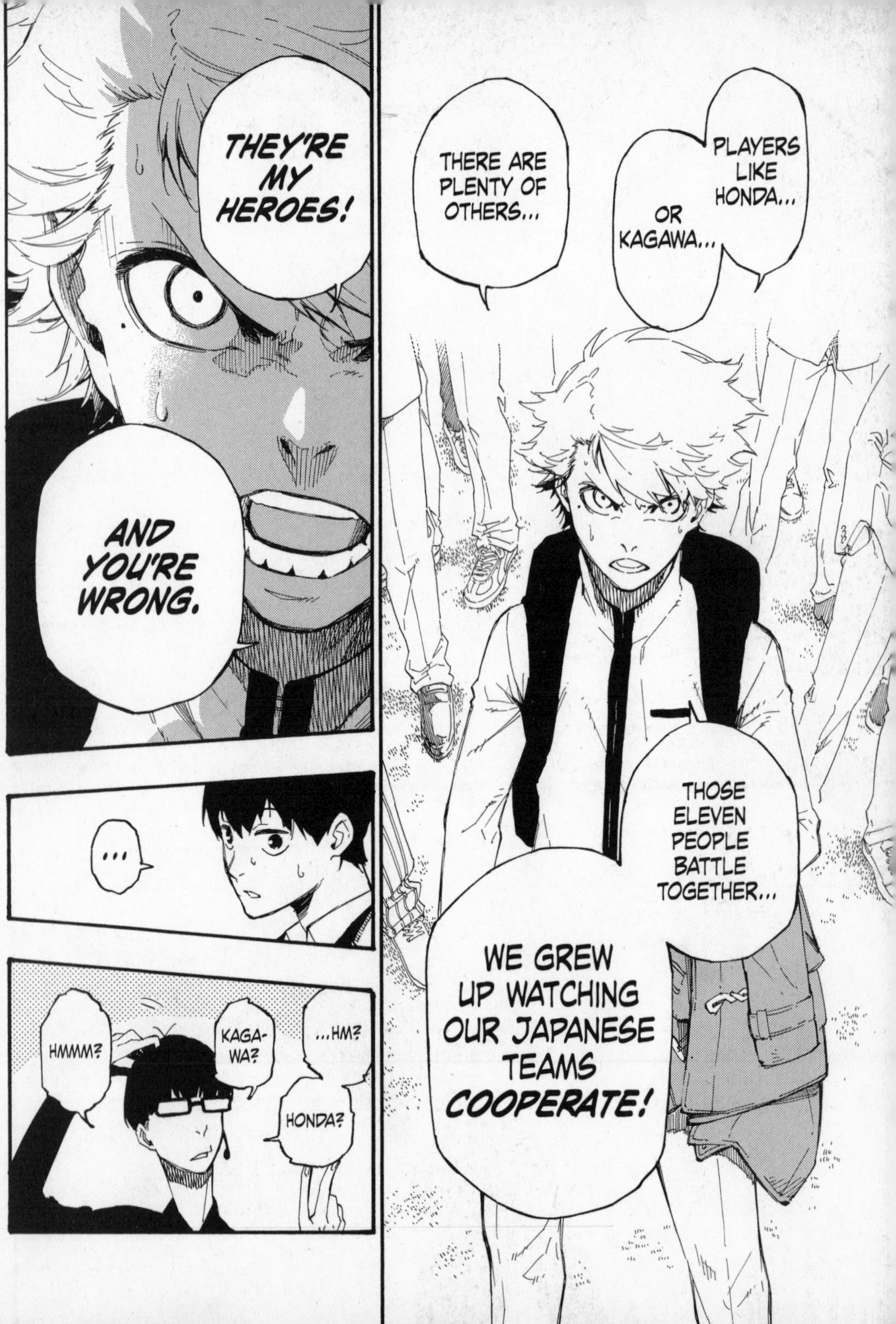
PLAYERS LIKE HONDA...
OR KAGAWA...
THERE ARE PLENTY OF OTHERS...
THOSE ELEVEN PEOPLE BATTLE TOGETHER...
WE GREW UP WATCHING OUR JAPANESE TEAMS COOPERATE!
THEY'RE MY HEROES!
AND YOU'RE WRONG.
...
...HM?
KAGA-WA?
HONDA?
HMMM?

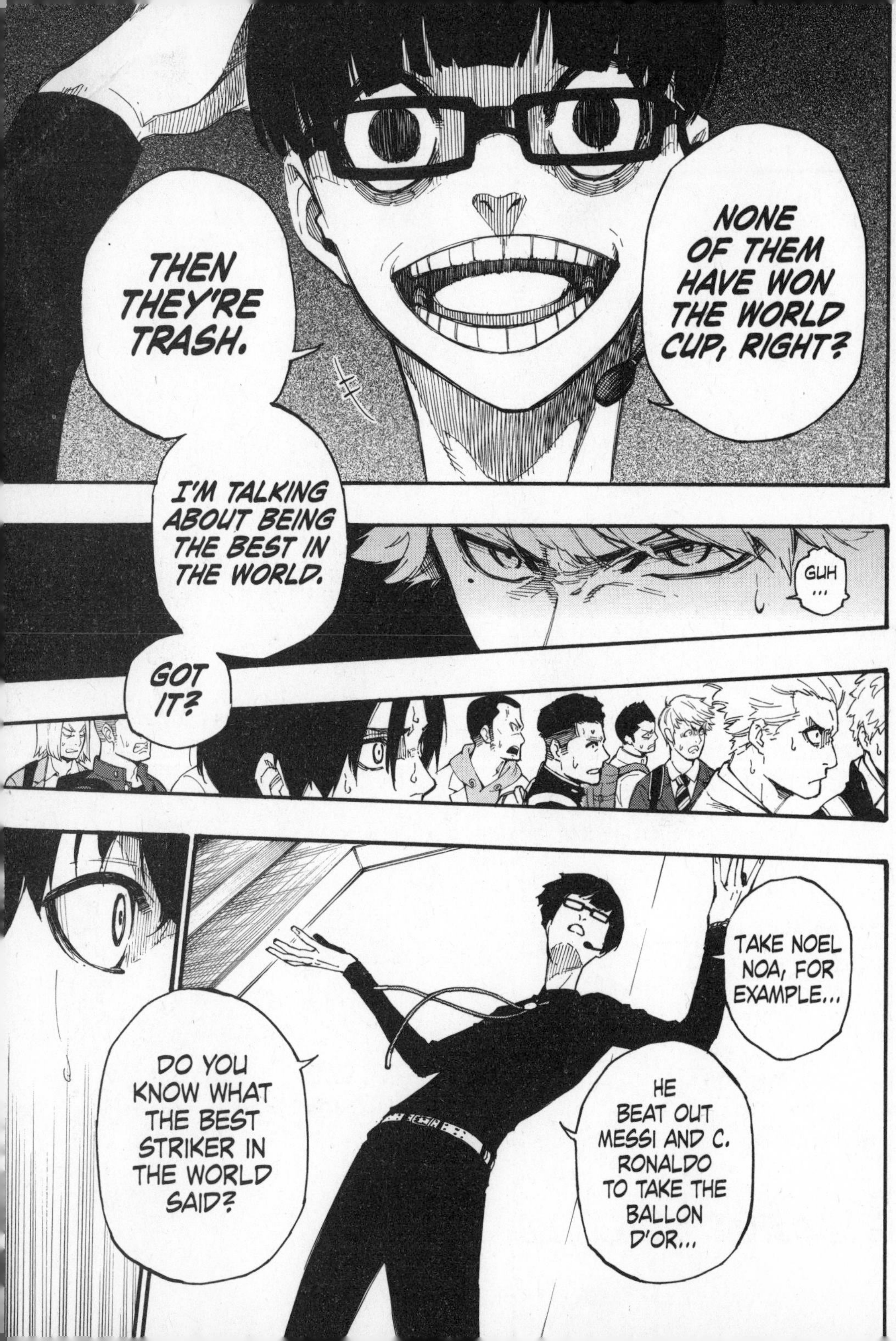
NONE OF THEM HAVE WON THE WORLD CUP, RIGHT?
THEN THEY'RE TRASH.
I'M TALKING ABOUT BEING THE BEST IN THE WORLD.
GUH...
GOT IT?
TAKE NOEL NOA, FOR EXAMPLE...
HE BEAT OUT MESSI AND C. RONALDO TO TAKE THE BALLON D'OR...
DO YOU KNOW WHAT THE BEST STRIKER IN THE WORLD SAID?

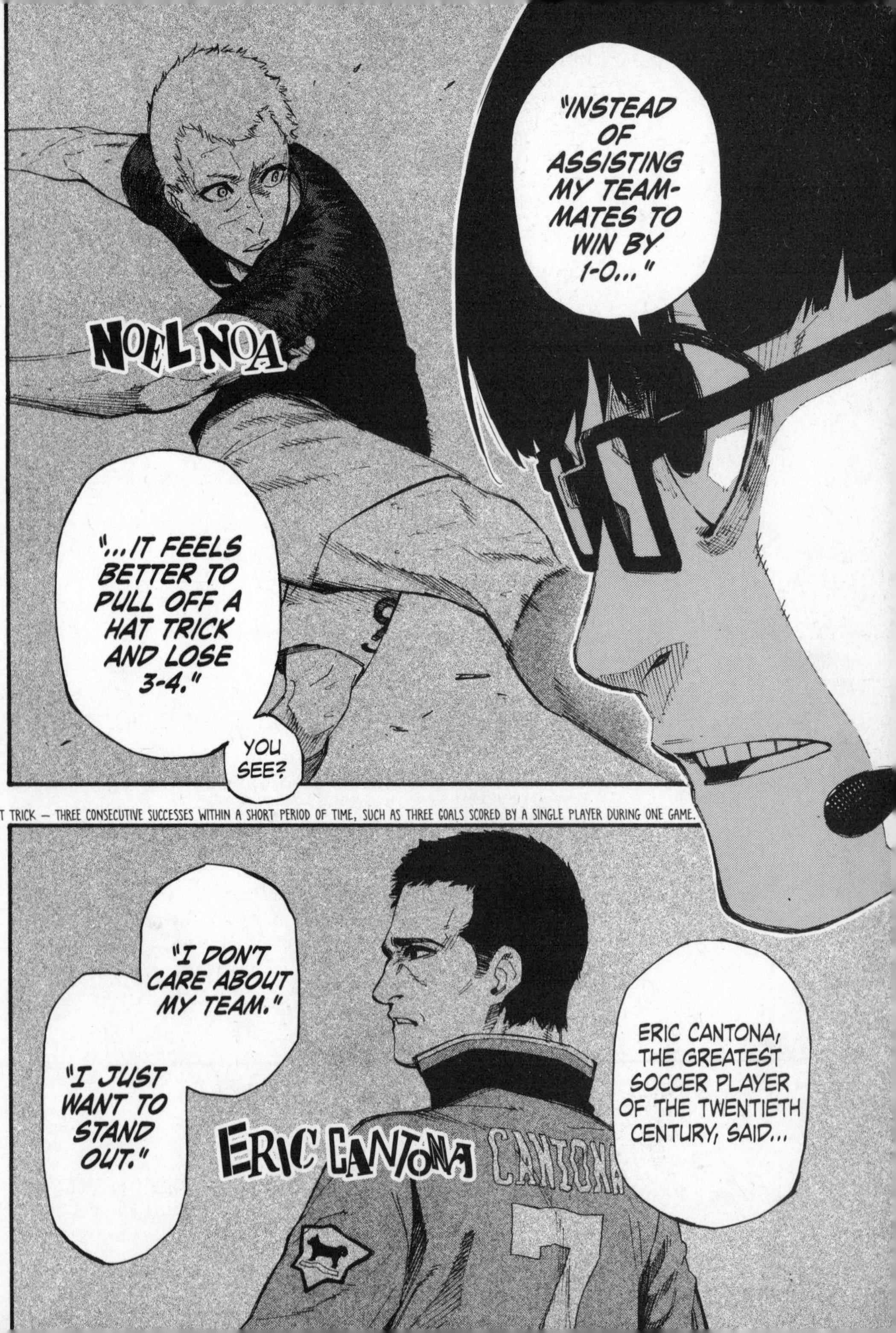
"INSTEAD OF ASSISTING MY TEAM-MATES TO WIN BY 1-0..."
NOEL NOA
"...IT FEELS BETTER TO PULL OFF A HAT TRICK AND LOSE 3-4."
YOU SEE?
ERIC CANTONA, THE GREATEST SOCCER PLAYER OF THE TWENTIETH CENTURY, SAID...
ERIC CANTONA
CANTONA
7
"I DON'T CARE ABOUT MY TEAM."
"I JUST WANT TO STAND OUT."

*HAT TRICK — THREE CONSECUTIVE SUCCESSES WITHIN A SHORT PERIOD OF TIME, SUCH AS THREE GOALS SCORED BY A SINGLE PLAYER DURING ONE GAME.

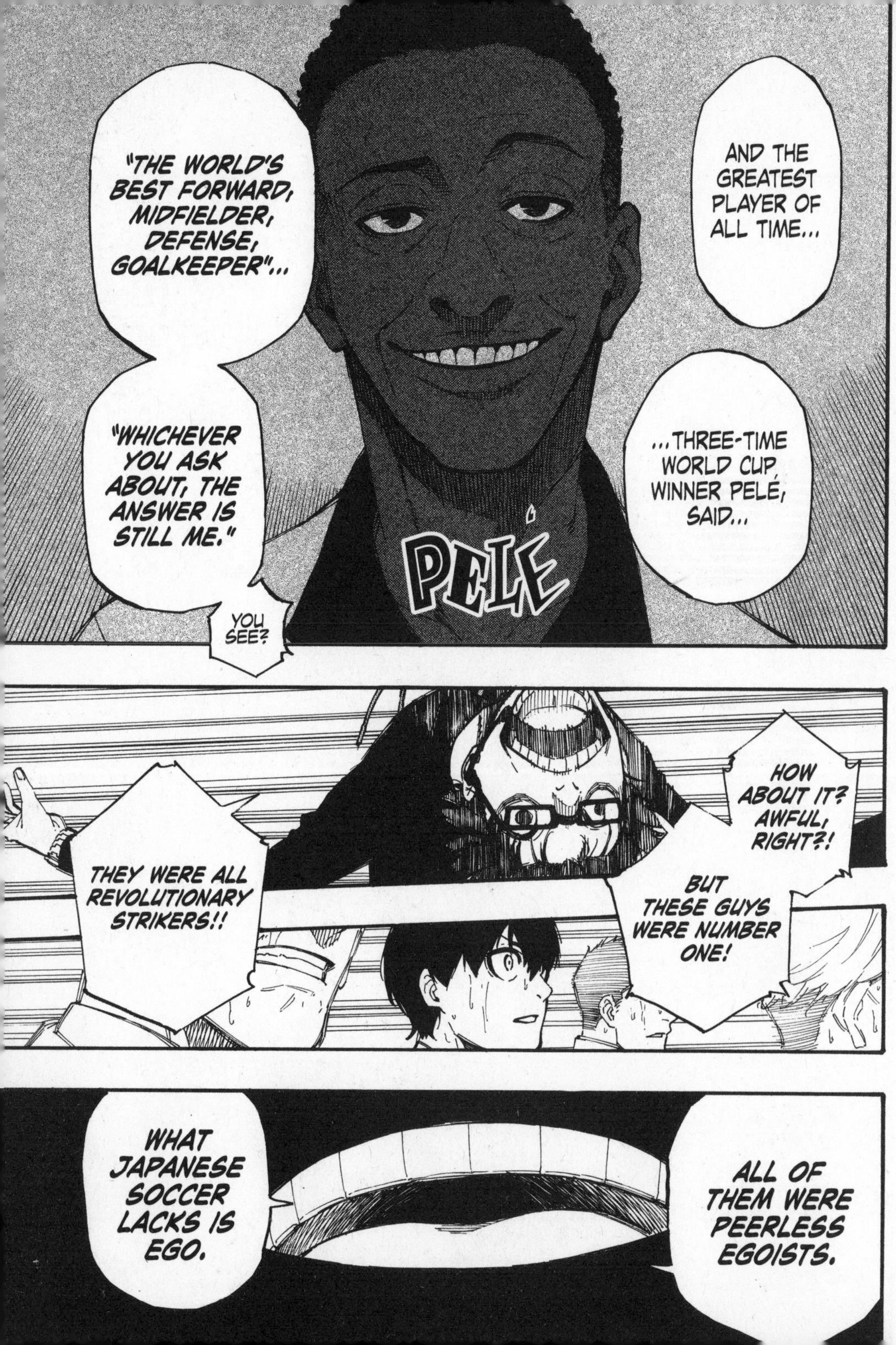
AND THE GREATEST PLAYER OF ALL TIME...
...THREE-TIME WORLD CUP WINNER PELÉ, SAID...
"THE WORLD'S BEST FORWARD, MIDFIELDER, DEFENSE, GOALKEEPER"...
PELE
"WHICHEVER YOU ASK ABOUT, THE ANSWER IS STILL ME."
YOU SEE?
HOW ABOUT IT? AWFUL, RIGHT?!
BUT THESE GUYS WERE NUMBER ONE!
THEY WERE ALL REVOLUTIONARY STRIKERS!!
ALL OF THEM WERE PEERLESS EGOISTS.
WHAT JAPANESE SOCCER LACKS IS EGO.

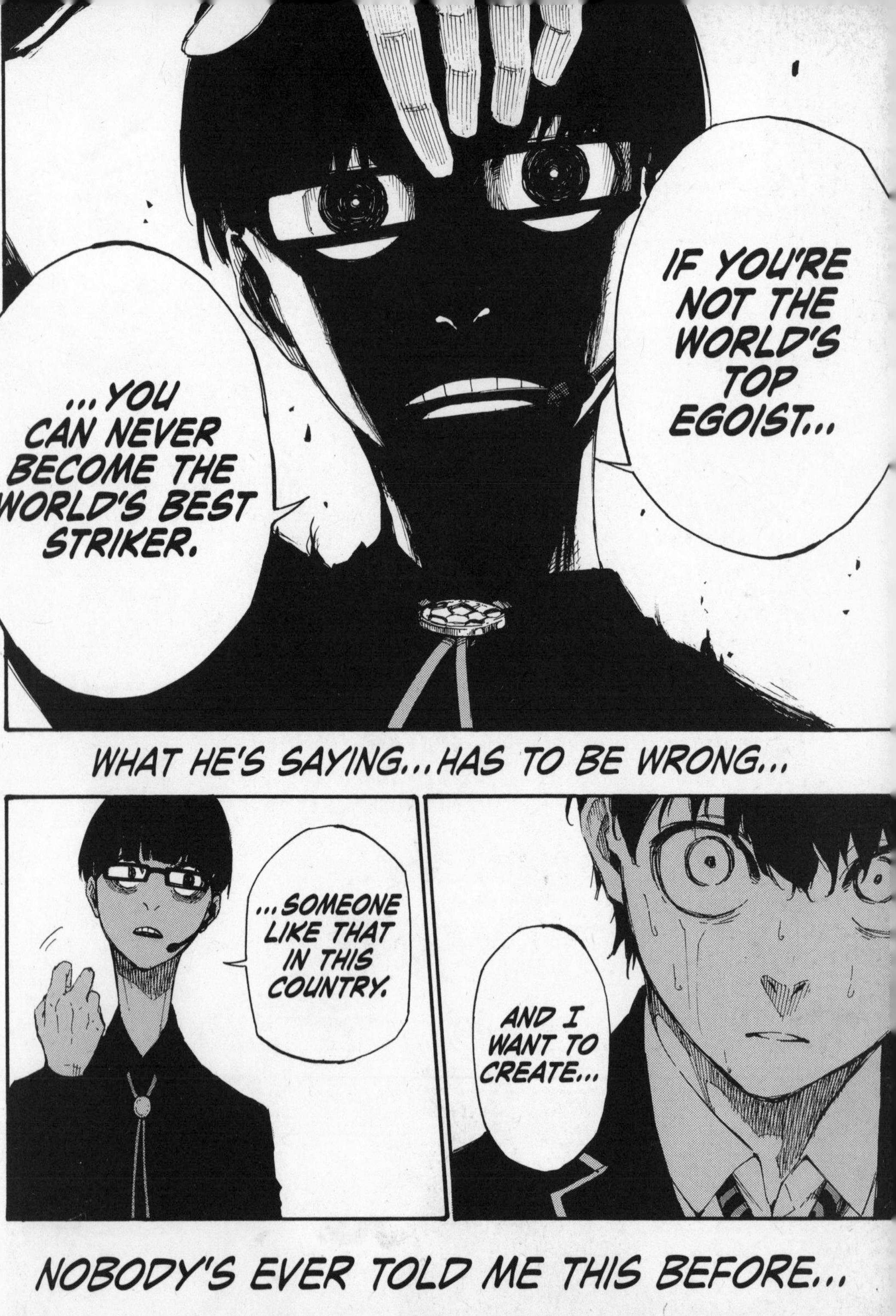
IF YOU'RE NOT THE WORLD'S TOP EGOIST...
...YOU CAN NEVER BECOME THE WORLD'S BEST STRIKER.
WHAT HE'S SAYING...HAS TO BE WRONG...
AND I WANT TO CREATE...
...SOMEONE LIKE THAT IN THIS COUNTRY.
NOBODY'S EVER TOLD ME THIS BEFORE...

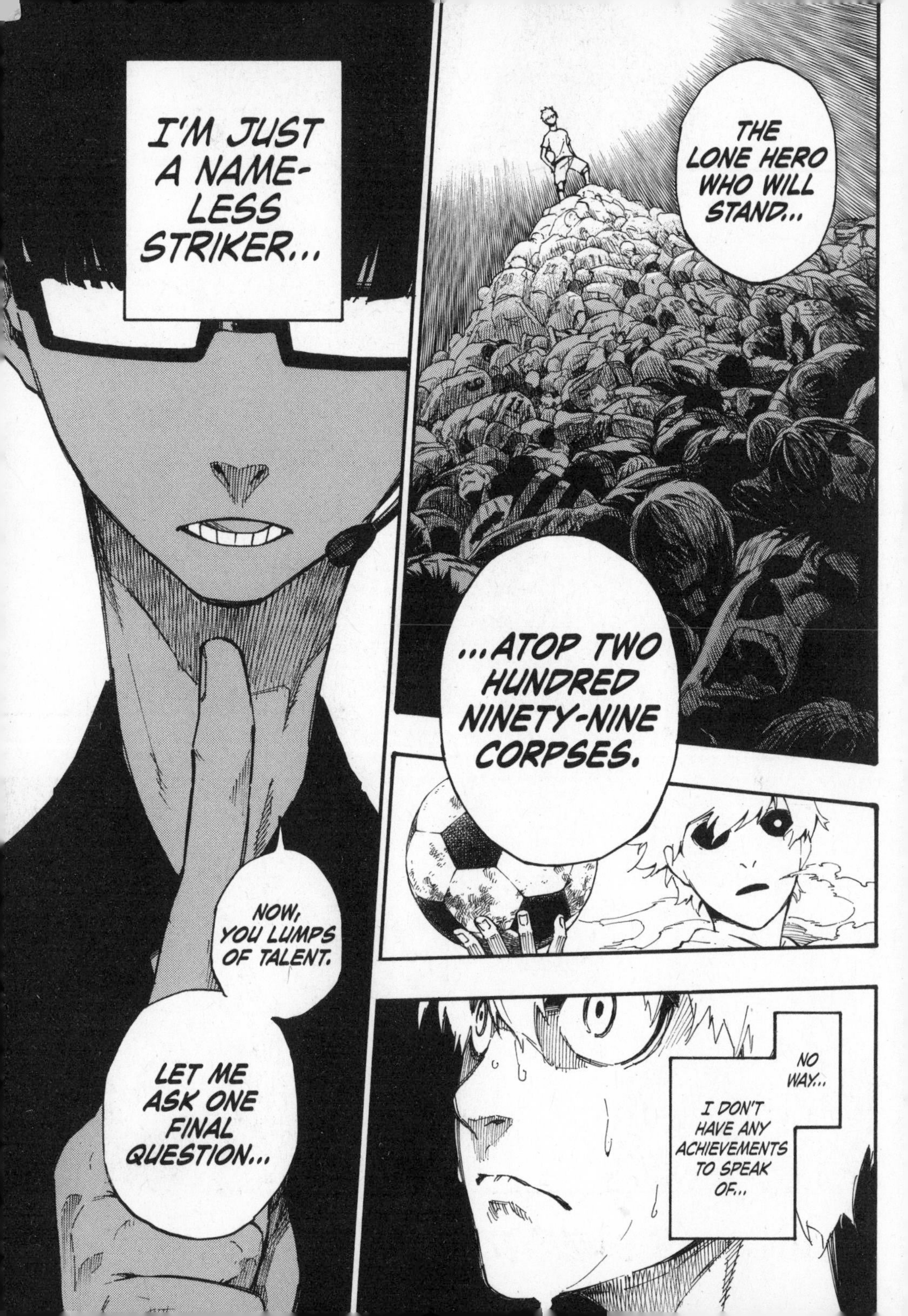
THE LONE HERO WHO WILL STAND...
...ATOP TWO HUNDRED NINETY-NINE CORPSES.
NO WAY...
I DON'T HAVE ANY ACHIEVEMENTS TO SPEAK OF...
I'M JUST A NAME-LESS STRIKER...
NOW, YOU LUMPS OF TALENT.
LET ME ASK ONE FINAL QUESTION...

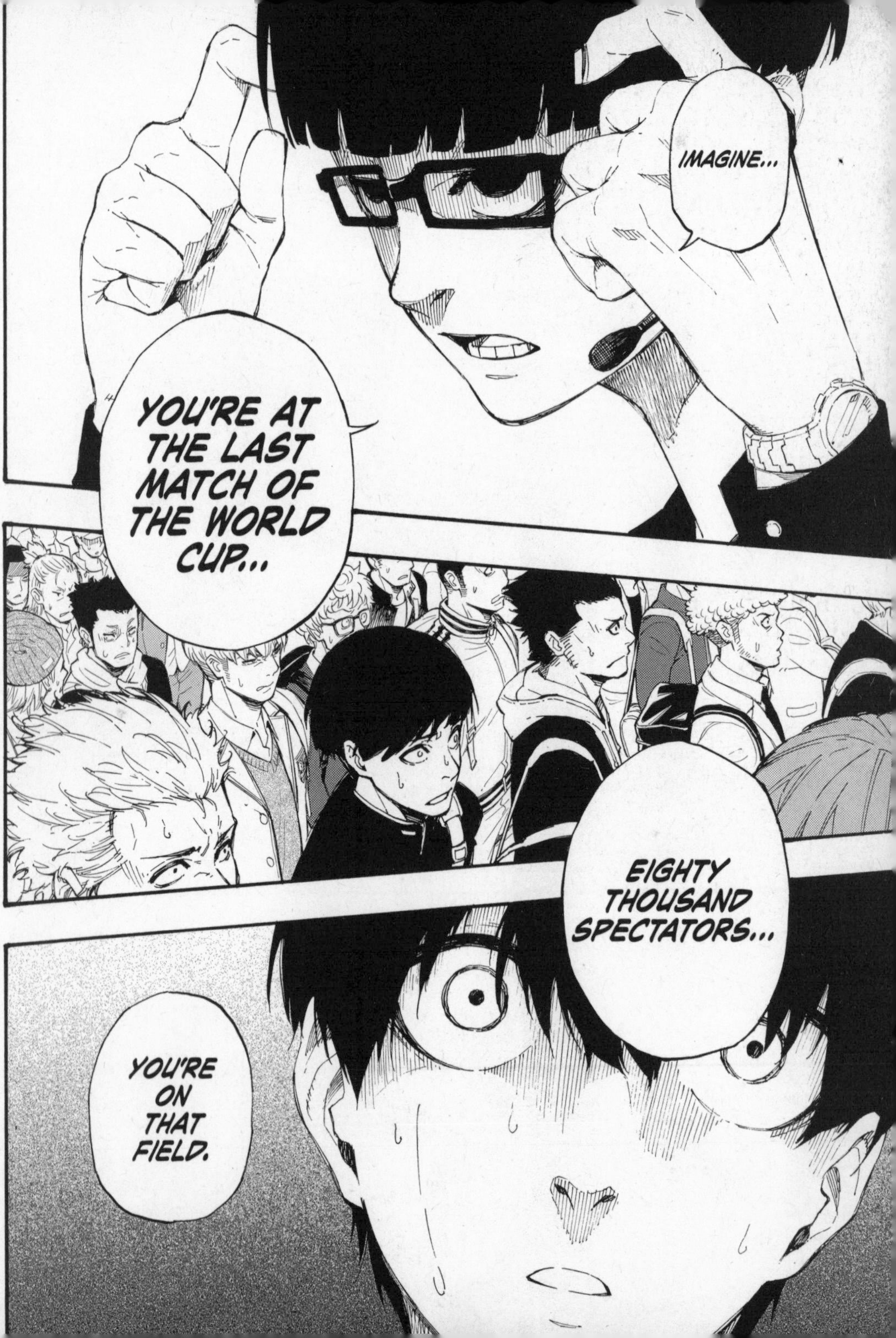
IMAGINE...
YOU'RE AT THE LAST MATCH OF THE WORLD CUP...
EIGHTY THOUSAND SPECTATORS...
YOU'RE ON THAT FIELD.

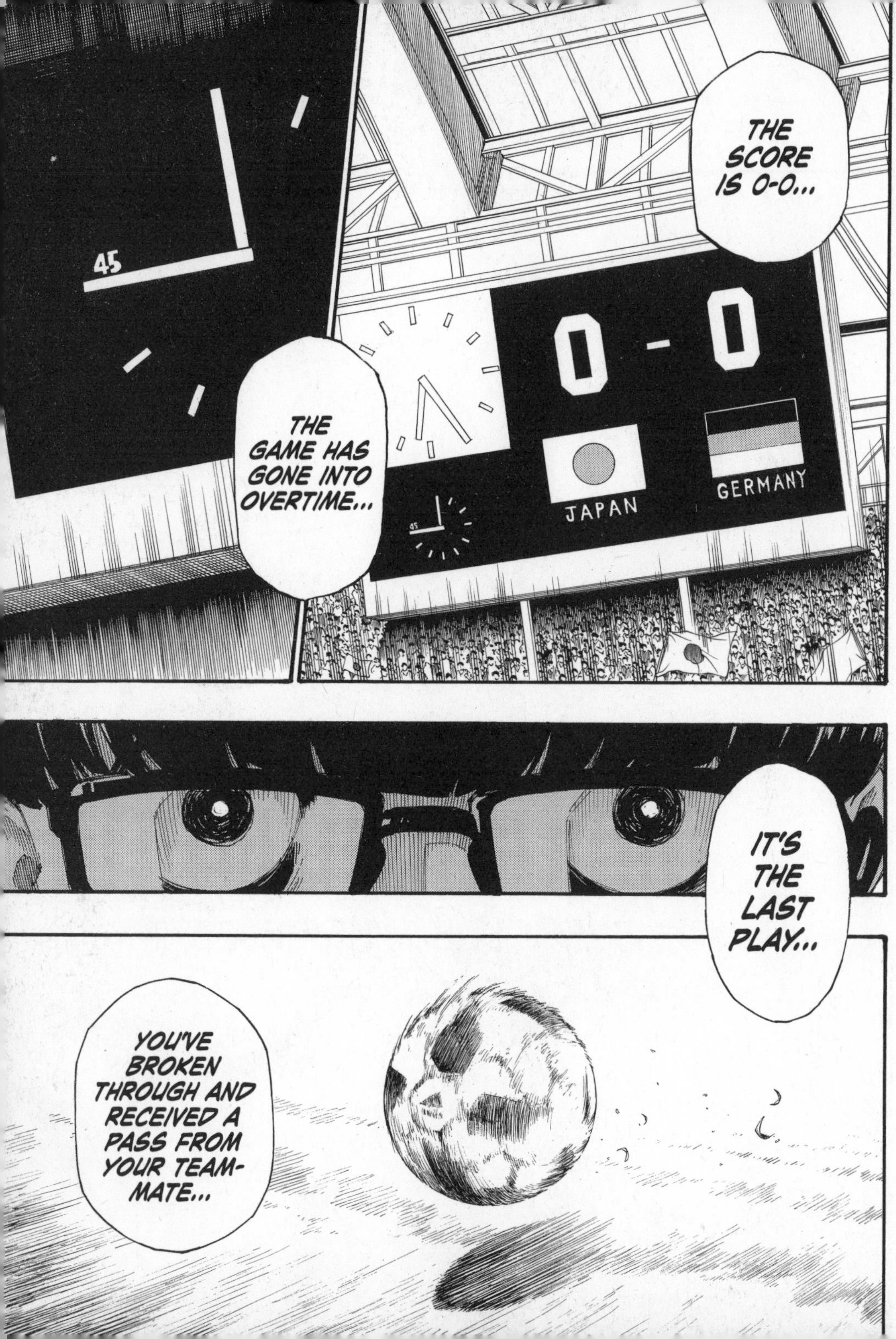
THE SCORE IS 0-0...
THE GAME HAS GONE INTO OVERTIME...
45
0 - 0
JAPAN
GERMANY
IT'S THE LAST PLAY...
YOU'VE BROKEN THROUGH AND RECEIVED A PASS FROM YOUR TEAM-MATE...

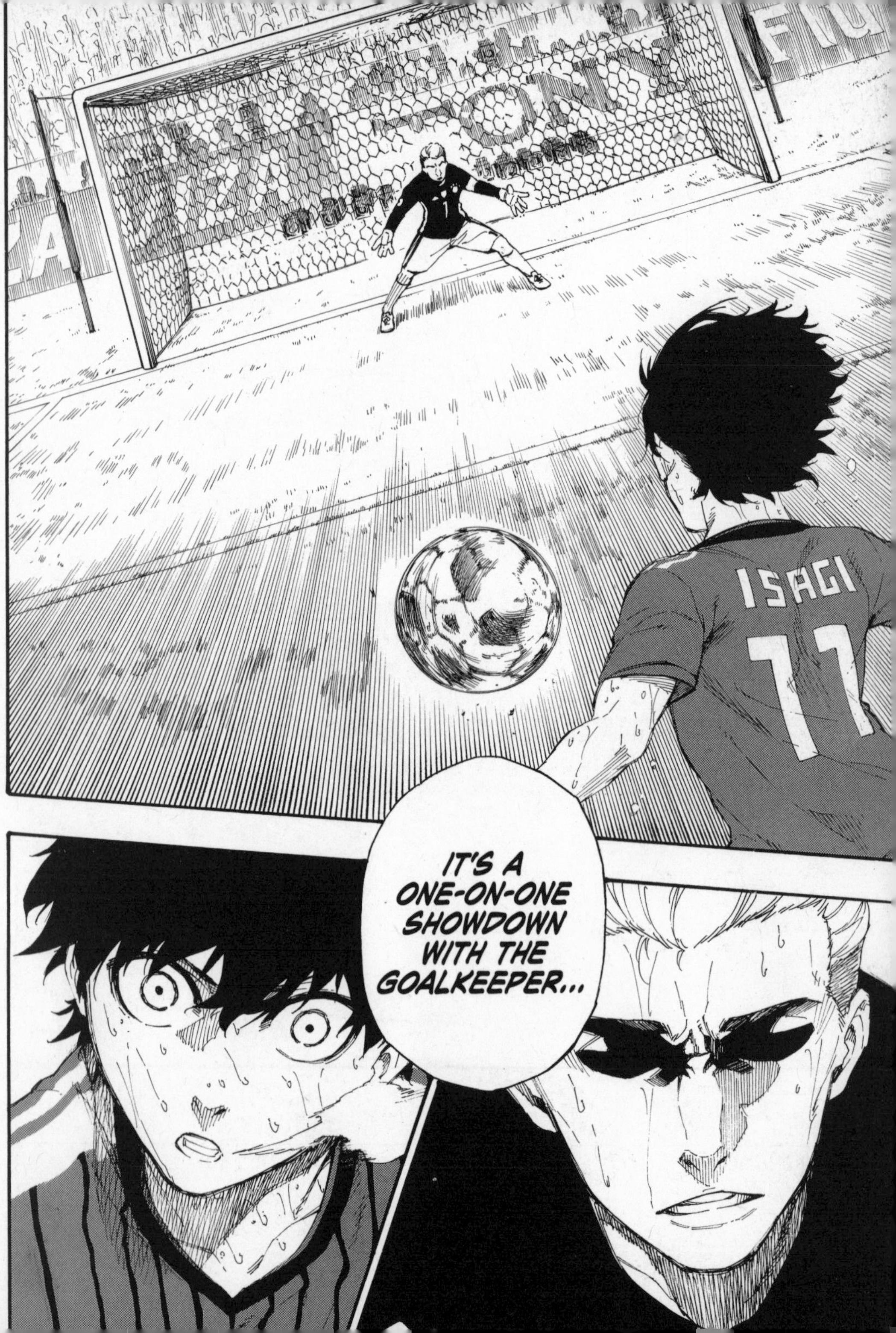
ISAGI
11
IT'S A ONE-ON-ONE SHOWDOWN WITH THE GOALKEEPER...

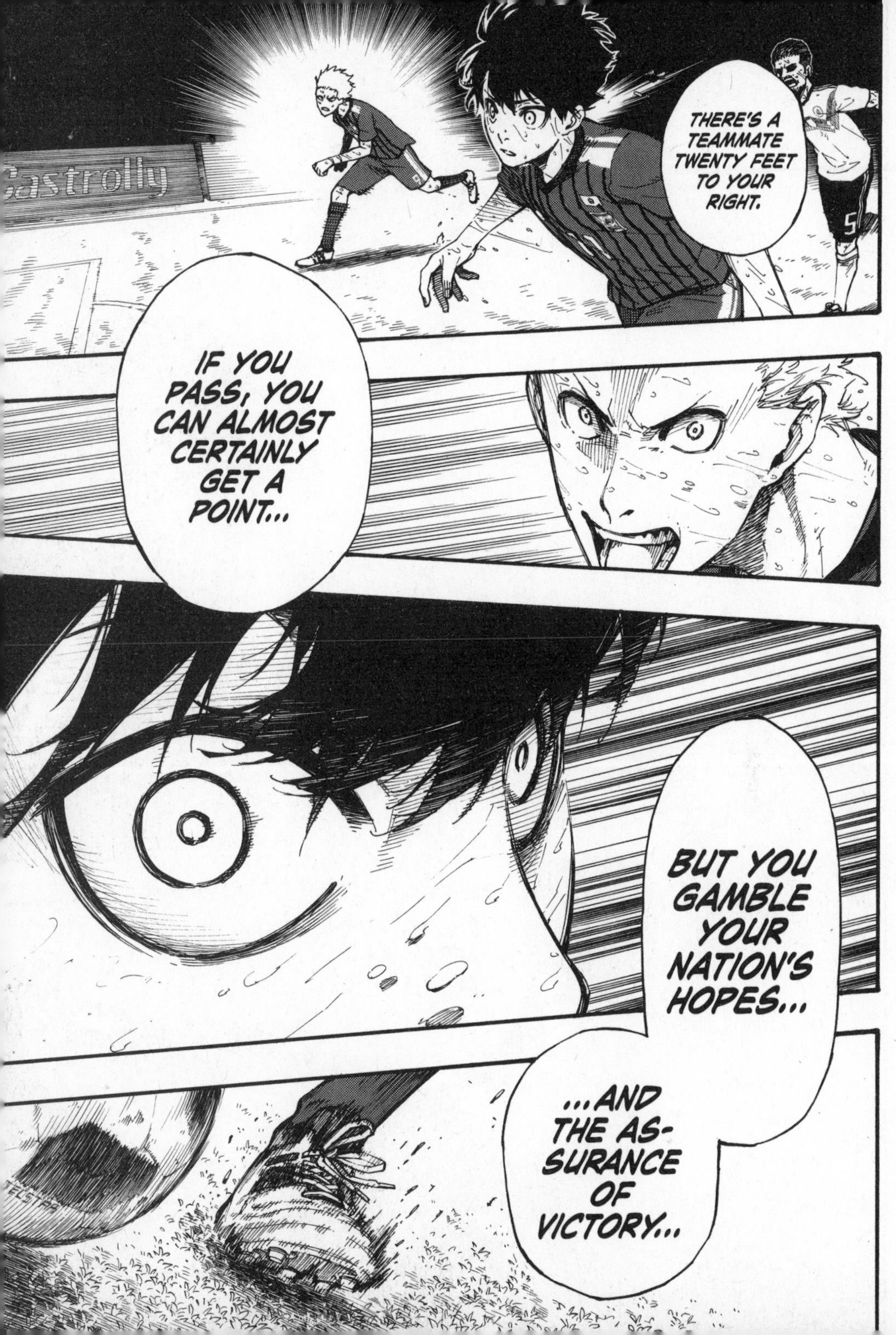
THERE'S A TEAMMATE TWENTY FEET TO YOUR RIGHT.
IF YOU PASS, YOU CAN ALMOST CERTAINLY GET A POINT...
BUT YOU GAMBLE YOUR NATION'S HOPES...
...AND THE AS-SURANCE OF VICTORY...

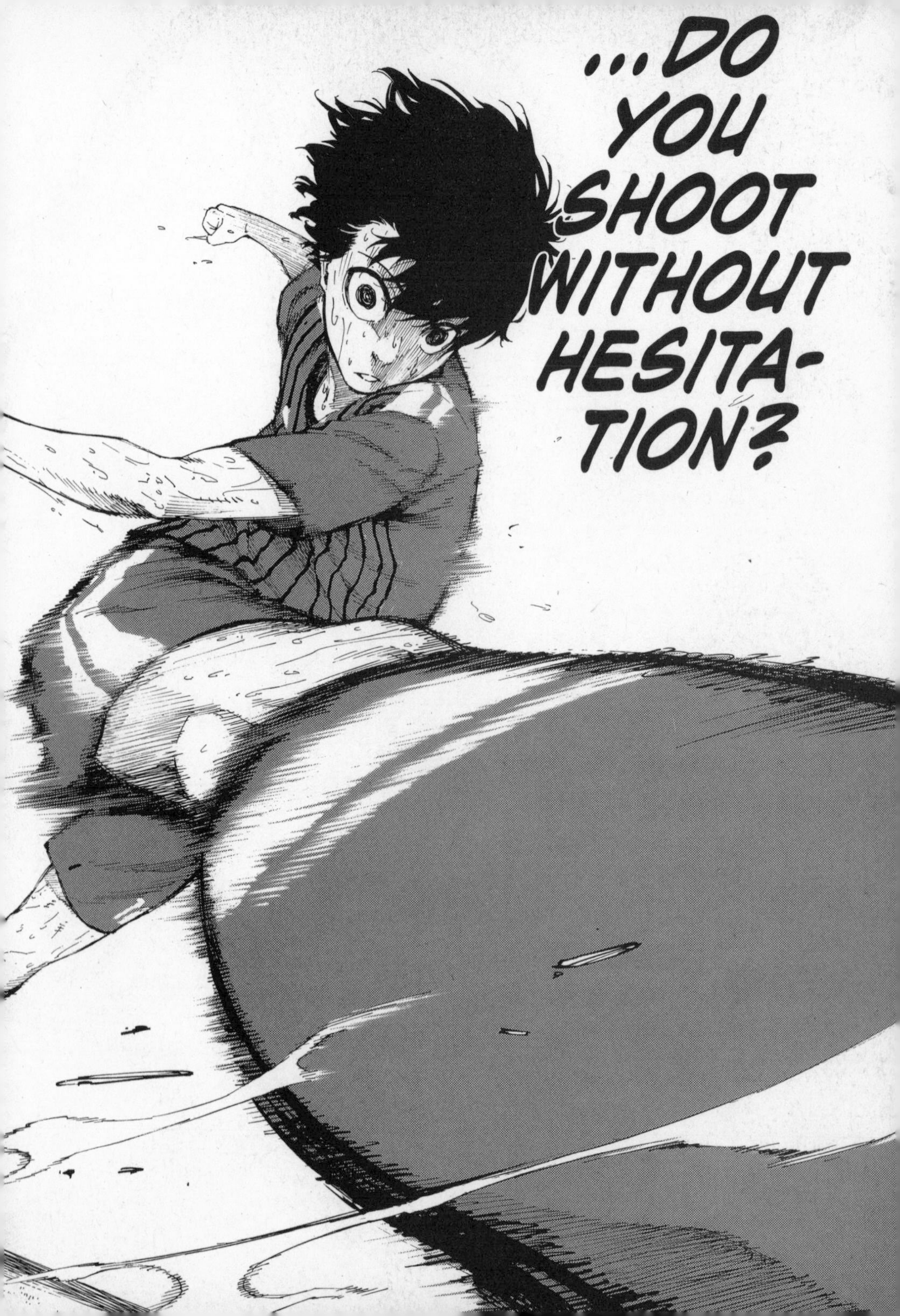
...DO YOU SHOOT WITHOUT HESITA-TION?

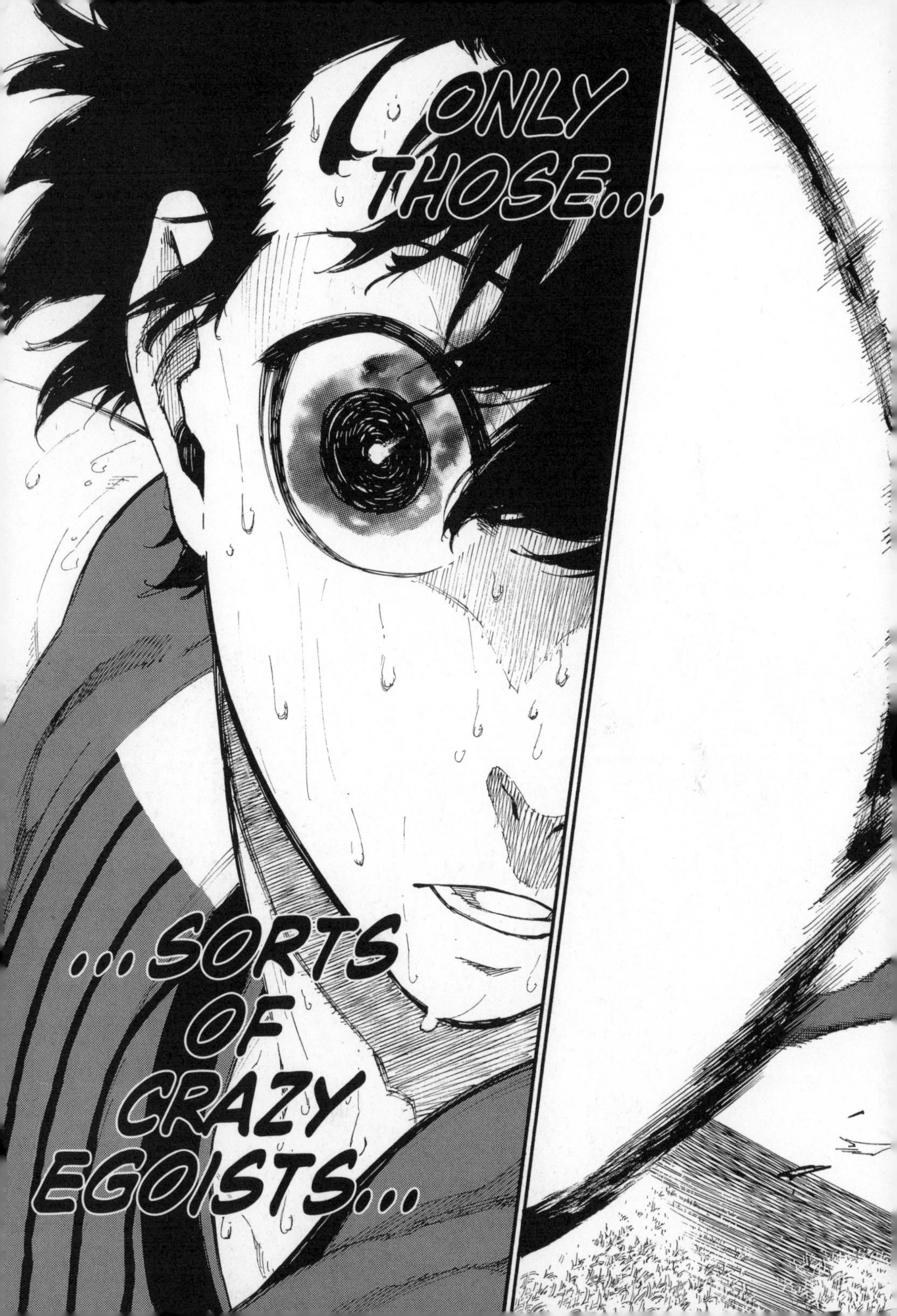
ONLY THOSE...
...SORTS OF CRAZY EGOISTS...

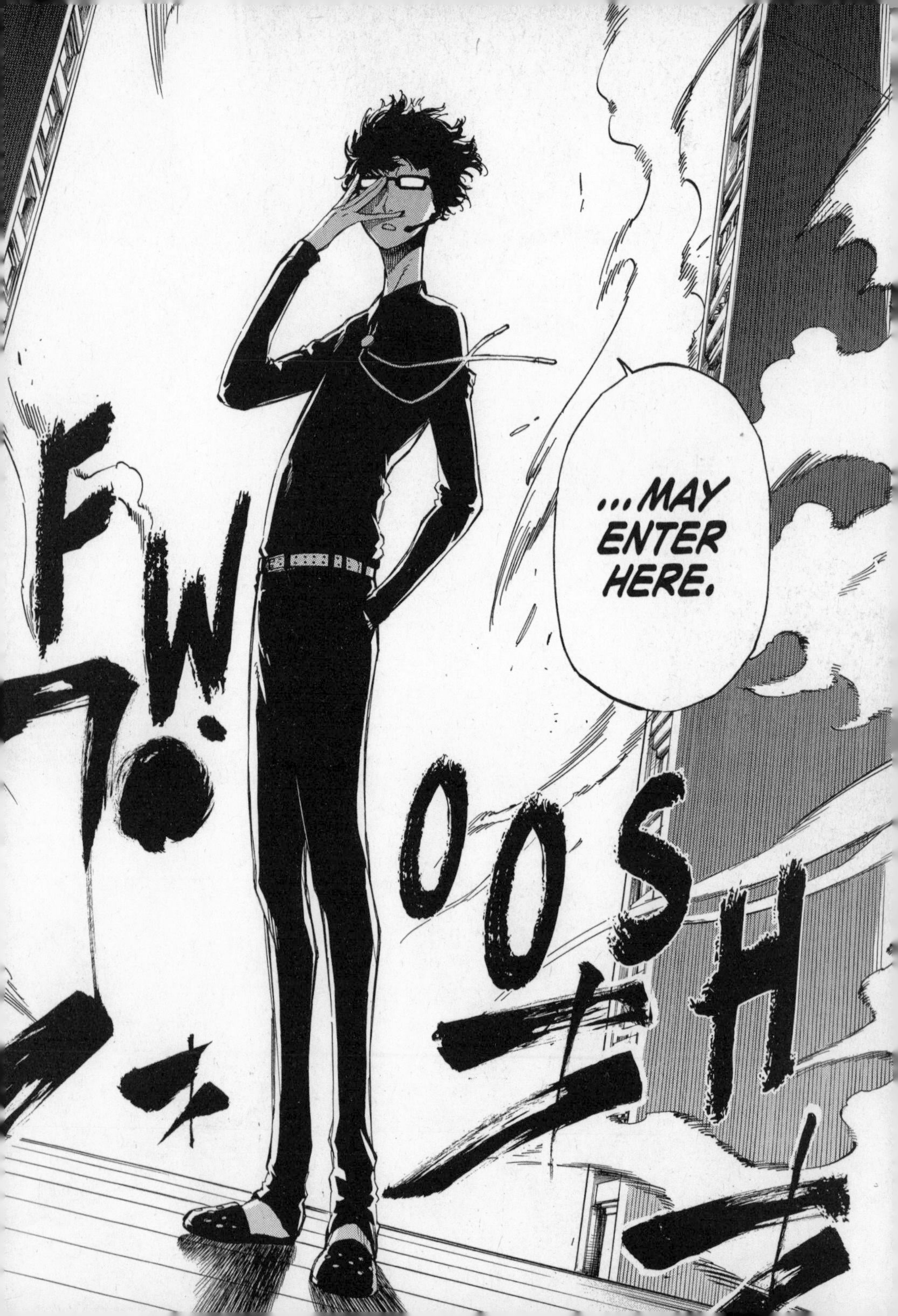
...MAY ENTER HERE.
FWOOSH

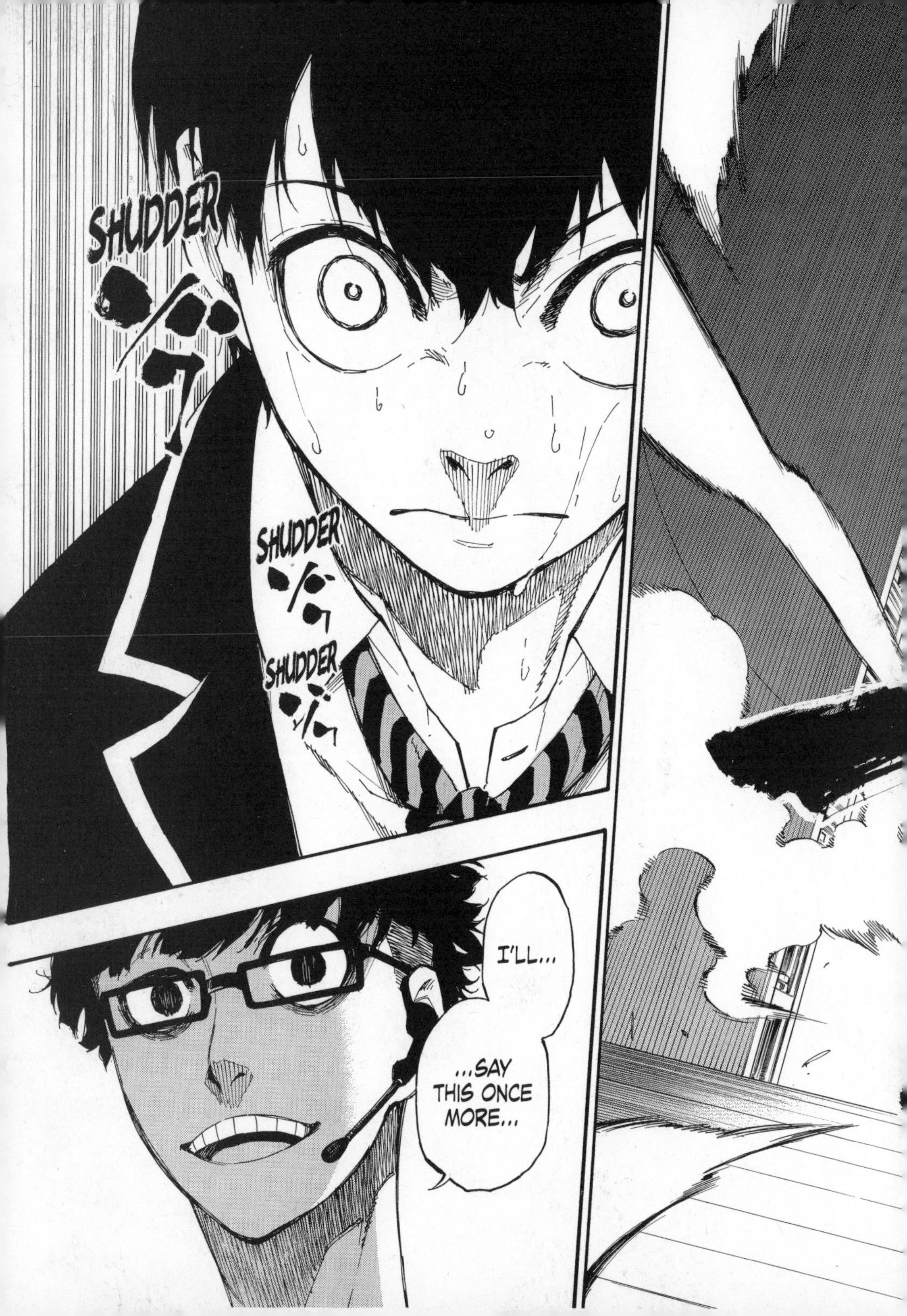
SHUDDER
SHUDDER
SHUDDER
I'LL...
...SAY THIS ONCE MORE...

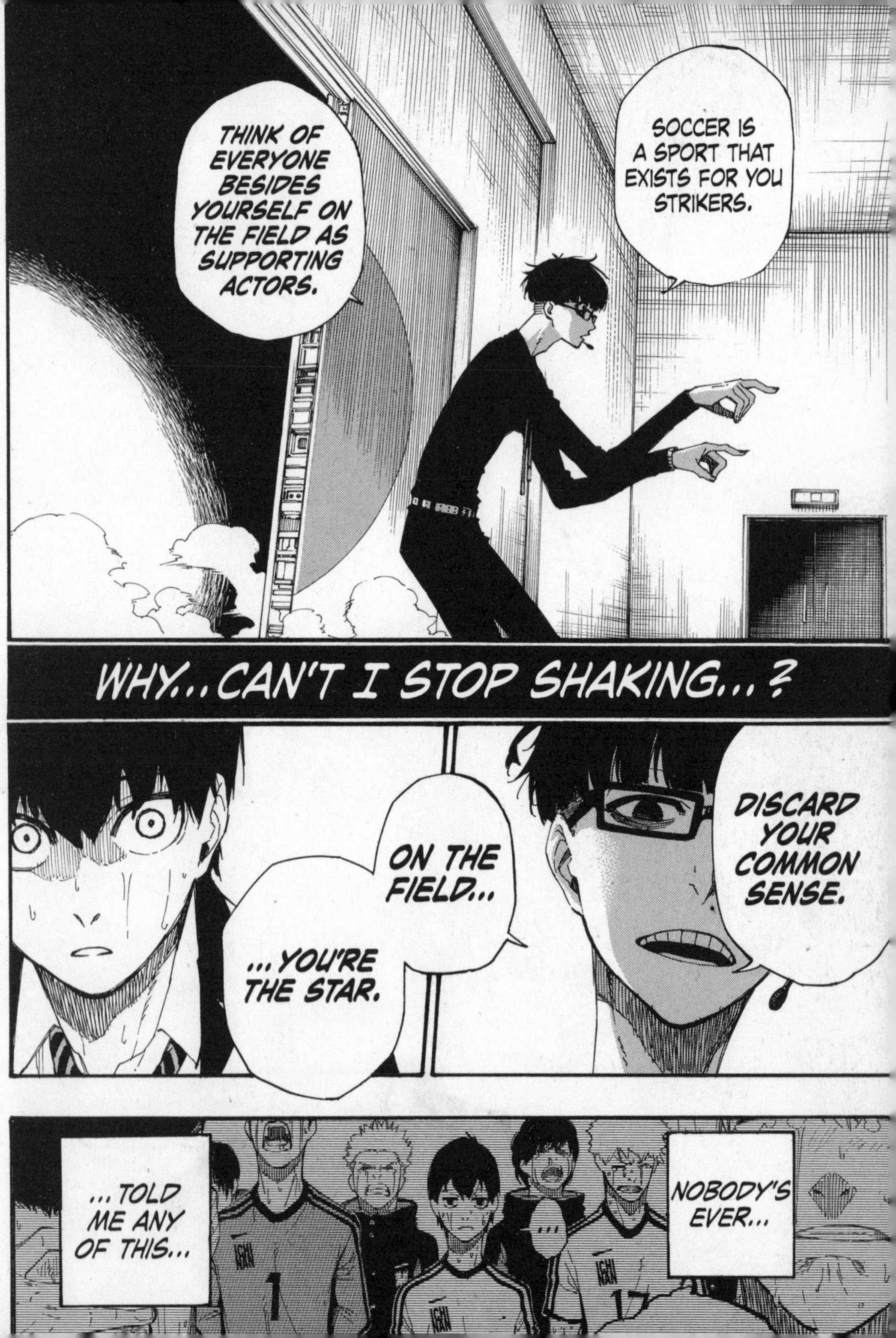
SOCCER IS A SPORT THAT EXISTS FOR YOU STRIKERS.
THINK OF EVERYONE BESIDES YOURSELF ON THE FIELD AS SUPPORTING ACTORS.
WHY...CAN'T I STOP SHAKING...?
DISCARD YOUR COMMON SENSE.
ON THE FIELD...
...YOU'RE THE STAR.
NOBODY'S EVER...
...
...TOLD ME ANY OF THIS...

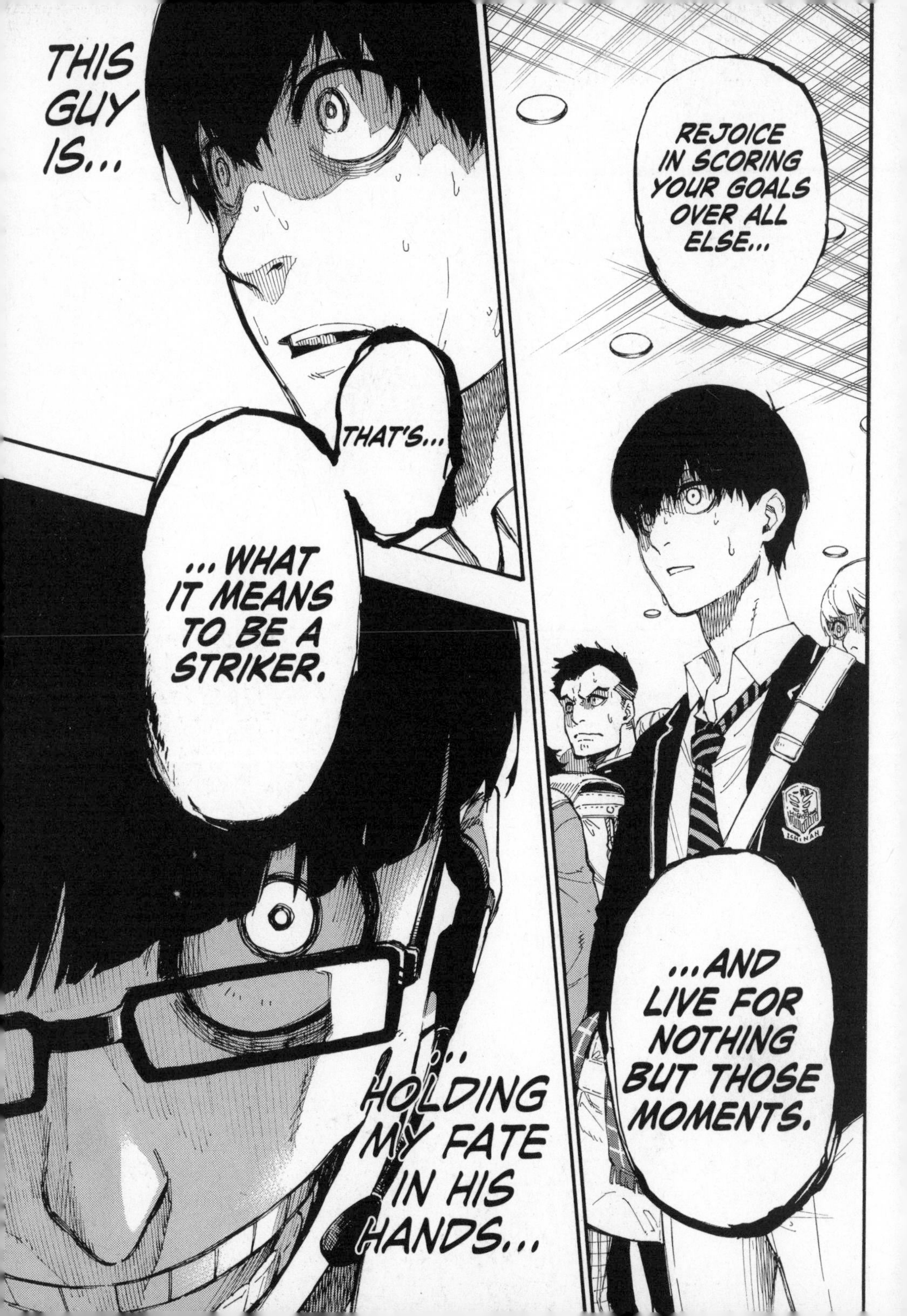
REJOICE IN SCORING YOUR GOALS OVER ALL ELSE...
...AND LIVE FOR NOTHING BUT THOSE MOMENTS.
THIS GUY IS...
THAT'S...
...WHAT IT MEANS TO BE A STRIKER.
...HOLDING MY FATE IN HIS HANDS...

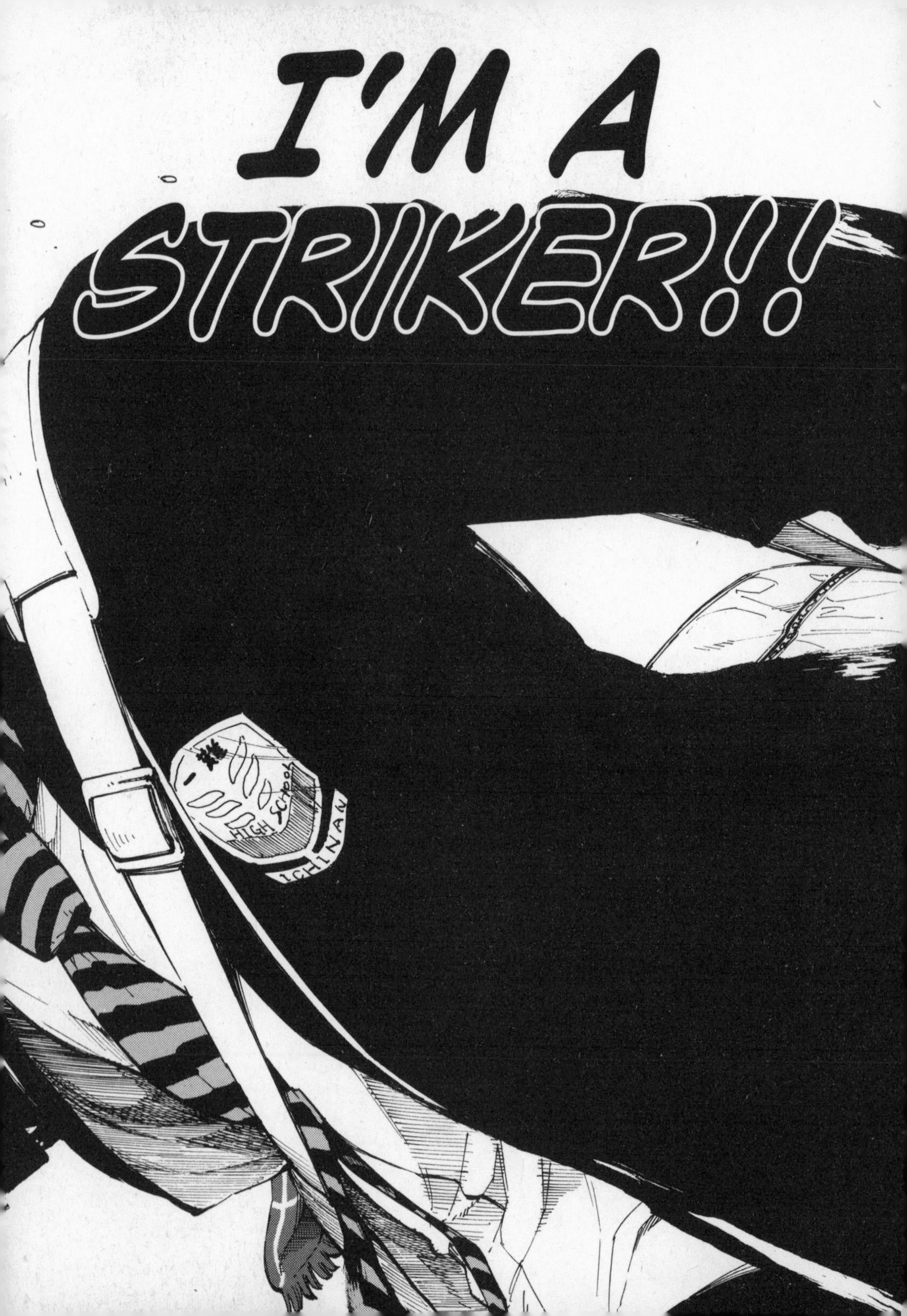
I'M A
STRIKER!!
ICHINAN
HIGH SCHOOL

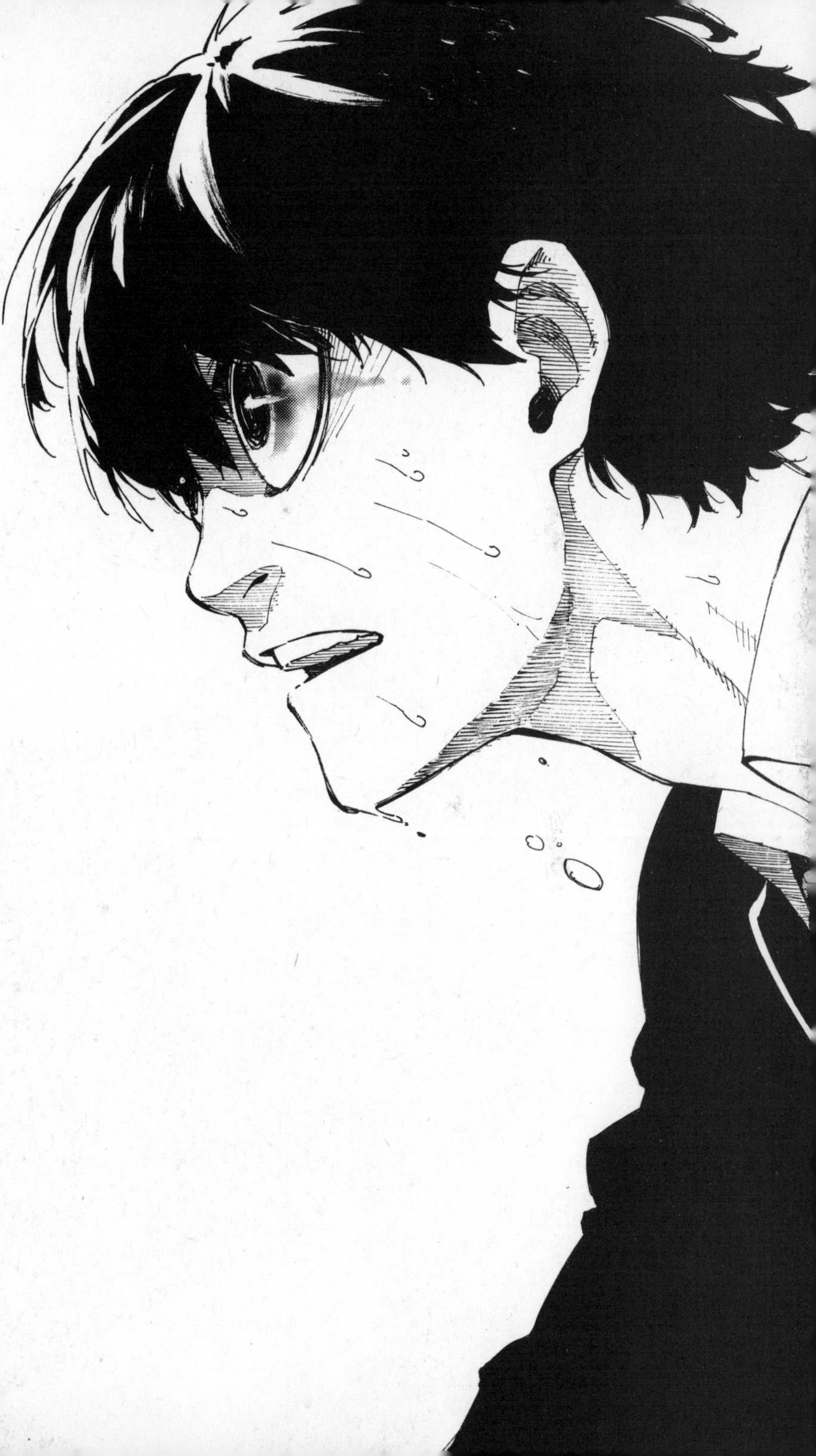

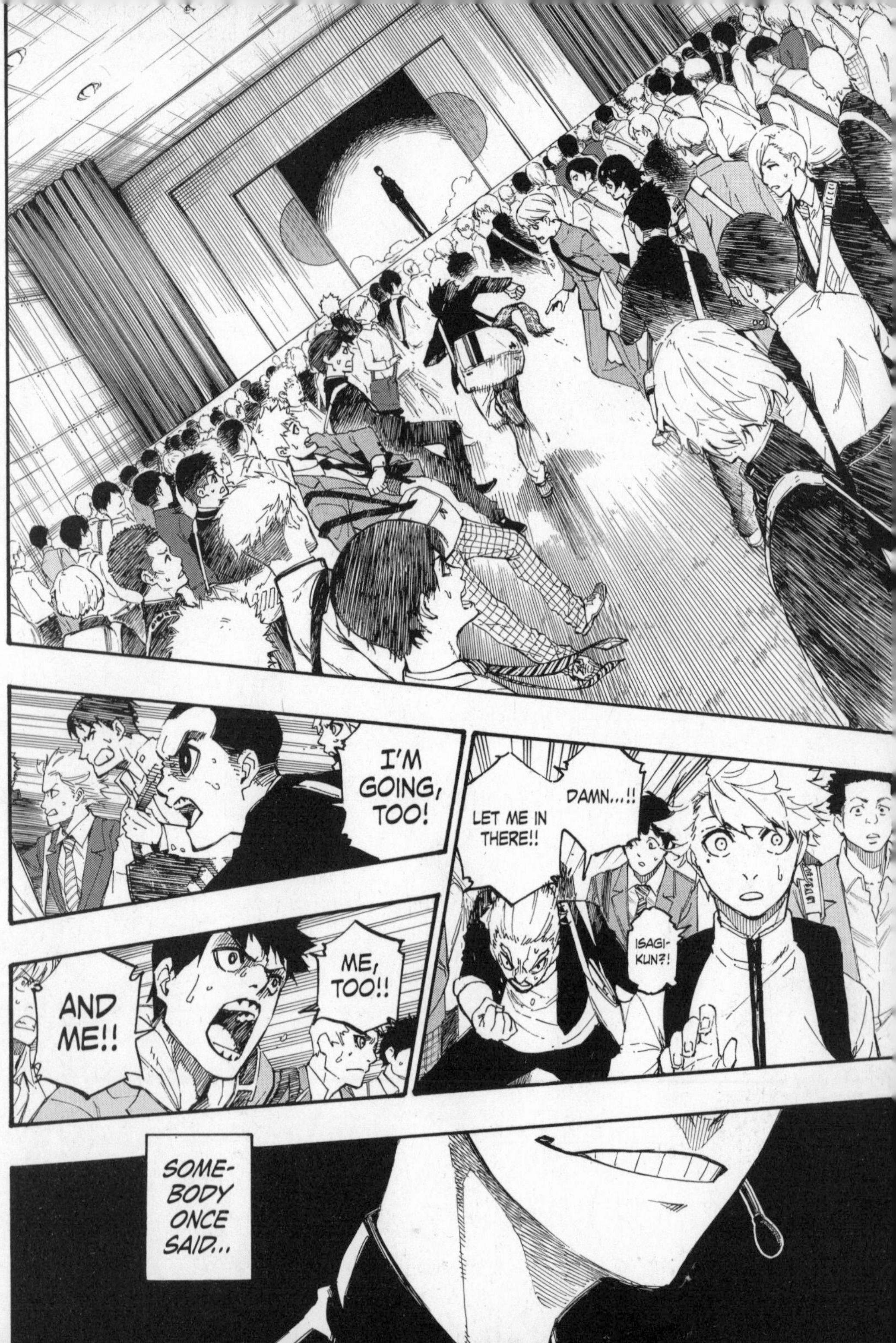
DAMN...!!
LET ME IN THERE!!
ISAGI-KUN?!
I'M GOING, TOO!
ME, TOO!!
AND ME!!
SOME-BODY ONCE SAID...

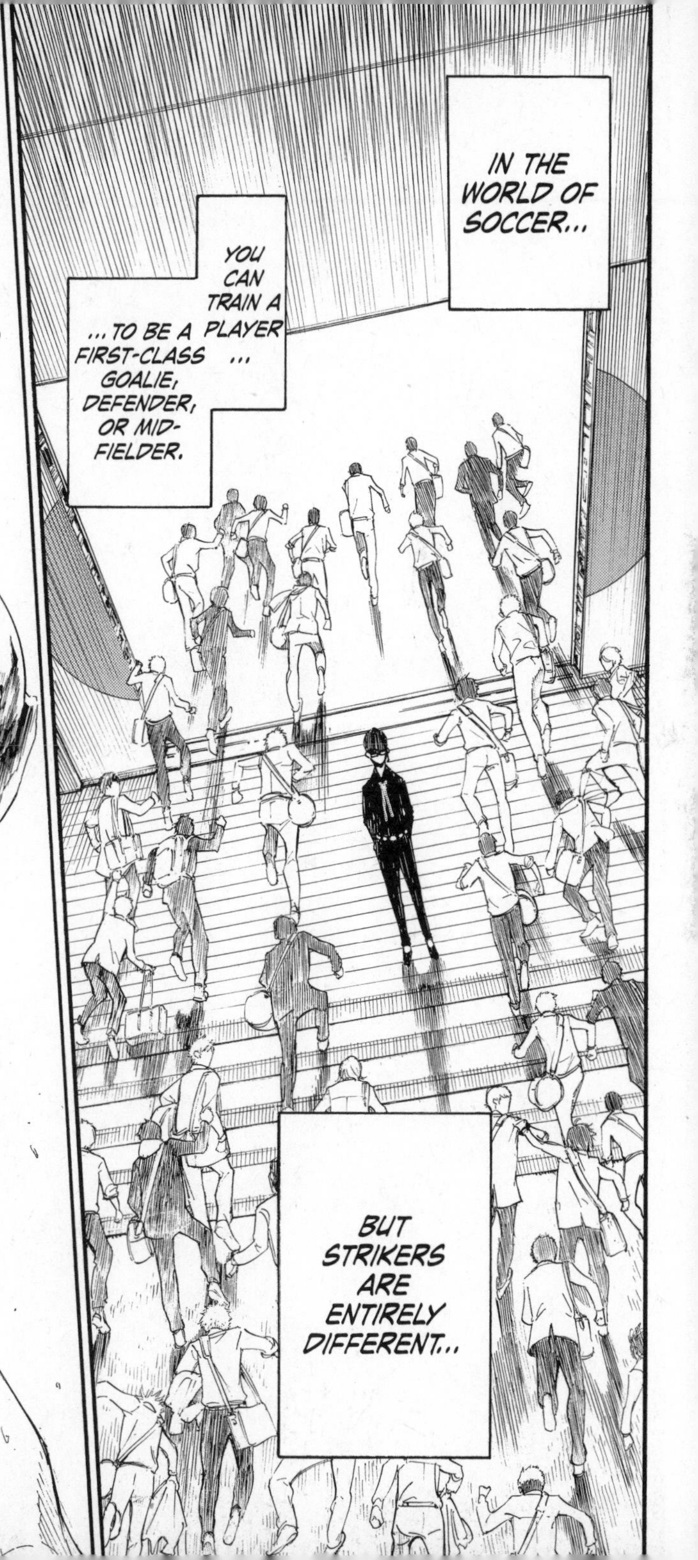
IN THE WORLD OF SOCCER...
YOU CAN TRAIN A PLAYER ...
...TO BE A FIRST-CLASS GOALIE, DEFENDER, OR MID-FIELDER.
BUT STRIKERS ARE ENTIRELY DIFFERENT...
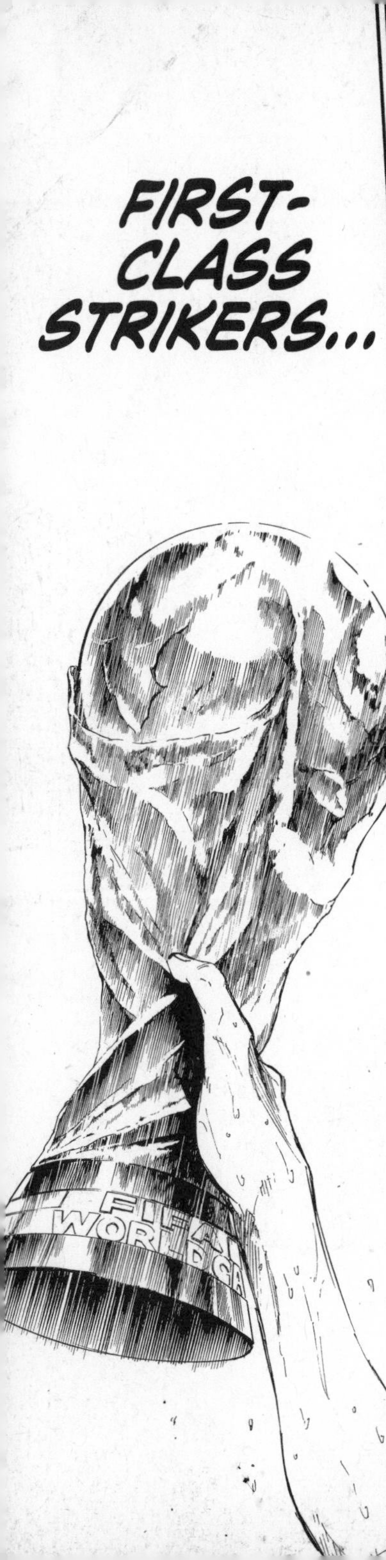
FIRST-CLASS STRIKERS...

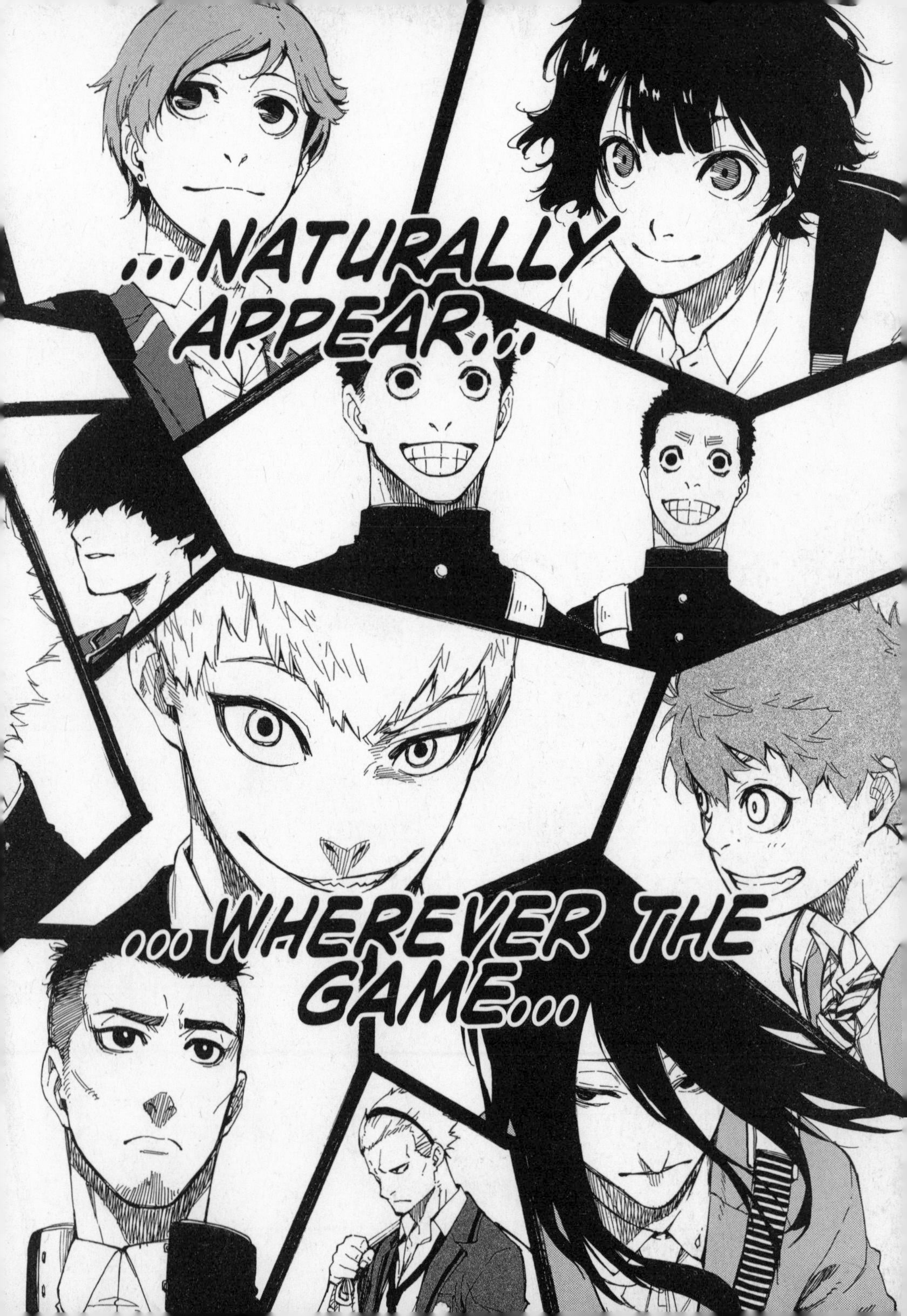
...NATURALLY APPEAR...
...WHEREVER THE GAME...

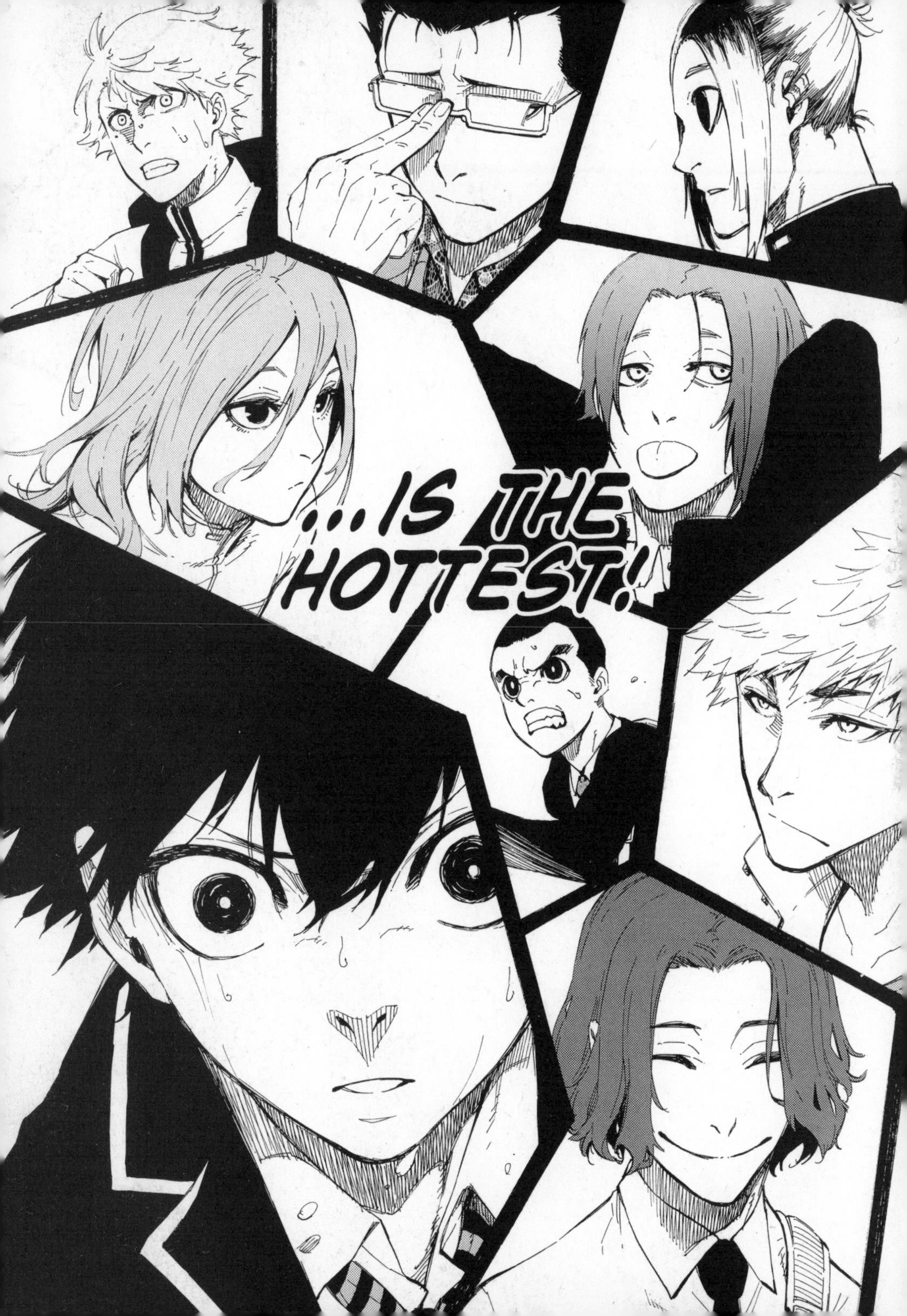
...IS THE HOTTEST!

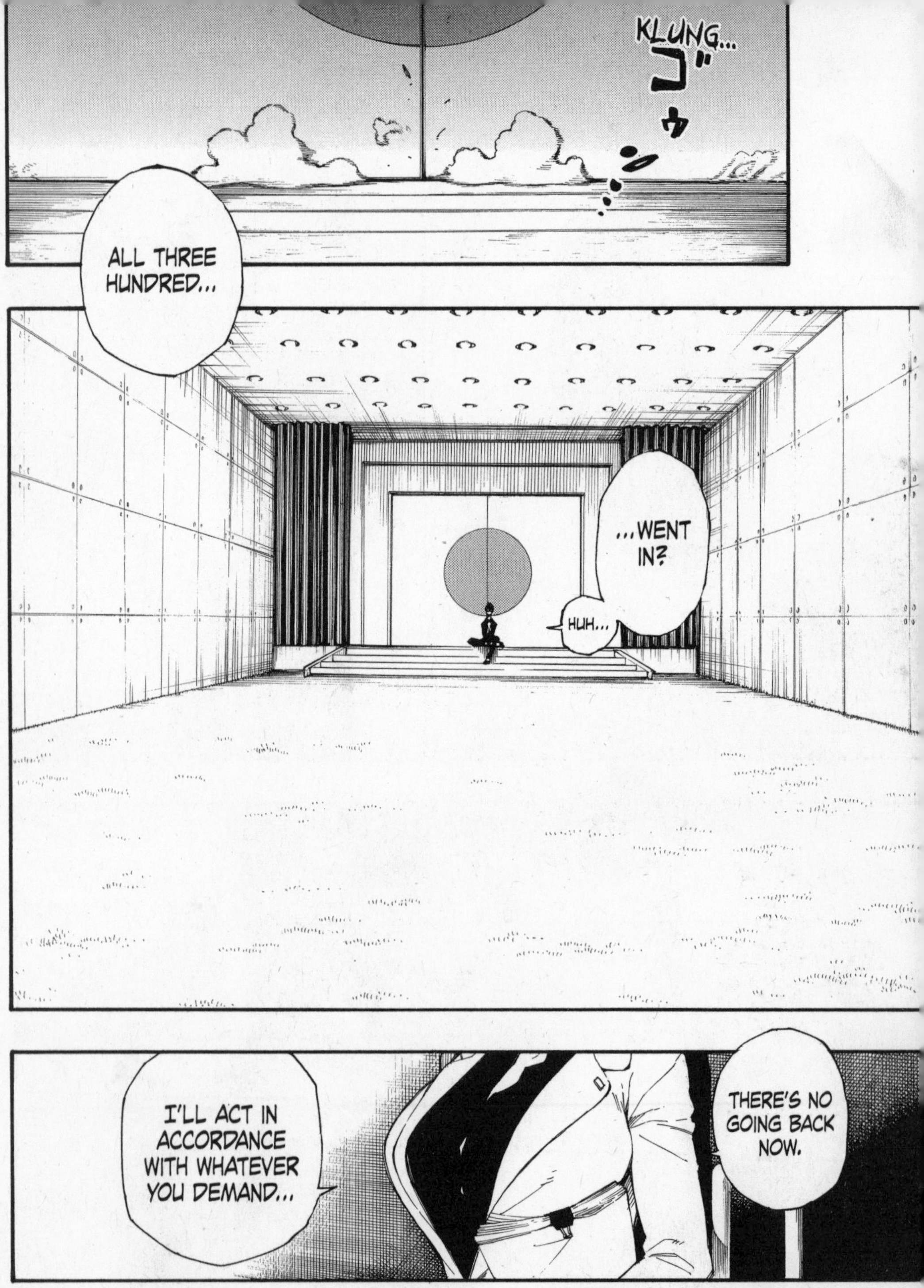
KLUNG...
ゴゥ
ALL THREE HUNDRED...
...WENT IN?
HUH...
THERE'S NO GOING BACK NOW.
I'LL ACT IN ACCORDANCE WITH WHATEVER YOU DEMAND...

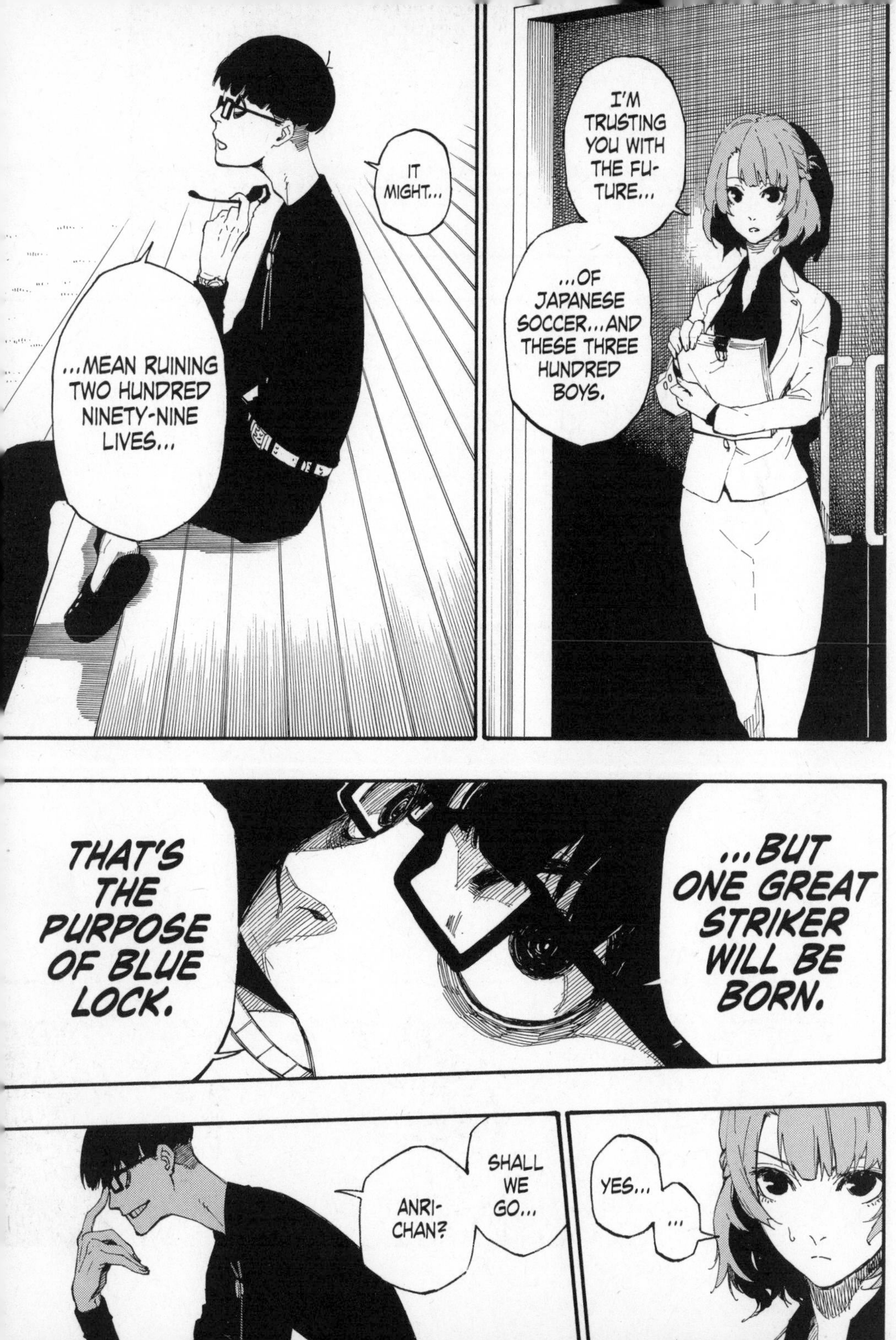

I'M TRUSTING YOU WITH THE FU-TURE...
...OF JAPANESE SOCCER...AND THESE THREE HUNDRED BOYS.
IT MIGHT...
...MEAN RUINING TWO HUNDRED NINETY-NINE LIVES...
...BUT ONE GREAT STRIKER WILL BE BORN.
THAT'S THE PURPOSE OF BLUE LOCK.
YES...
...
SHALL WE GO...
ANRI-CHAN?

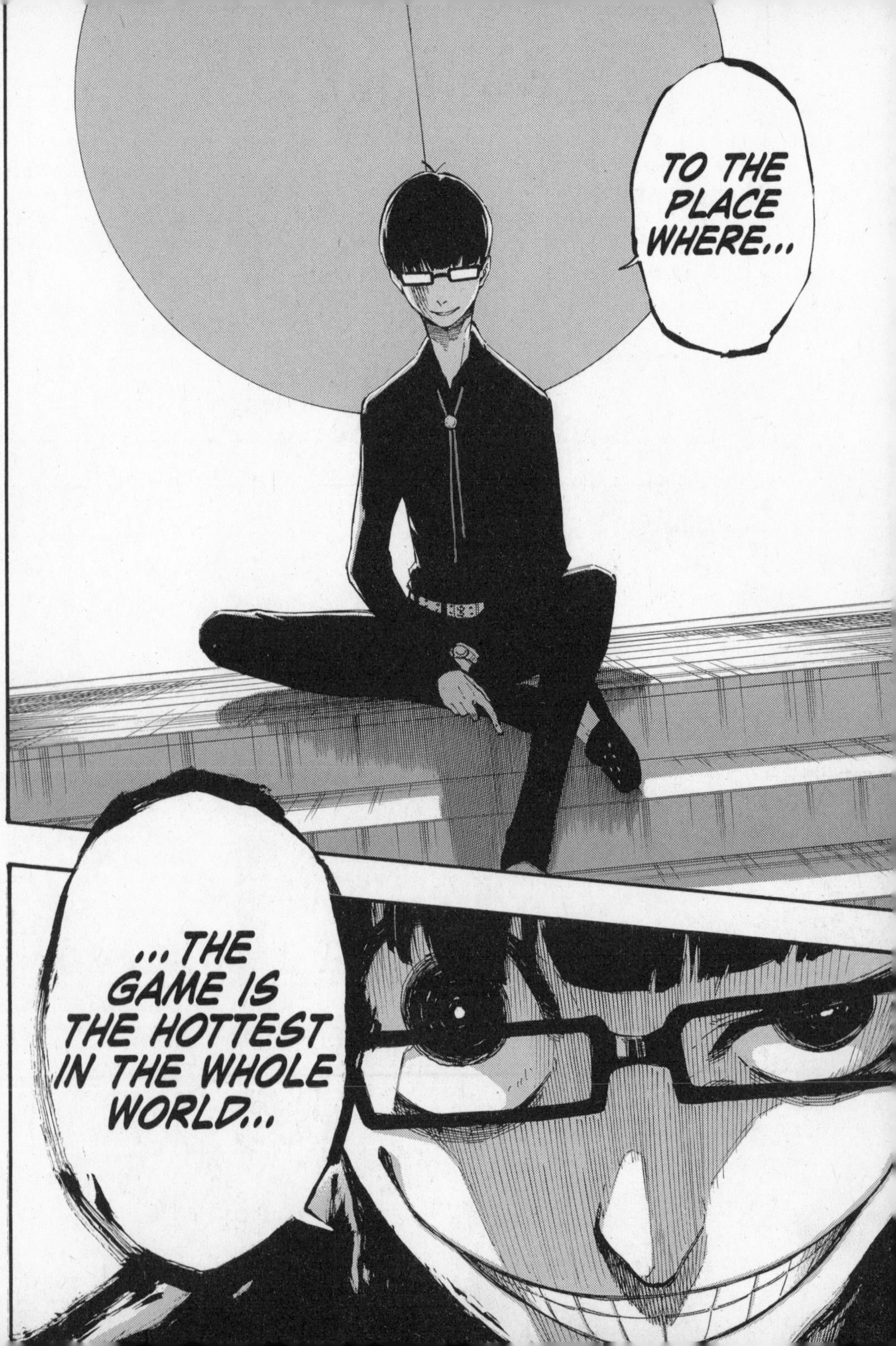
TO THE PLACE WHERE...
...THE GAME IS THE HOTTEST IN THE WHOLE WORLD...

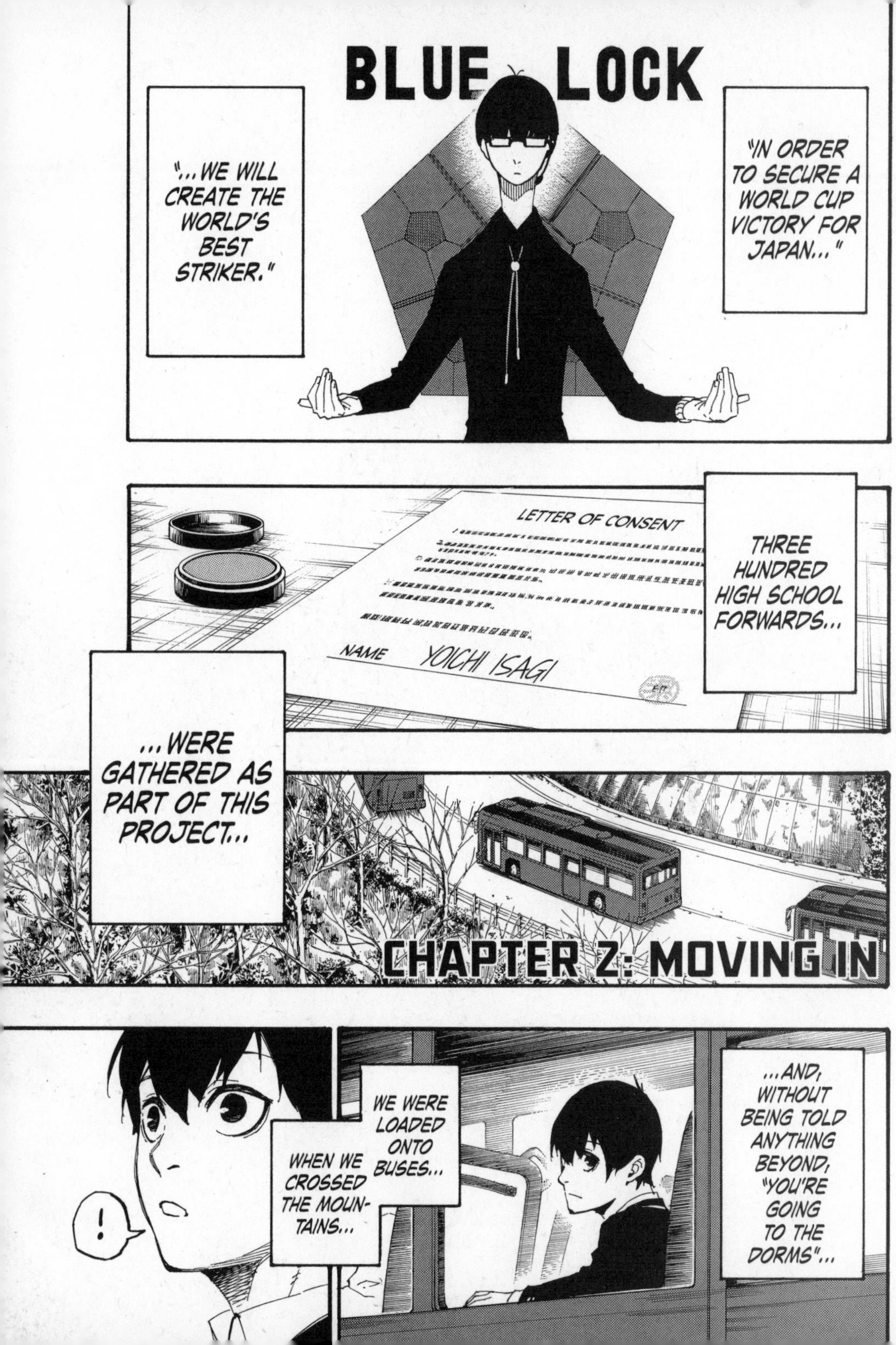
BLUE LOCK
"IN ORDER TO SECURE A WORLD CUP VICTORY FOR JAPAN..."
"...WE WILL CREATE THE WORLD'S BEST STRIKER."
THREE HUNDRED HIGH SCHOOL FORWARDS...
LETTER OF CONSENT
NAME YOICHI ISAGI
...WERE GATHERED AS PART OF THIS PROJECT...
CHAPTER 2: MOVING IN
...AND, WITHOUT BEING TOLD ANYTHING BEYOND, "YOU'RE GOING TO THE DORMS"...
WE WERE LOADED ONTO BUSES...
WHEN WE CROSSED THE MOUNTAINS...
!

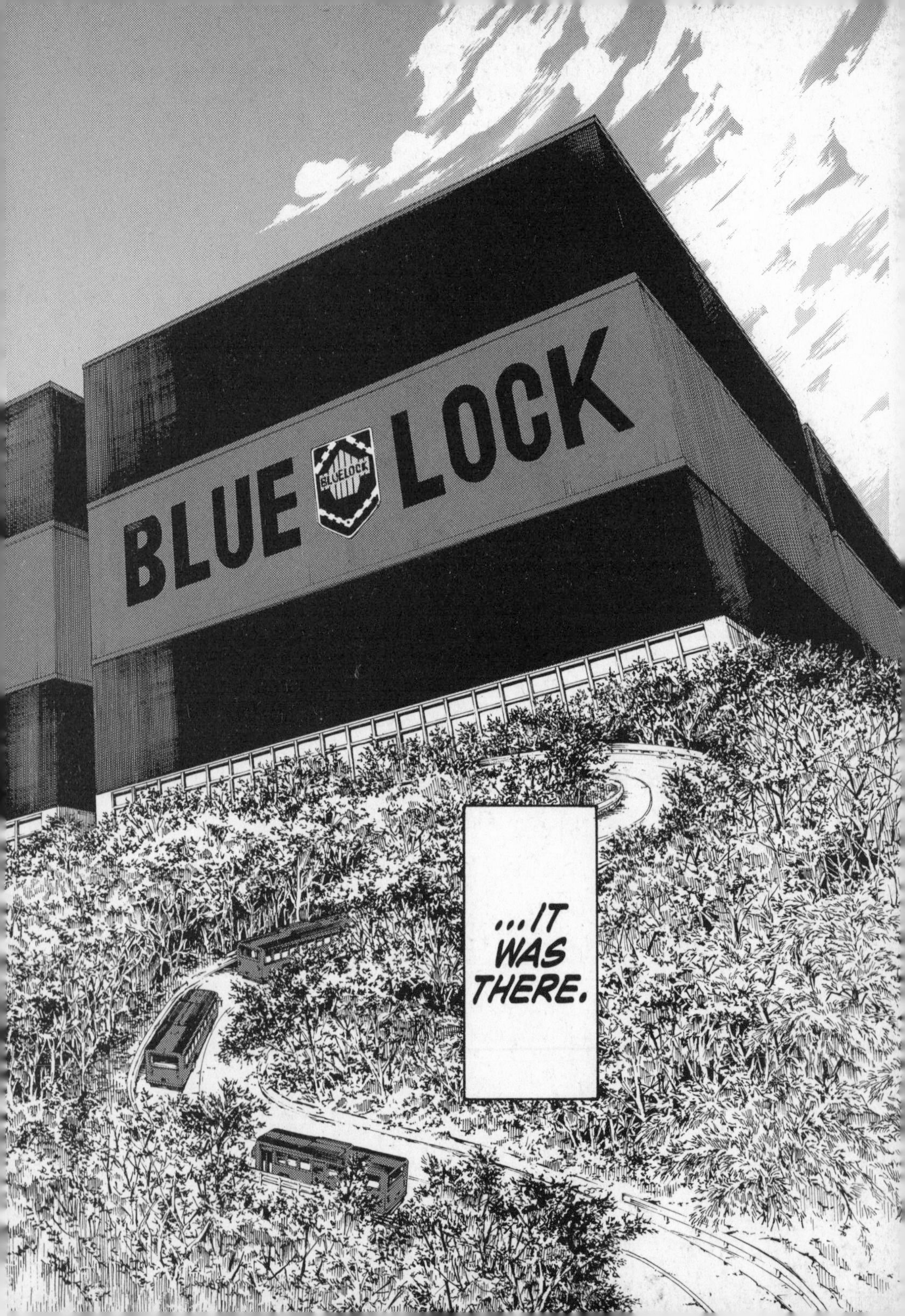
BLUE LOCK
BLUELOCK
...IT WAS THERE.

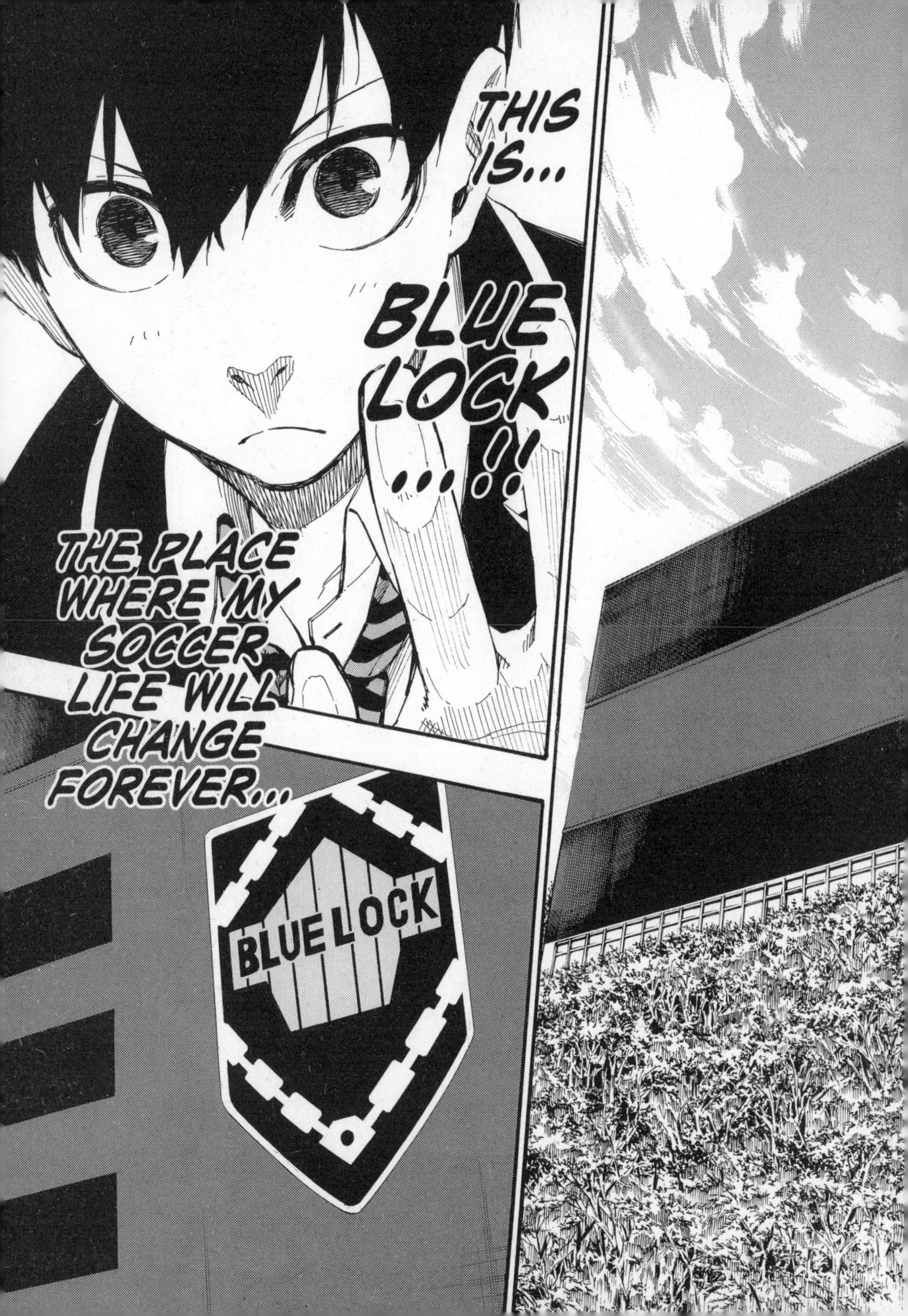
THIS IS...
BLUE LOCK...!!
THE PLACE WHERE MY SOCCER LIFE WILL CHANGE FOREVER...
BLUE LOCK

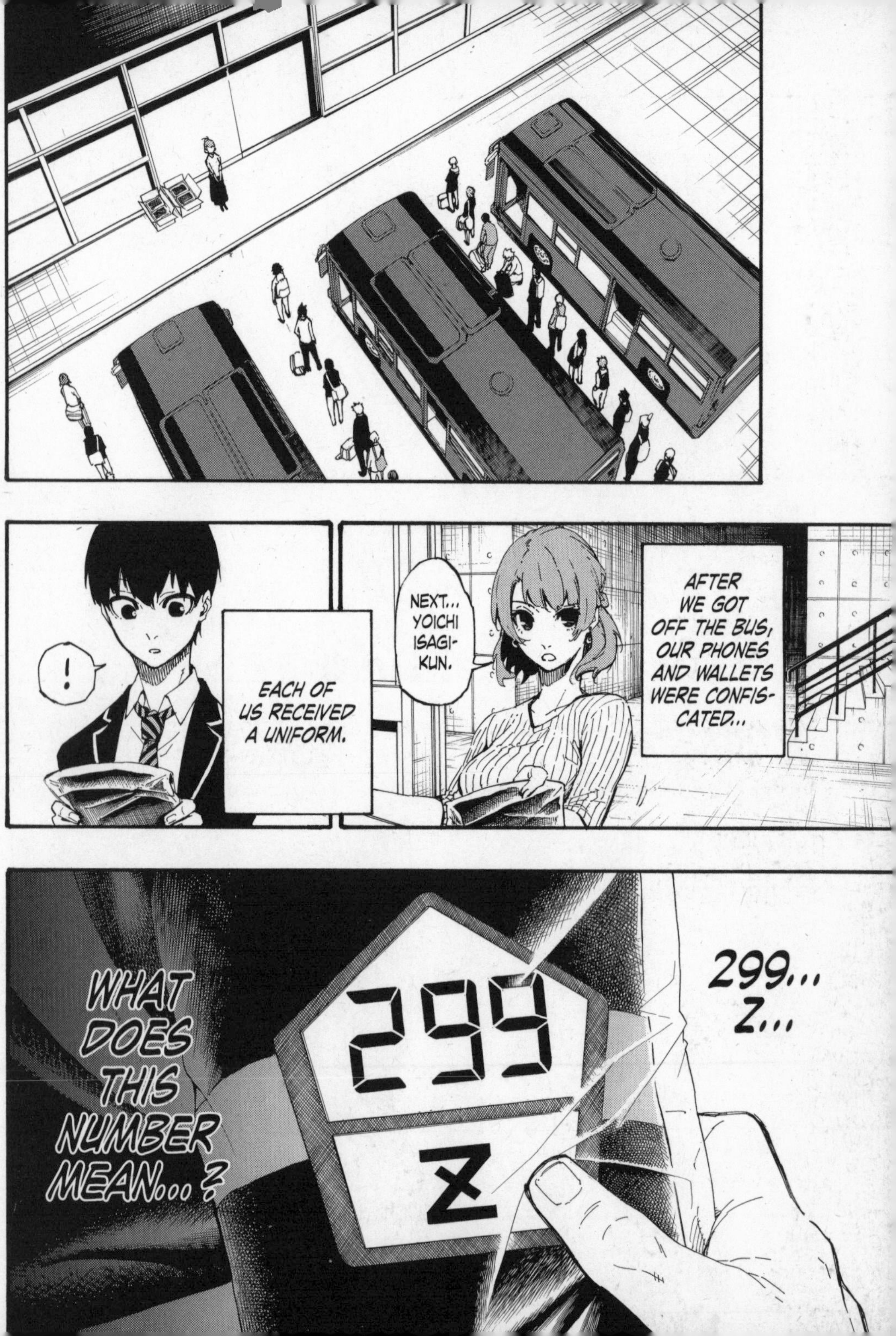
AFTER WE GOT OFF THE BUS, OUR PHONES AND WALLETS WERE CONFISCATED...
NEXT... YOICHI ISAGI-KUN.
EACH OF US RECEIVED A UNIFORM.
!
299
Z
299... Z...
WHAT DOES THIS NUMBER MEAN...?

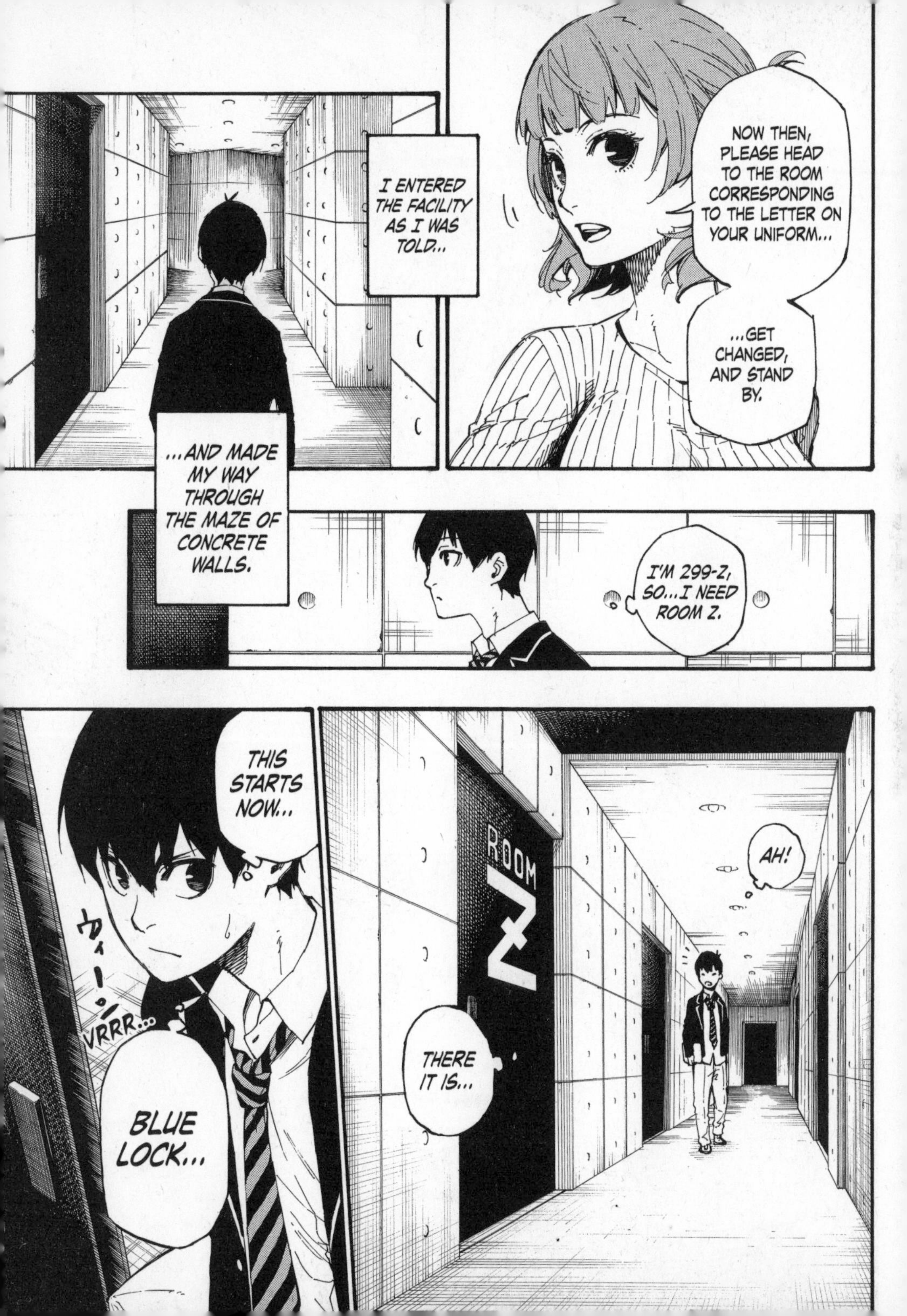
NOW THEN, PLEASE HEAD TO THE ROOM CORRESPONDING TO THE LETTER ON YOUR UNIFORM...
...GET CHANGED, AND STAND BY.
I ENTERED THE FACILITY AS I WAS TOLD...
...AND MADE MY WAY THROUGH THE MAZE OF CONCRETE WALLS.
I'M 299-Z, SO...I NEED ROOM Z.
AH!
ROOM Z
THERE IT IS...
THIS STARTS NOW...
VRRR...
BLUE LOCK...

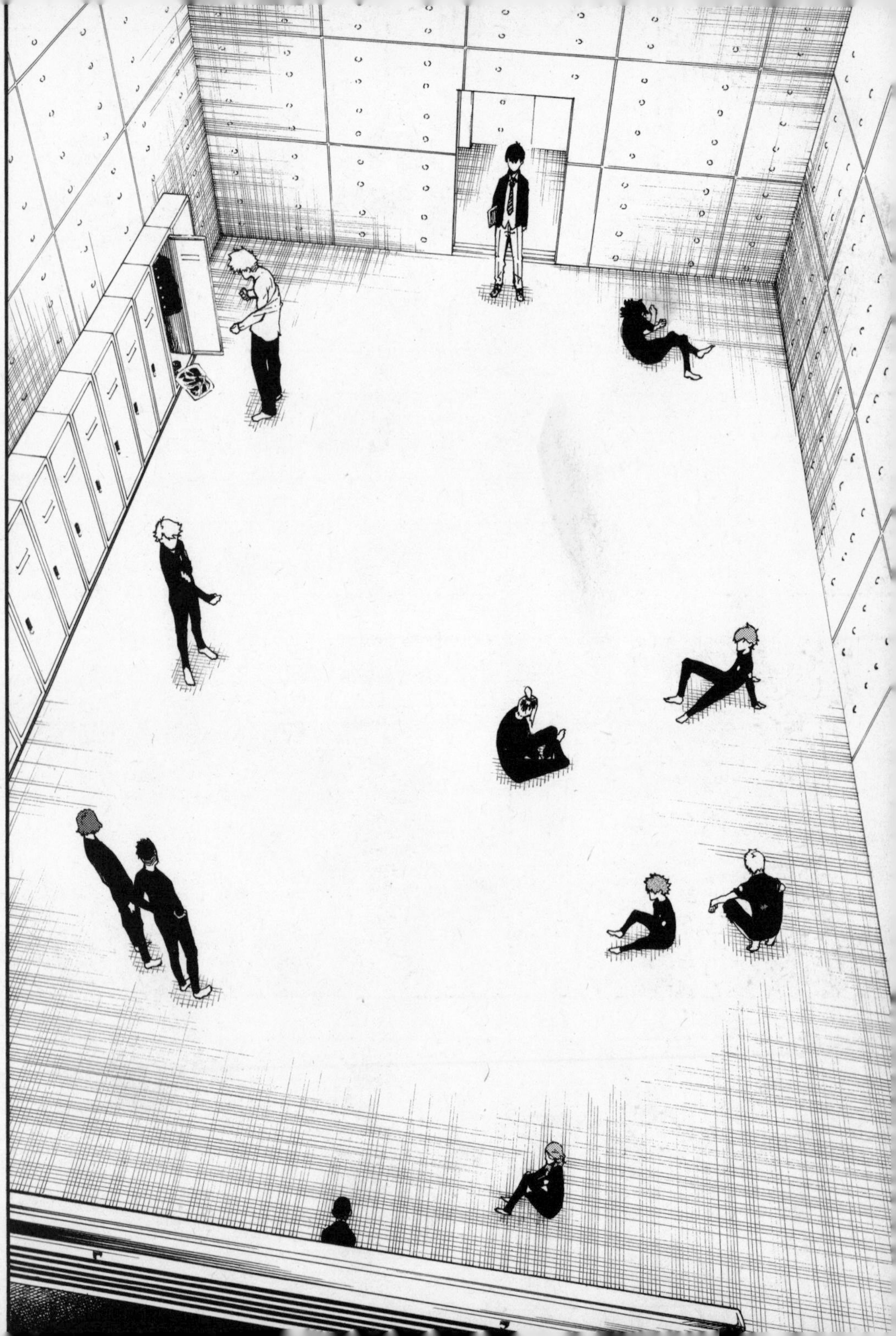

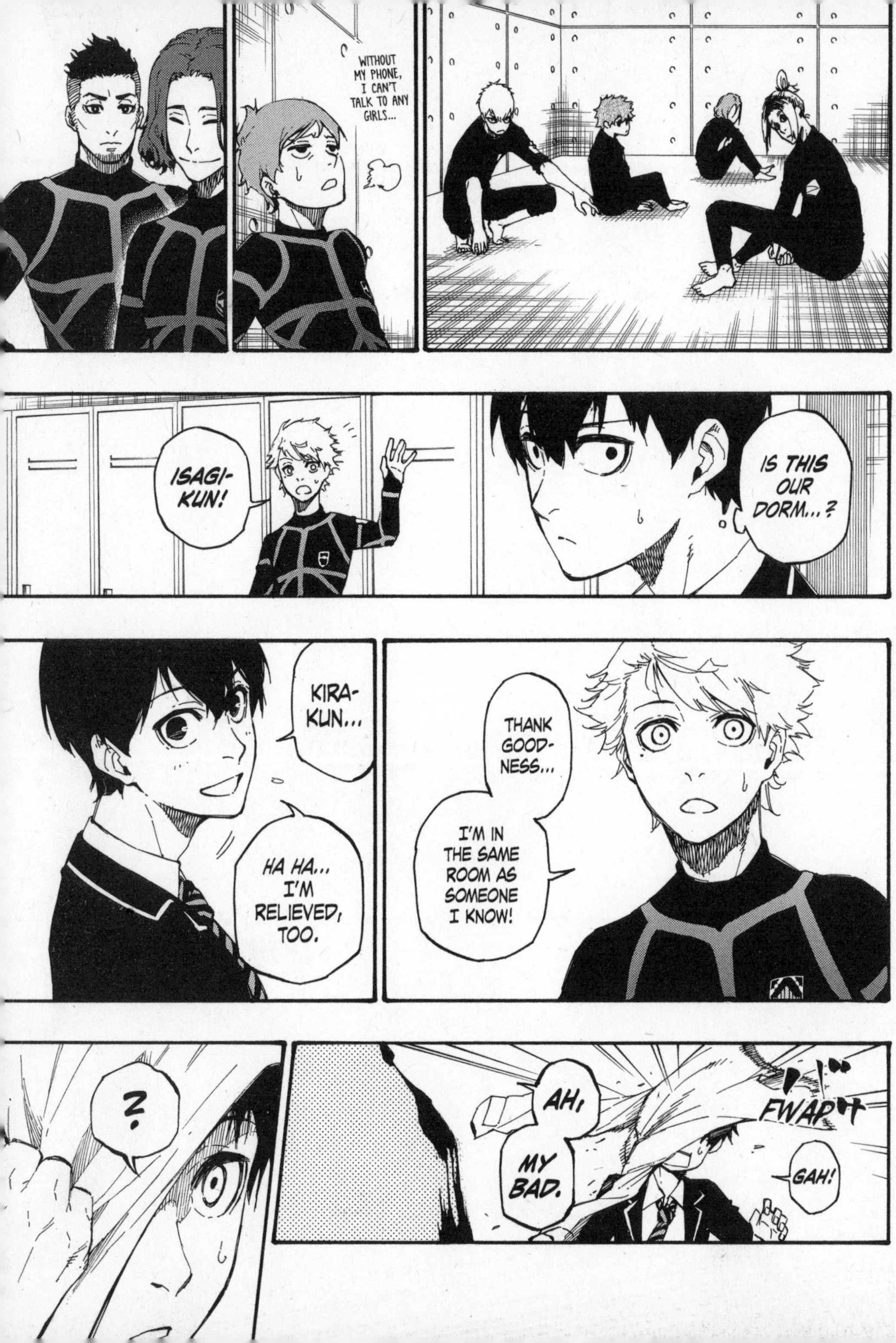
WITHOUT MY PHONE, I CAN'T TALK TO ANY GIRLS...
IS THIS OUR DORM...?
ISAGI-KUN!
THANK GOODNESS...
I'M IN THE SAME ROOM AS SOMEONE I KNOW!
KIRA-KUN...
HA HA... I'M RELIEVED, TOO.
FWAP
GAH!
AH, MY BAD.
?

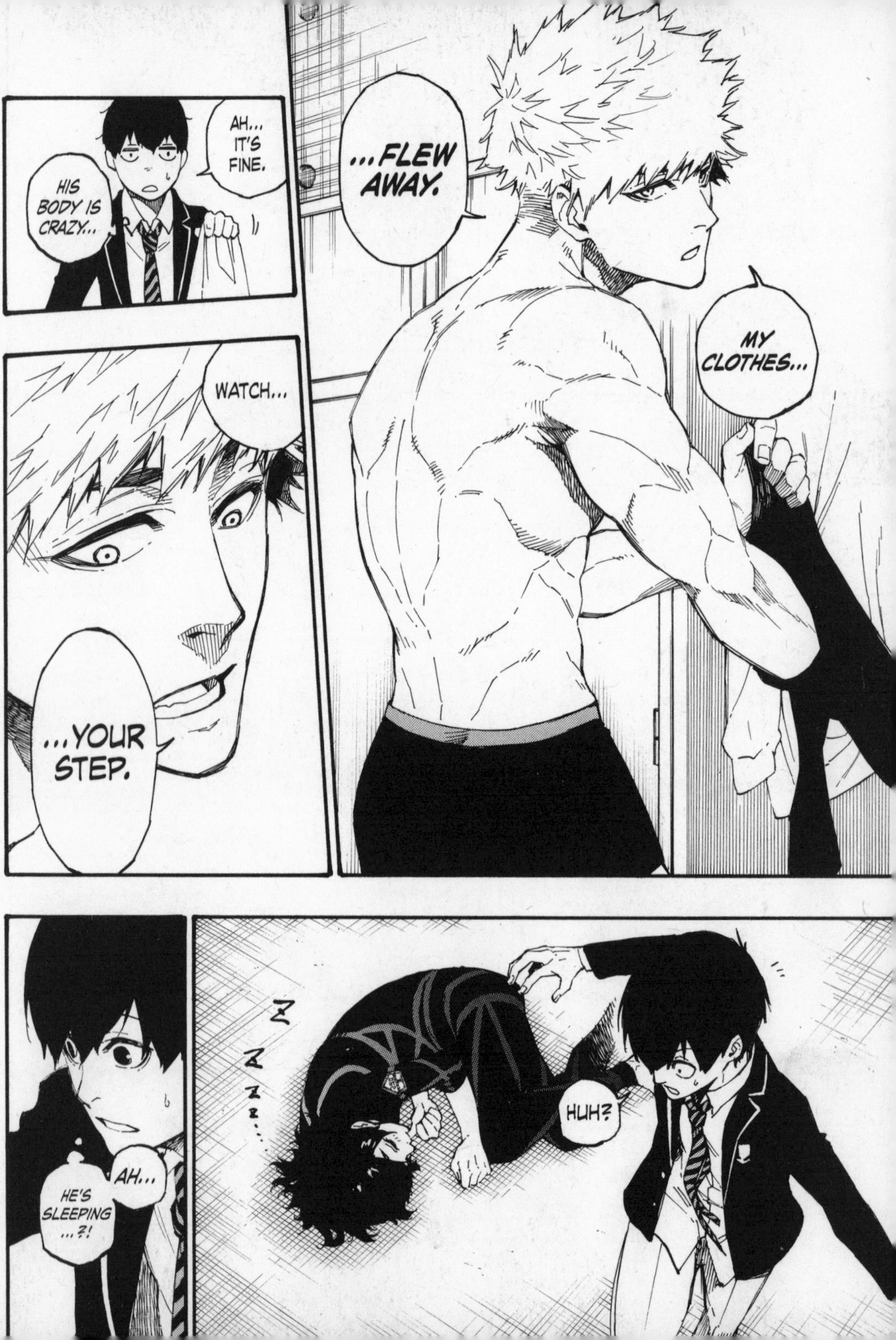
MY CLOTHES...
...FLEW AWAY.
AH... IT'S FINE.
HIS BODY IS CRAZY...
WATCH...
...YOUR STEP.
HUH?
Z Z Z...
AH...
HE'S SLEEPING ...?!

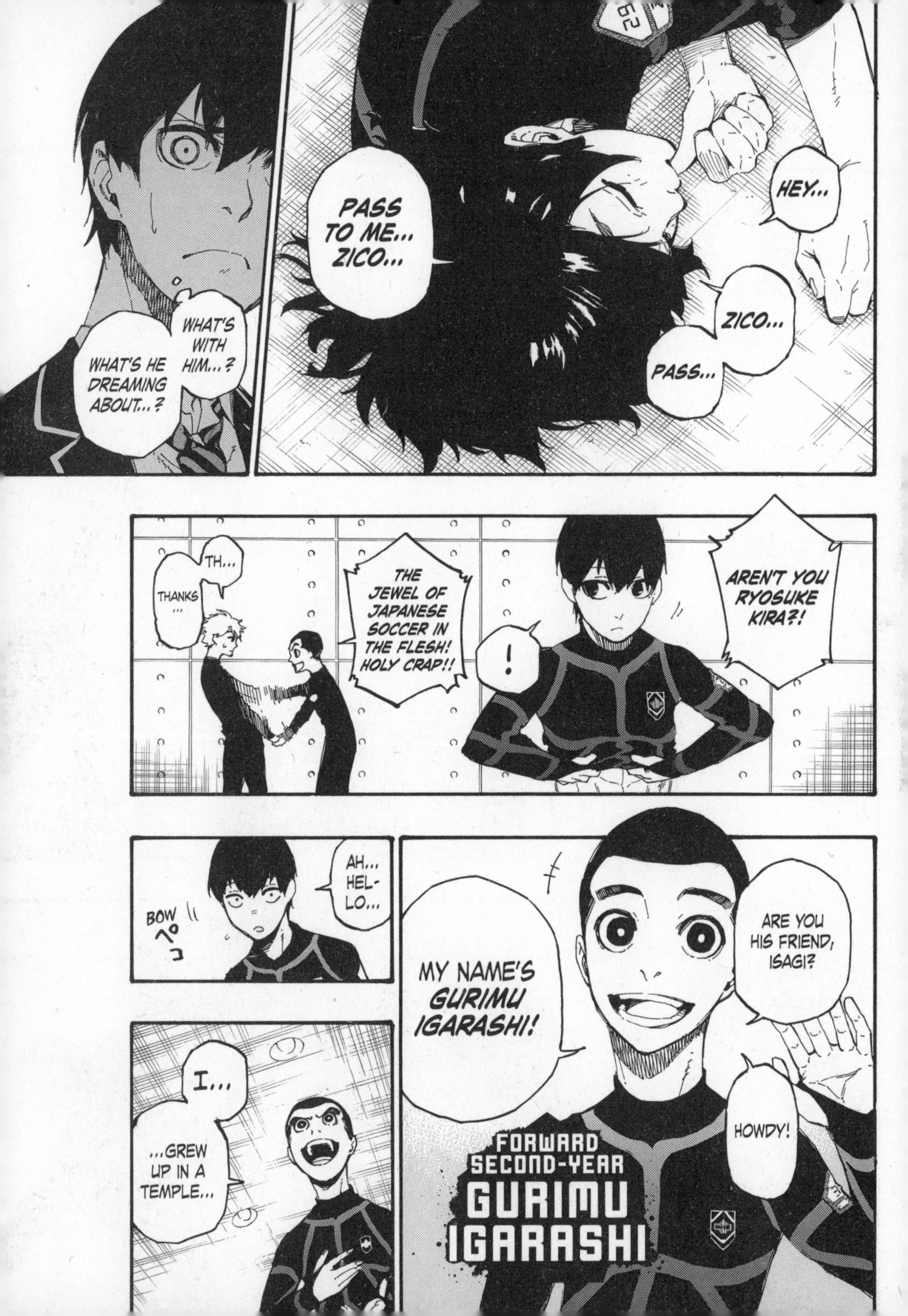
HEY...
PASS TO ME... ZICO...
ZICO...
PASS...
WHAT'S WITH HIM...?
WHAT'S HE DREAMING ABOUT...?
AREN'T YOU RYOSUKE KIRA?!
!
THE JEWEL OF JAPANESE SOCCER IN THE FLESH! HOLY CRAP!!
TH...
THANKS...
ARE YOU HIS FRIEND, ISAGI?
MY NAME'S GURIMU IGARASHI!
HOWDY!
FORWARD SECOND-YEAR
GURIMU IGARASHI
AH... HEL-LO...
BOW
ペコ
I...
...GREW UP IN A TEMPLE...

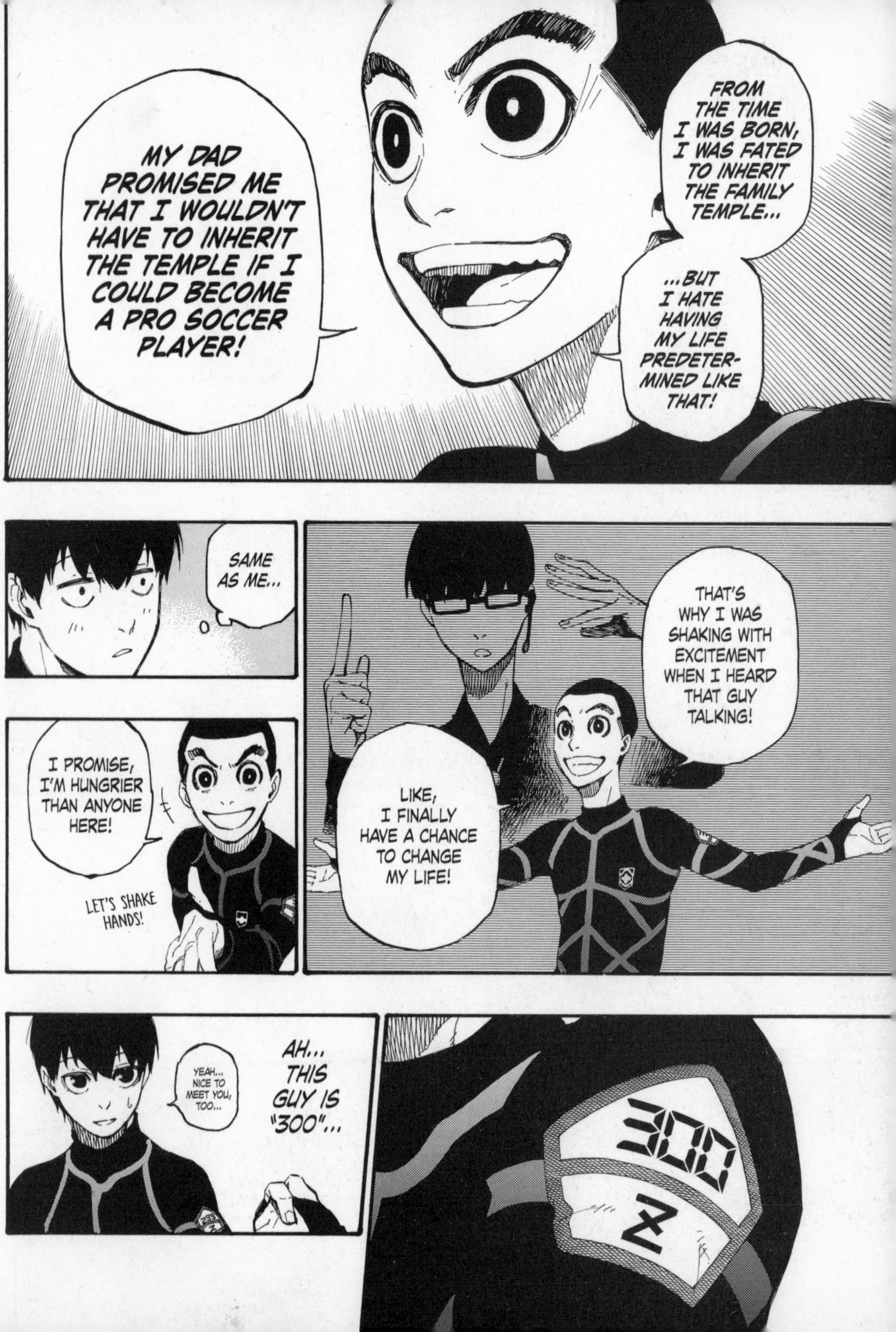
FROM THE TIME I WAS BORN, I WAS FATED TO INHERIT THE FAMILY TEMPLE...
...BUT I HATE HAVING MY LIFE PREDETER-MINED LIKE THAT!
MY DAD PROMISED ME THAT I WOULDN'T HAVE TO INHERIT THE TEMPLE IF I COULD BECOME A PRO SOCCER PLAYER!
THAT'S WHY I WAS SHAKING WITH EXCITEMENT WHEN I HEARD THAT GUY TALKING!
LIKE, I FINALLY HAVE A CHANCE TO CHANGE MY LIFE!
SAME AS ME...
I PROMISE, I'M HUNGRIER THAN ANYONE HERE!
LET'S SHAKE HANDS!
300
Z
AH... THIS GUY IS "300"...
YEAH... NICE TO MEET YOU, TOO...

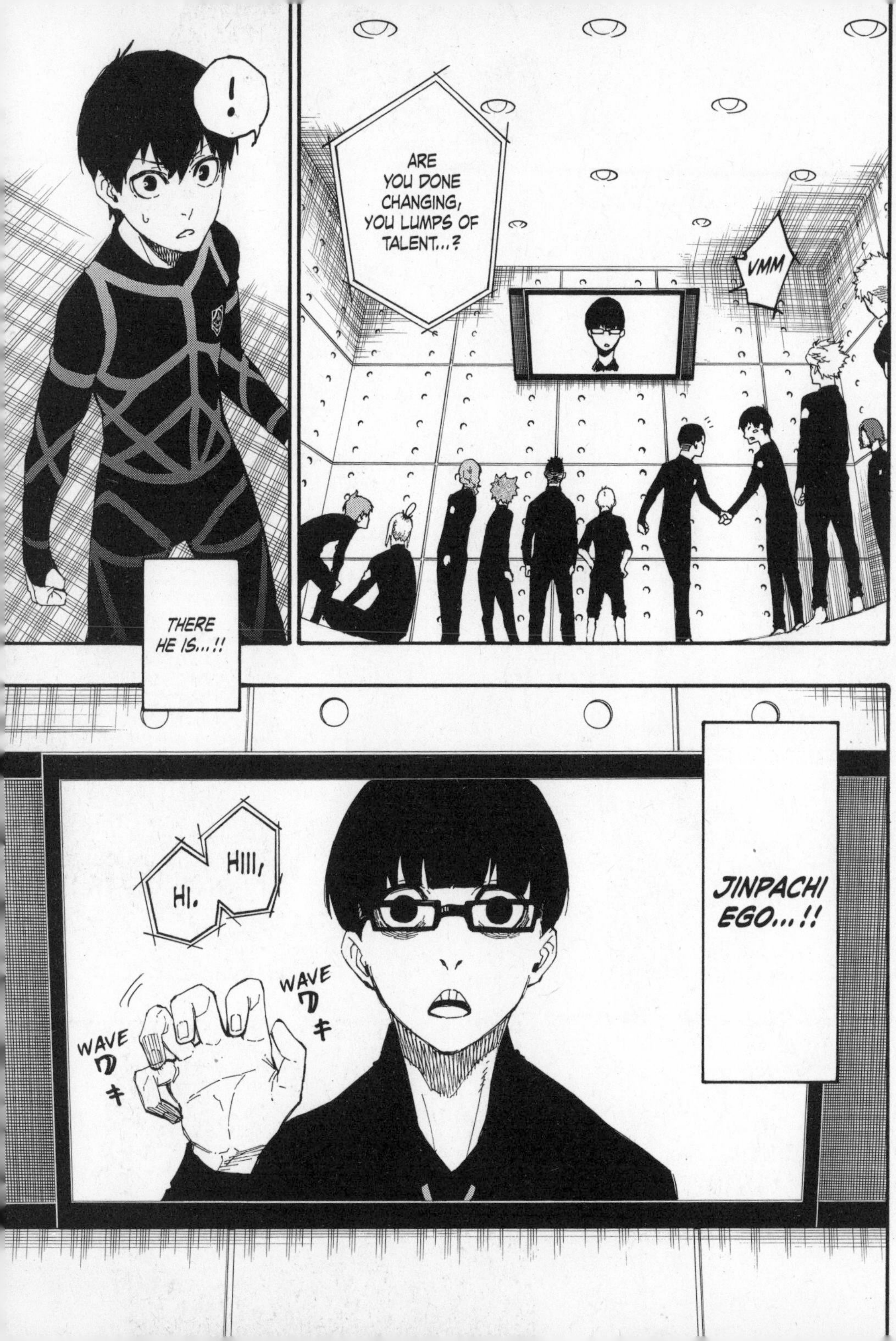
ARE YOU DONE CHANGING, YOU LUMPS OF TALENT...?
VMM
!
THERE HE IS...!!
JINPACHI EGO...!!
HIIII, HI.
WAVE ワキ
WAVE ワキ

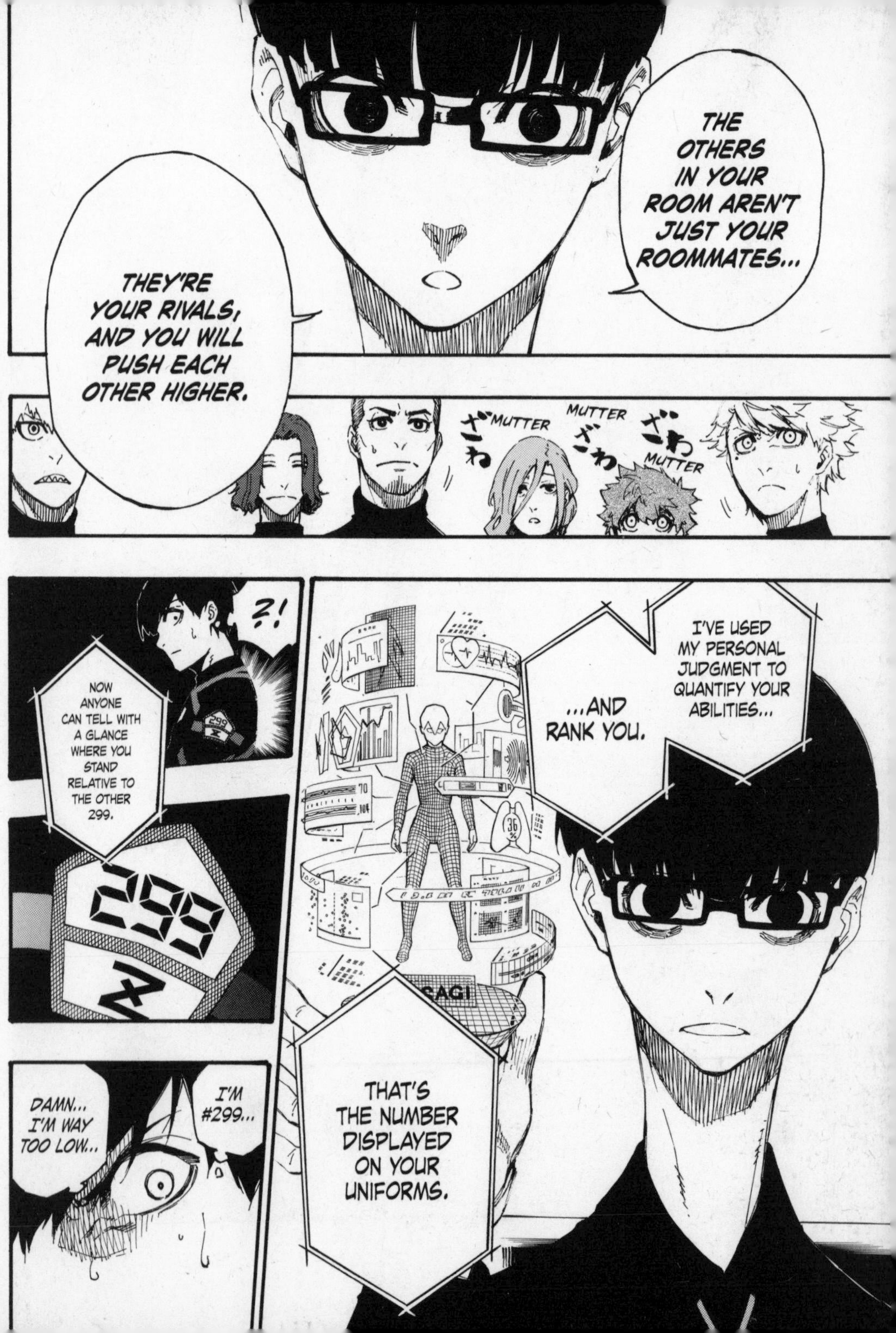
THE OTHERS IN YOUR ROOM AREN'T JUST YOUR ROOMMATES...
THEY'RE YOUR RIVALS, AND YOU WILL PUSH EACH OTHER HIGHER.
ざわ MUTTER
MUTTER ざわ
ざわ MUTTER
I'VE USED MY PERSONAL JUDGMENT TO QUANTIFY YOUR ABILITIES...
...AND RANK YOU.
THAT'S THE NUMBER DISPLAYED ON YOUR UNIFORMS.
?!
NOW ANYONE CAN TELL WITH A GLANCE WHERE YOU STAND RELATIVE TO THE OTHER 299.
299
I'M #299...
DAMN... I'M WAY TOO LOW...

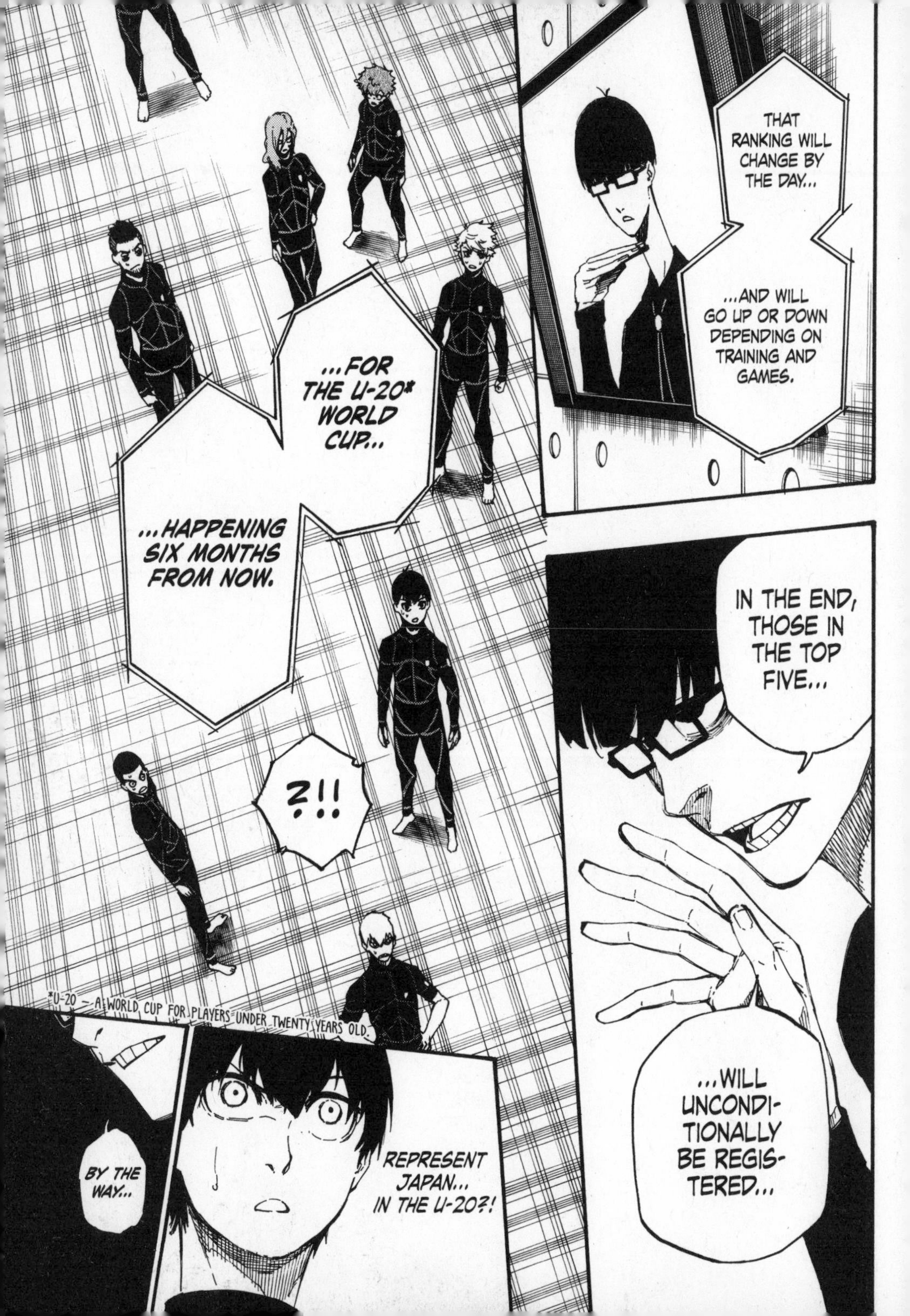
THAT RANKING WILL CHANGE BY THE DAY...
...AND WILL GO UP OR DOWN DEPENDING ON TRAINING AND GAMES.
IN THE END, THOSE IN THE TOP FIVE...
...WILL UNCONDITIONALLY BE REGISTERED...
...FOR THE U-20* WORLD CUP...
...HAPPENING SIX MONTHS FROM NOW.
?!!
REPRESENT JAPAN... IN THE U-20?!
BY THE WAY...
*U-20 — A WORLD CUP FOR PLAYERS UNDER TWENTY YEARS OLD.

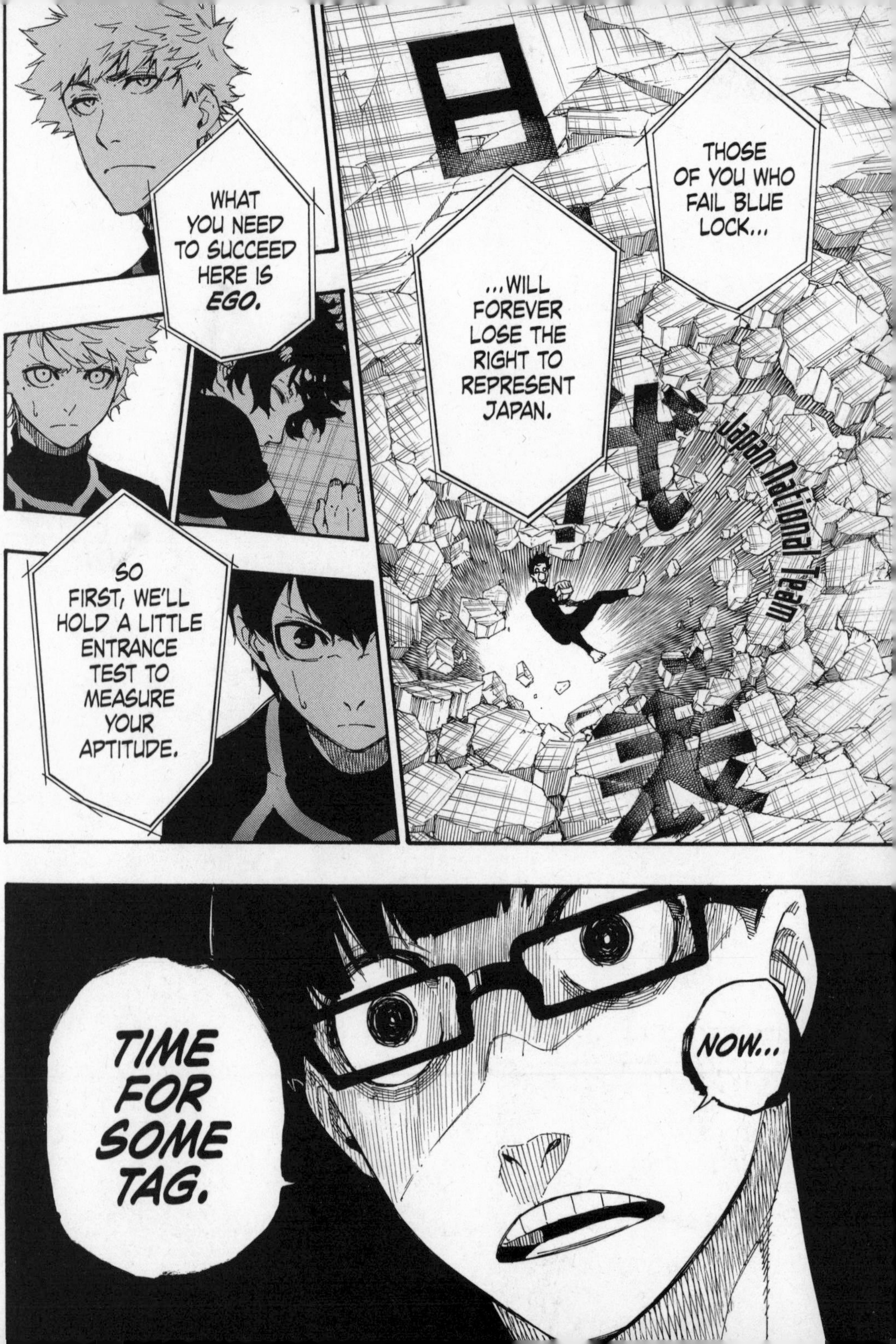
THOSE OF YOU WHO FAIL BLUE LOCK...
...WILL FOREVER LOSE THE RIGHT TO REPRESENT JAPAN.
Japan National Team
WHAT YOU NEED TO SUCCEED HERE IS *EGO.*
SO FIRST, WE'LL HOLD A LITTLE ENTRANCE TEST TO MEASURE YOUR APTITUDE.
NOW...
TIME FOR SOME TAG.

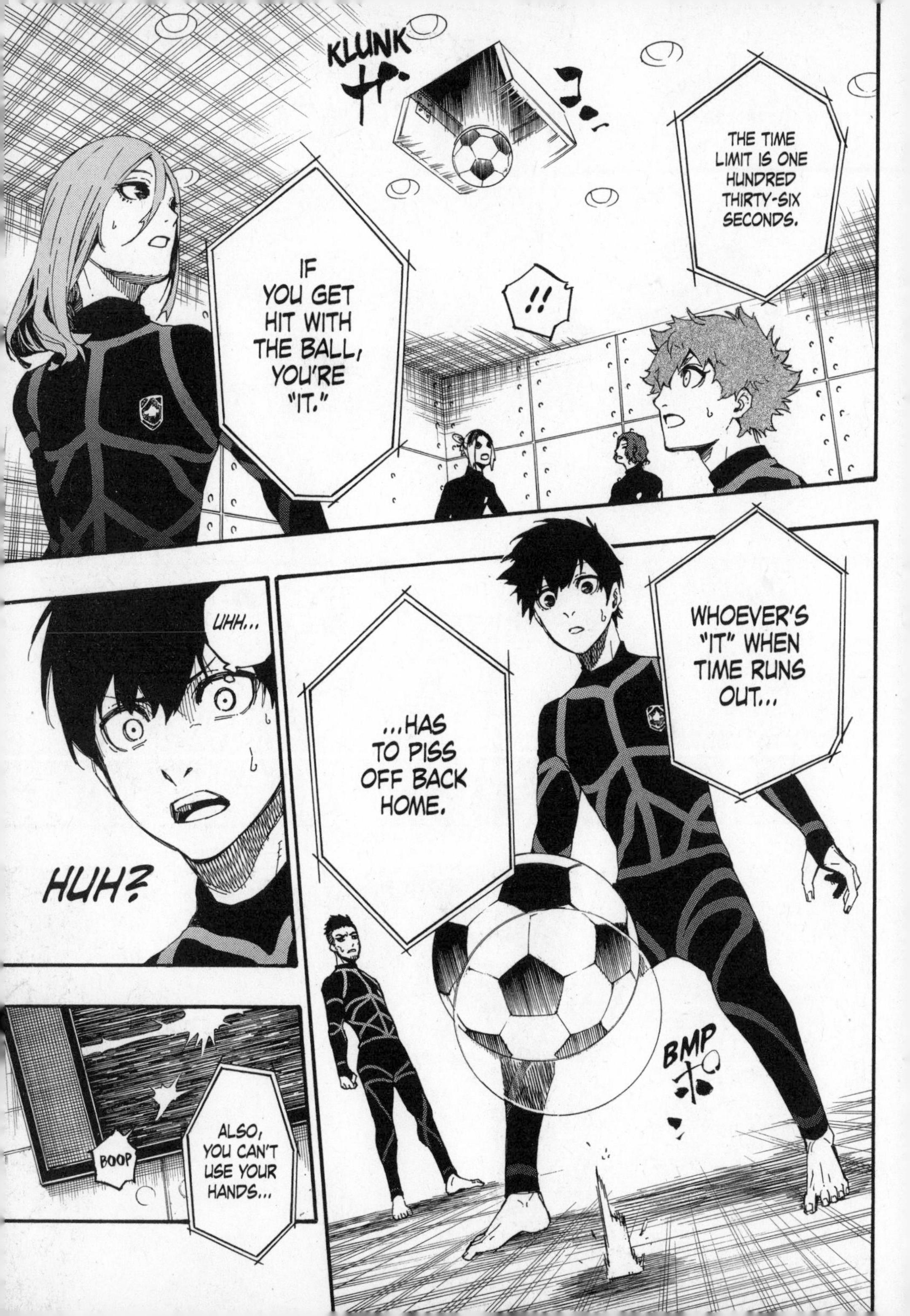
KLUNK
THE TIME LIMIT IS ONE HUNDRED THIRTY-SIX SECONDS.
!!
IF YOU GET HIT WITH THE BALL, YOU'RE "IT."
WHOEVER'S "IT" WHEN TIME RUNS OUT...
...HAS TO PISS OFF BACK HOME.
BMP
UHH...
HUH?
ALSO, YOU CAN'T USE YOUR HANDS...
BOOP

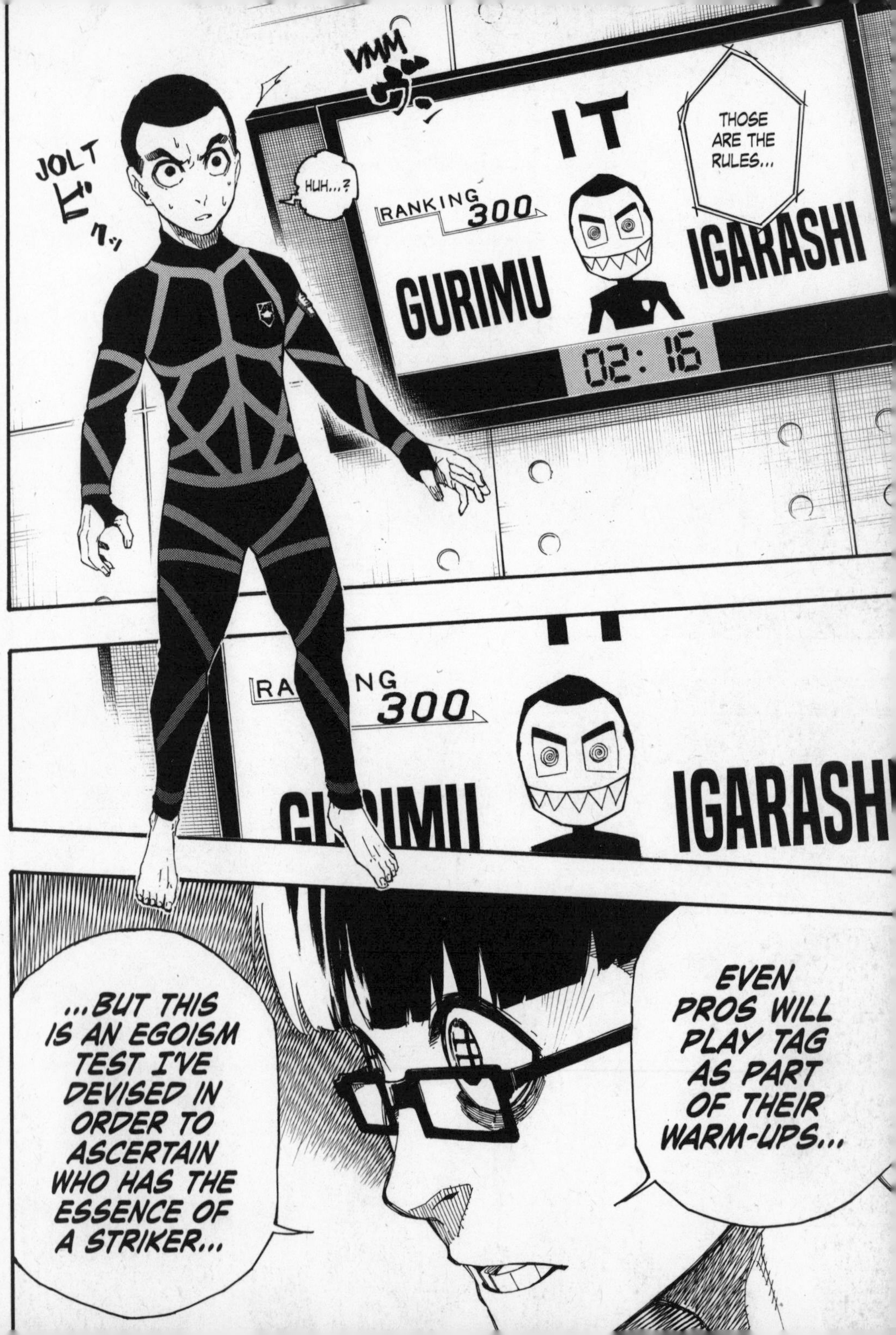
THOSE ARE THE RULES...
IT
VMM
HUH...?
RANKING 300
IGARASHI
GURIMU
02:16
JOLT
300
IGARASHI
EVEN PROS WILL PLAY TAG AS PART OF THEIR WARM-UPS...
...BUT THIS IS AN EGOISM TEST I'VE DEVISED IN ORDER TO ASCERTAIN WHO HAS THE ESSENCE OF A STRIKER...

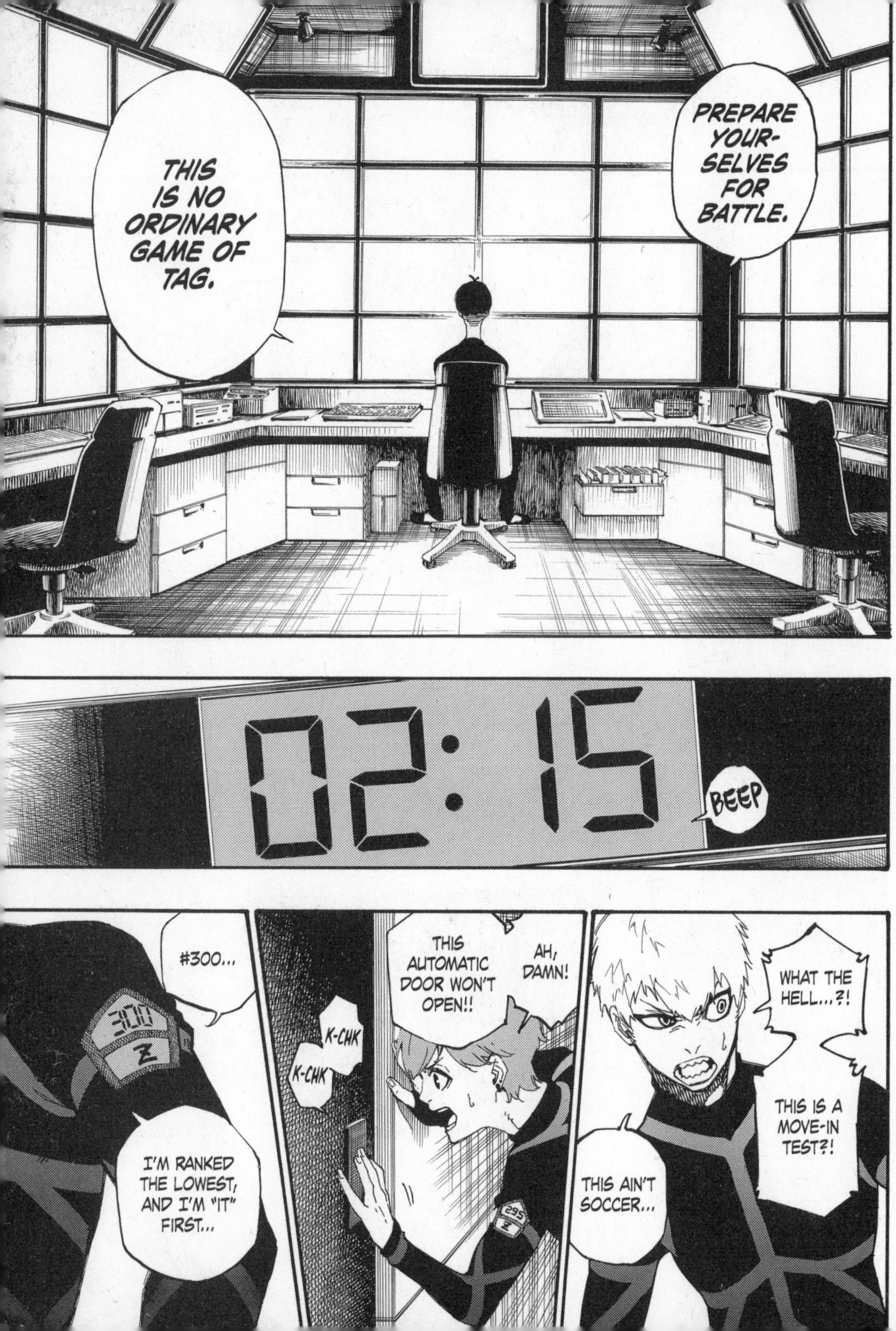
PREPARE YOURSELVES FOR BATTLE.
THIS IS NO ORDINARY GAME OF TAG.
02:15
BEEP
WHAT THE HELL...?!
THIS IS A MOVE-IN TEST?!
THIS AIN'T SOCCER...
AH, DAMN!
THIS AUTOMATIC DOOR WON'T OPEN!!
K-CHK
K-CHK
#300...
I'M RANKED THE LOWEST, AND I'M "IT" FIRST...

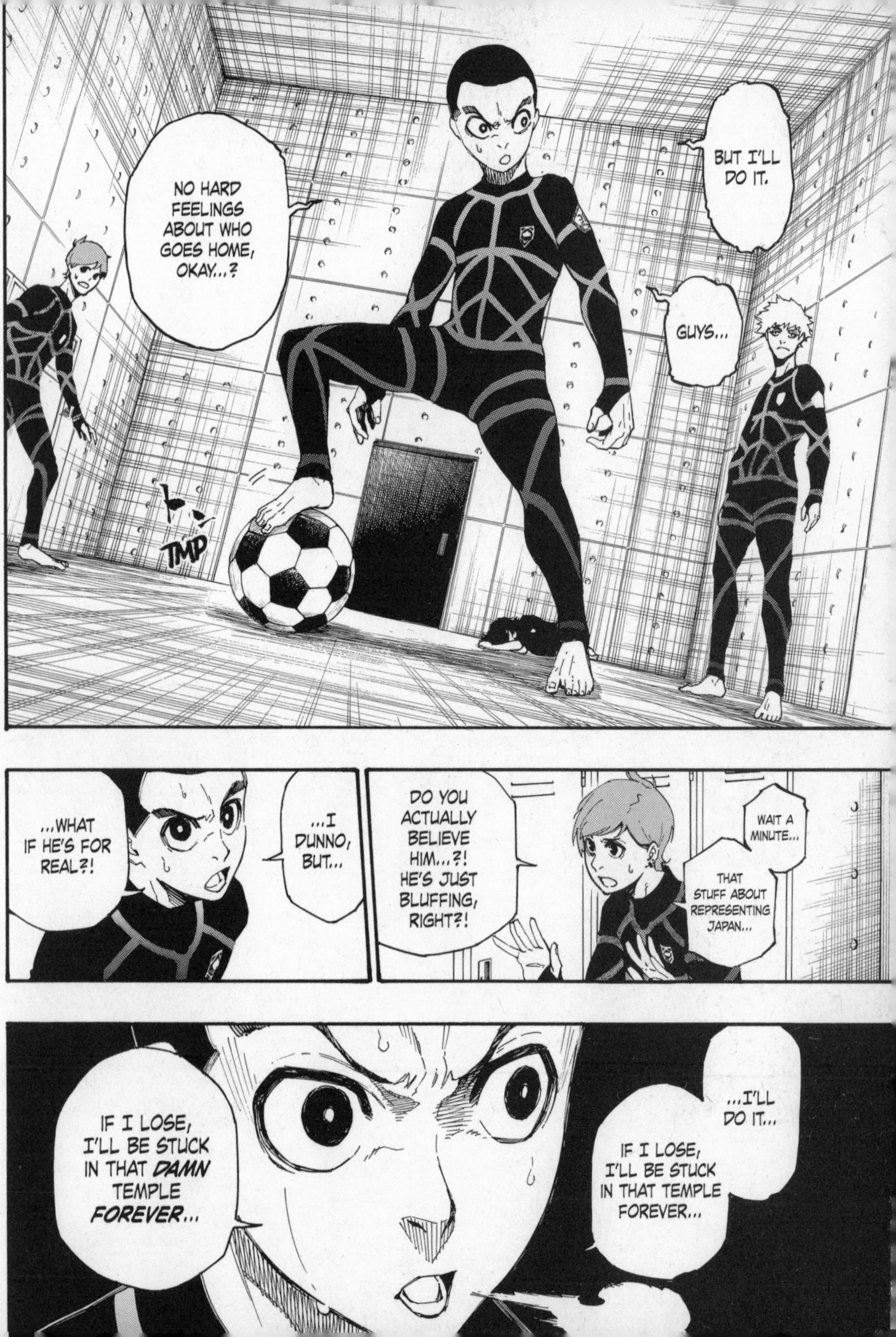
BUT I'LL DO IT.
NO HARD FEELINGS ABOUT WHO GOES HOME, OKAY...?
GUYS...
TMP
WAIT A MINUTE...
THAT STUFF ABOUT REPRESENTING JAPAN...
DO YOU ACTUALLY BELIEVE HIM...?! HE'S JUST BLUFFING, RIGHT?!
...I DUNNO, BUT...
...WHAT IF HE'S FOR REAL?!
...I'LL DO IT...
IF I LOSE, I'LL BE STUCK IN THAT TEMPLE FOREVER...
IF I LOSE, I'LL BE STUCK IN THAT *DAMN* TEMPLE ***FOREVER***...

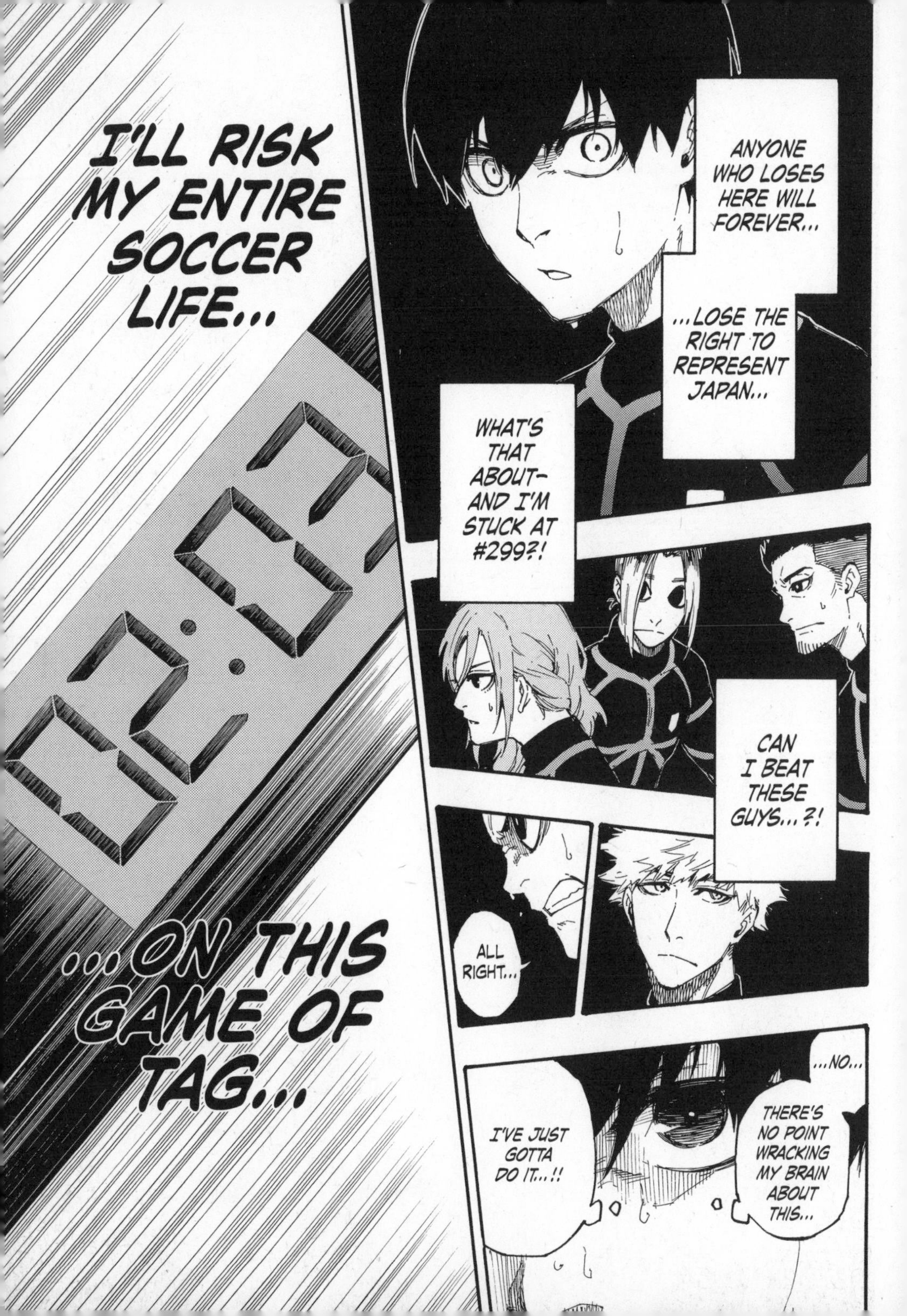
ANYONE WHO LOSES HERE WILL FOREVER...
...LOSE THE RIGHT TO REPRESENT JAPAN...
WHAT'S THAT ABOUT- AND I'M STUCK AT #299?!
CAN I BEAT THESE GUYS...?!
ALL RIGHT...
...NO...
THERE'S NO POINT WRACKING MY BRAIN ABOUT THIS...
I'VE JUST GOTTA DO IT...!!
I'LL RISK MY ENTIRE SOCCER LIFE...
...ON THIS GAME OF TAG...

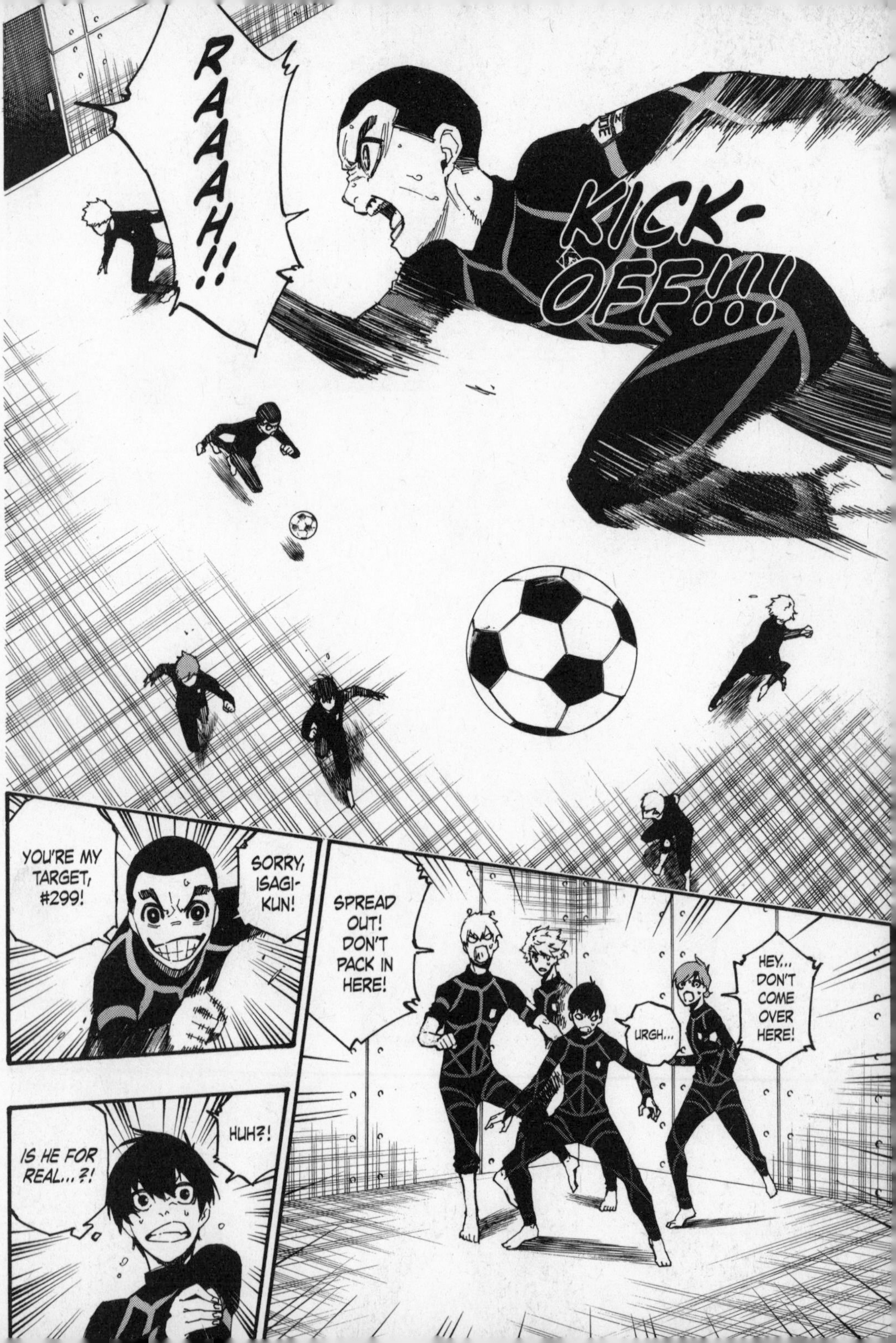
RAAAAH!!
KICK-OFF!!!
HEY... DON'T COME OVER HERE!
URGH...
SPREAD OUT! DON'T PACK IN HERE!
SORRY, ISAGI-KUN!
YOU'RE MY TARGET, #299!
HUH?!
IS HE FOR REAL...?!

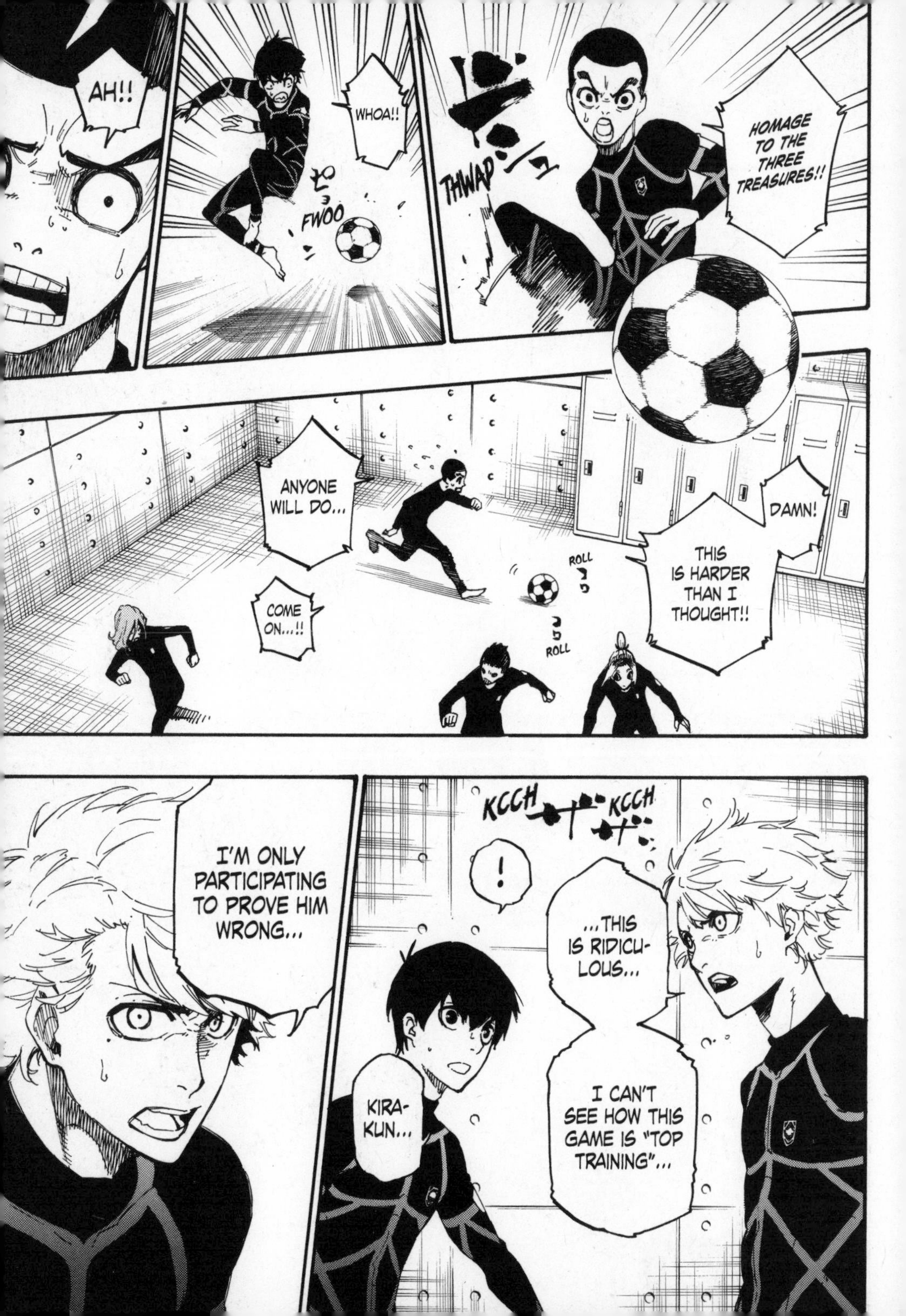
HOMAGE TO THE THREE TREASURES!!
THWAP
WHOA!!
FWOO
AH!!
DAMN!
THIS IS HARDER THAN I THOUGHT!!
ANYONE WILL DO...
ROLL
ROLL
COME ON...!!
KCCH KCCH
!
...THIS IS RIDICU-LOUS...
I CAN'T SEE HOW THIS GAME IS "TOP TRAINING"...
KIRA-KUN...
I'M ONLY PARTICIPATING TO PROVE HIM WRONG...

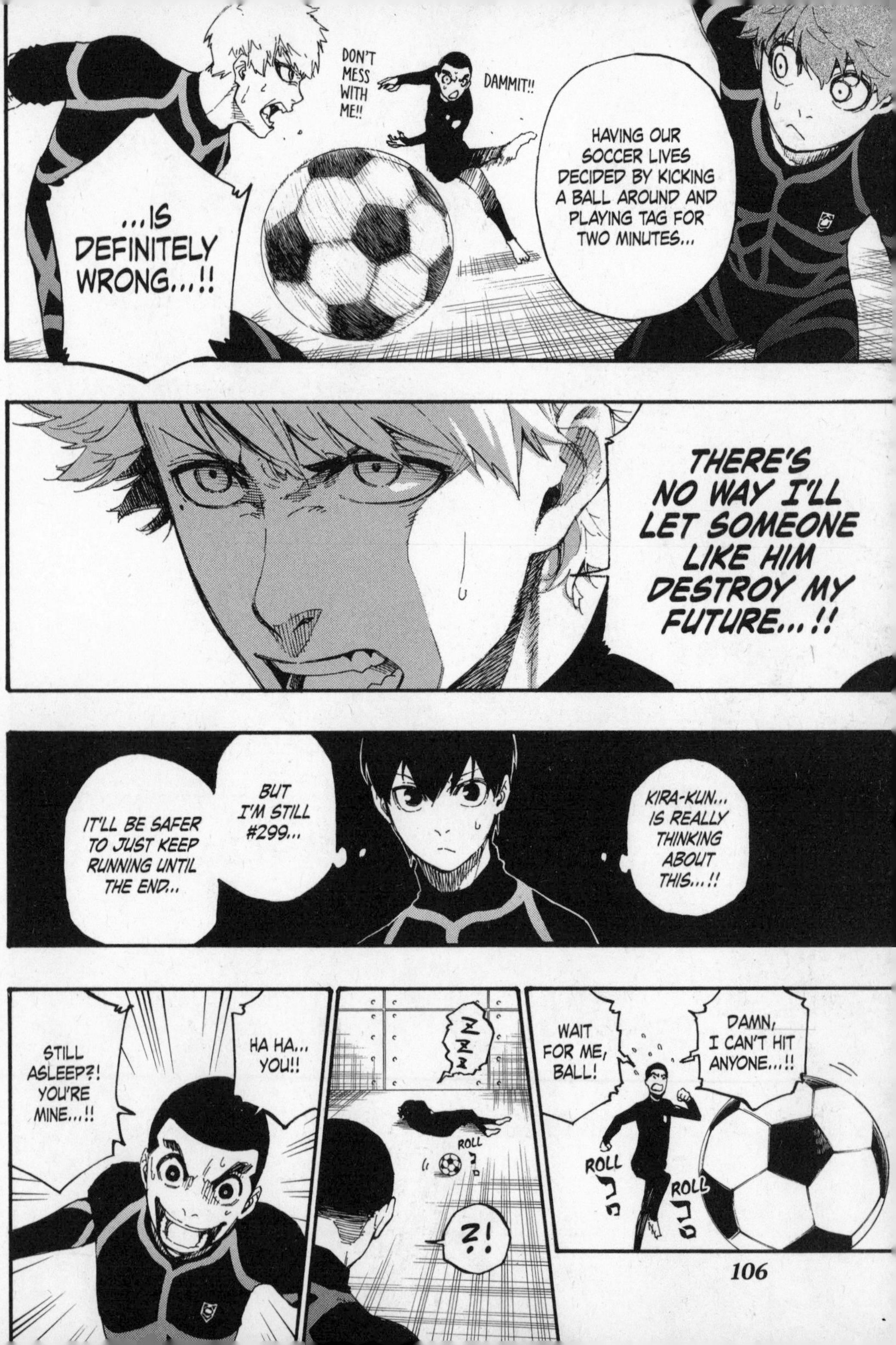
HAVING OUR SOCCER LIVES DECIDED BY KICKING A BALL AROUND AND PLAYING TAG FOR TWO MINUTES...
DAMMIT!!
DON'T MESS WITH ME!!
...IS DEFINITELY WRONG...!!
THERE'S NO WAY I'LL LET SOMEONE LIKE HIM DESTROY MY FUTURE...!!
KIRA-KUN... IS REALLY THINKING ABOUT THIS...!!
BUT I'M STILL #299...
IT'LL BE SAFER TO JUST KEEP RUNNING UNTIL THE END...
DAMN, I CAN'T HIT ANYONE...!!
WAIT FOR ME, BALL!
ROLL
ROLL
ZZZ
ROLL
?!
HA HA... YOU!!
STILL ASLEEP?! YOU'RE MINE...!!

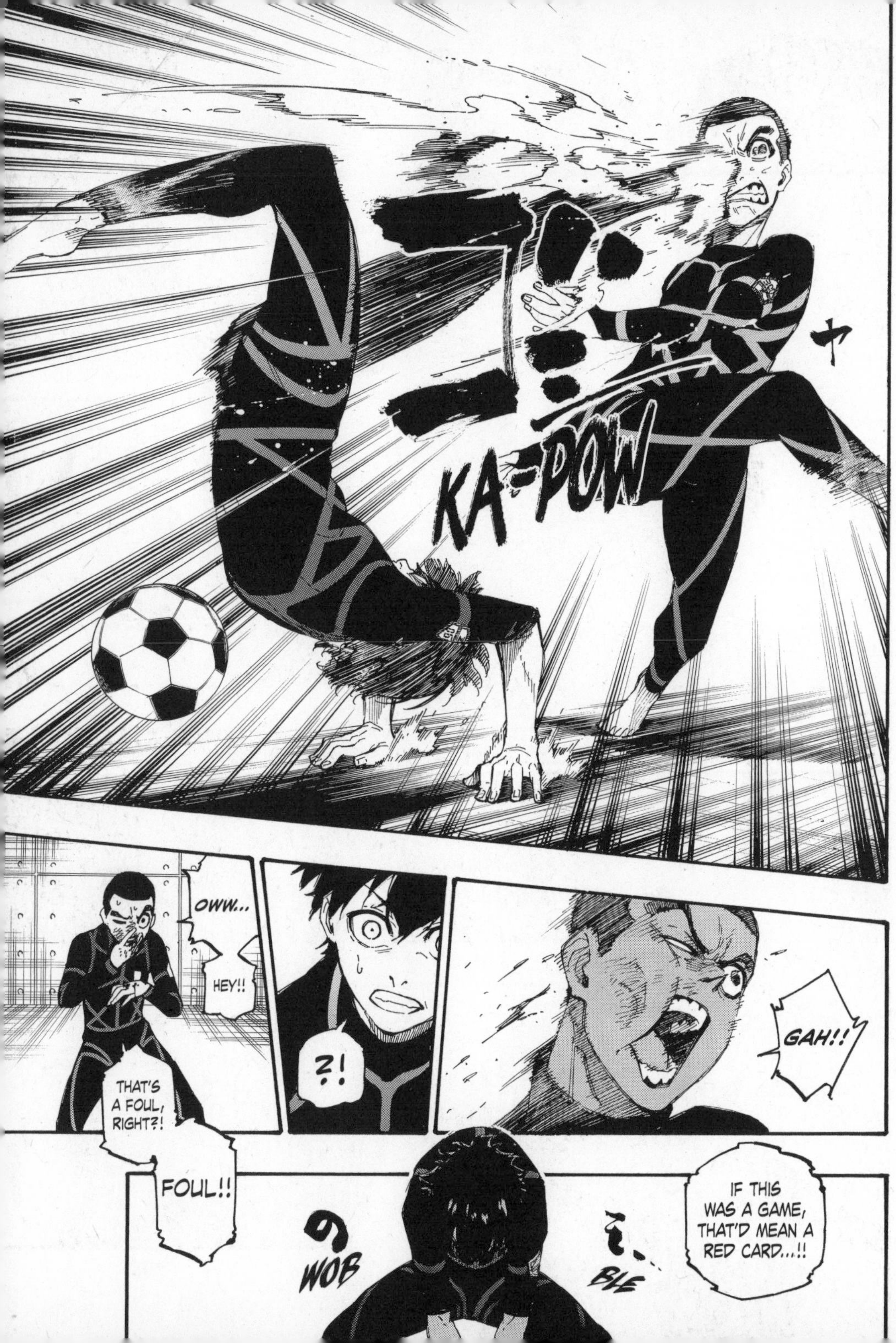
KA-POW
GAH!!
?!
OWW...
HEY!!
THAT'S A FOUL, RIGHT?!
IF THIS WAS A GAME, THAT'D MEAN A RED CARD...!!
BLE
WOB
FOUL!!

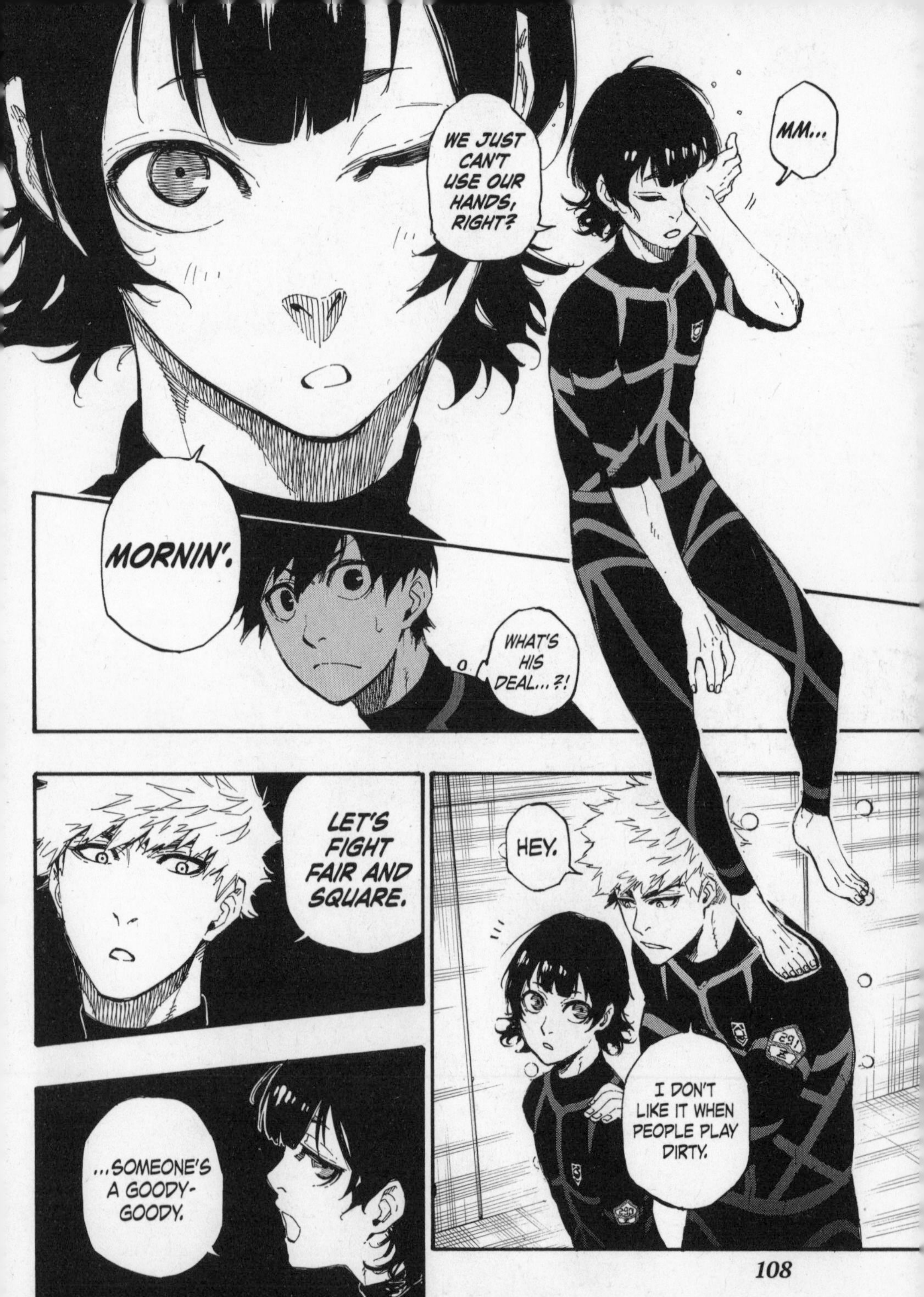
MM...
WE JUST CAN'T USE OUR HANDS, RIGHT?
MORNIN'.
WHAT'S HIS DEAL...?!
HEY.
I DON'T LIKE IT WHEN PEOPLE PLAY DIRTY.
LET'S FIGHT FAIR AND SQUARE.
...SOMEONE'S A GOODY-GOODY.

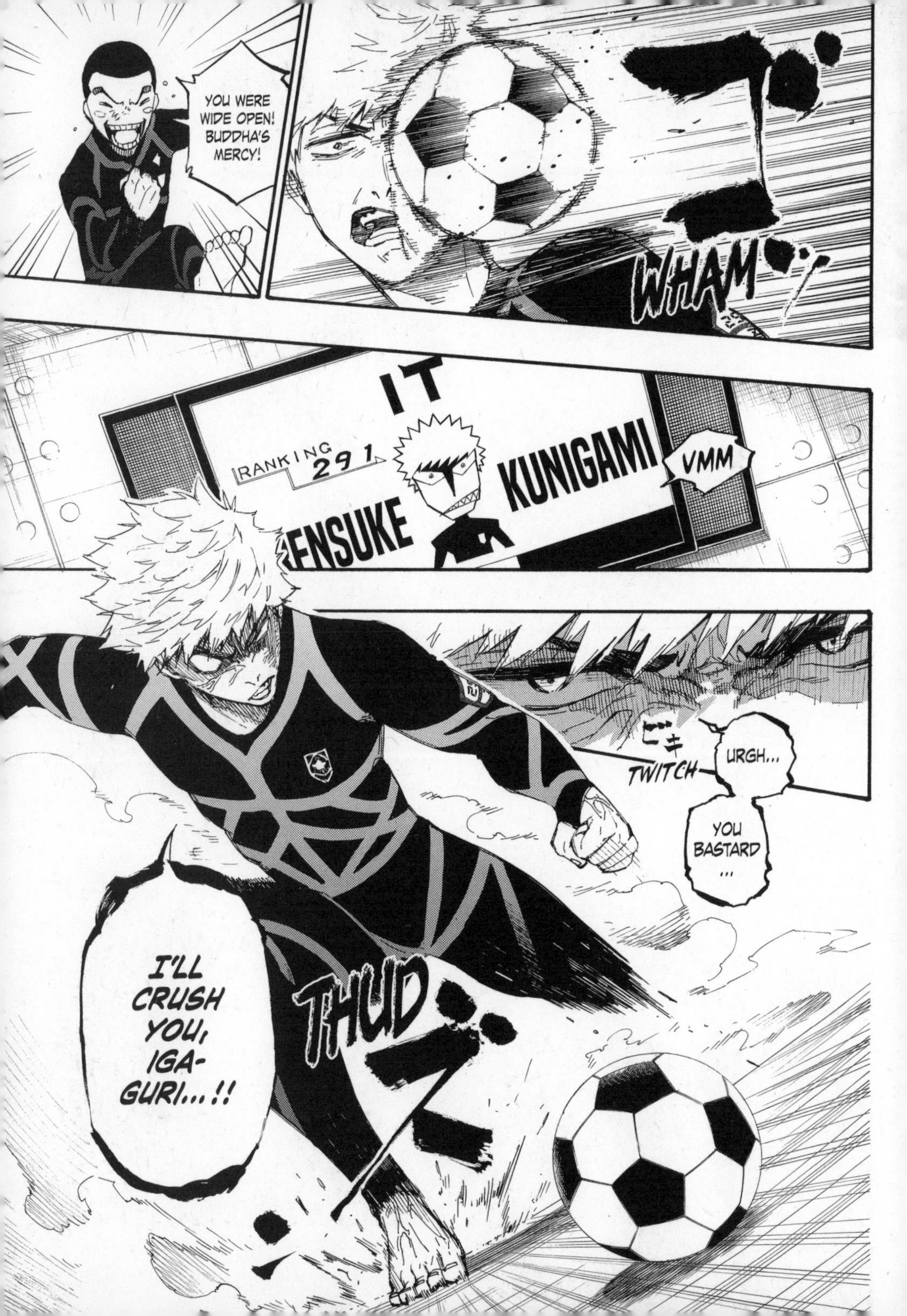
WHAM
YOU WERE WIDE OPEN! BUDDHA'S MERCY!
IT
RANKING 291
ENSUKE KUNIGAMI
VMM
TWITCH
URGH...
YOU BASTARD ...
THUD
I'LL CRUSH YOU, IGA-GURI...!!

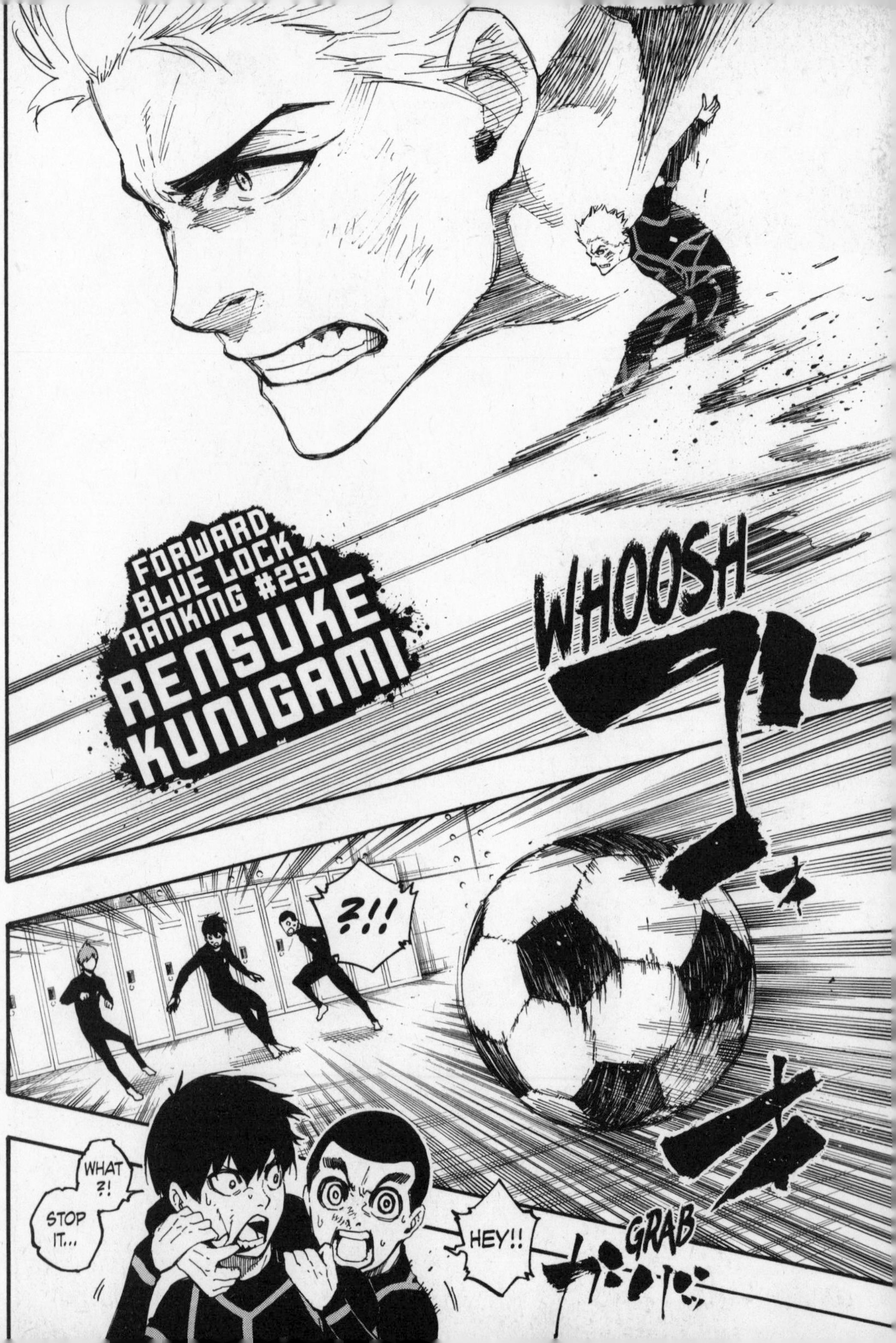
FORWARD
BLUE LOCK
RANKING #291
RENSUKE KUNIGAMI
WHOOSH
?!!
HEY!!
WHAT ?!
STOP IT...
GRAB

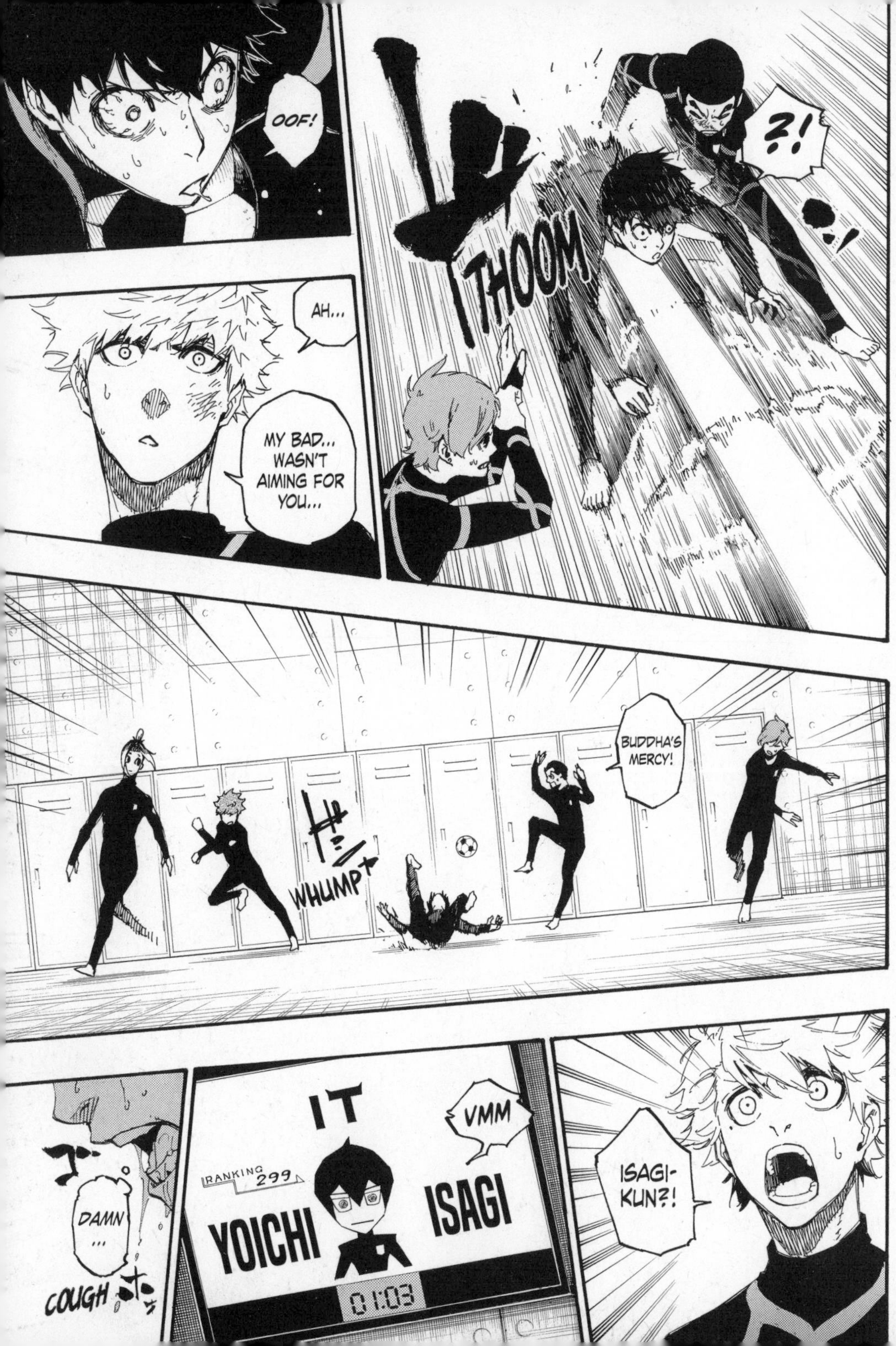
?!
?!
THOOM
OOF!
AH...
MY BAD... WASN'T AIMING FOR YOU...
BUDDHA'S MERCY!
WHUMP
ISAGI-KUN?!
IT
VMM
RANKING 299
YOICHI ISAGI
01:03
DAMN...
COUGH

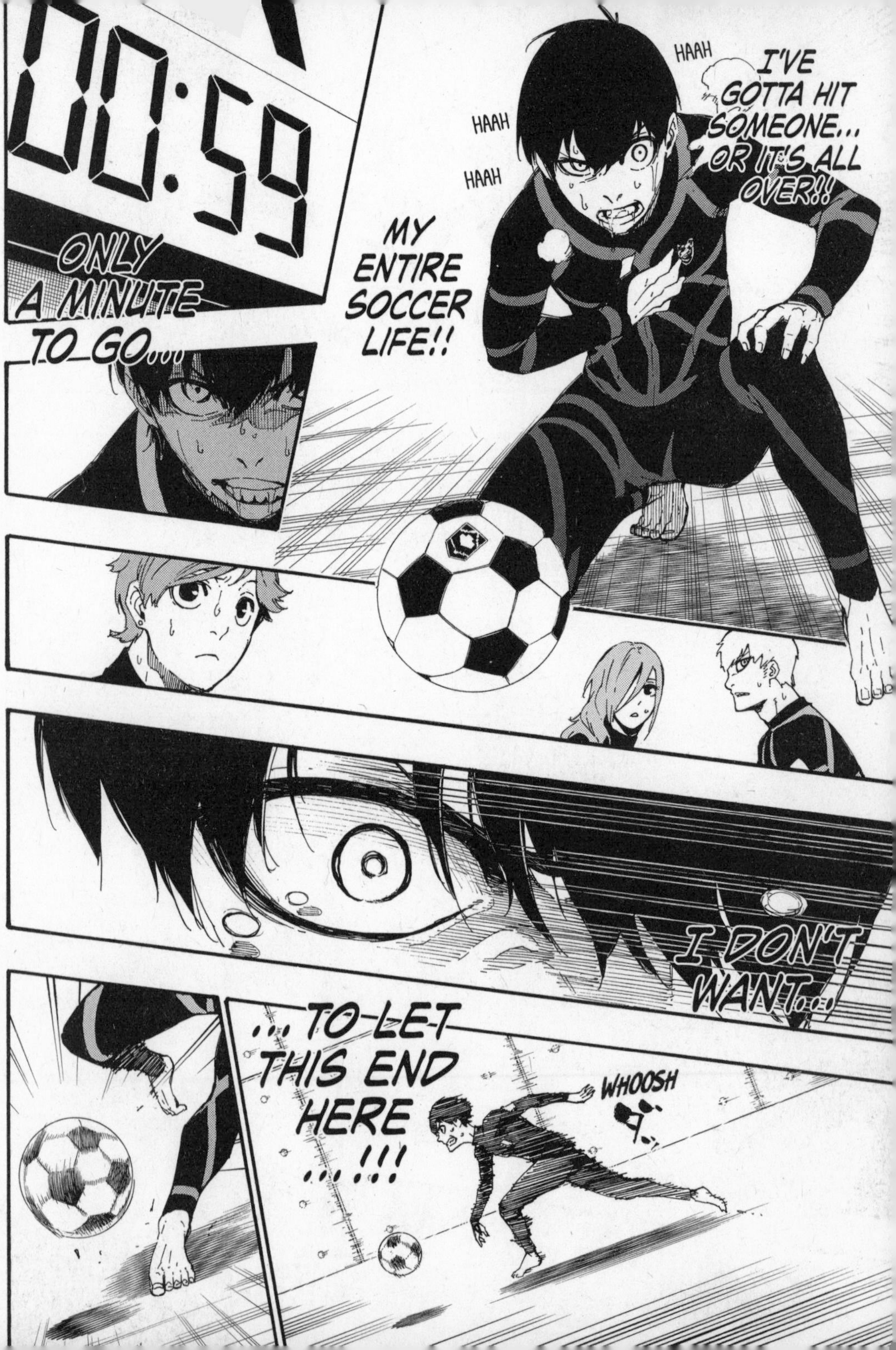
HAAH
I'VE GOTTA HIT SOMEONE... OR IT'S ALL OVER!!
HAAH
HAAH
MY ENTIRE SOCCER LIFE!!
00:59
ONLY A MINUTE TO GO...
I DON'T WANT...
...TO LET THIS END HERE...!!!
WHOOSH

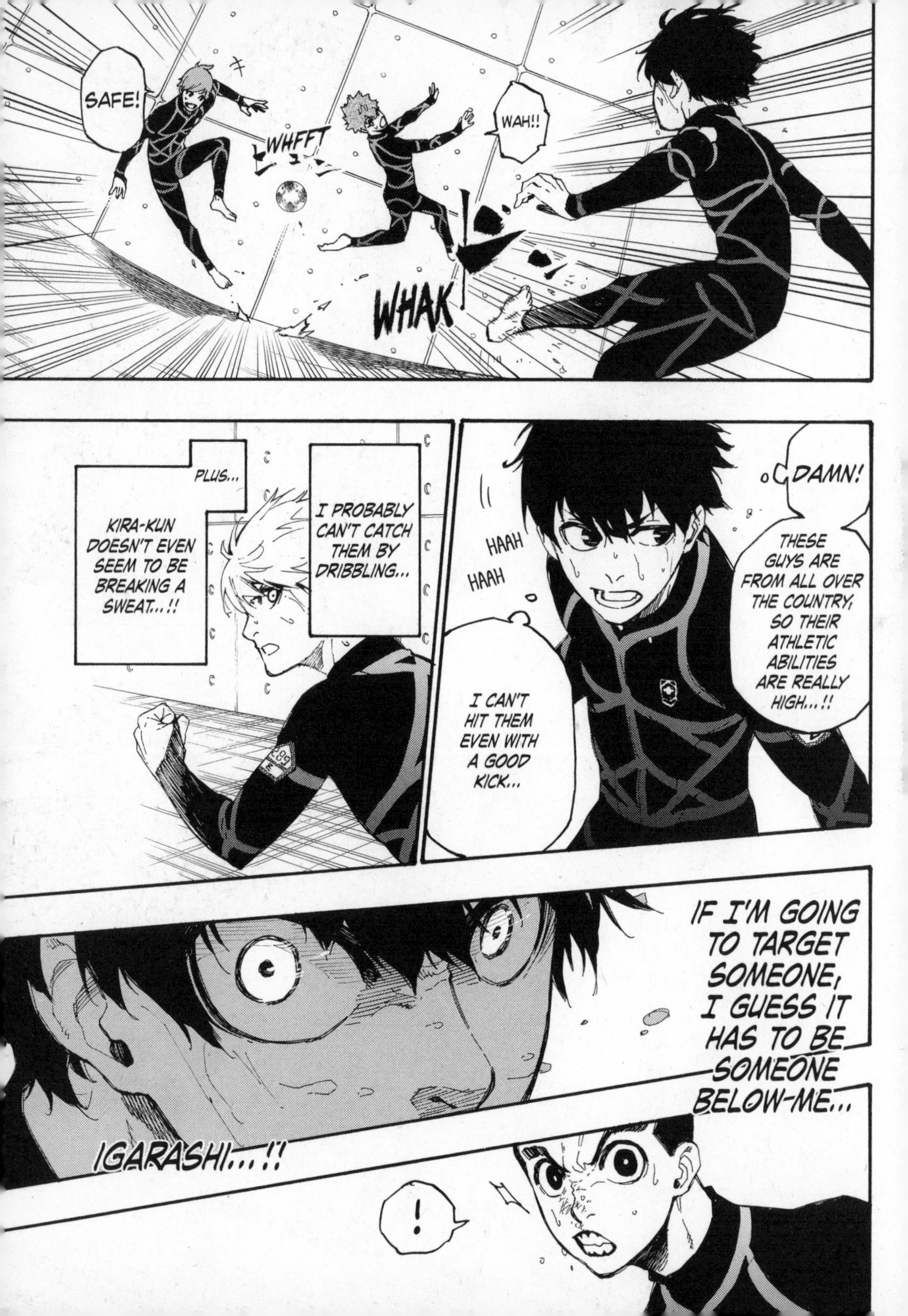
WAH!!
WHFFT
SAFE!
WHAK
DAMN!
THESE GUYS ARE FROM ALL OVER THE COUNTRY, SO THEIR ATHLETIC ABILITIES ARE REALLY HIGH...!!
HAAH HAAH
I CAN'T HIT THEM EVEN WITH A GOOD KICK...
I PROBABLY CAN'T CATCH THEM BY DRIBBLING...
PLUS...
KIRA-KUN DOESN'T EVEN SEEM TO BE BREAKING A SWEAT...!!
IF I'M GOING TO TARGET SOMEONE, I GUESS IT HAS TO BE SOMEONE BELOW ME...
IGARASHI...!!
!

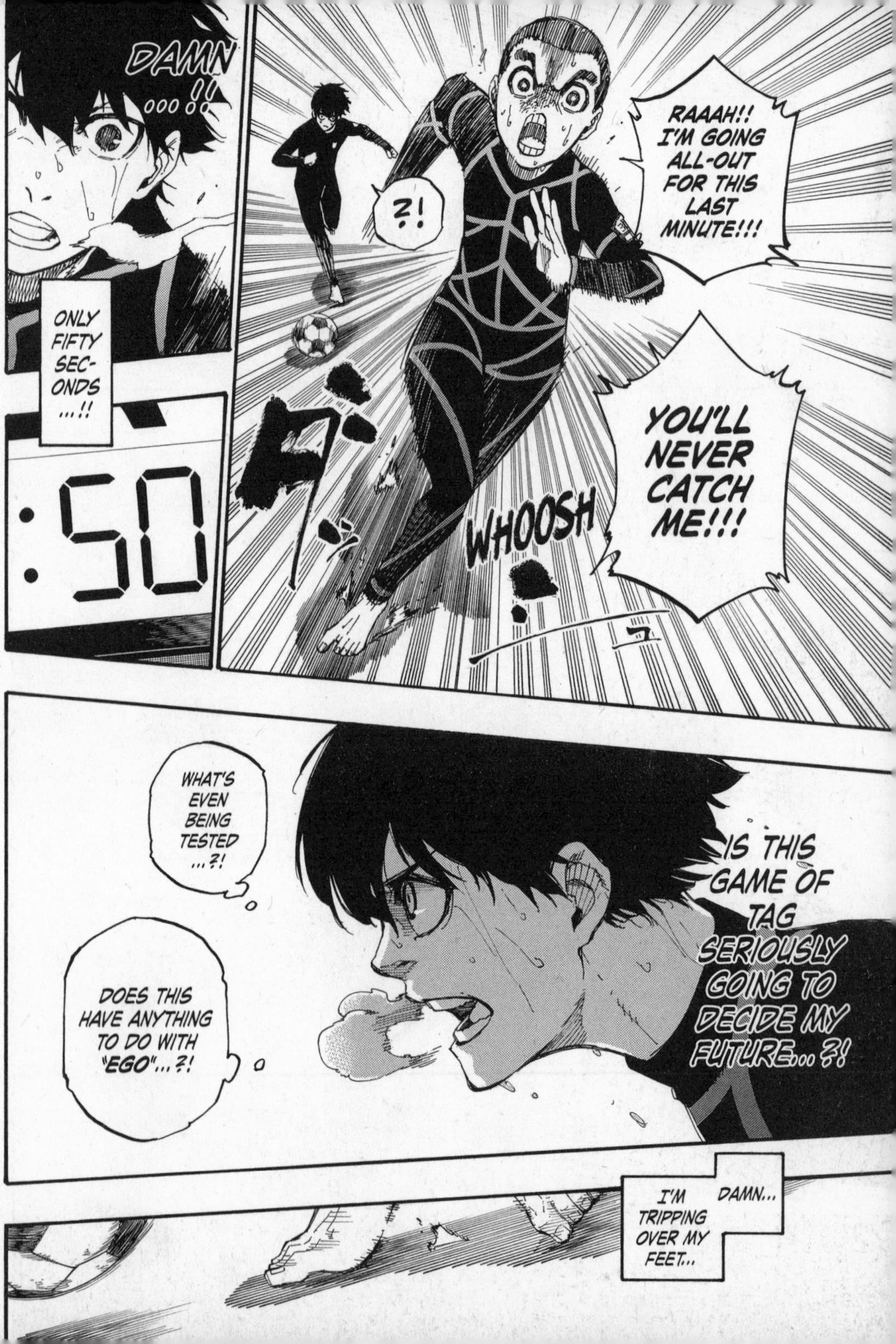
RAAAH!! I'M GOING ALL-OUT FOR THIS LAST MINUTE!!!
?!
YOU'LL NEVER CATCH ME!!!
WHOOSH
DAMN ooo!!
ONLY FIFTY SEC-ONDS...!!
:50
IS THIS GAME OF TAG SERIOUSLY GOING TO DECIDE MY FUTURE...?!
WHAT'S EVEN BEING TESTED...?!
DOES THIS HAVE ANYTHING TO DO WITH "EGO"...?!
DAMN...
I'M TRIPPING OVER MY FEET...

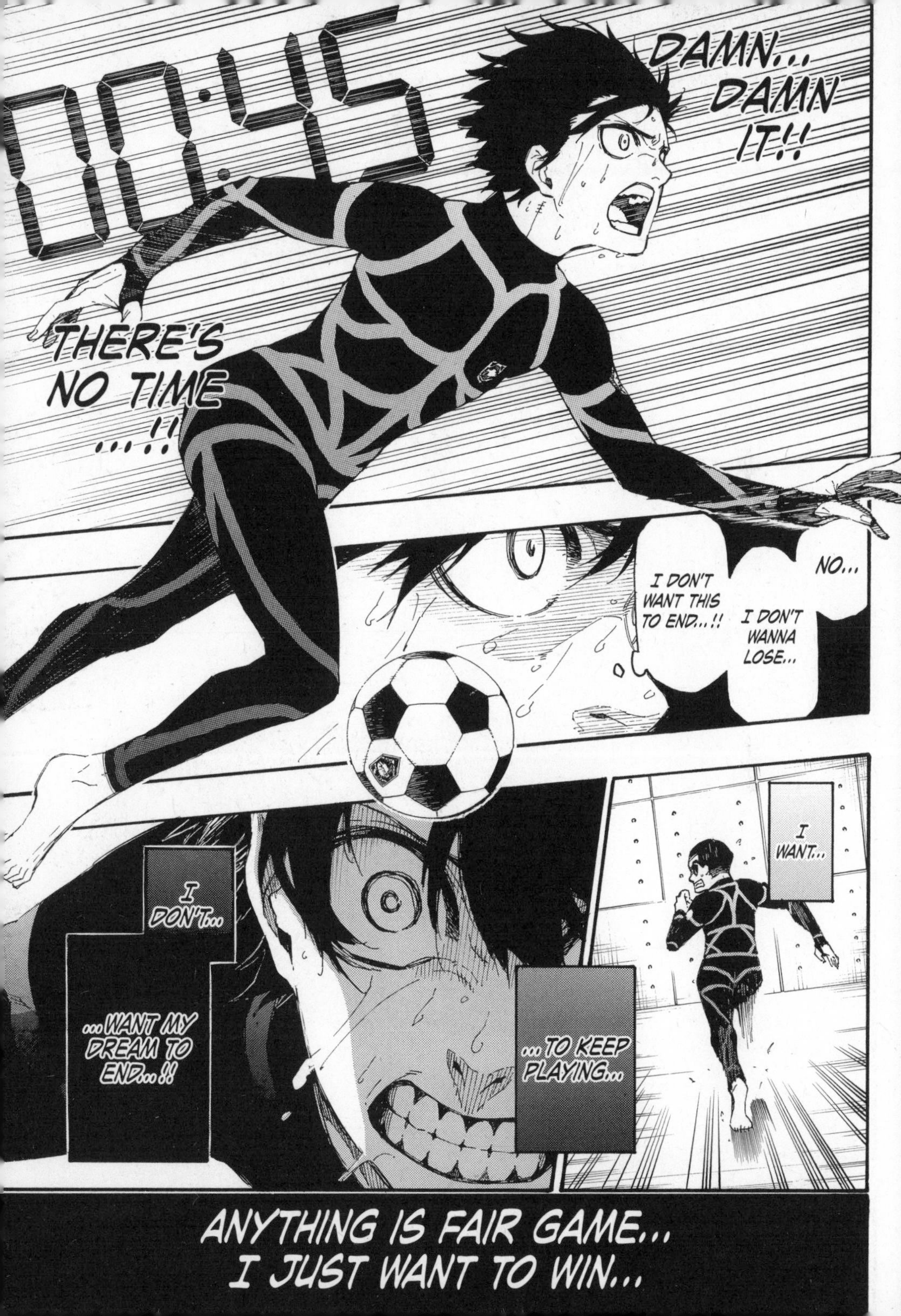
00:45
DAMN... DAMN IT!!
THERE'S NO TIME ...!!
NO...
I DON'T WANNA LOSE...
I DON'T WANT THIS TO END...!!
I WANT...
...TO KEEP PLAYING...
I DON'T...
...WANT MY DREAM TO END...!!
ANYTHING IS FAIR GAME...
I JUST WANT TO WIN...

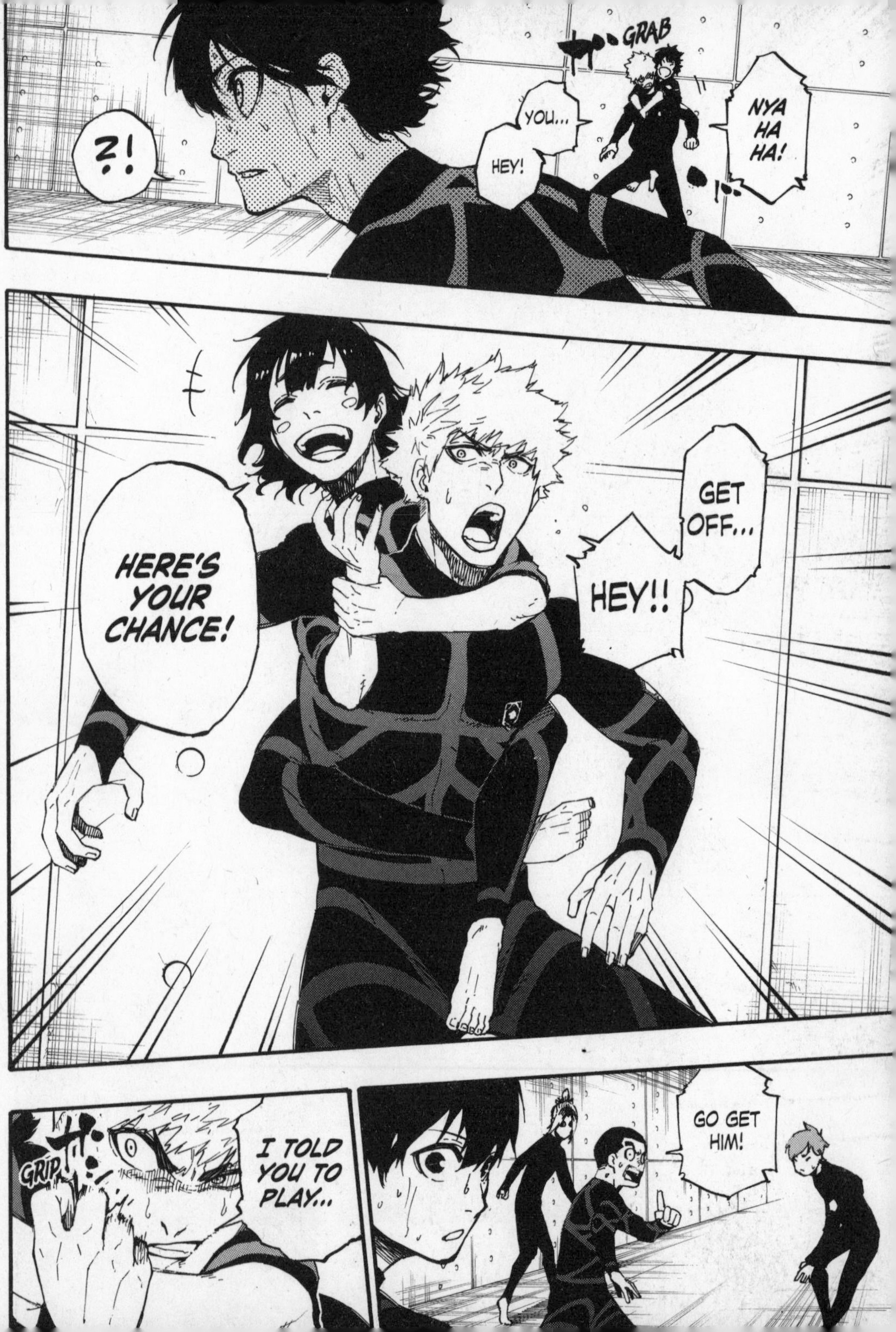
GRAB
NYA HA HA!
YOU...
HEY!
?!
GET OFF...
HEY!!
HERE'S YOUR CHANCE!
GO GET HIM!
I TOLD YOU TO PLAY...
GRIP

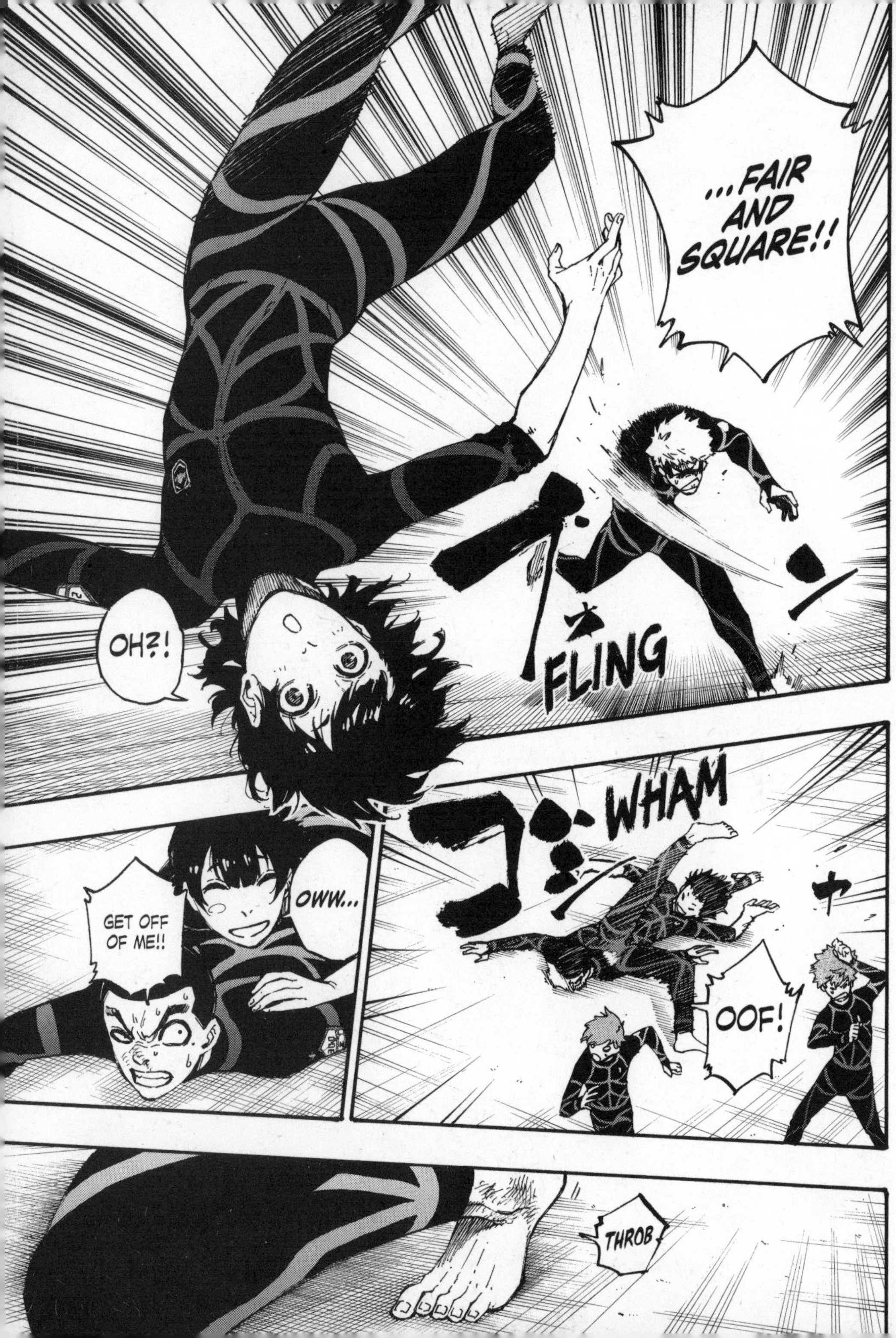
...FAIR AND SQUARE!!
FLING
OH?!
WHAM
OOF!
OWW...
GET OFF OF ME!!
THROB

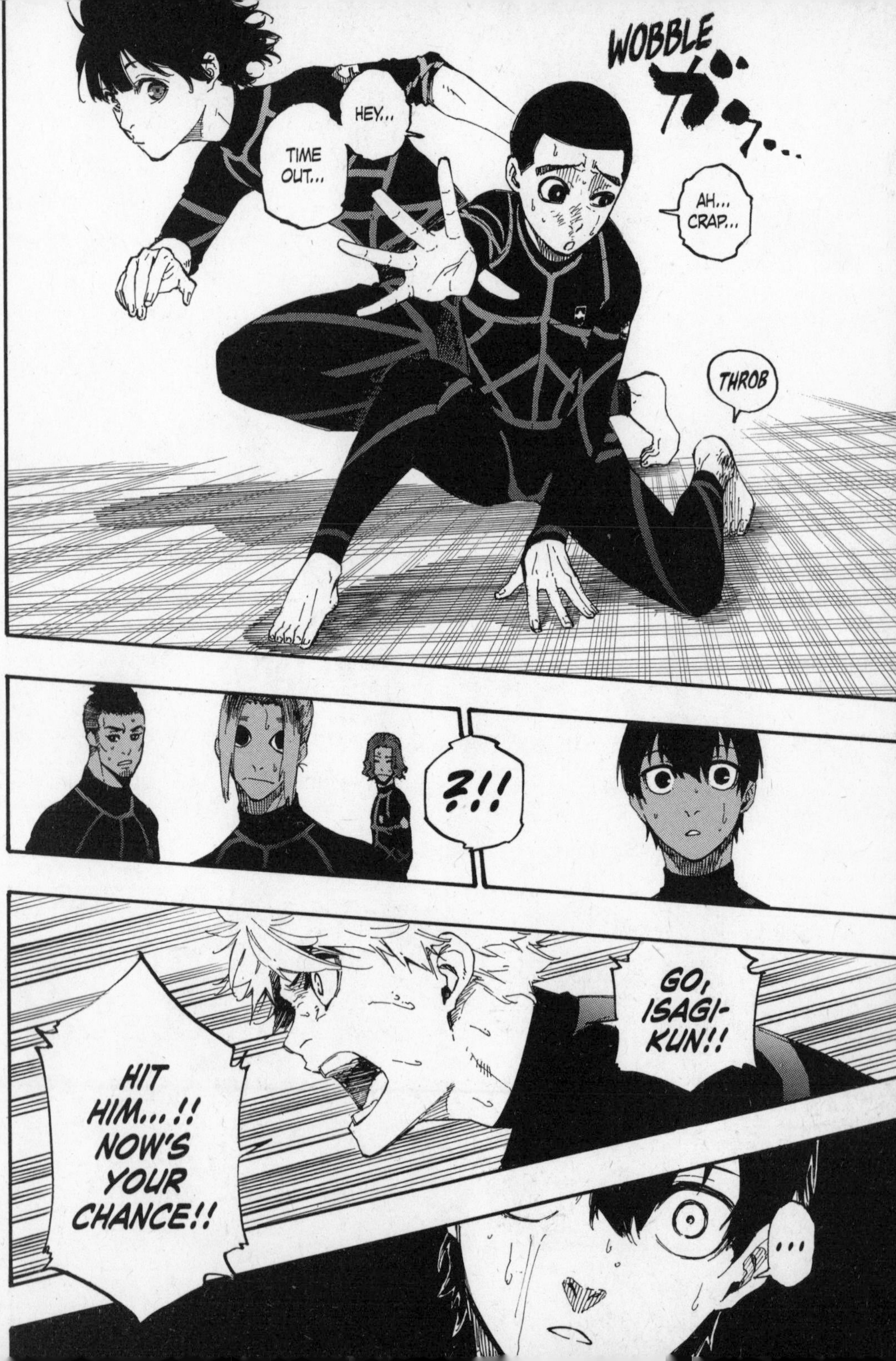
WOBBLE
AH... CRAP...
HEY...
TIME OUT...
THROB
?!!
GO, ISAGI-KUN!!
HIT HIM...!! NOW'S YOUR CHANCE!!
...

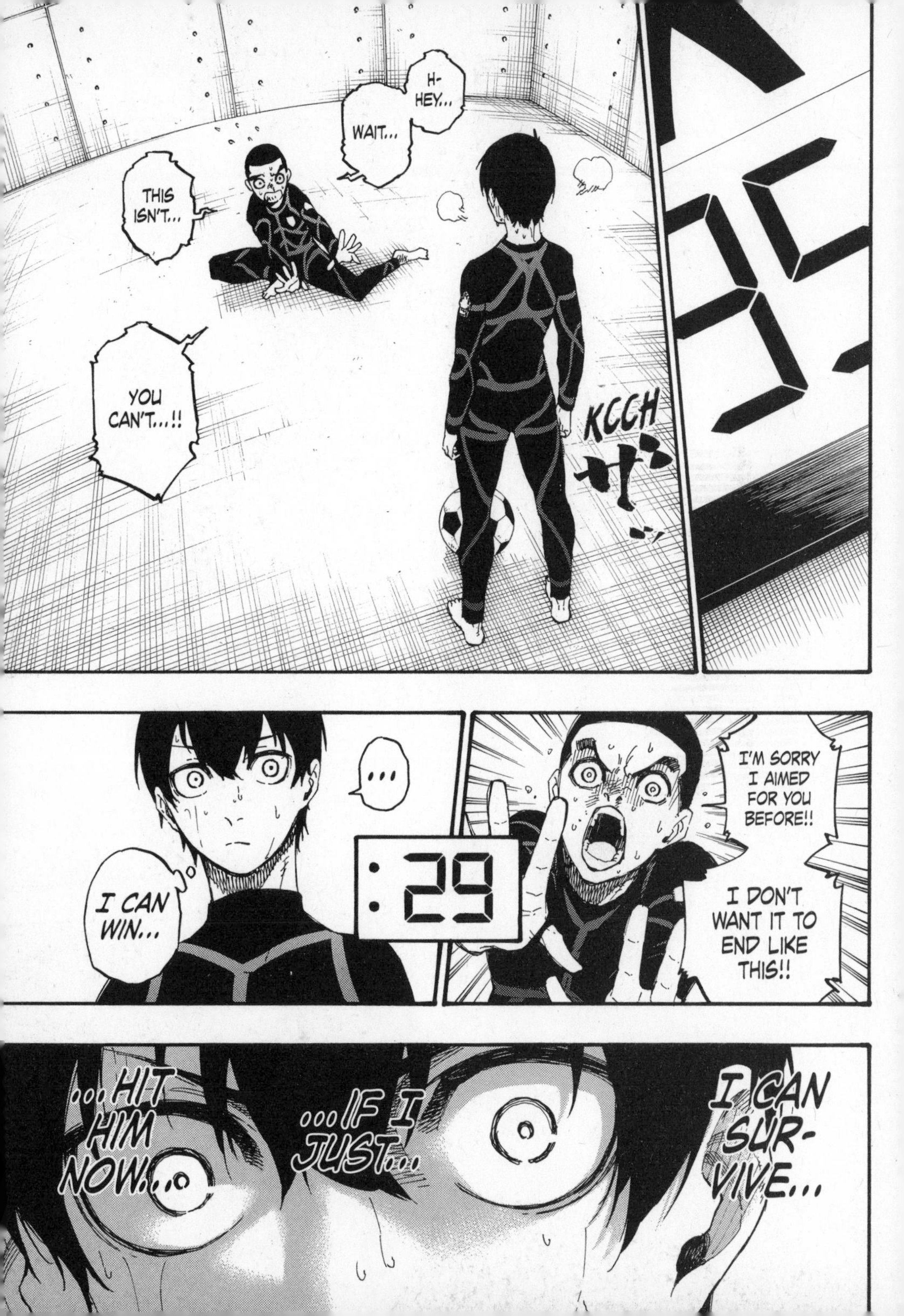
H-
HEY...
WAIT...
THIS ISN'T...
KCCH
YOU CAN'T...!!
I'M SORRY I AIMED FOR YOU BEFORE!!
I DON'T WANT IT TO END LIKE THIS!!
...
:29
I CAN WIN...
I CAN SUR-VIVE...
...IF I JUST...
...HIT HIM NOW...

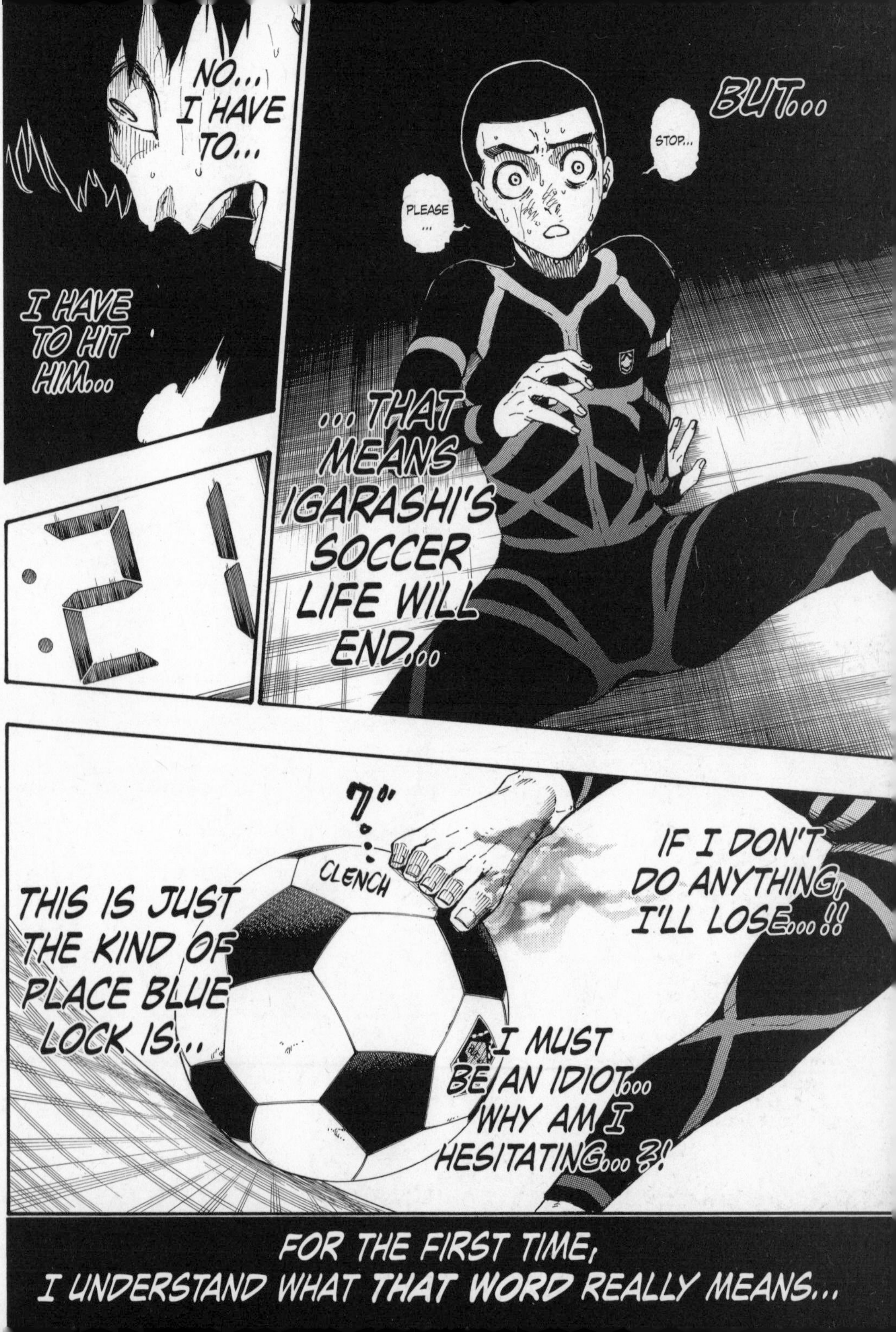
BUT...
STOP...
PLEASE...
...THAT MEANS IGARASHI'S SOCCER LIFE WILL END...
NO... I HAVE TO...
I HAVE TO HIT HIM...
21
IF I DON'T DO ANYTHING, I'LL LOSE...!!
CLENCH
THIS IS JUST THE KIND OF PLACE BLUE LOCK IS...
I MUST BE AN IDIOT... WHY AM I HESITATING...?!
FOR THE FIRST TIME,
I UNDERSTAND WHAT THAT WORD REALLY MEANS...

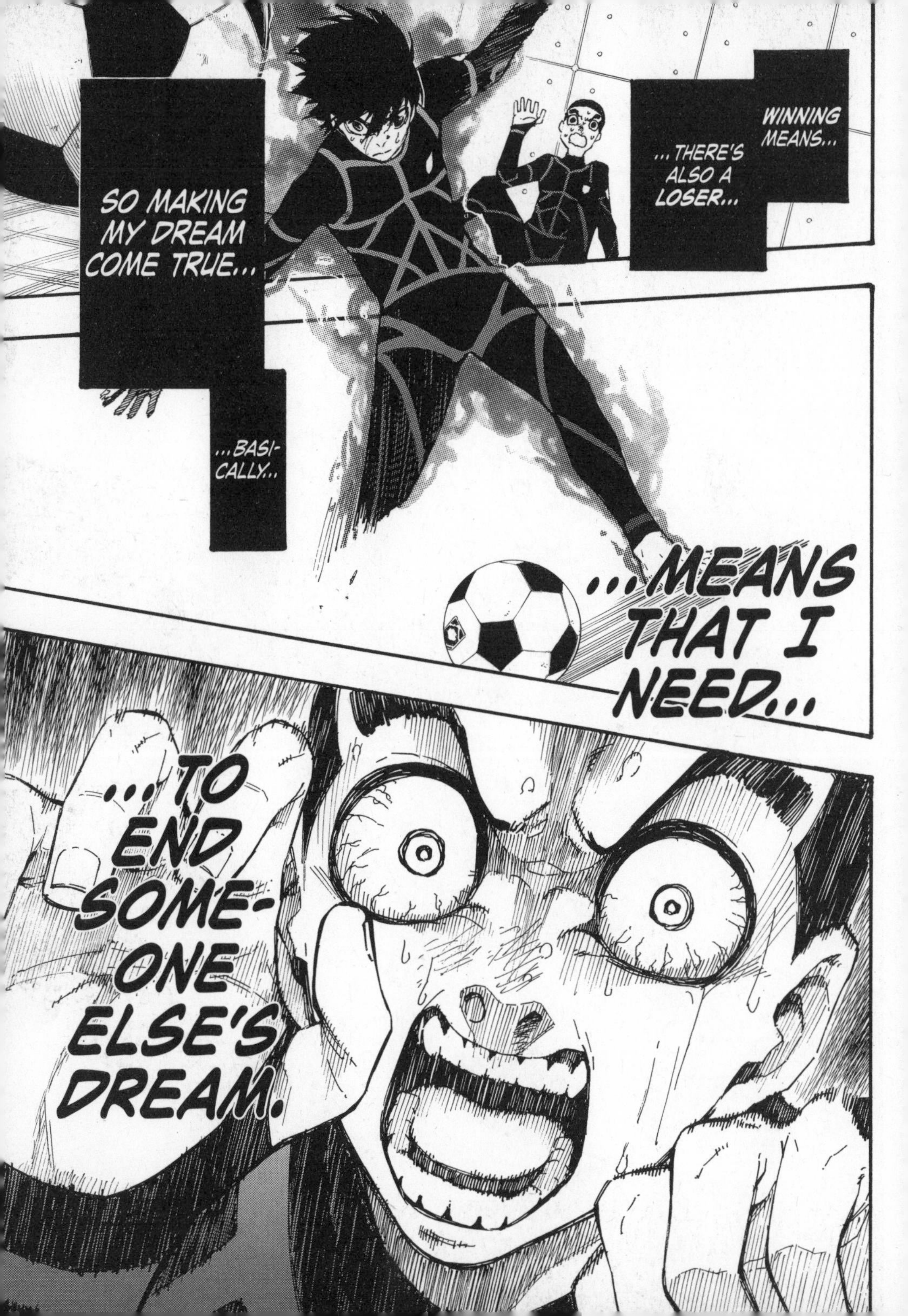
WINNING MEANS...
...THERE'S ALSO A LOSER...
SO MAKING MY DREAM COME TRUE...
...BASI- CALLY...
...MEANS THAT I NEED...
...TO END SOME- ONE ELSE'S DREAM.

FREEZE

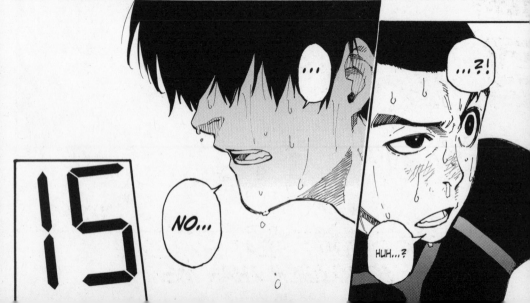

15

NO...

...

...?!

HUH...?

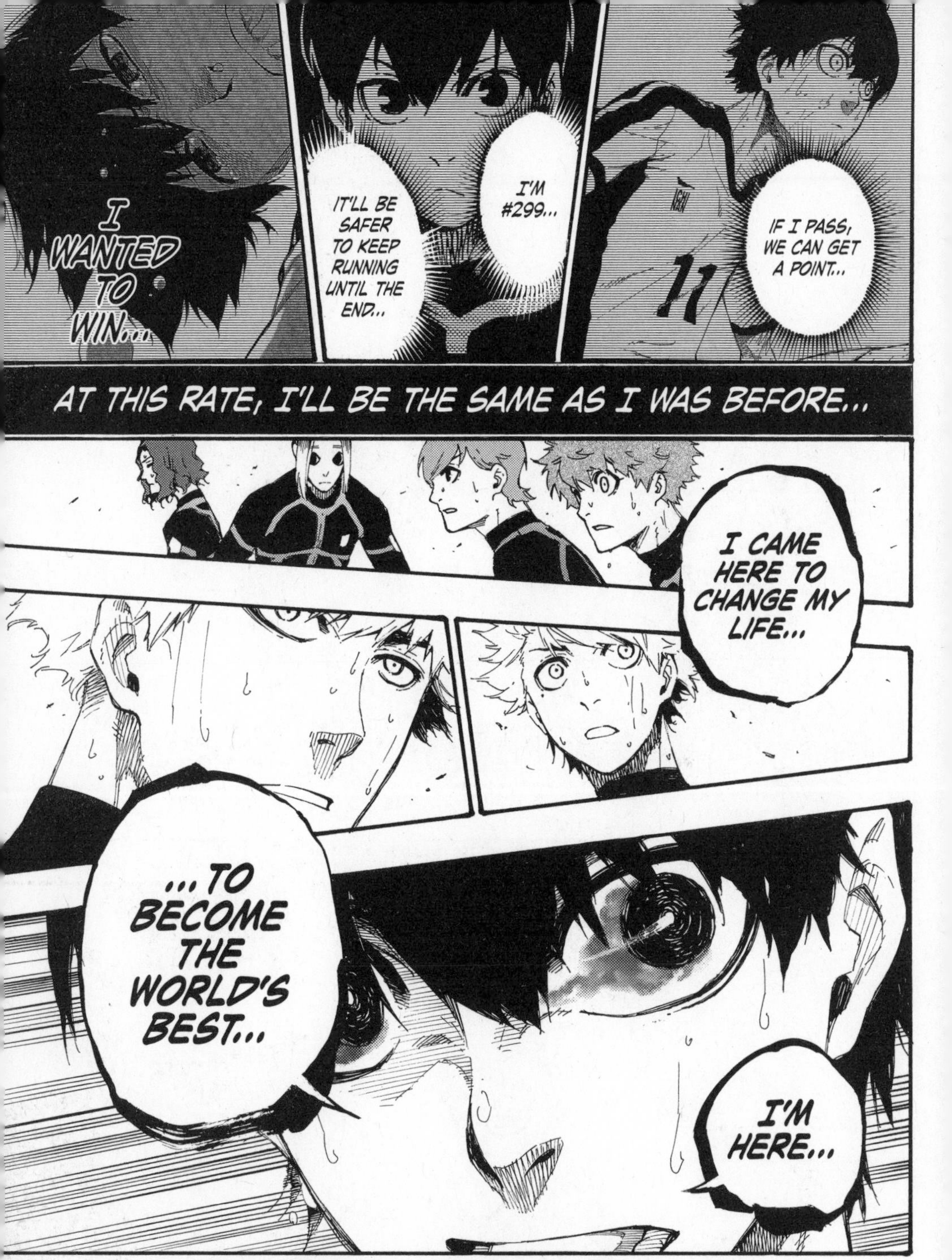
IF I PASS, WE CAN GET A POINT...
I'M #299...
IT'LL BE SAFER TO KEEP RUNNING UNTIL THE END...
I WANTED TO WIN...
AT THIS RATE, I'LL BE THE SAME AS I WAS BEFORE...
I CAME HERE TO CHANGE MY LIFE...
...TO BECOME THE WORLD'S BEST...
I'M HERE...

IF I DON'T BEAT SOMEONE STRONGER THAN ME...

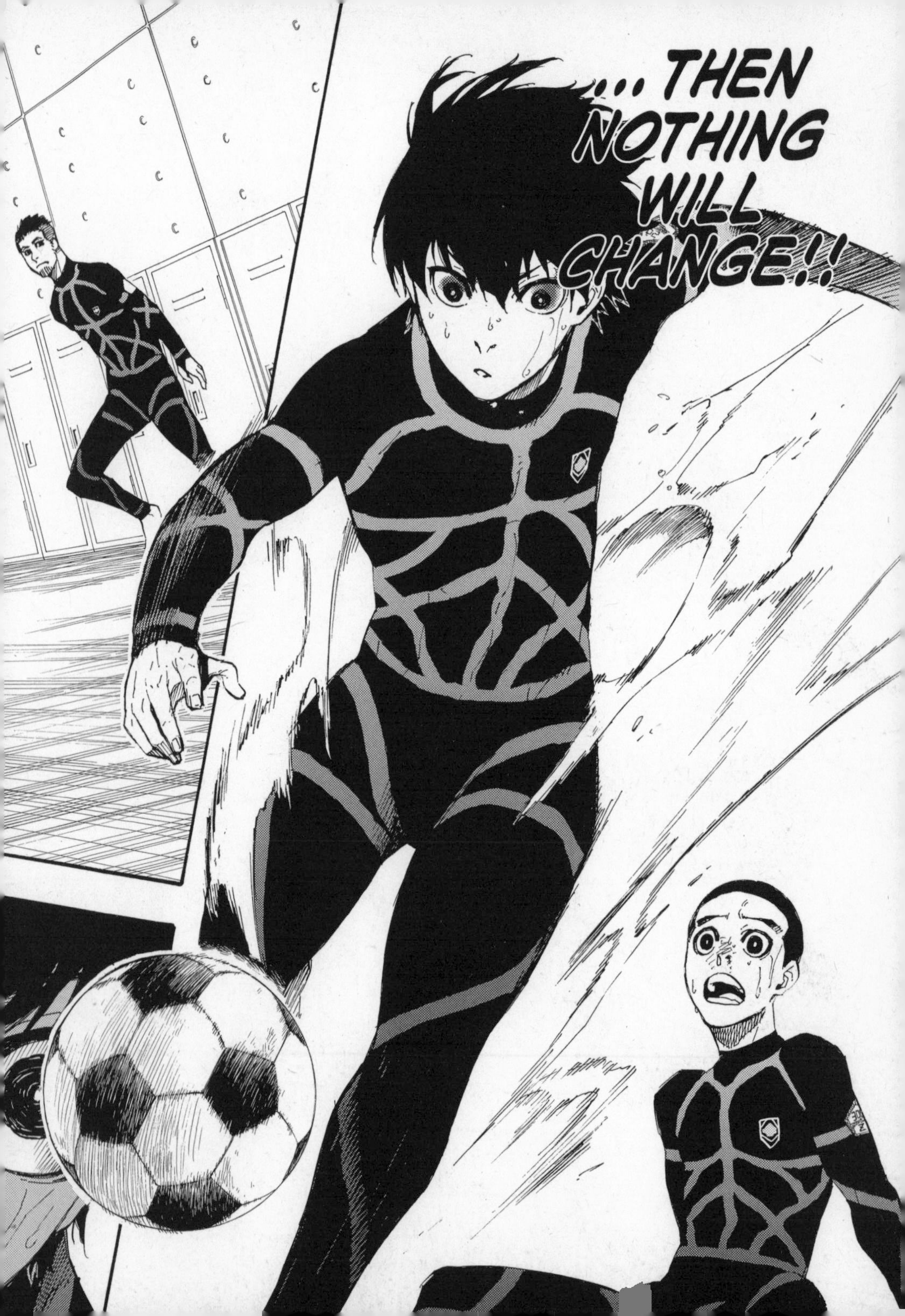
...THEN NOTHING WILL CHANGE!!

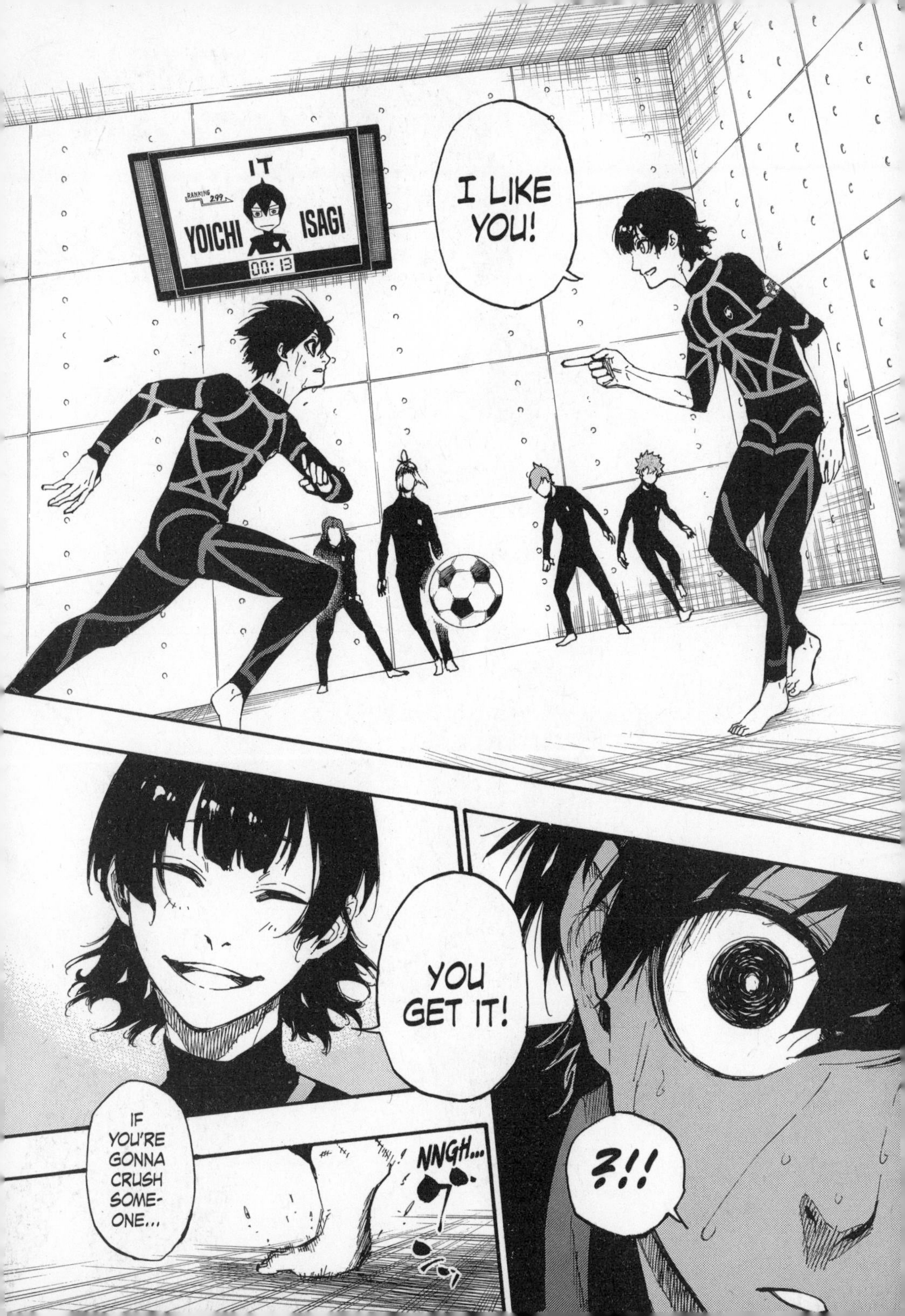
IT
RANKING 299
YOICHI
ISAGI
00:13
I LIKE YOU!
?!!
YOU GET IT!
NNGH...
IF YOU'RE GONNA CRUSH SOME-ONE...

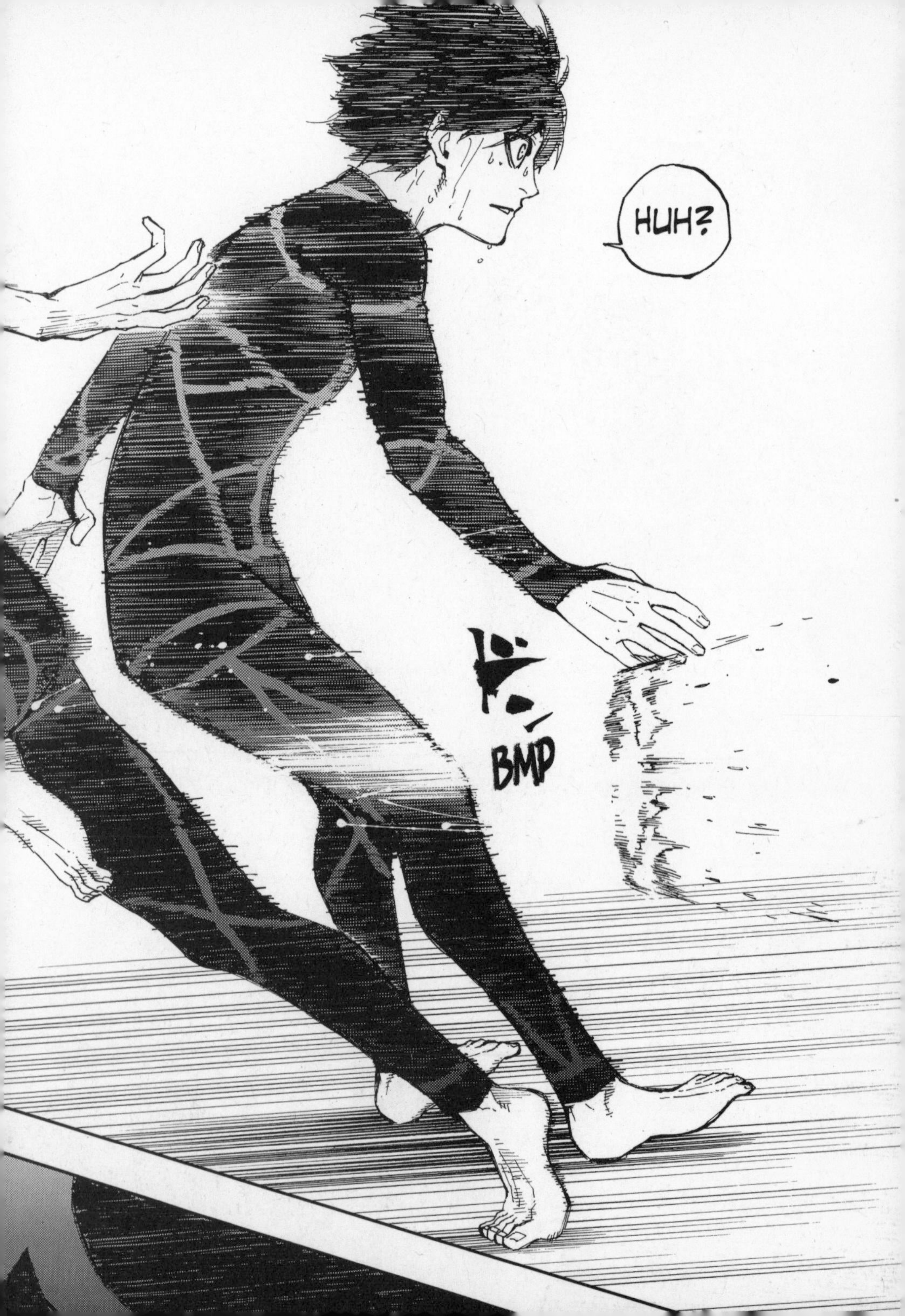
HUH?
ド
BMP

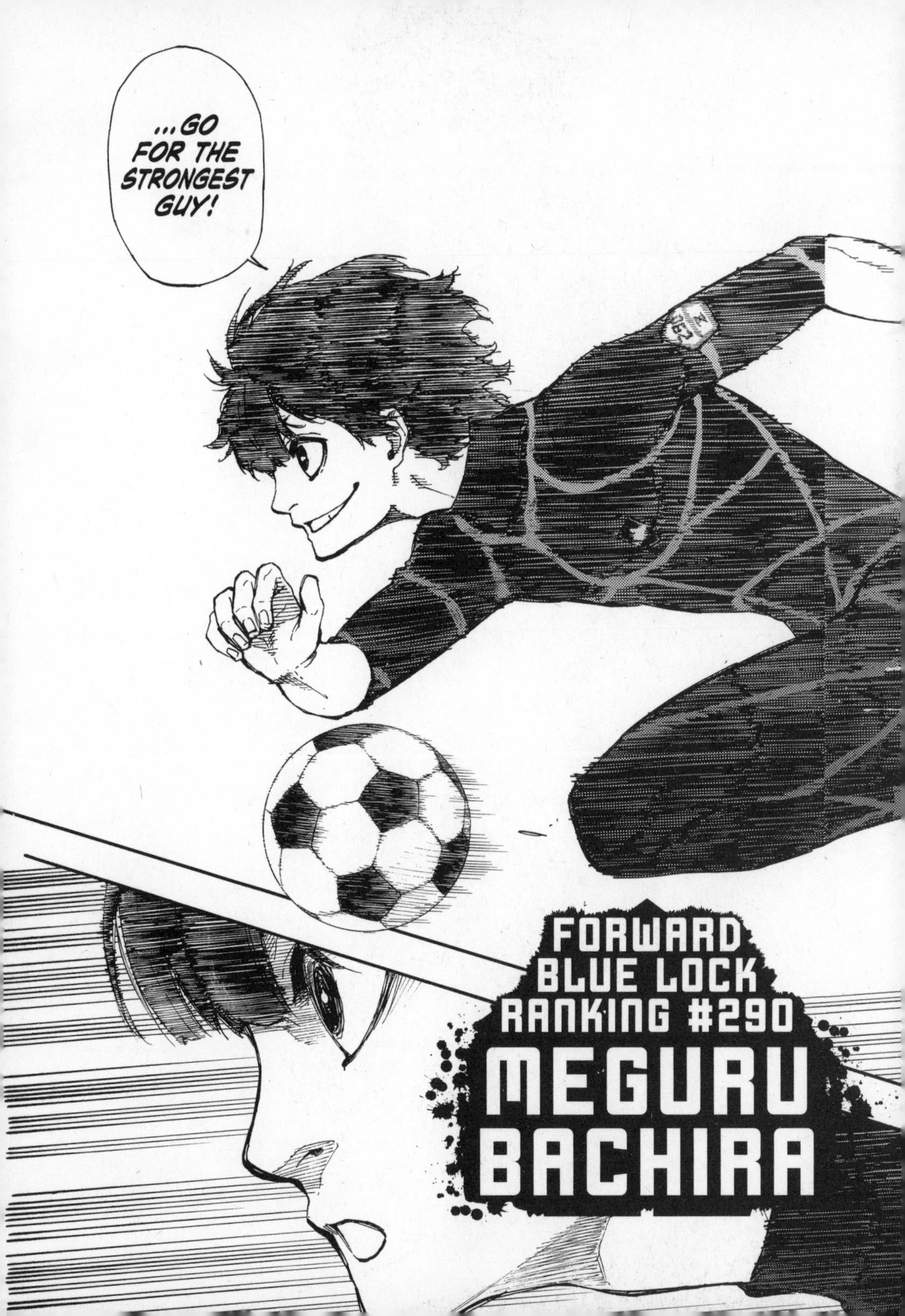
...GO FOR THE STRONGEST GUY!
FORWARD
BLUE LOCK
RANKING #290
MEGURU
BACHIRA

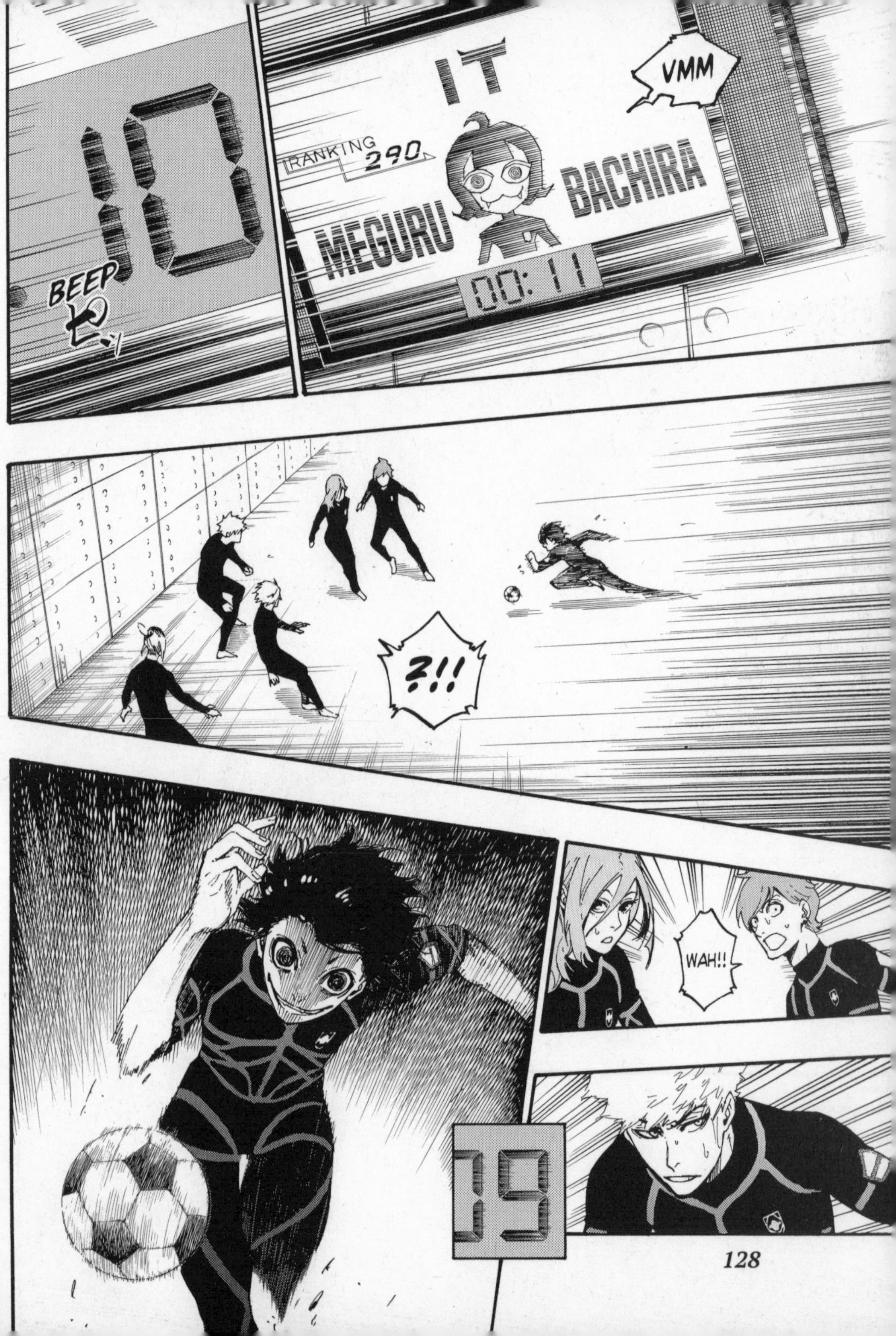
VMM
IT
RANKING 290
MEGURU BACHIRA
00:11
10
BEEP
ピッ
?!!
WAH!!
19

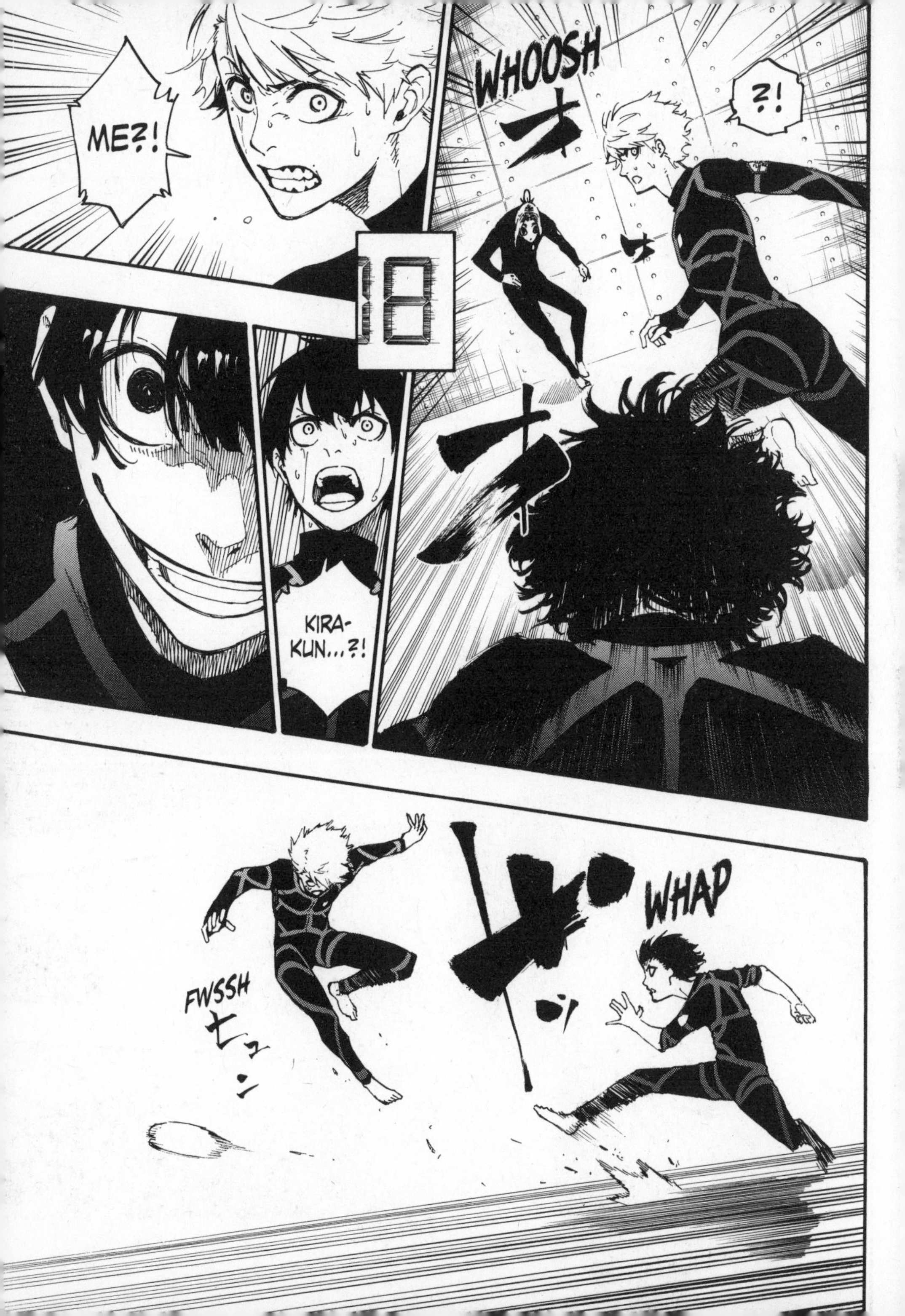

WHOOSH
?!
ME?!
18
KIRA-KUN...?!
WHAP
FWSSH

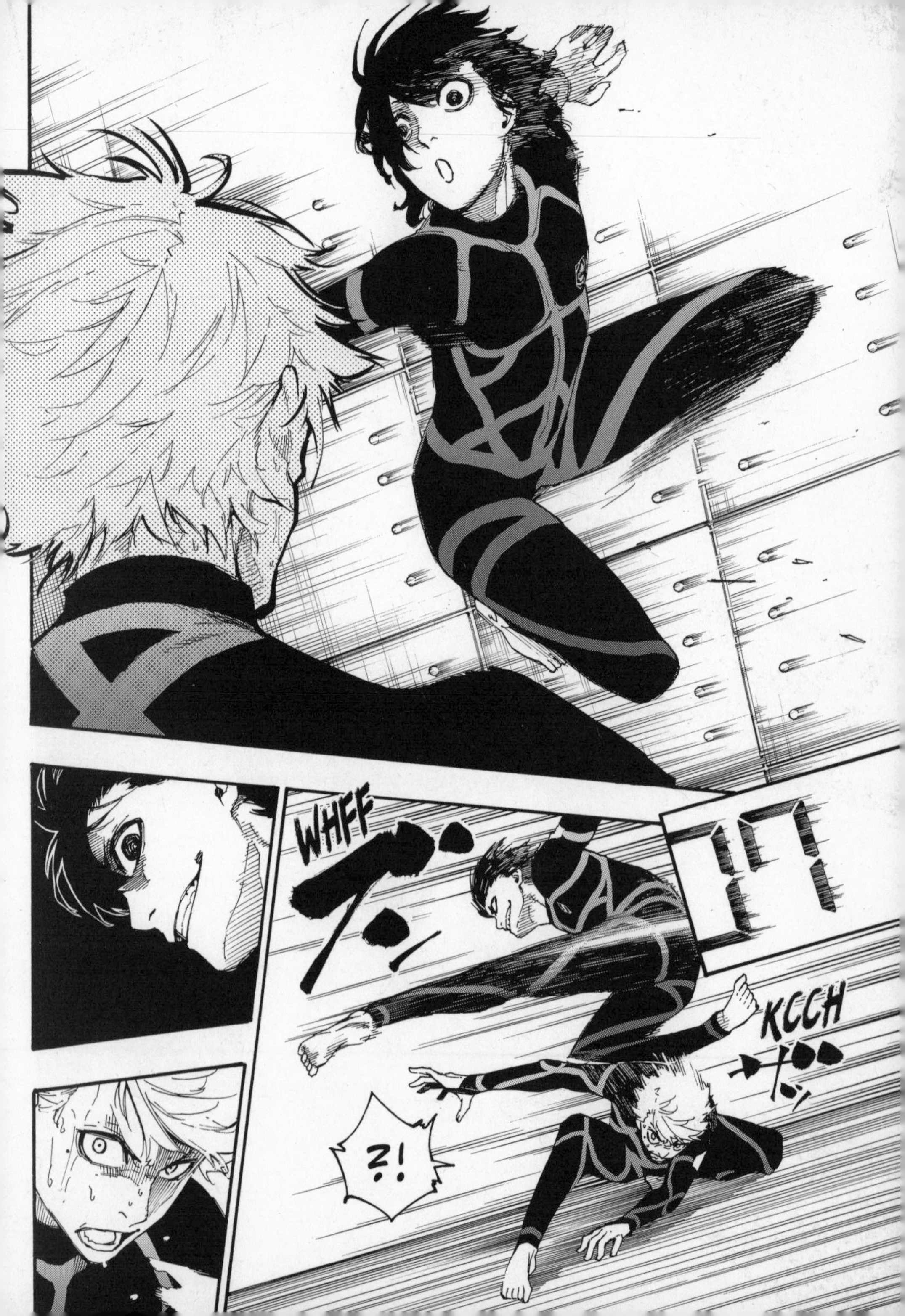
WHFF
KCCH
?!

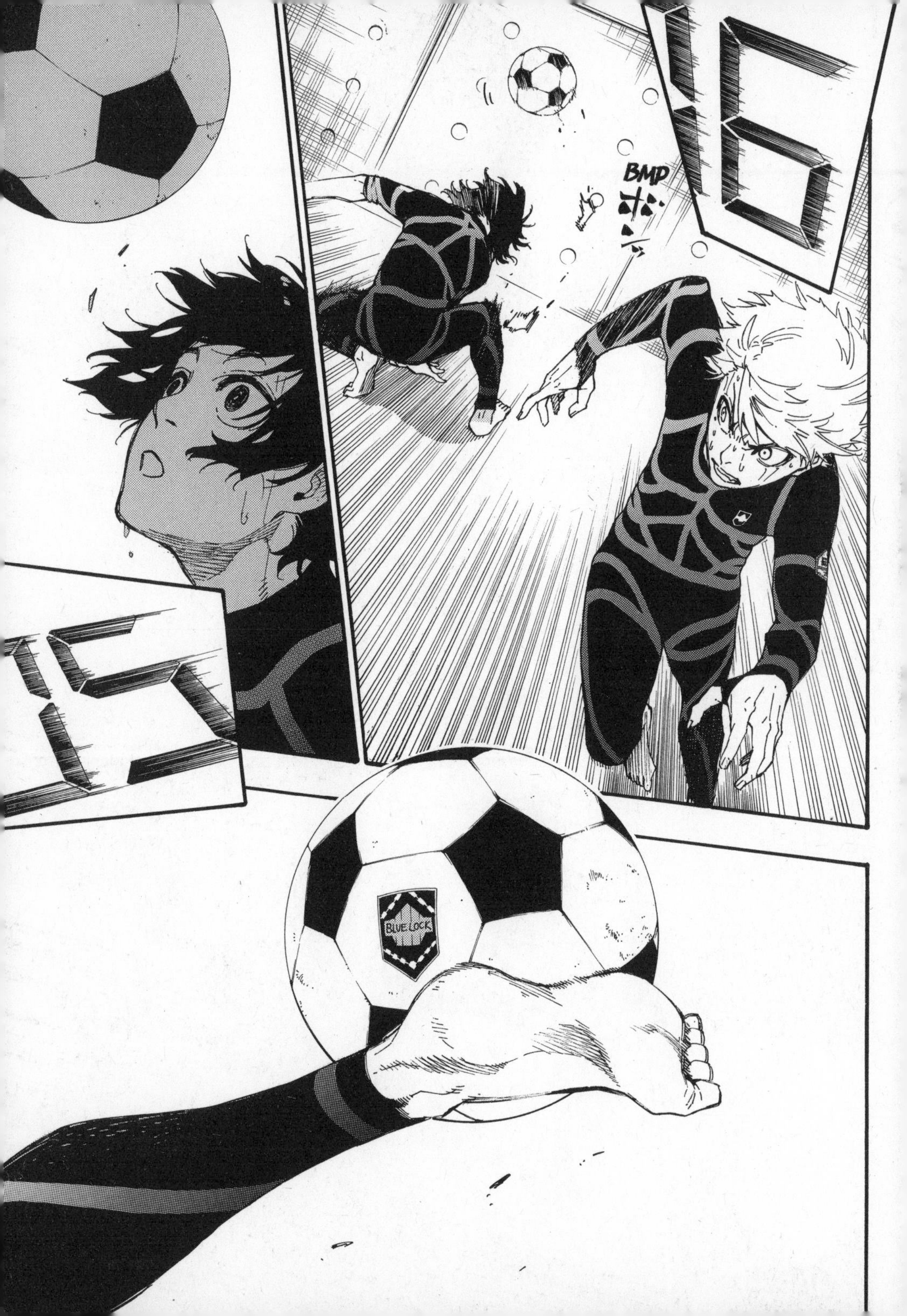
16
BMP
ボッ
15

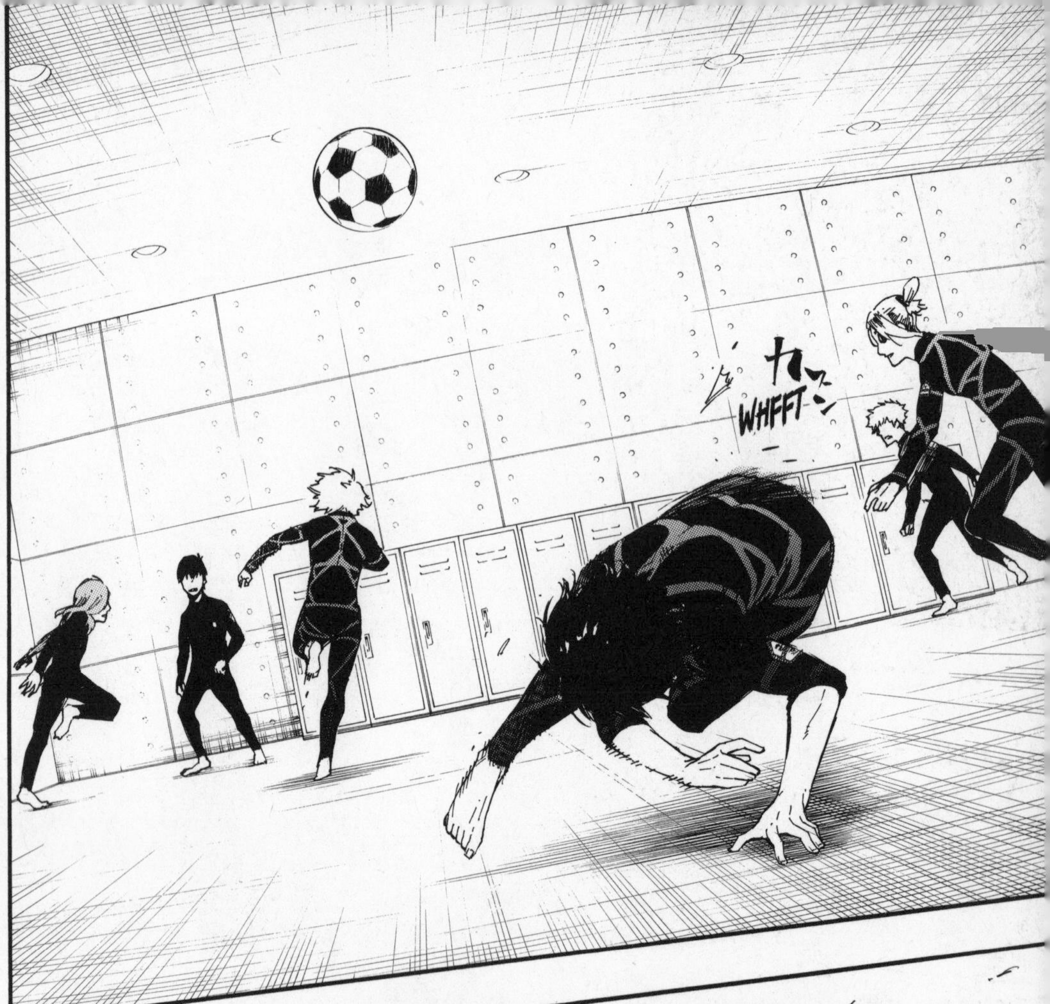
WHFFT
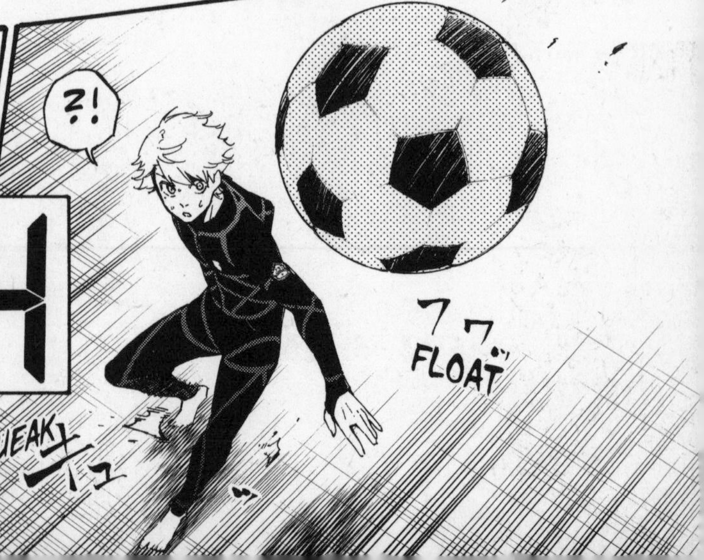
?!
FLOAT
SQUEAK
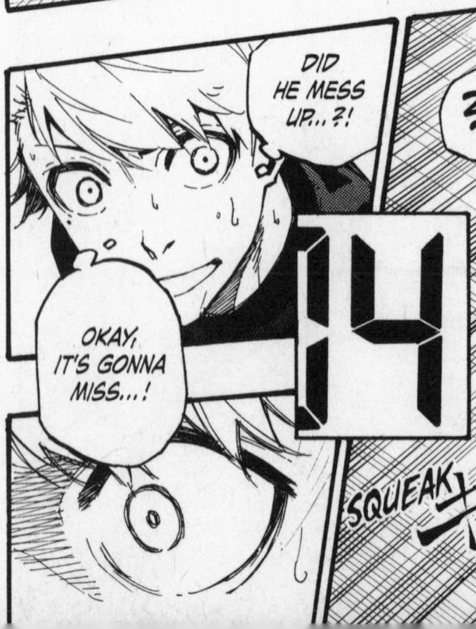
DID HE MESS UP...?!
14
OKAY, IT'S GONNA MISS...!

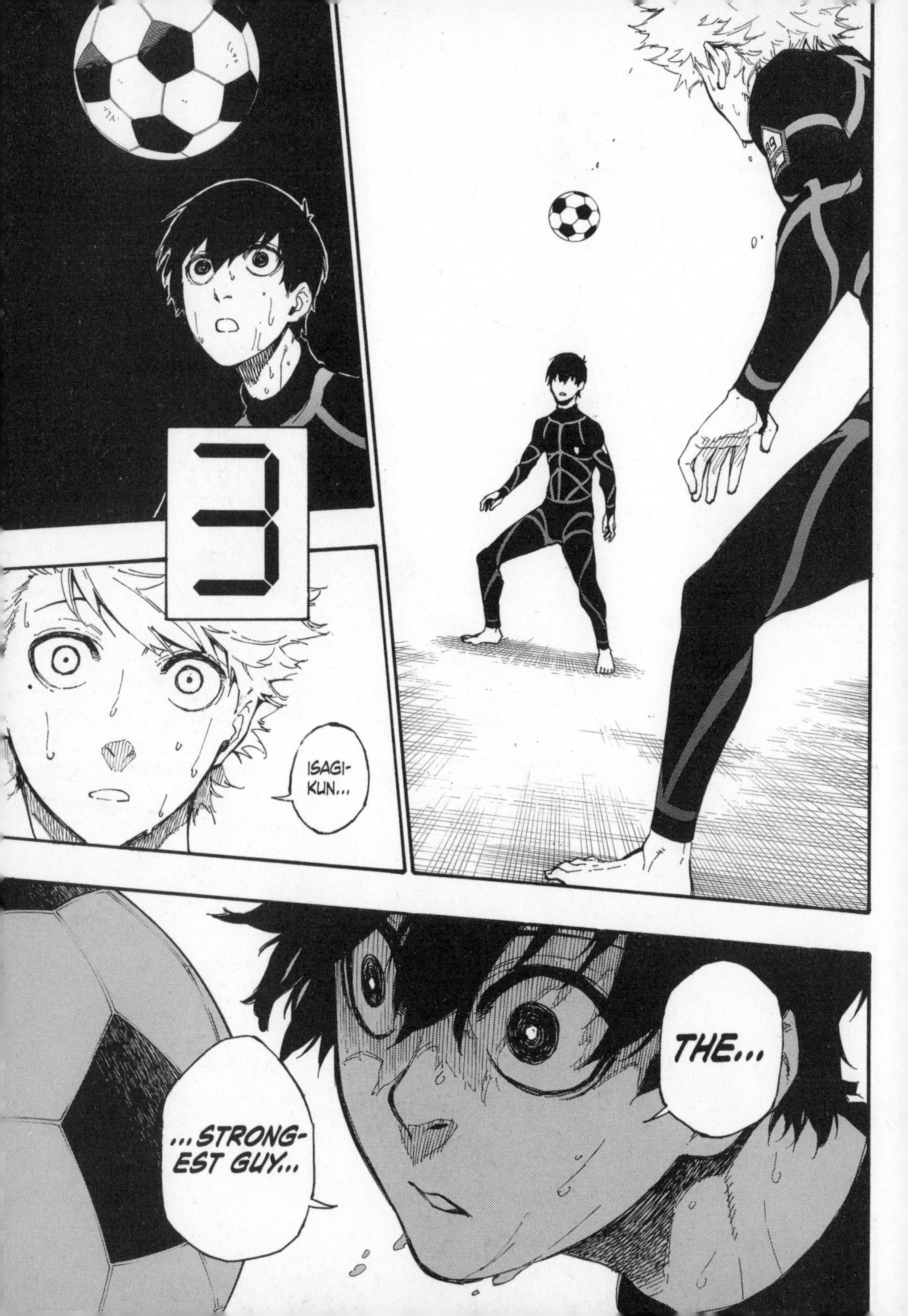
3
ISAGI-KUN...
THE...
...STRONG-EST GUY...

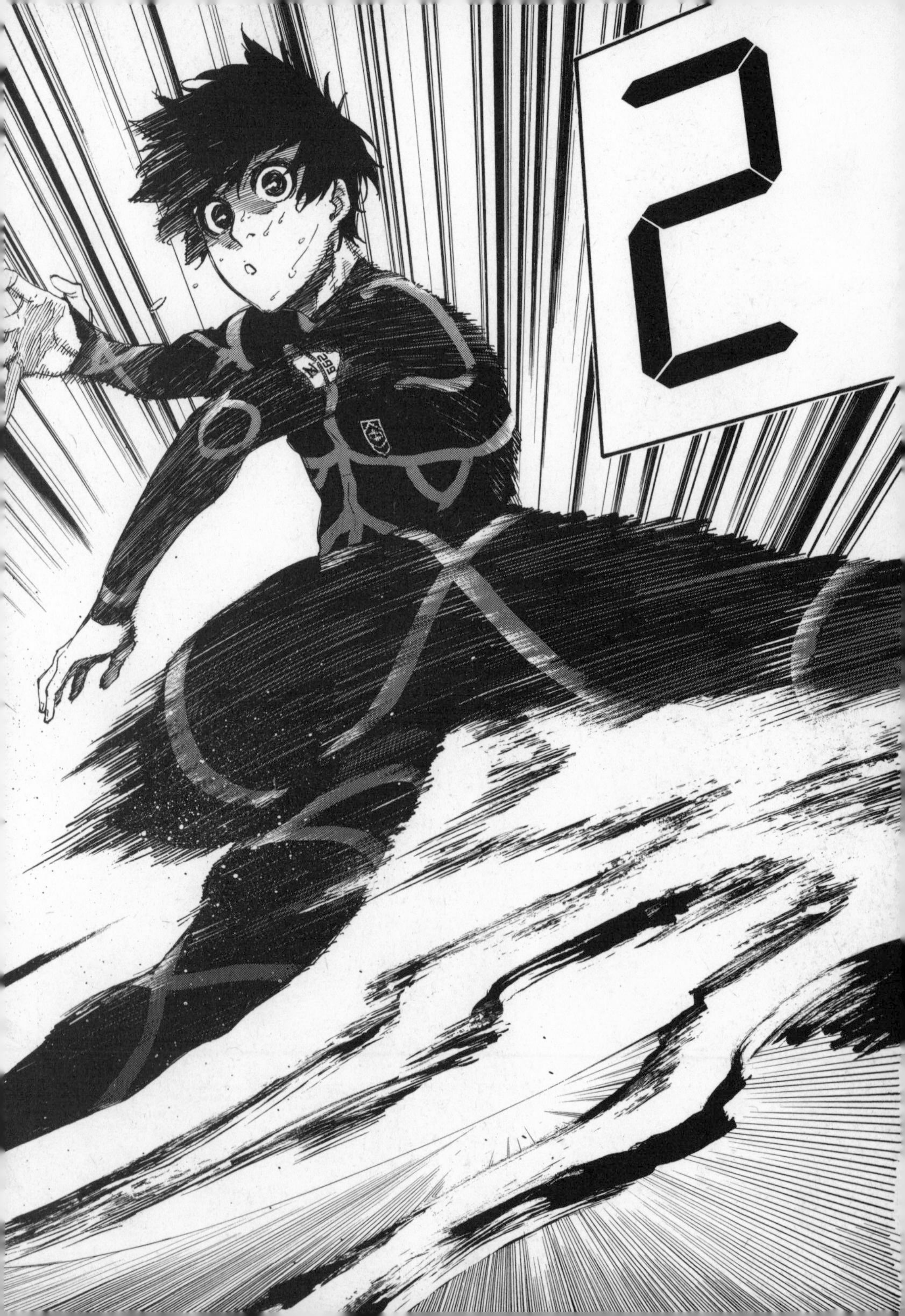
2

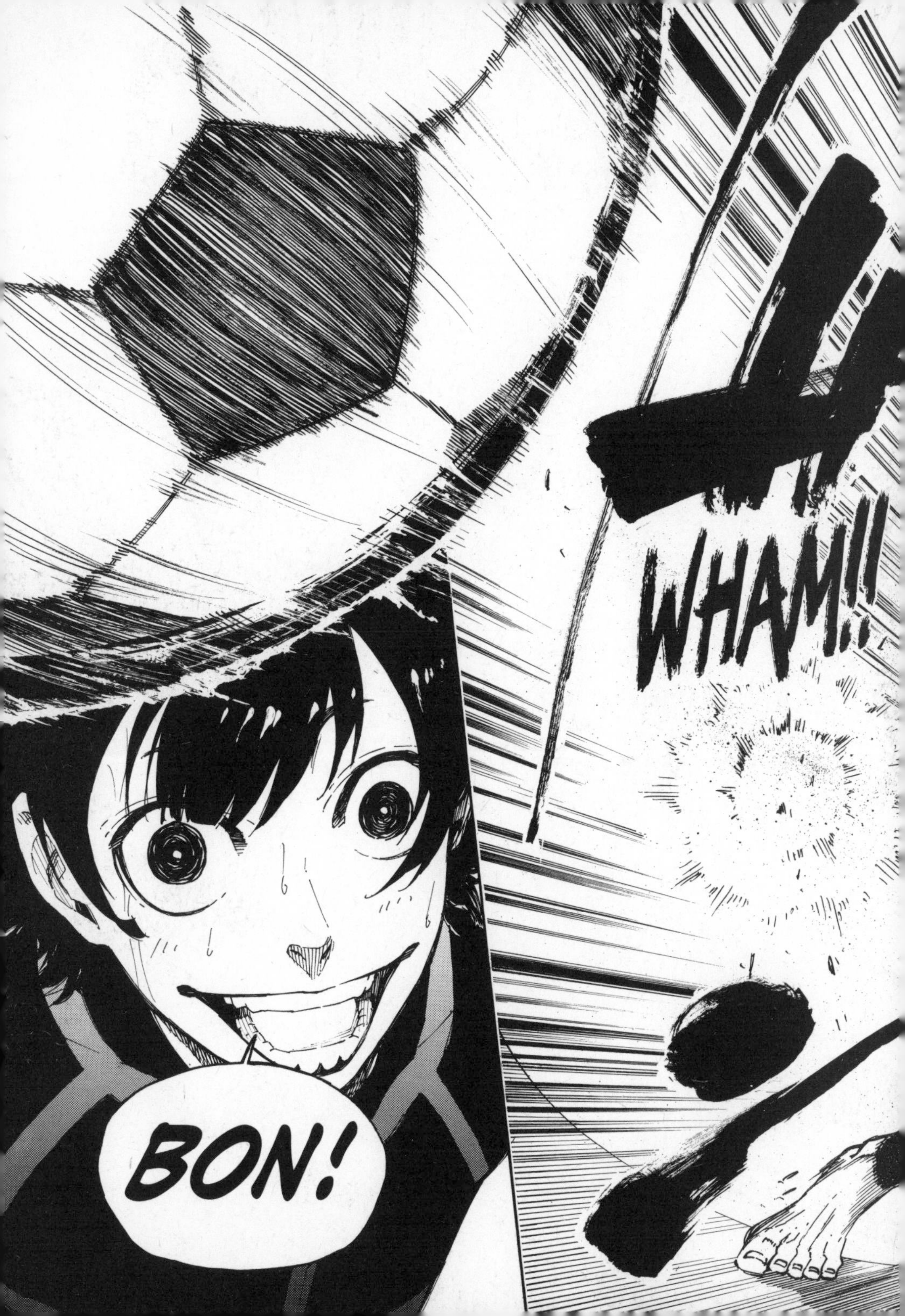
WHAM!!
BON!

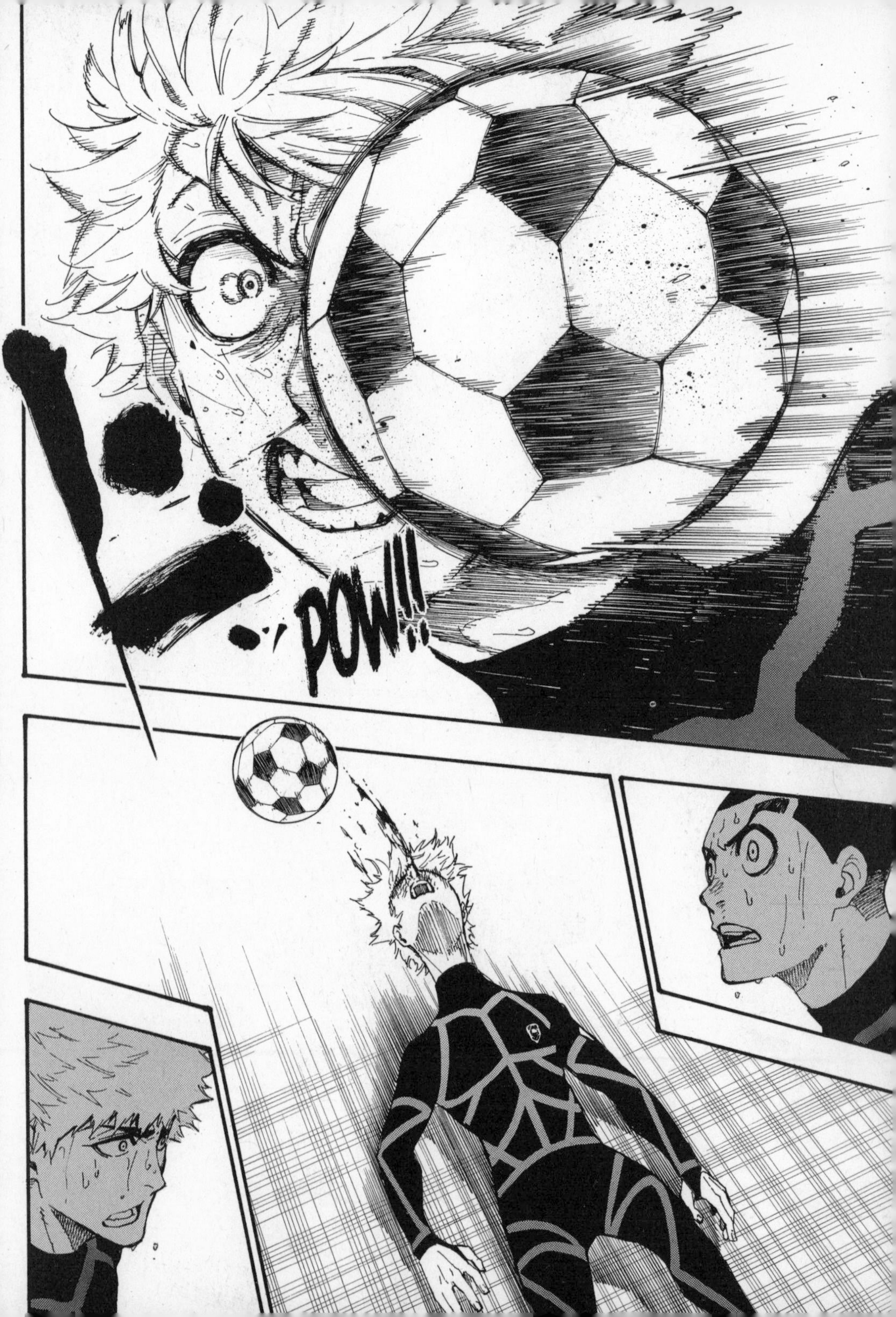
POW!!

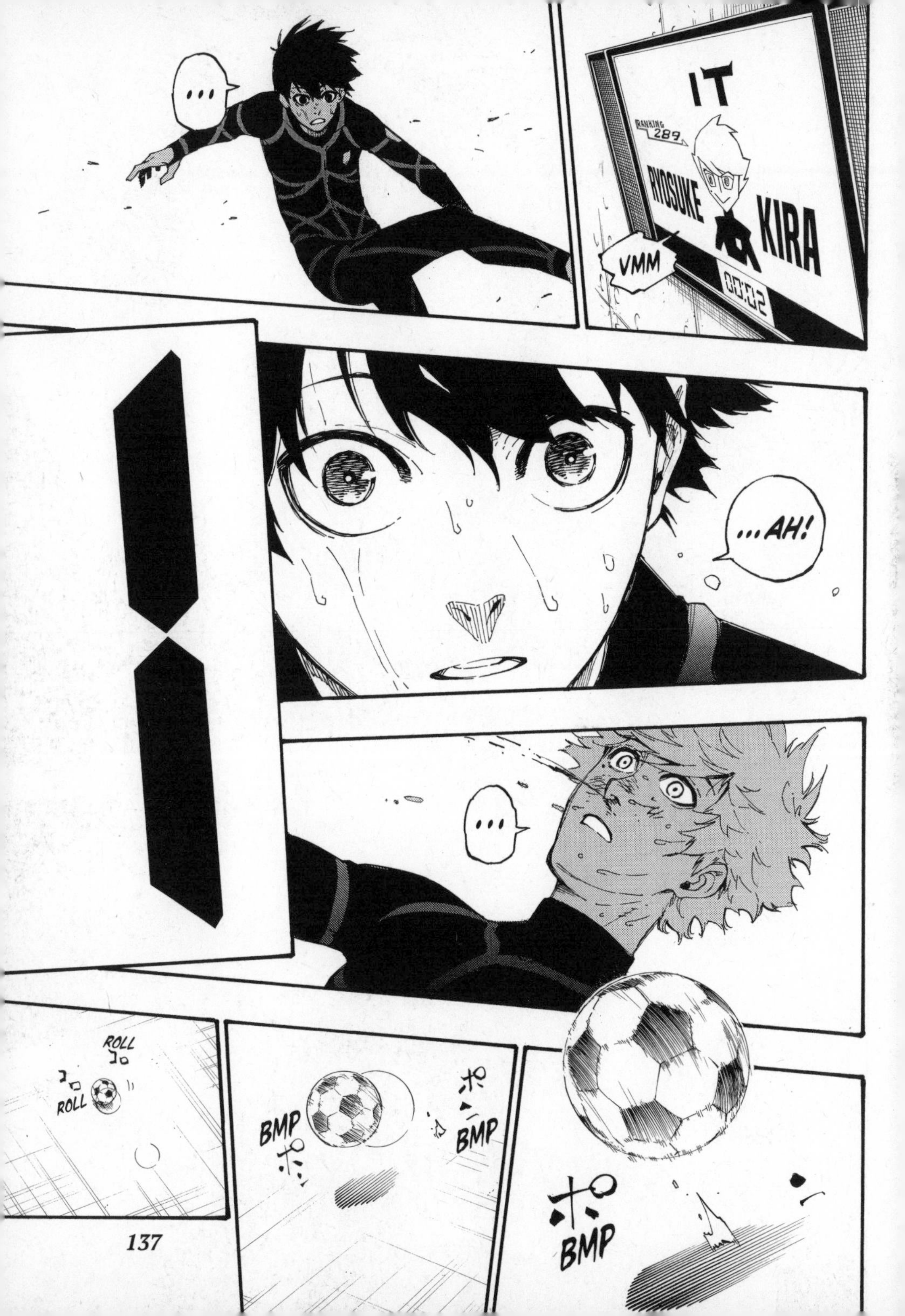
IT
RANKING 289
RYOSUKE KIRA
00:02
VMM
...
...AH!
...
BMP
BMP
BMP
ROLL
ROLL

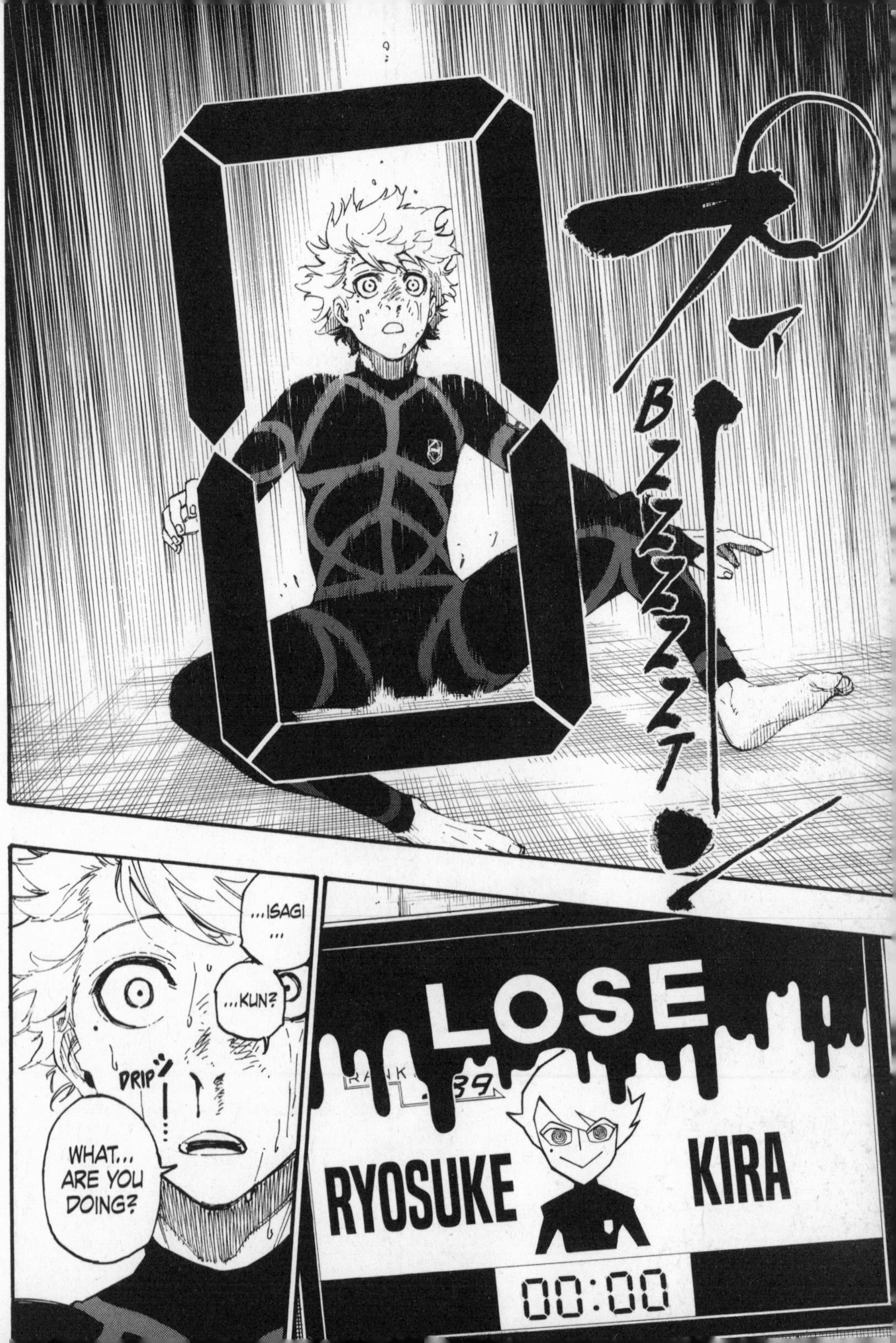
BZZZZZT
LOSE
RYOSUKE
KIRA
00:00
...ISAGI ...
...KUN?
DRIP
WHAT... ARE YOU DOING?

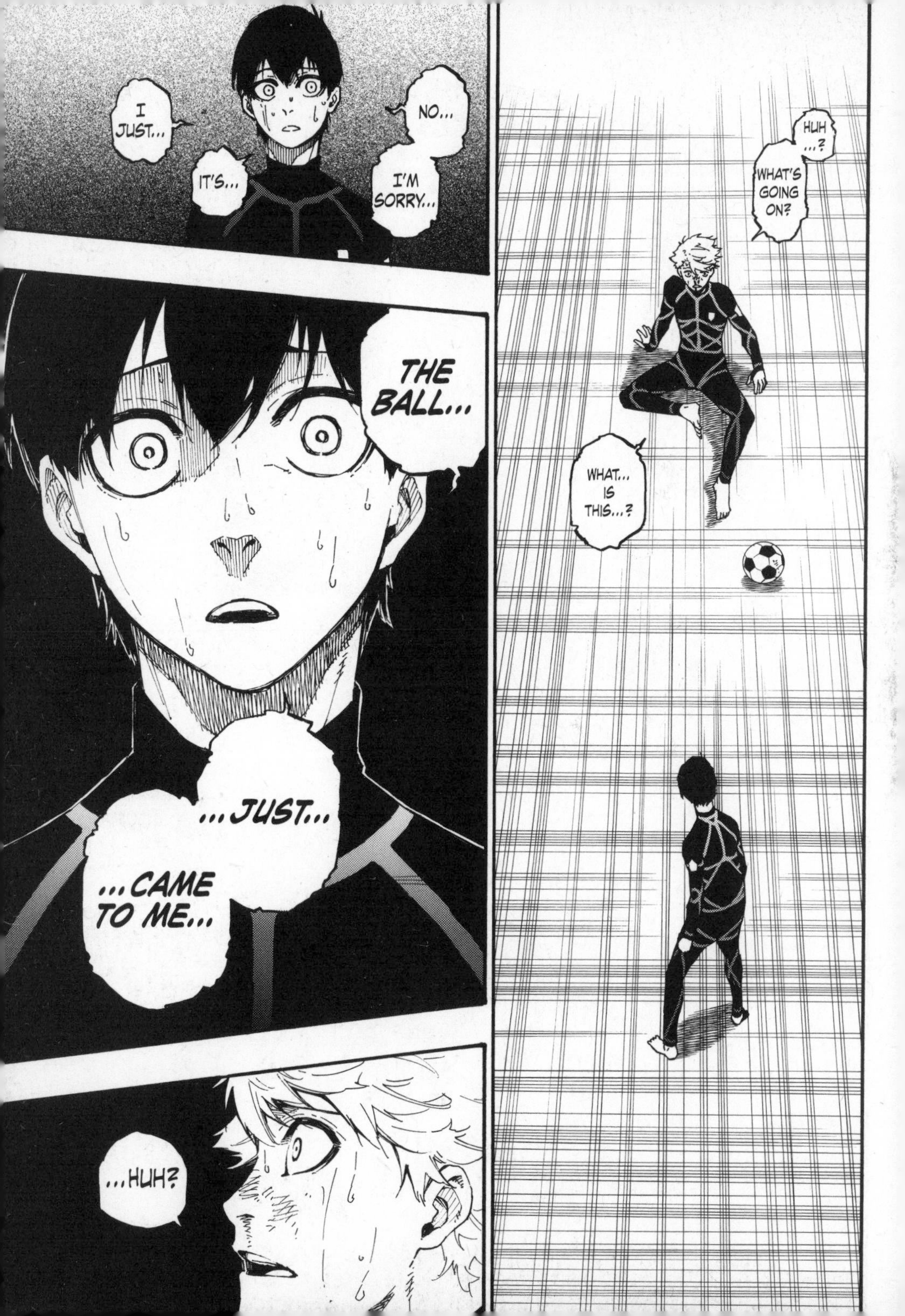
HUH ...?
WHAT'S GOING ON?
WHAT... IS THIS...?
NO...
I'M SORRY...
I JUST...
IT'S...
THE BALL...
...JUST...
...CAME TO ME...
...HUH?

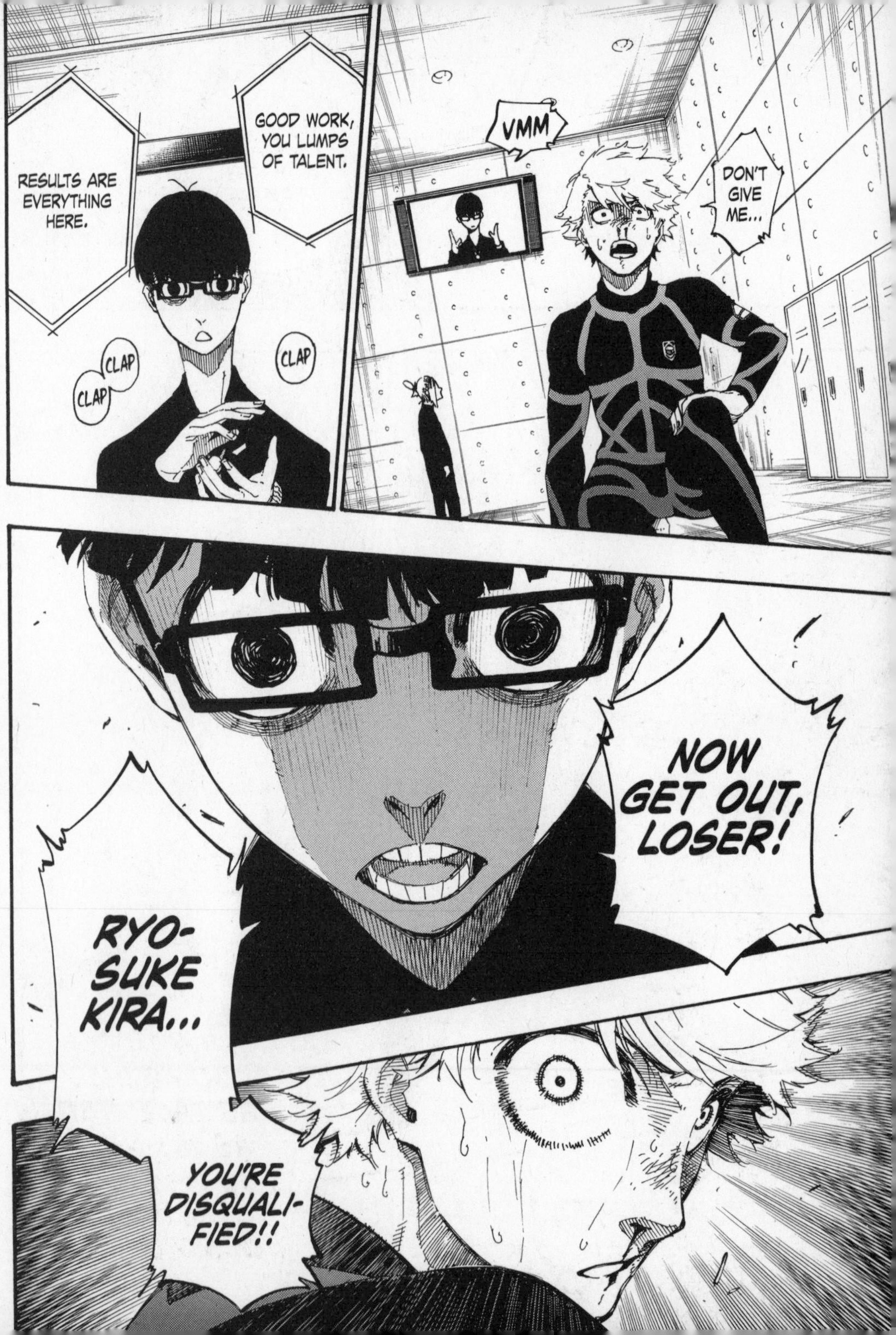
VMM
DON'T GIVE ME...
GOOD WORK, YOU LUMPS OF TALENT.
RESULTS ARE EVERYTHING HERE.
CLAP
CLAP
CLAP
NOW GET OUT, LOSER!
RYO-SUKE KIRA...
YOU'RE DISQUALI-FIED!!

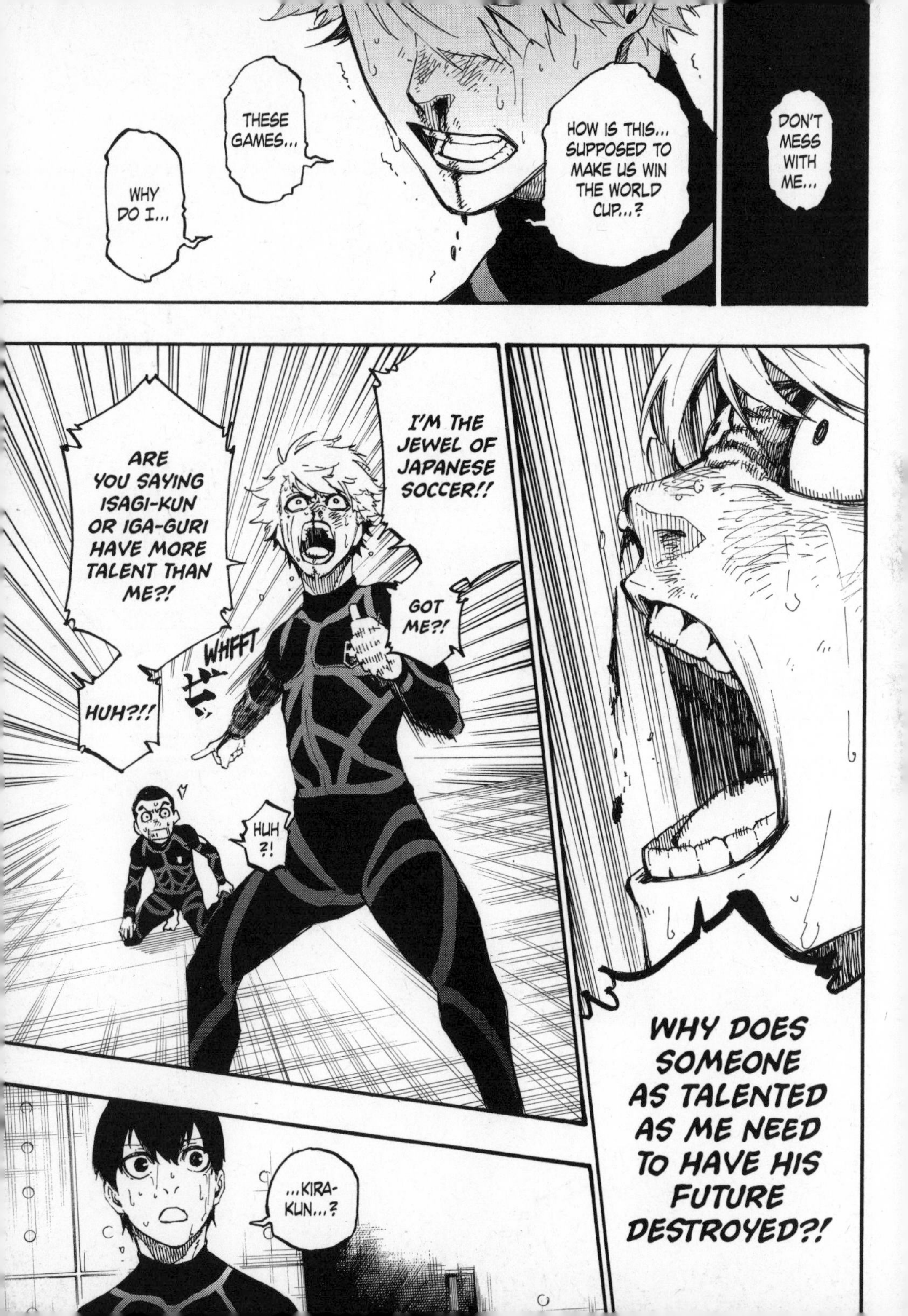
DON'T MESS WITH ME...
HOW IS THIS... SUPPOSED TO MAKE US WIN THE WORLD CUP...?
THESE GAMES...
WHY DO I...
WHY DOES SOMEONE AS TALENTED AS ME NEED TO HAVE HIS FUTURE DESTROYED?!
I'M THE JEWEL OF JAPANESE SOCCER!!
ARE YOU SAYING ISAGI-KUN OR IGA-GURI HAVE MORE TALENT THAN ME?!
GOT ME?!
WHFFT
HUH?!!
HUH ?!
...KIRA-KUN...?

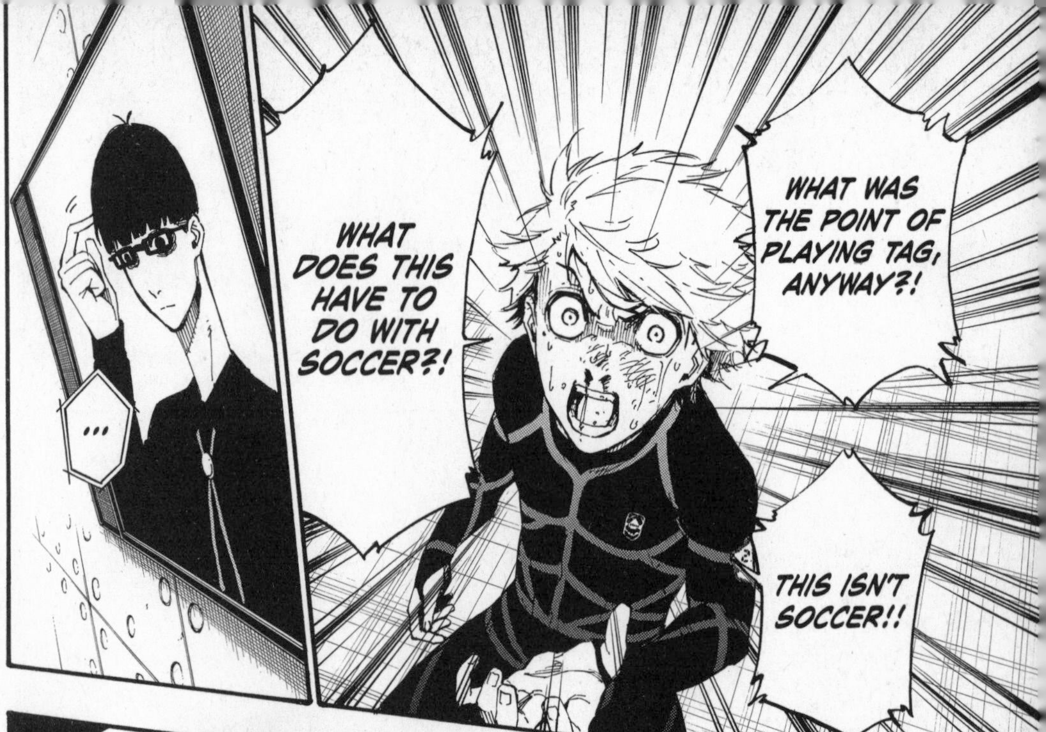
WHAT WAS THE POINT OF PLAYING TAG, ANYWAY?!
WHAT DOES THIS HAVE TO DO WITH SOCCER?!
THIS ISN'T SOCCER!!
...

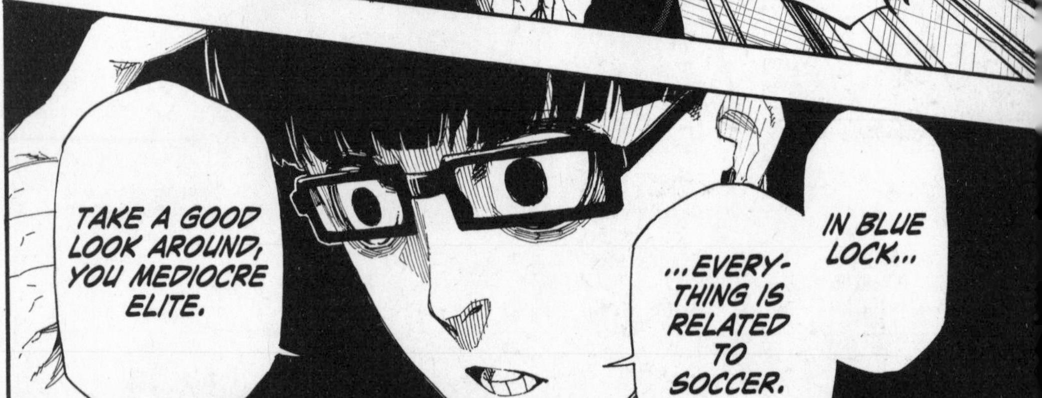
IN BLUE LOCK...
...EVERY-THING IS RELATED TO SOCCER.
TAKE A GOOD LOOK AROUND, YOU MEDIOCRE ELITE.

*ABOUT 54 X 132 FEET.

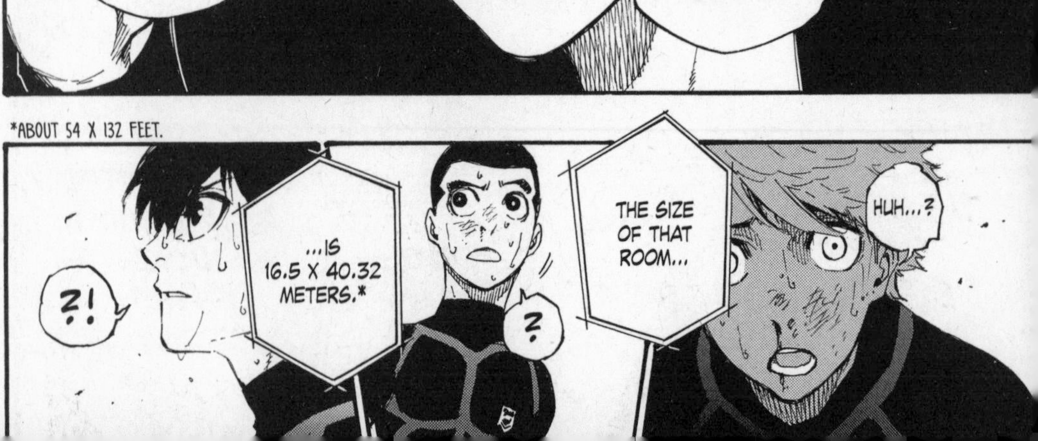
HUH...?
THE SIZE OF THAT ROOM...
...IS 16.5 X 40.32 METERS.*
?
?!

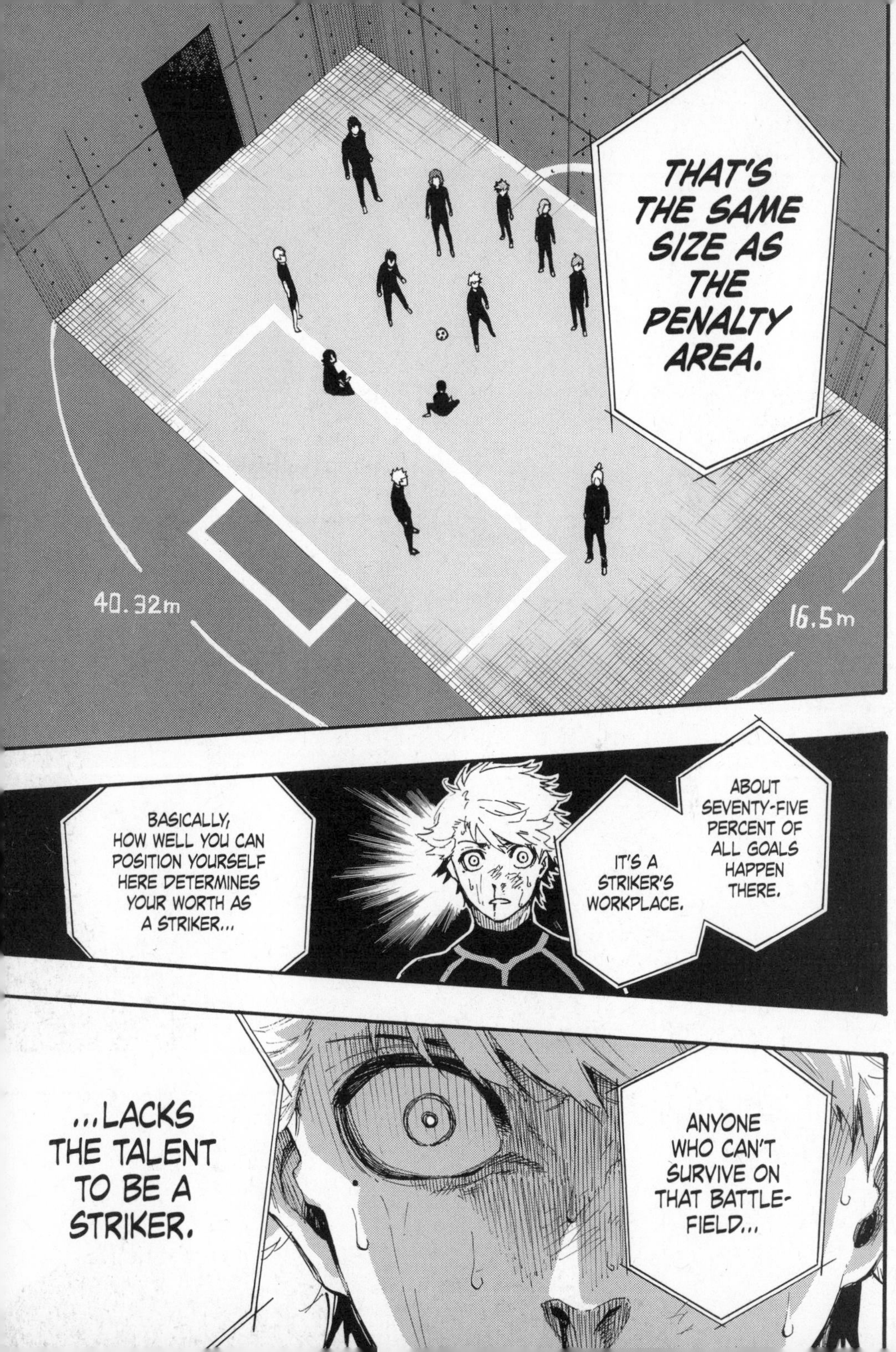
THAT'S THE SAME SIZE AS THE PENALTY AREA.
16.5m
40.32m
ABOUT SEVENTY-FIVE PERCENT OF ALL GOALS HAPPEN THERE.
IT'S A STRIKER'S WORKPLACE.
BASICALLY, HOW WELL YOU CAN POSITION YOURSELF HERE DETERMINES YOUR WORTH AS A STRIKER...
ANYONE WHO CAN'T SURVIVE ON THAT BATTLE-FIELD...
...LACKS THE TALENT TO BE A STRIKER.

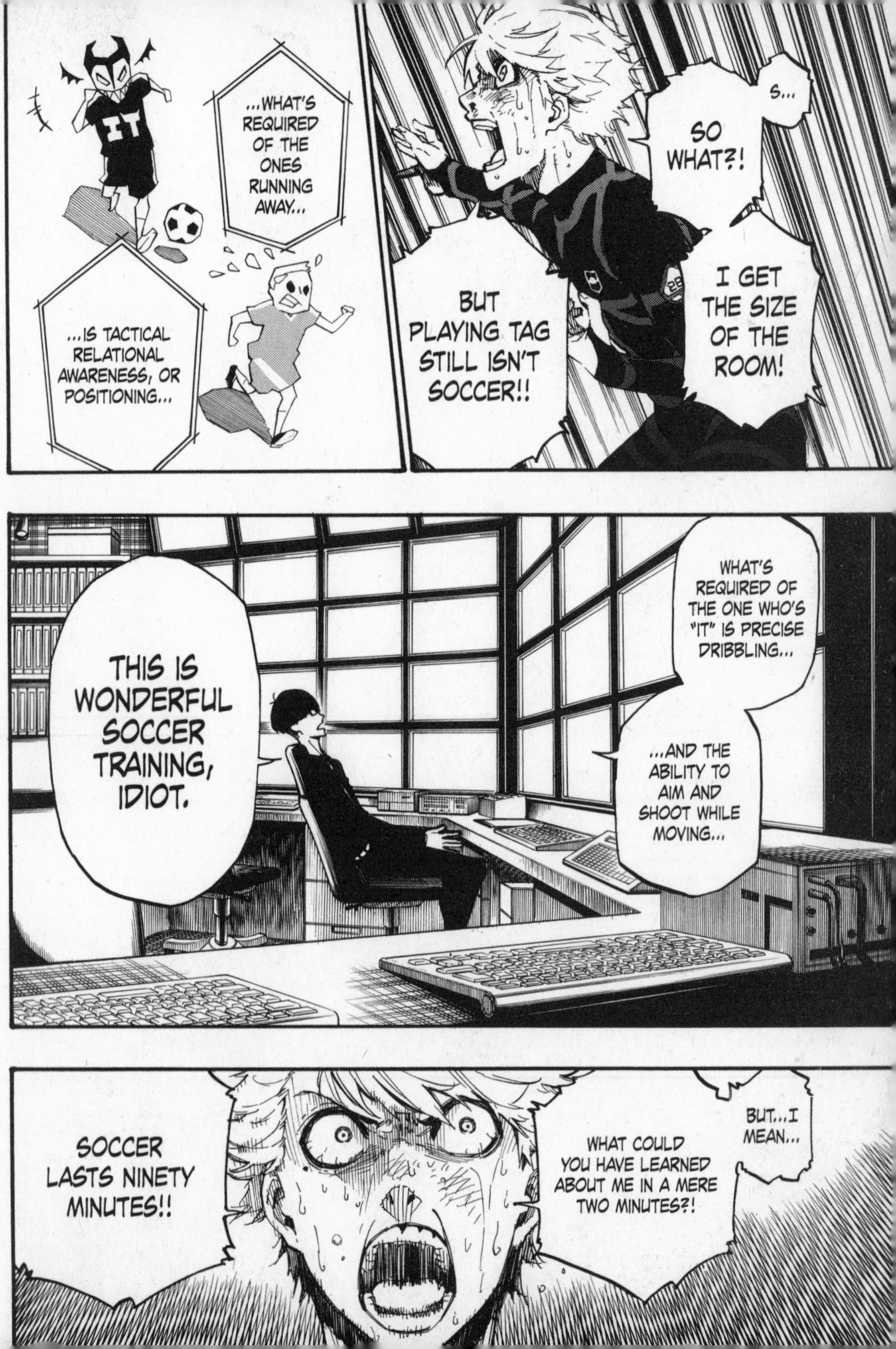
S...
SO WHAT?!
I GET THE SIZE OF THE ROOM!
BUT PLAYING TAG STILL ISN'T SOCCER!!
...WHAT'S REQUIRED OF THE ONES RUNNING AWAY...
IT
...IS TACTICAL RELATIONAL AWARENESS, OR POSITIONING...
WHAT'S REQUIRED OF THE ONE WHO'S "IT" IS PRECISE DRIBBLING...
...AND THE ABILITY TO AIM AND SHOOT WHILE MOVING...
THIS IS WONDERFUL SOCCER TRAINING, IDIOT.
BUT...I MEAN...
WHAT COULD YOU HAVE LEARNED ABOUT ME IN A MERE TWO MINUTES?!
SOCCER LASTS NINETY MINUTES!!

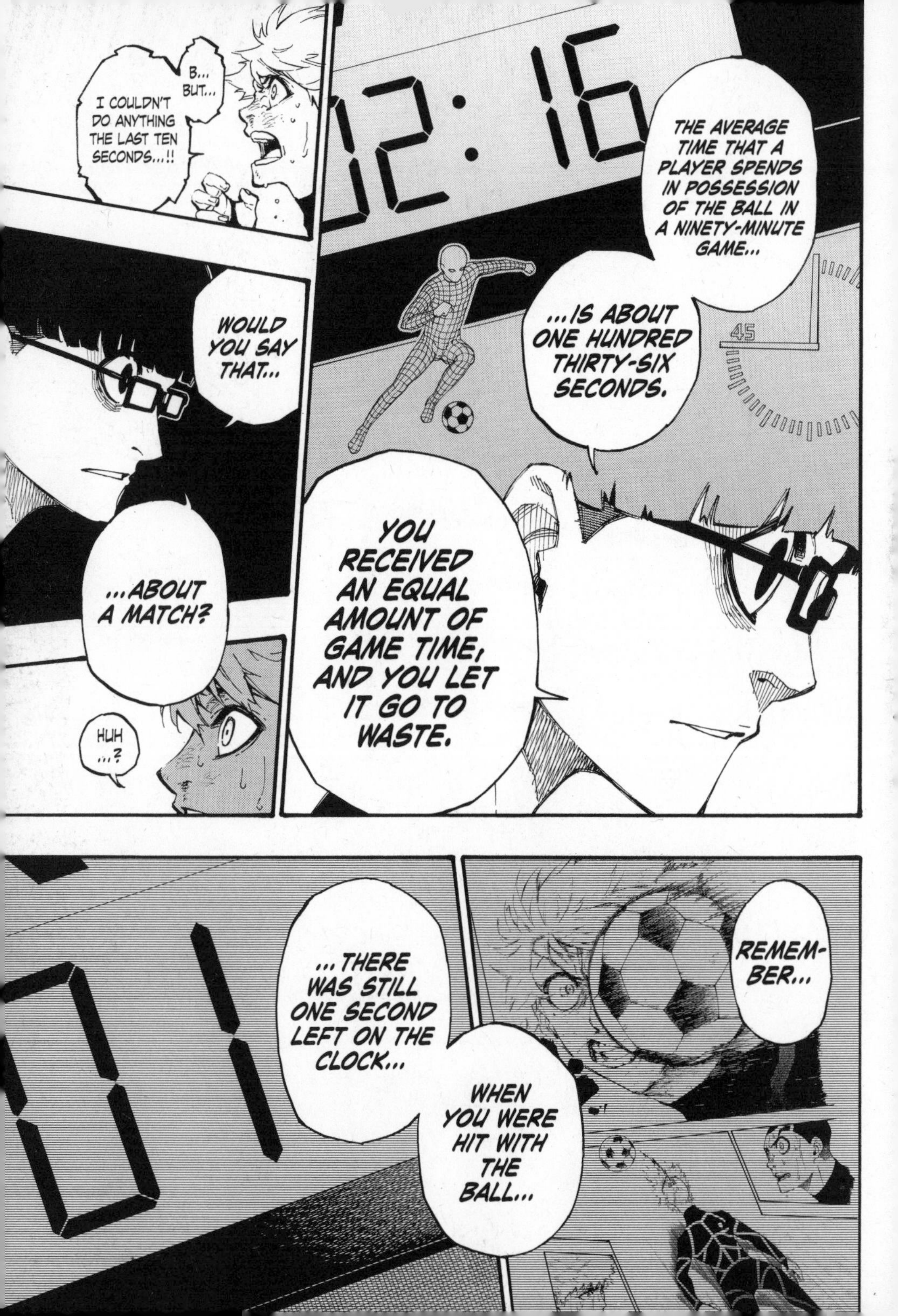
B... BUT...
I COULDN'T DO ANYTHING THE LAST TEN SECONDS...!!
WOULD YOU SAY THAT...
...ABOUT A MATCH?
HUH ...?
THE AVERAGE TIME THAT A PLAYER SPENDS IN POSSESSION OF THE BALL IN A NINETY-MINUTE GAME...
...IS ABOUT ONE HUNDRED THIRTY-SIX SECONDS.
YOU RECEIVED AN EQUAL AMOUNT OF GAME TIME, AND YOU LET IT GO TO WASTE.
REMEMBER...
...THERE WAS STILL ONE SECOND LEFT ON THE CLOCK...
WHEN YOU WERE HIT WITH THE BALL...

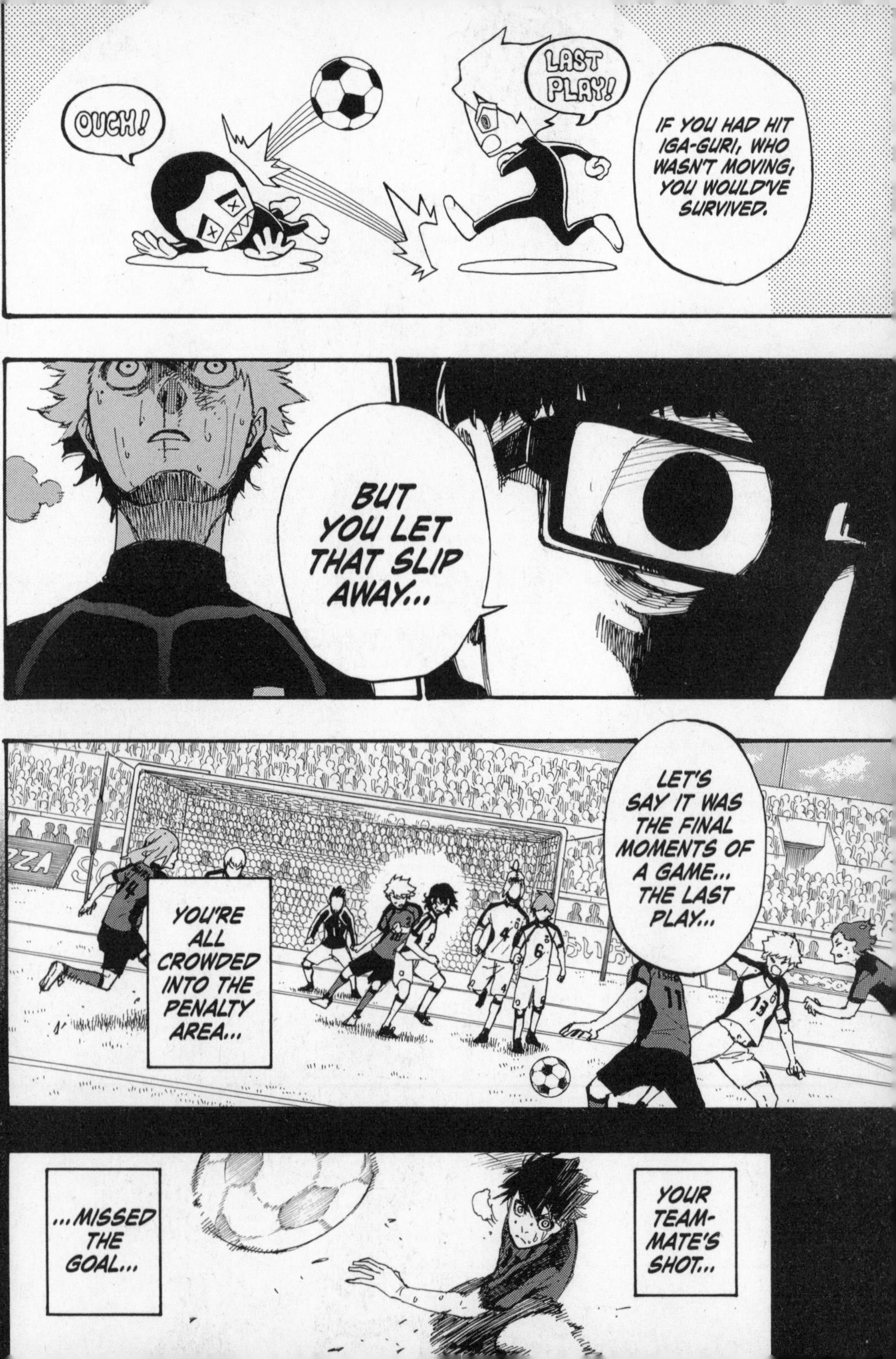
IF YOU HAD HIT IGA-GURI, WHO WASN'T MOVING, YOU WOULD'VE SURVIVED.
LAST PLAY!
OUCH!
BUT YOU LET THAT SLIP AWAY...
LET'S SAY IT WAS THE FINAL MOMENTS OF A GAME... THE LAST PLAY...
YOU'RE ALL CROWDED INTO THE PENALTY AREA...
YOUR TEAM-MATE'S SHOT...
...MISSED THE GOAL...

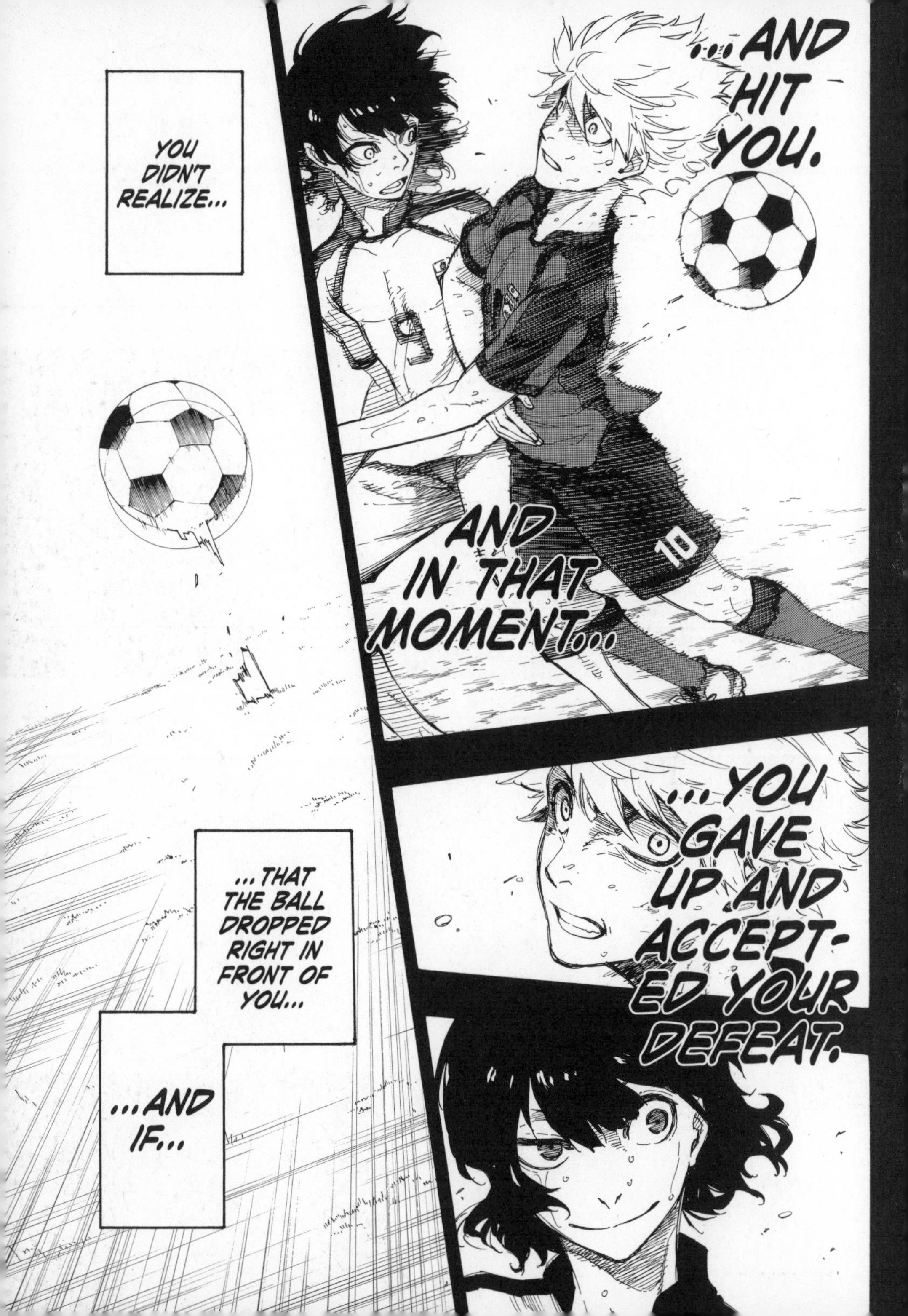
YOU DIDN'T REALIZE...
...THAT THE BALL DROPPED RIGHT IN FRONT OF YOU...
...AND IF...
...AND HIT YOU.
AND IN THAT MOMENT...
...YOU GAVE UP AND ACCEPT-ED YOUR DEFEAT.

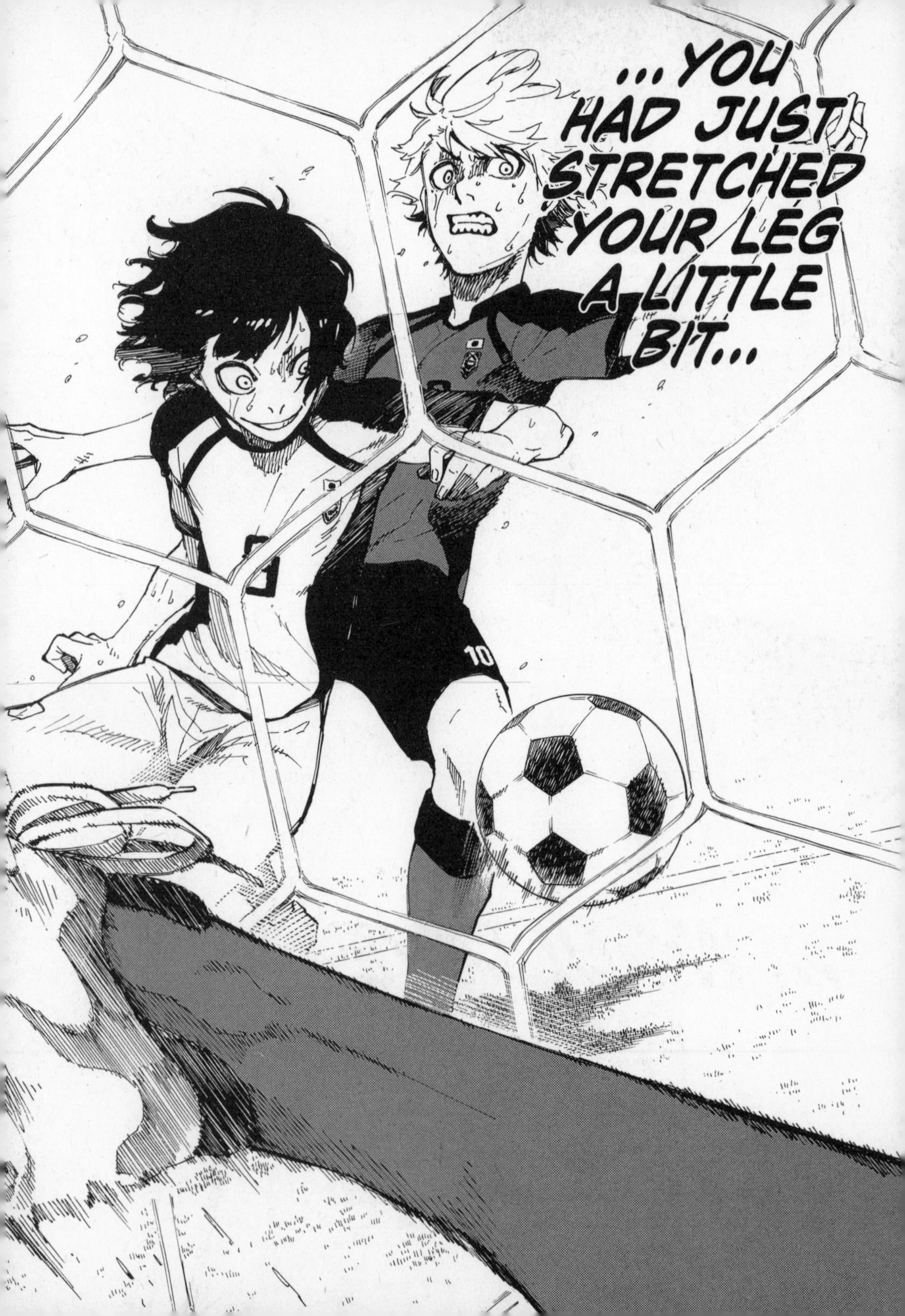
...YOU HAD JUST STRETCHED YOUR LEG A LITTLE BIT...

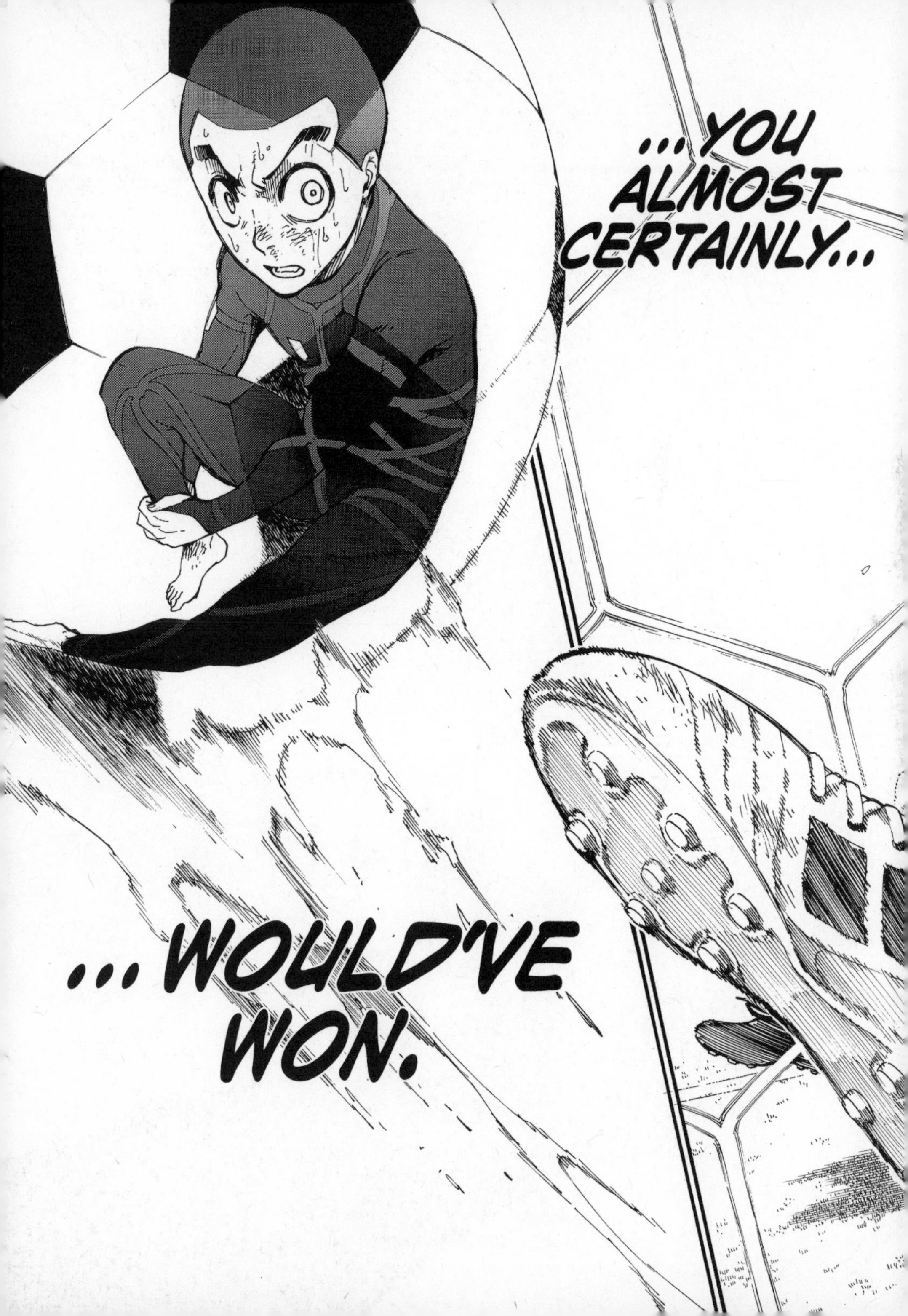
...YOU ALMOST CERTAINLY...
...WOULD'VE WON.

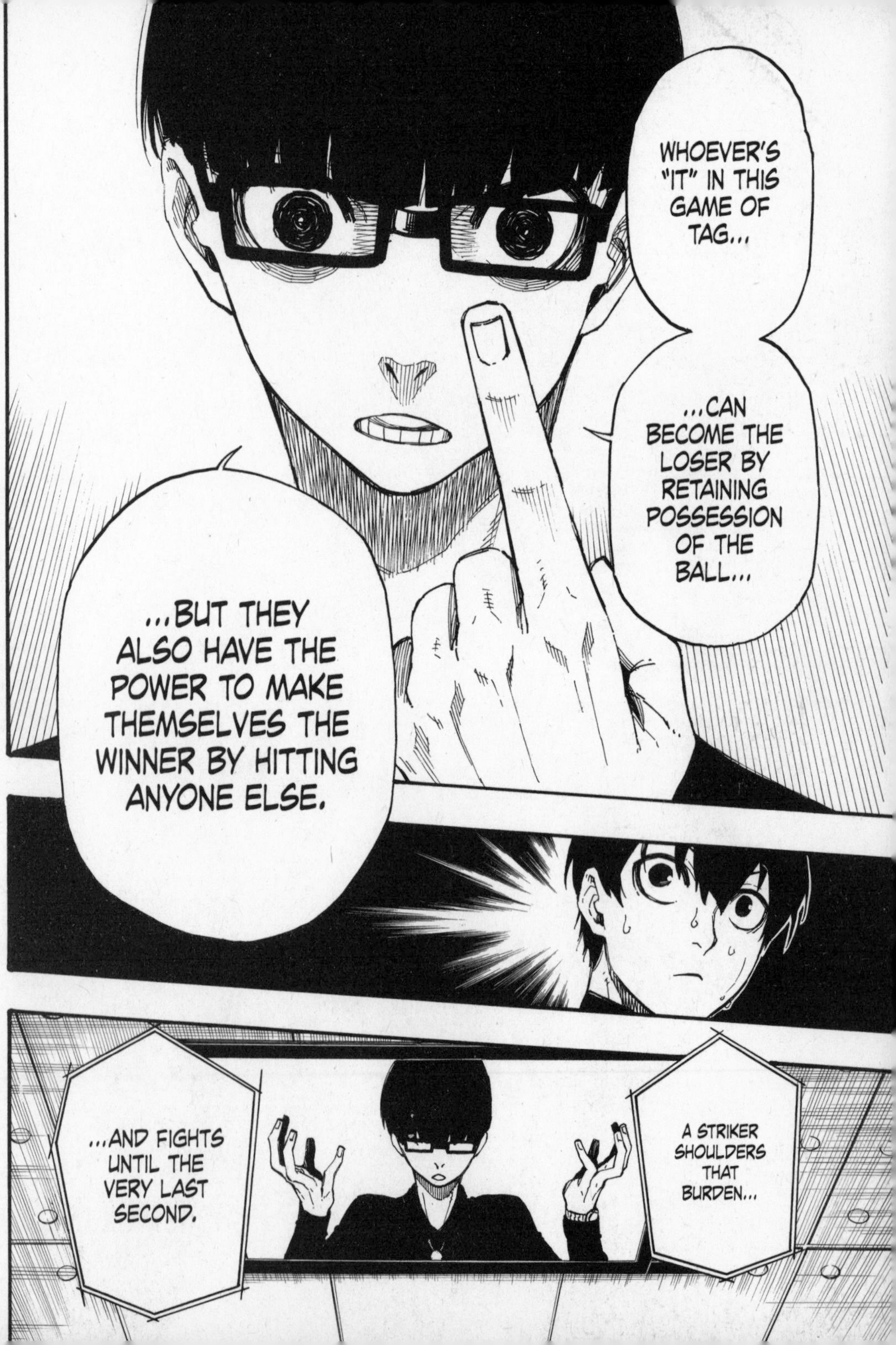
WHOEVER'S "IT" IN THIS GAME OF TAG...
...CAN BECOME THE LOSER BY RETAINING POSSESSION OF THE BALL...
...BUT THEY ALSO HAVE THE POWER TO MAKE THEMSELVES THE WINNER BY HITTING ANYONE ELSE.
A STRIKER SHOULDERS THAT BURDEN...
...AND FIGHTS UNTIL THE VERY LAST SECOND.

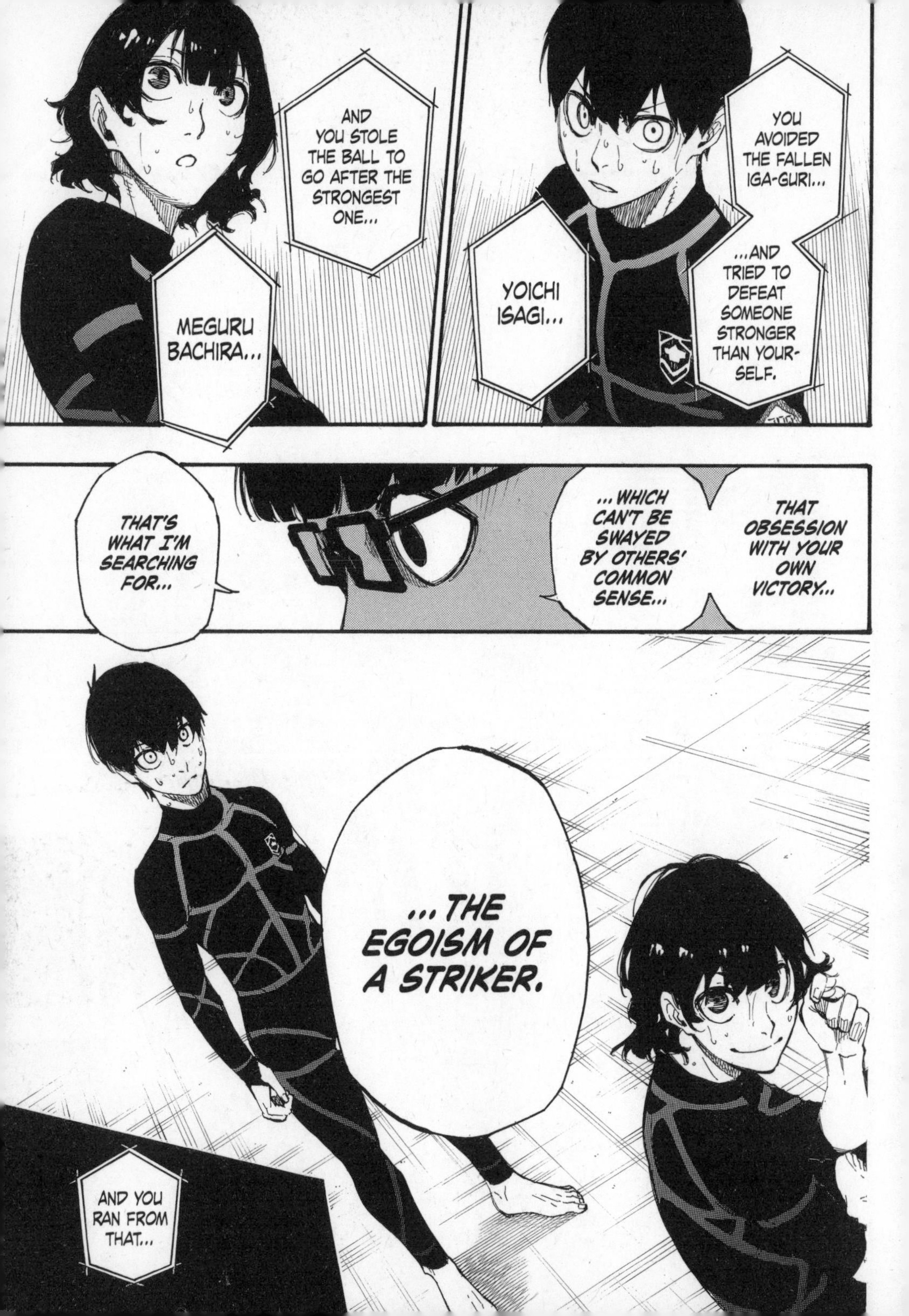
YOU AVOIDED THE FALLEN IGA-GURI...
...AND TRIED TO DEFEAT SOMEONE STRONGER THAN YOUR-SELF.
YOICHI ISAGI...
AND YOU STOLE THE BALL TO GO AFTER THE STRONGEST ONE...
MEGURU BACHIRA...
THAT OBSESSION WITH YOUR OWN VICTORY...
...WHICH CAN'T BE SWAYED BY OTHERS' COMMON SENSE...
THAT'S WHAT I'M SEARCHING FOR...
...THE EGOISM OF A STRIKER.
AND YOU RAN FROM THAT...

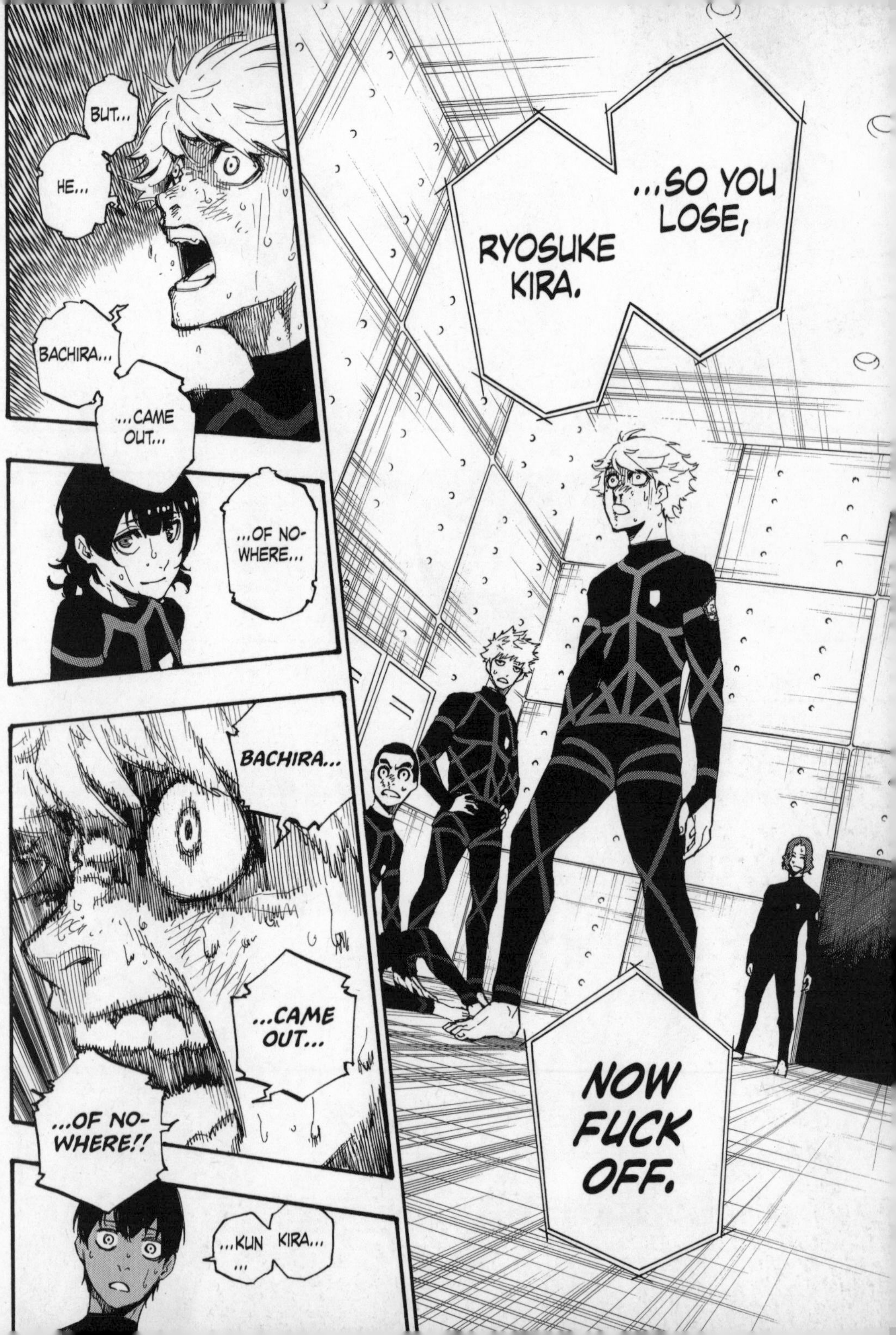
...SO YOU LOSE,
RYOSUKE KIRA.
NOW FUCK OFF.
BUT...
HE...
BACHIRA...
...CAME OUT...
...OF NO-WHERE...
BACHIRA...
...CAME OUT...
...OF NO-WHERE!!
KIRA...
...KUN
...

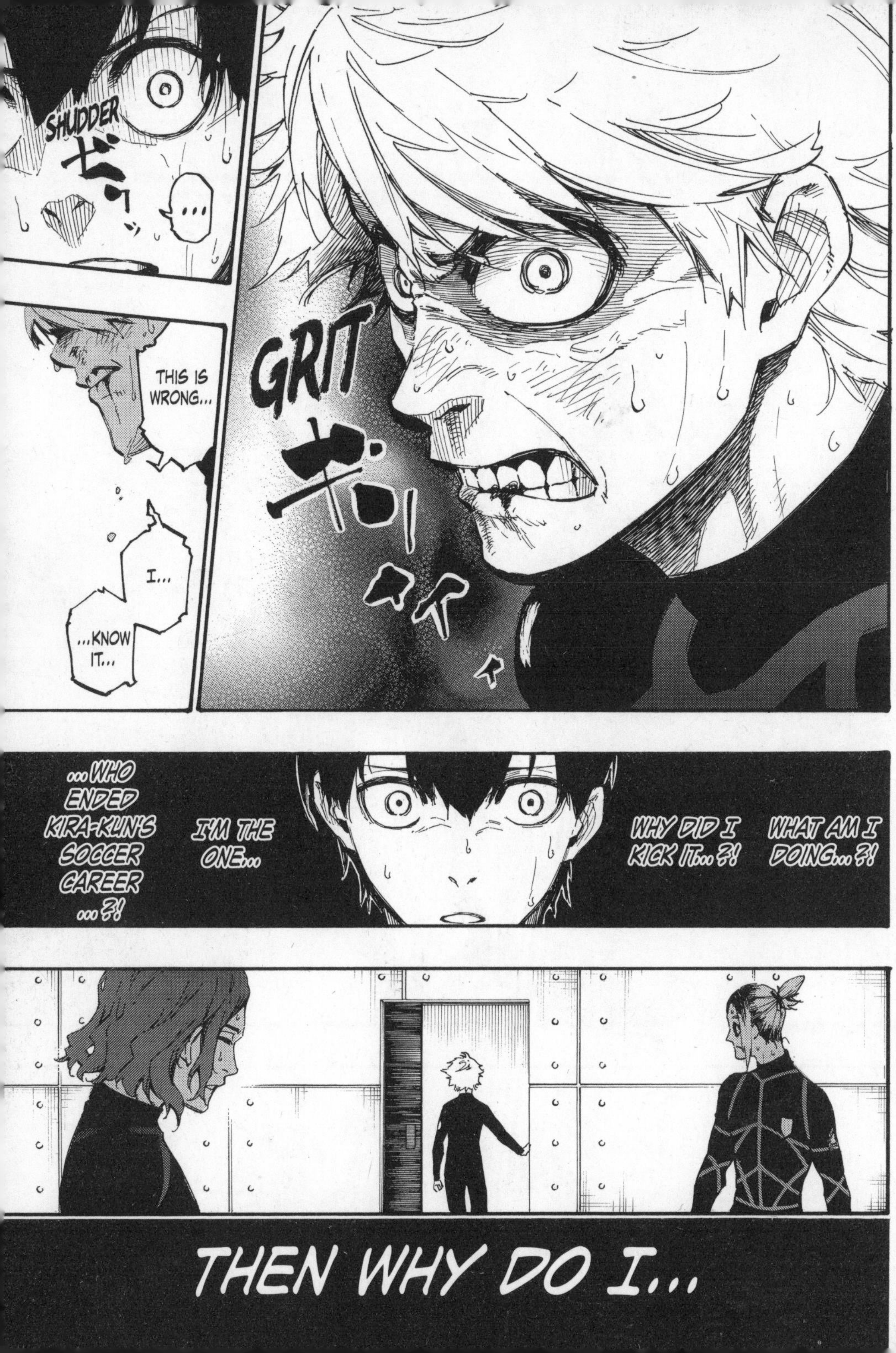
GRIT
SHUDDER
...
THIS IS WRONG...
I...
...KNOW IT...
WHAT AM I DOING...?!
WHY DID I KICK IT...?!
I'M THE ONE...
...WHO ENDED KIRA-KUN'S SOCCER CAREER ...?!
THEN WHY DO I...

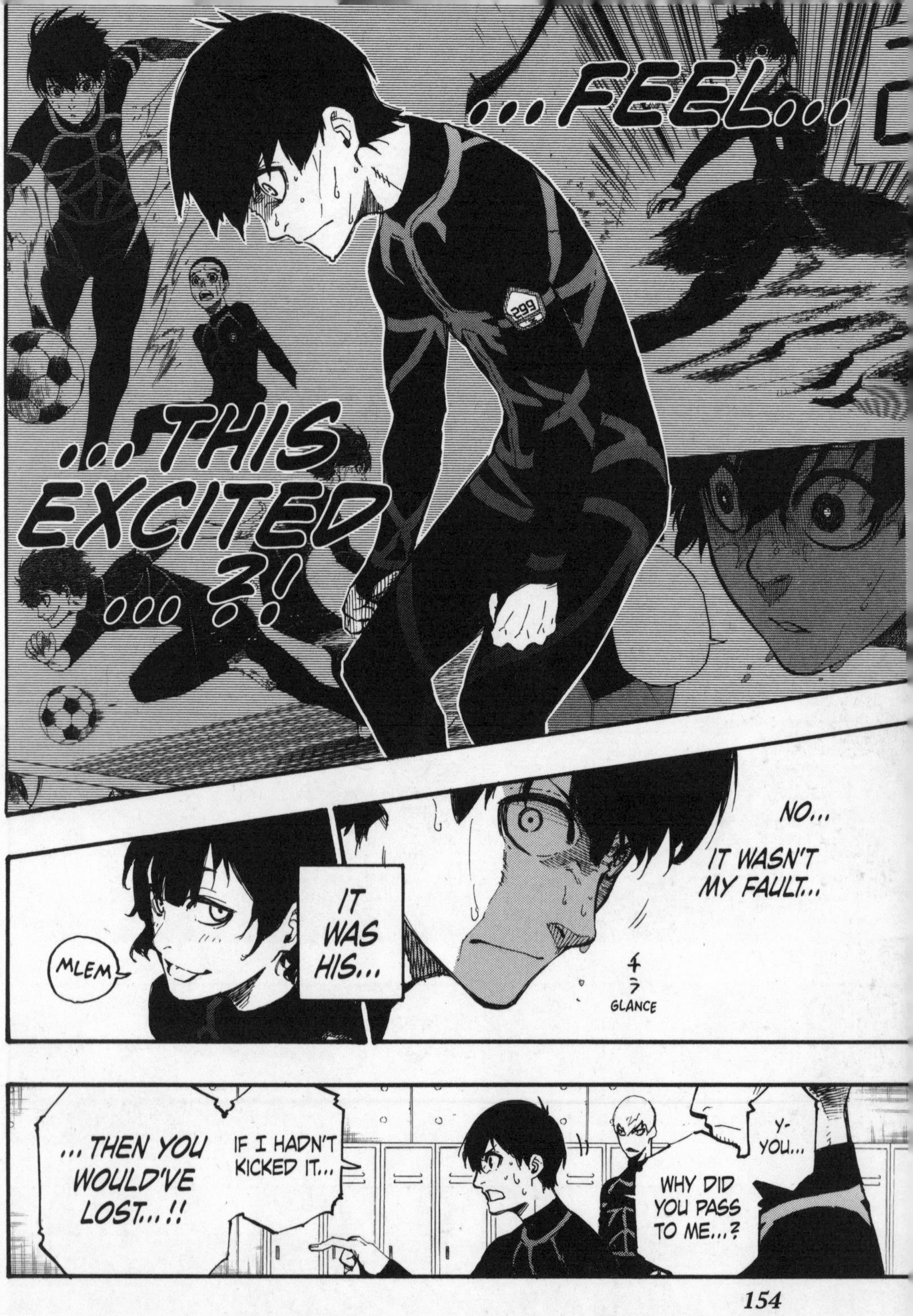
...FEEL...
...THIS EXCITED ...?!
NO...
IT WASN'T MY FAULT...
チラ
GLANCE
IT WAS HIS...
MLEM
Y-YOU...
WHY DID YOU PASS TO ME...?
IF I HADN'T KICKED IT...
...THEN YOU WOULD'VE LOST...!!

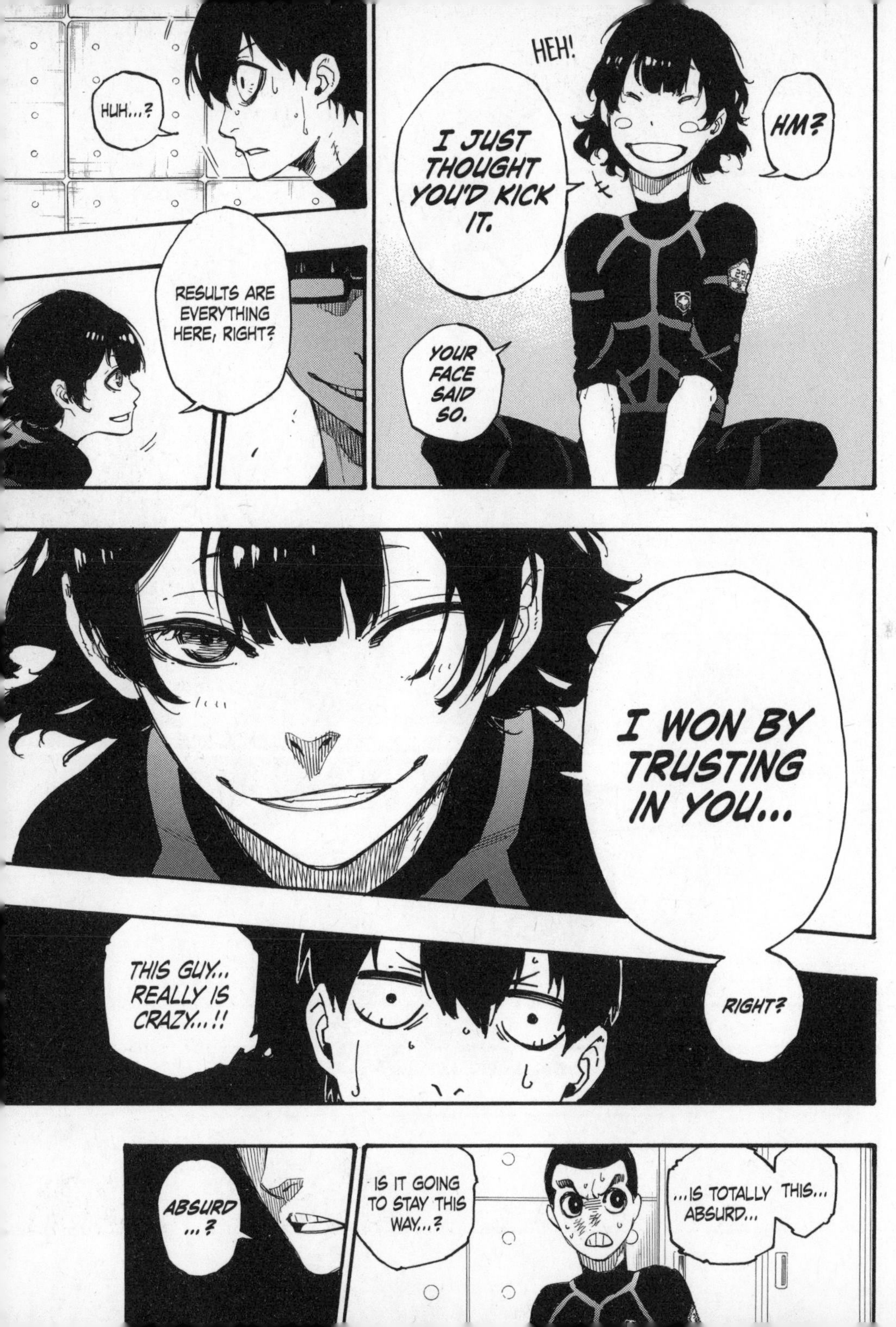
HEH!
HM?
I JUST THOUGHT YOU'D KICK IT.
YOUR FACE SAID SO.
HUH...?
RESULTS ARE EVERYTHING HERE, RIGHT?
I WON BY TRUSTING IN YOU...
RIGHT?
THIS GUY... REALLY IS CRAZY...!!
...IS TOTALLY THIS... ABSURD...
IS IT GOING TO STAY THIS WAY...?
ABSURD...?

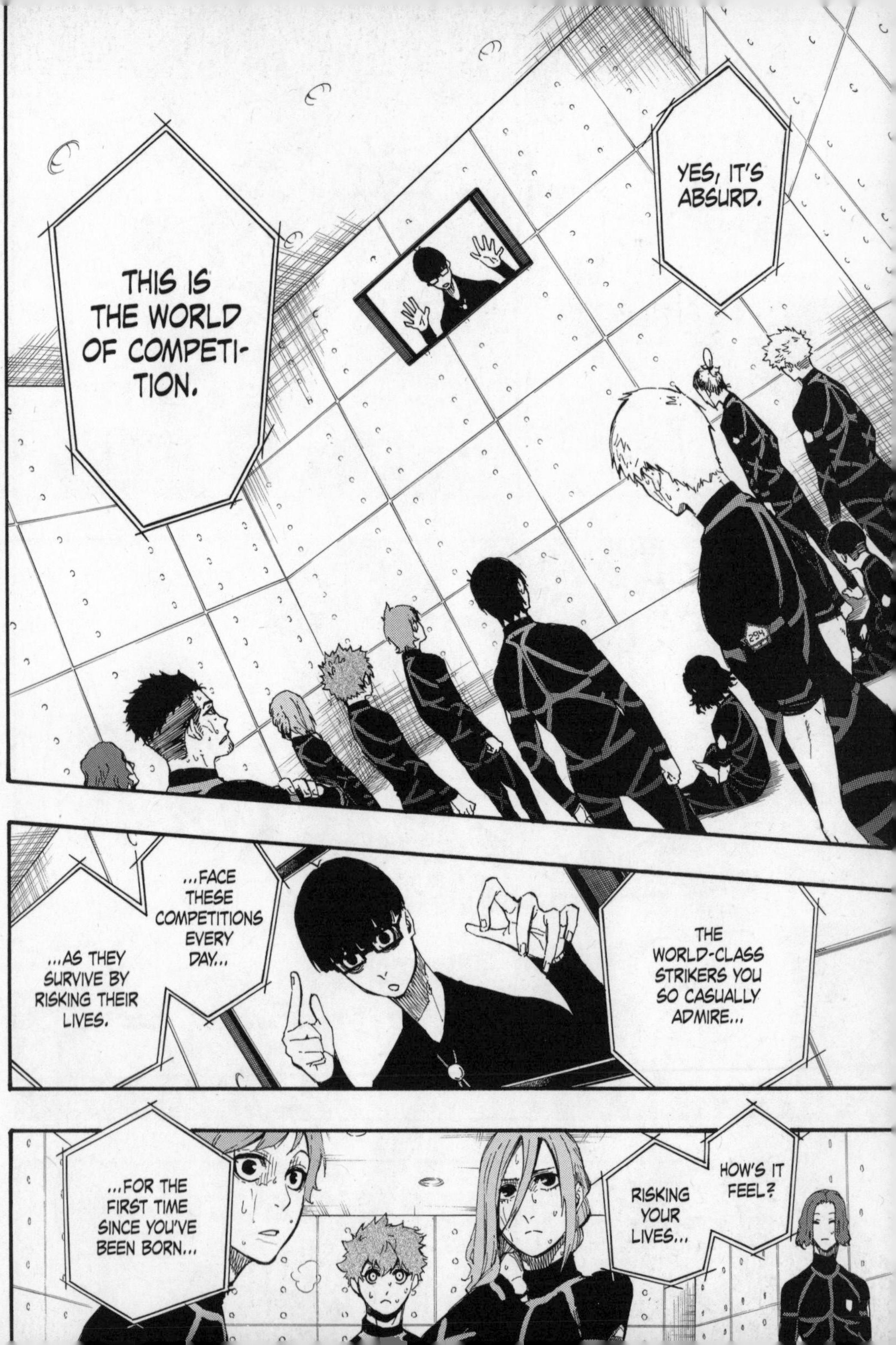
YES, IT'S ABSURD.
THIS IS THE WORLD OF COMPETI-TION.
THE WORLD-CLASS STRIKERS YOU SO CASUALLY ADMIRE...
...FACE THESE COMPETITIONS EVERY DAY...
...AS THEY SURVIVE BY RISKING THEIR LIVES.
HOW'S IT FEEL?
RISKING YOUR LIVES...
...FOR THE FIRST TIME SINCE YOU'VE BEEN BORN...

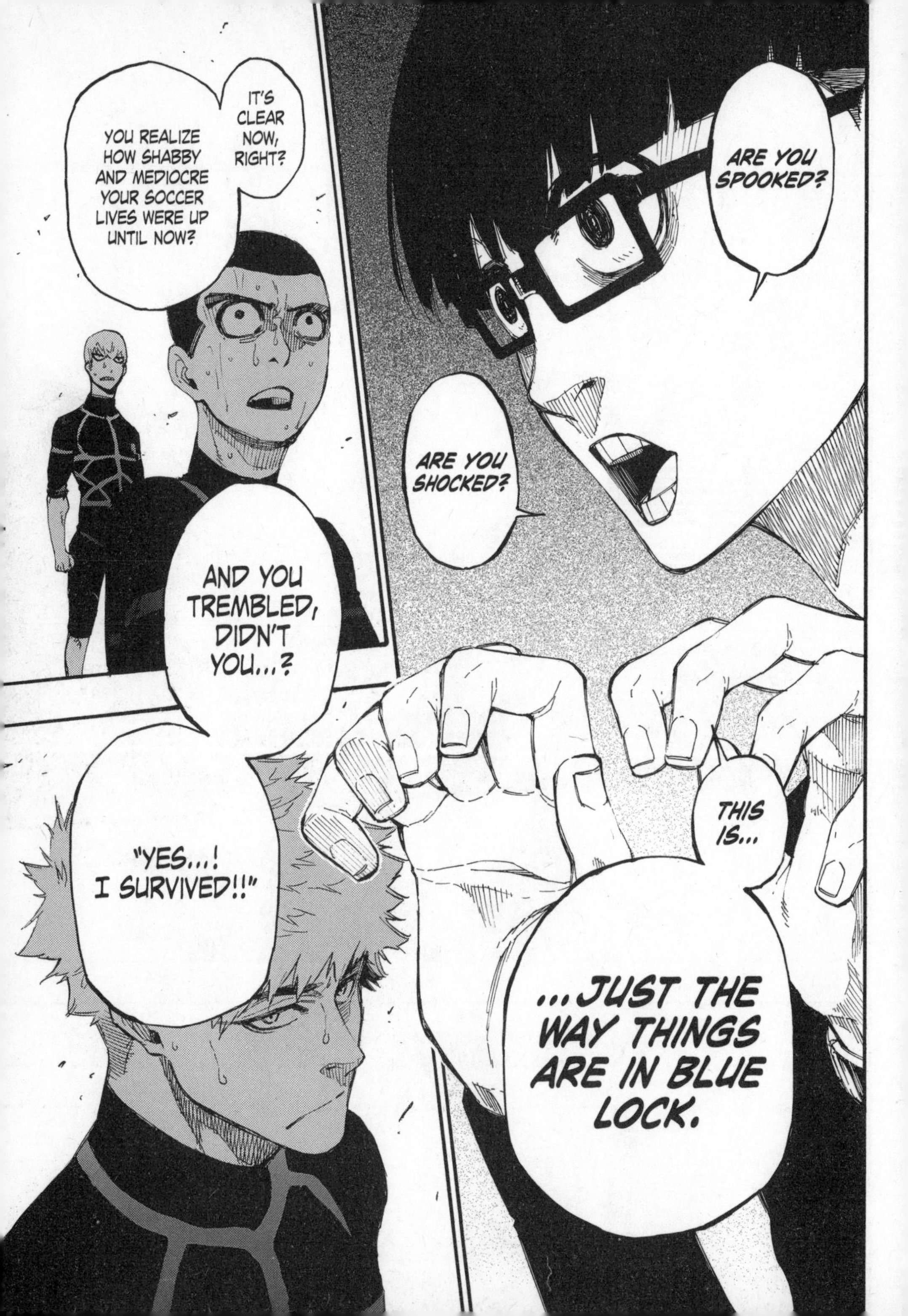
ARE YOU SPOOKED?
ARE YOU SHOCKED?
IT'S CLEAR NOW, RIGHT?
YOU REALIZE HOW SHABBY AND MEDIOCRE YOUR SOCCER LIVES WERE UP UNTIL NOW?
AND YOU TREMBLED, DIDN'T YOU...?
"YES...! I SURVIVED!!"
THIS IS...
...JUST THE WAY THINGS ARE IN BLUE LOCK.

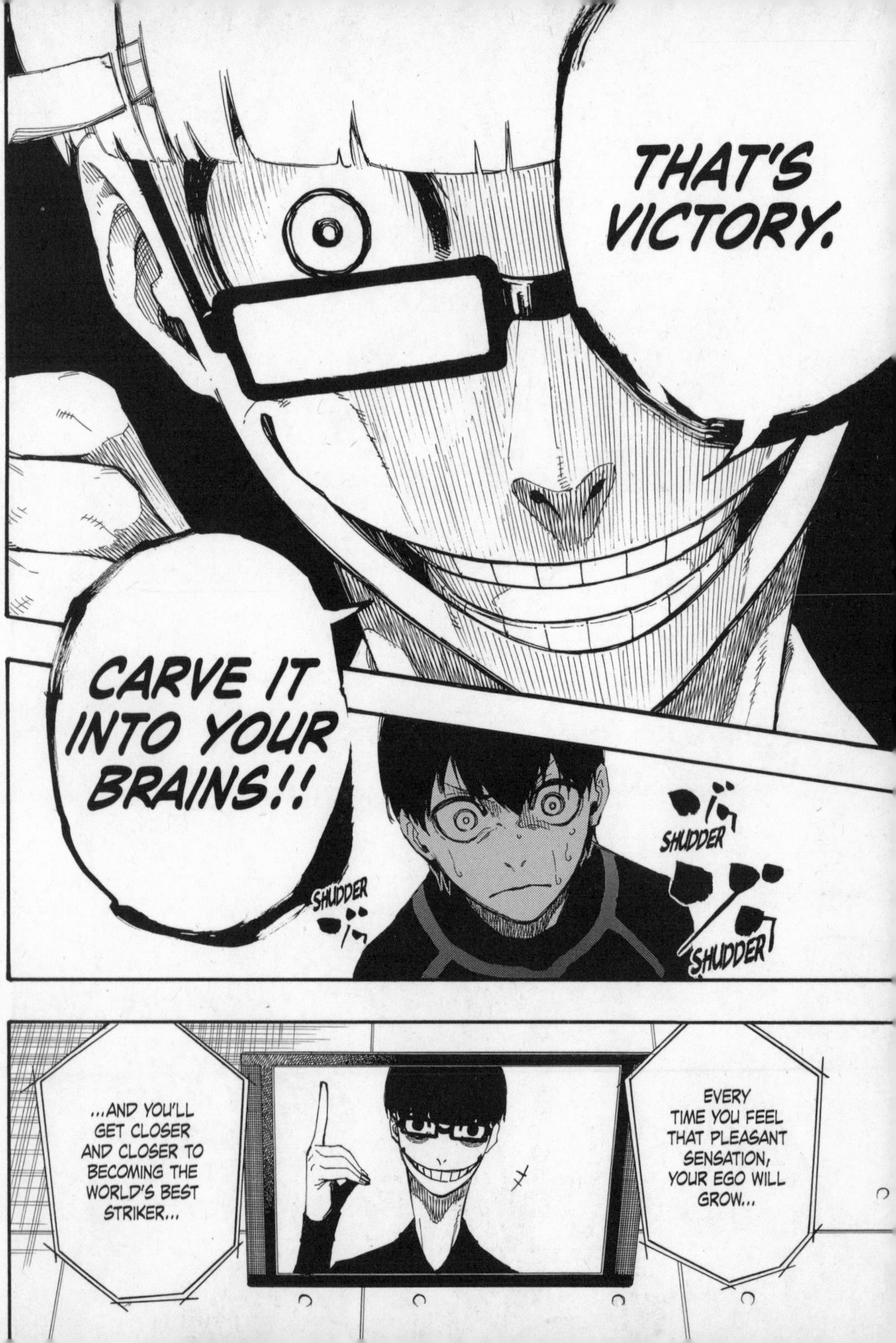
THAT'S VICTORY.
CARVE IT INTO YOUR BRAINS!!
SHUDDER
SHUDDER
SHUDDER
EVERY TIME YOU FEEL THAT PLEASANT SENSATION, YOUR EGO WILL GROW...
...AND YOU'LL GET CLOSER AND CLOSER TO BECOMING THE WORLD'S BEST STRIKER...

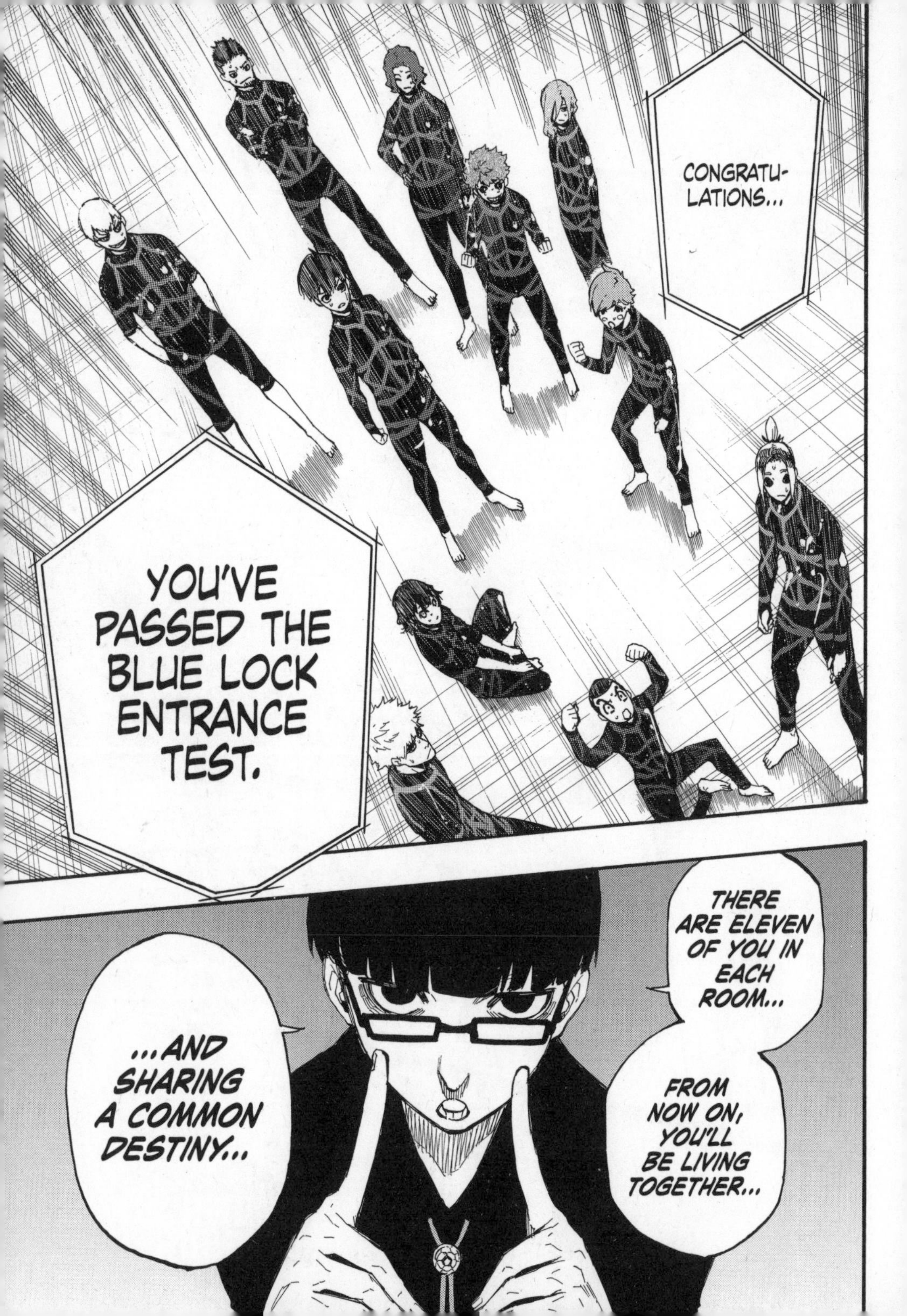
CONGRATU-LATIONS...
YOU'VE PASSED THE BLUE LOCK ENTRANCE TEST.
THERE ARE ELEVEN OF YOU IN EACH ROOM...
FROM NOW ON, YOU'LL BE LIVING TOGETHER...
...AND SHARING A COMMON DESTINY...

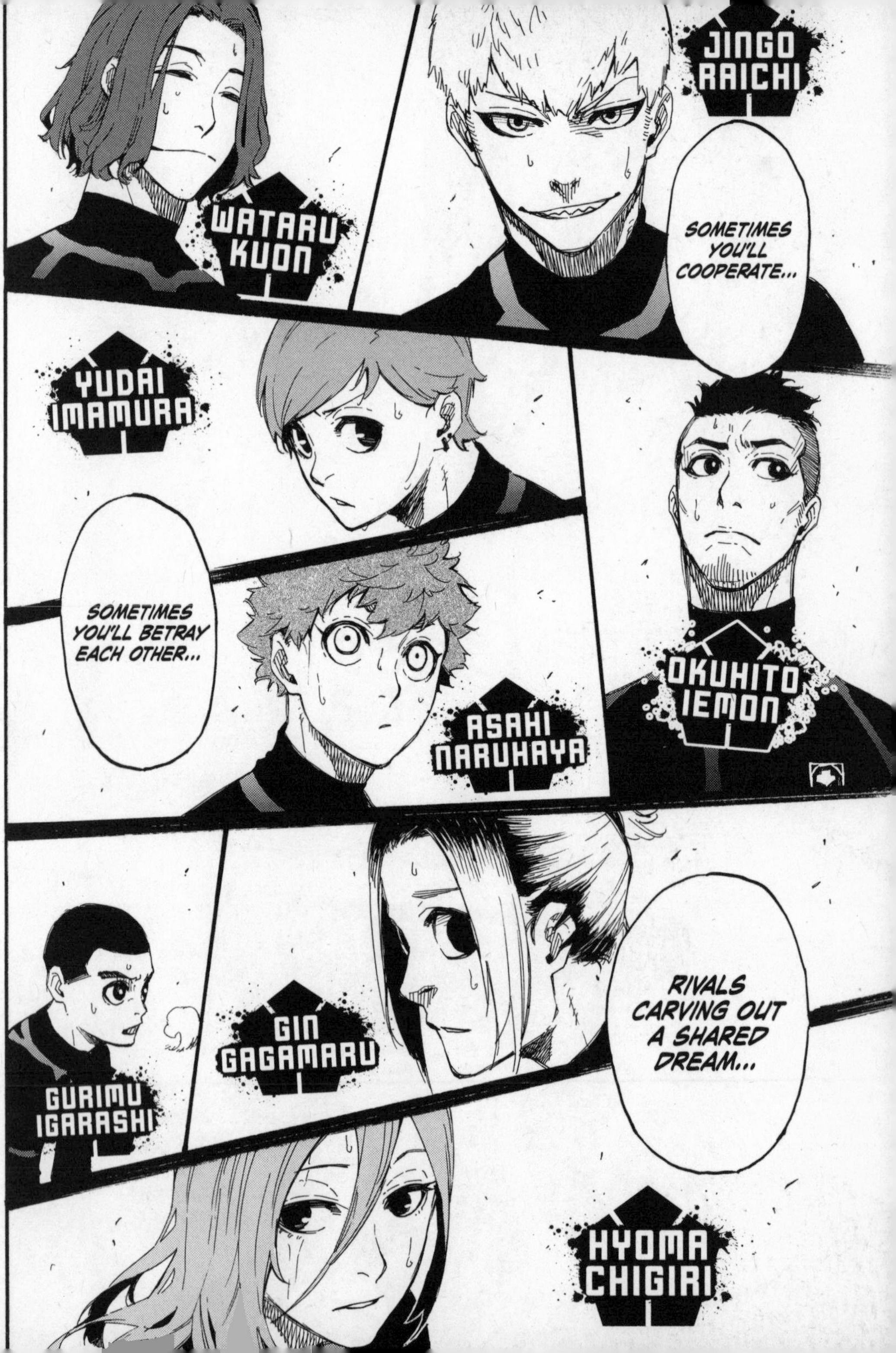
JINGO RAICHI
SOMETIMES YOU'LL COOPERATE...
WATARU KUON
OKUHITO IEMON
YUDAI IMAMURA
SOMETIMES YOU'LL BETRAY EACH OTHER...
ASAHI NARUHAYA
RIVALS CARVING OUT A SHARED DREAM...
GIN GAGAMARU
GURIMU IGARASHI
HYOMA CHIGIRI

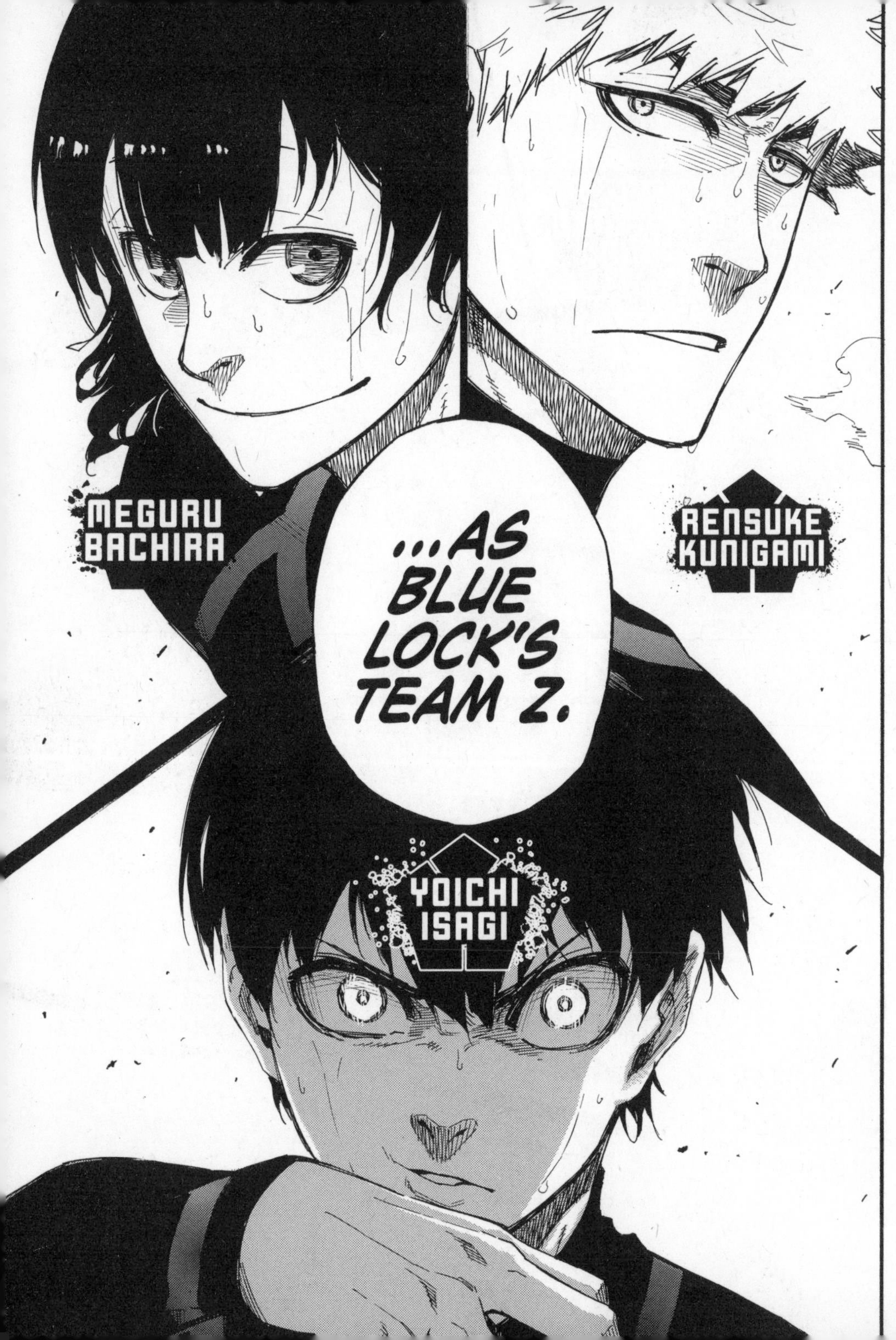
...AS BLUE LOCK'S TEAM Z.
RENSUKE KUNIGAMI
MEGURU BACHIRA
YOICHI ISAGI

BLUELOCK

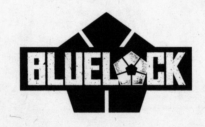

CHAPTER 3: MONSTER

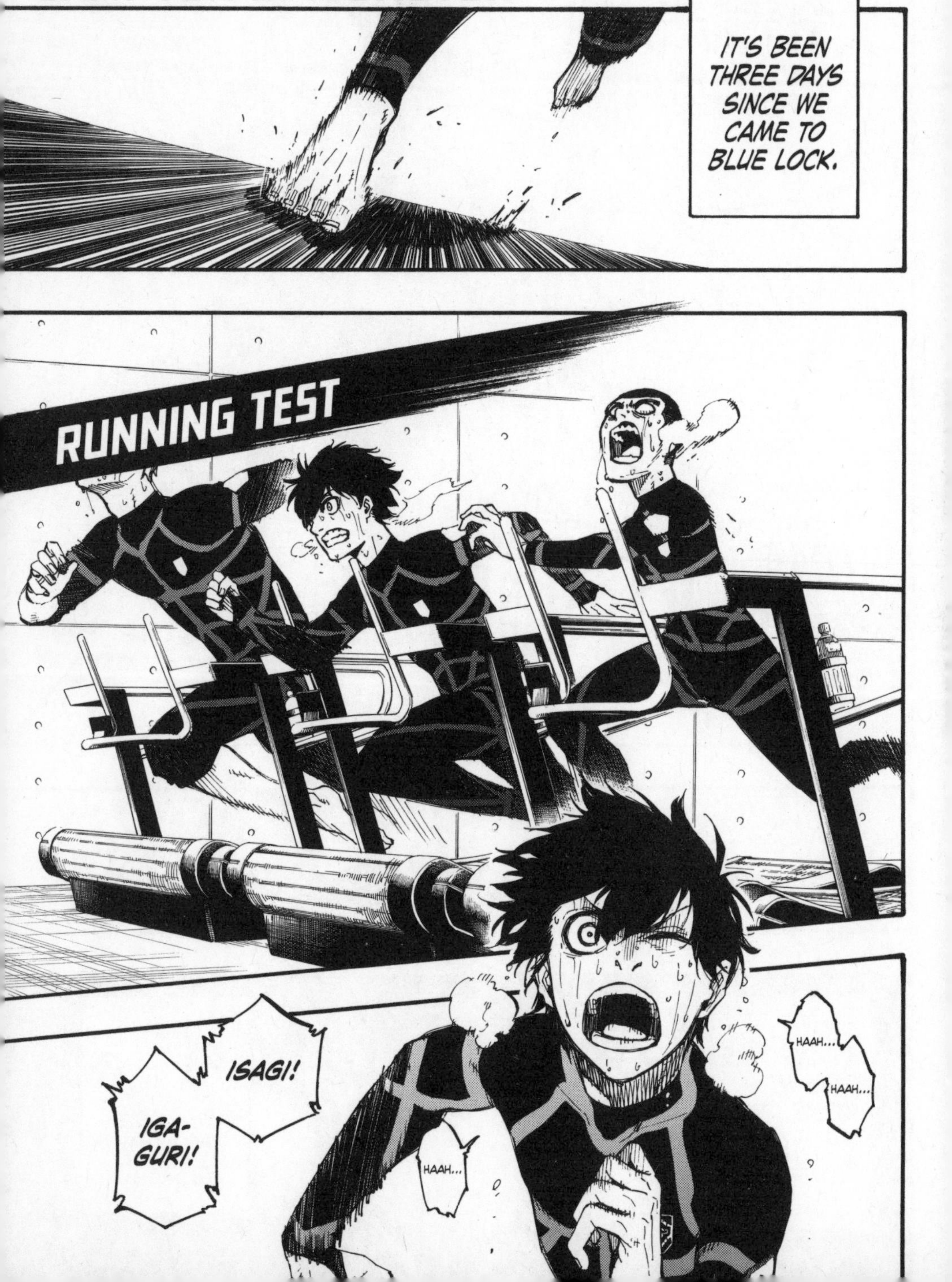
IT'S BEEN THREE DAYS SINCE WE CAME TO BLUE LOCK.
RUNNING TEST
HAAH...
HAAH...
HAAH...
ISAGI!
IGA-GURI!

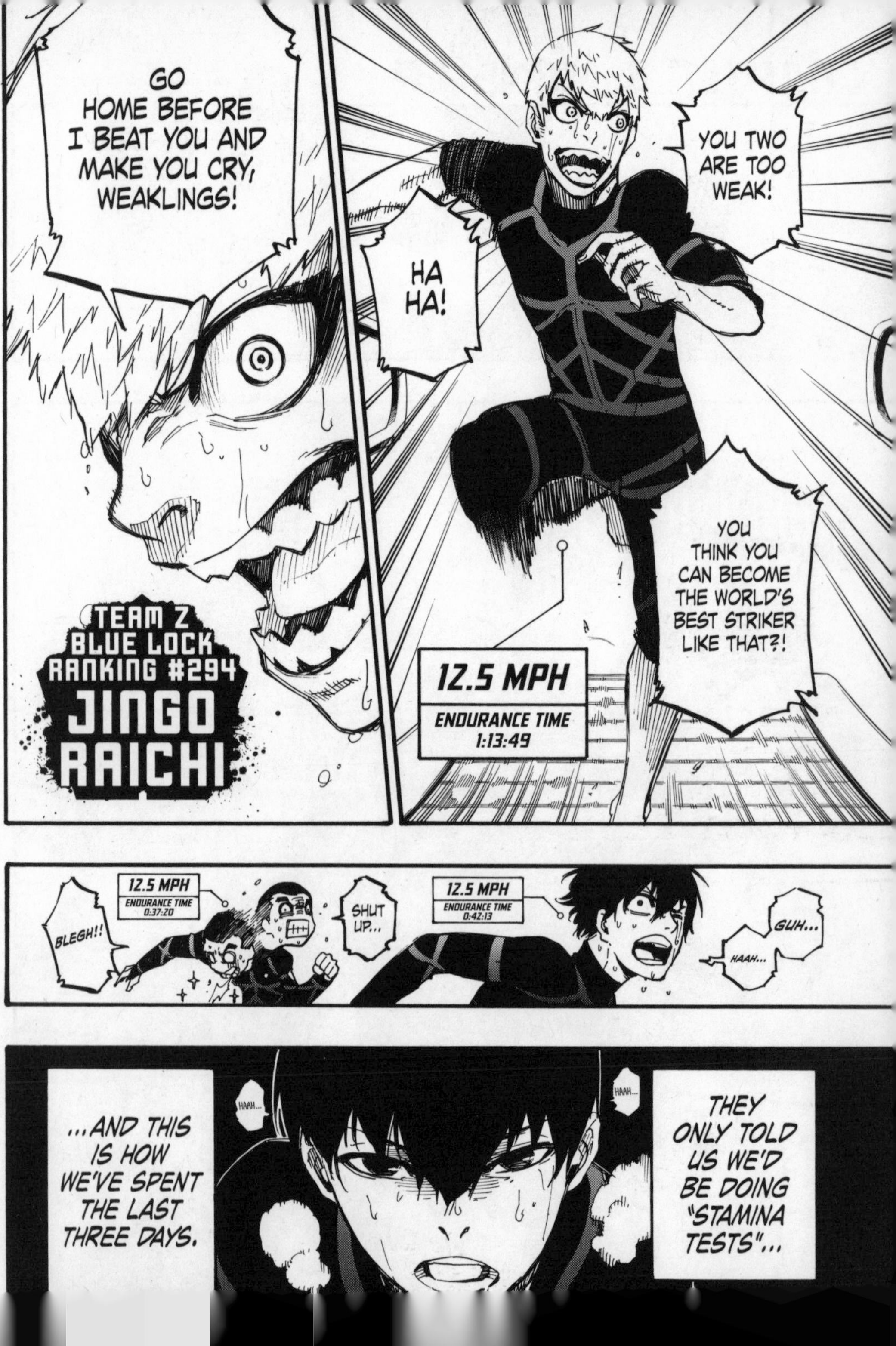
YOU TWO ARE TOO WEAK!
HA HA!
YOU THINK YOU CAN BECOME THE WORLD'S BEST STRIKER LIKE THAT?!
12.5 MPH
ENDURANCE TIME 1:13:49
GO HOME BEFORE I BEAT YOU AND MAKE YOU CRY, WEAKLINGS!
TEAM Z BLUE LOCK RANKING #294
JINGO RAICHI
GUH...
HAAH...
12.5 MPH
ENDURANCE TIME 0:42:13
SHUT UP...
12.5 MPH
ENDURANCE TIME 0:37:20
BLEGH!!
THEY ONLY TOLD US WE'D BE DOING "STAMINA TESTS"...
HAAH...
HAAH...
...AND THIS IS HOW WE'VE SPENT THE LAST THREE DAYS.

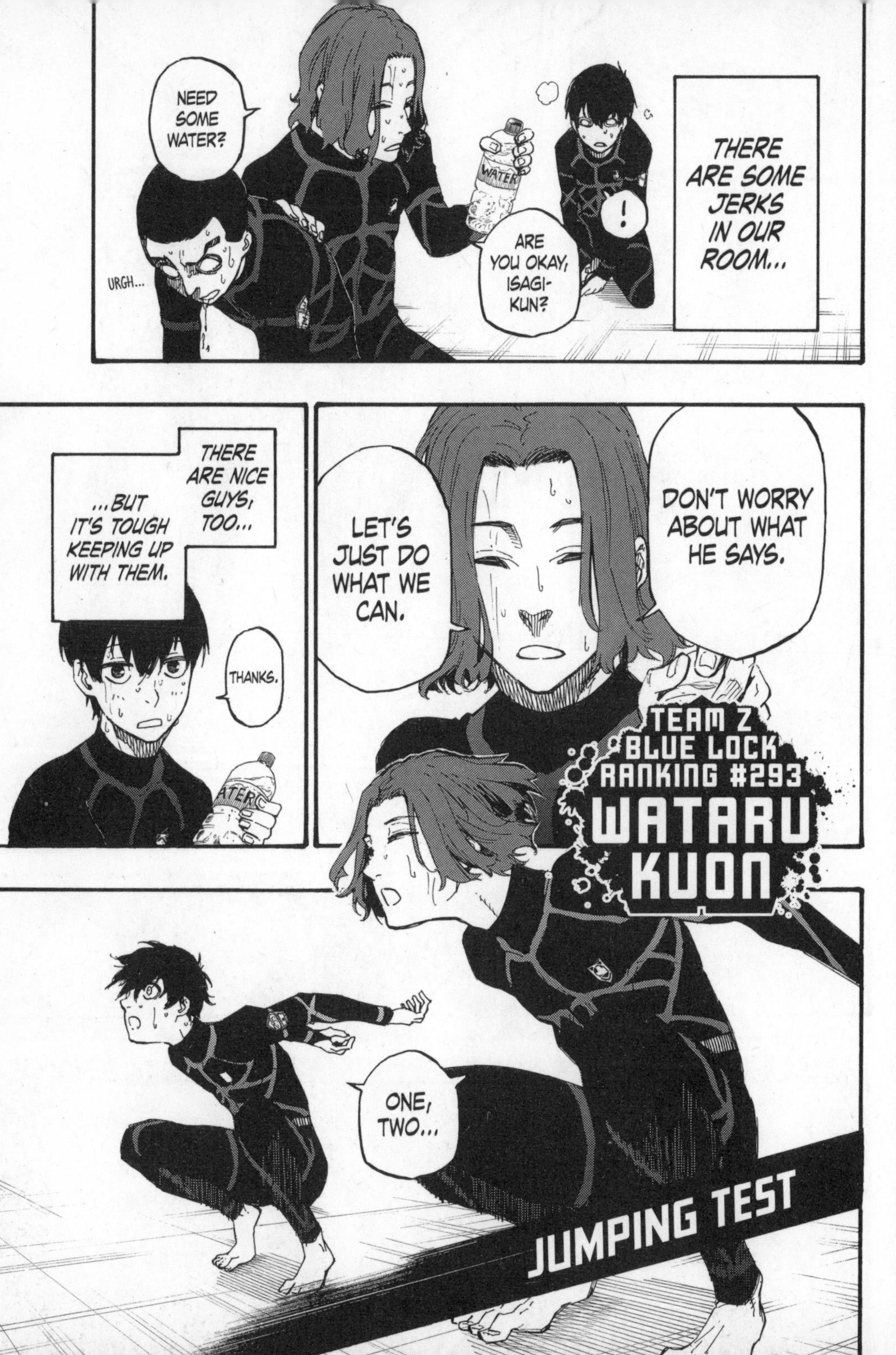
THERE ARE SOME JERKS IN OUR ROOM...
!
ARE YOU OKAY, ISAGI-KUN?
NEED SOME WATER?
WATER
URGH...
DON'T WORRY ABOUT WHAT HE SAYS.
LET'S JUST DO WHAT WE CAN.
THERE ARE NICE GUYS, TOO...
...BUT IT'S TOUGH KEEPING UP WITH THEM.
THANKS.
TEAM Z BLUE LOCK RANKING #293
WATARU KUON
ONE, TWO...
JUMPING TEST

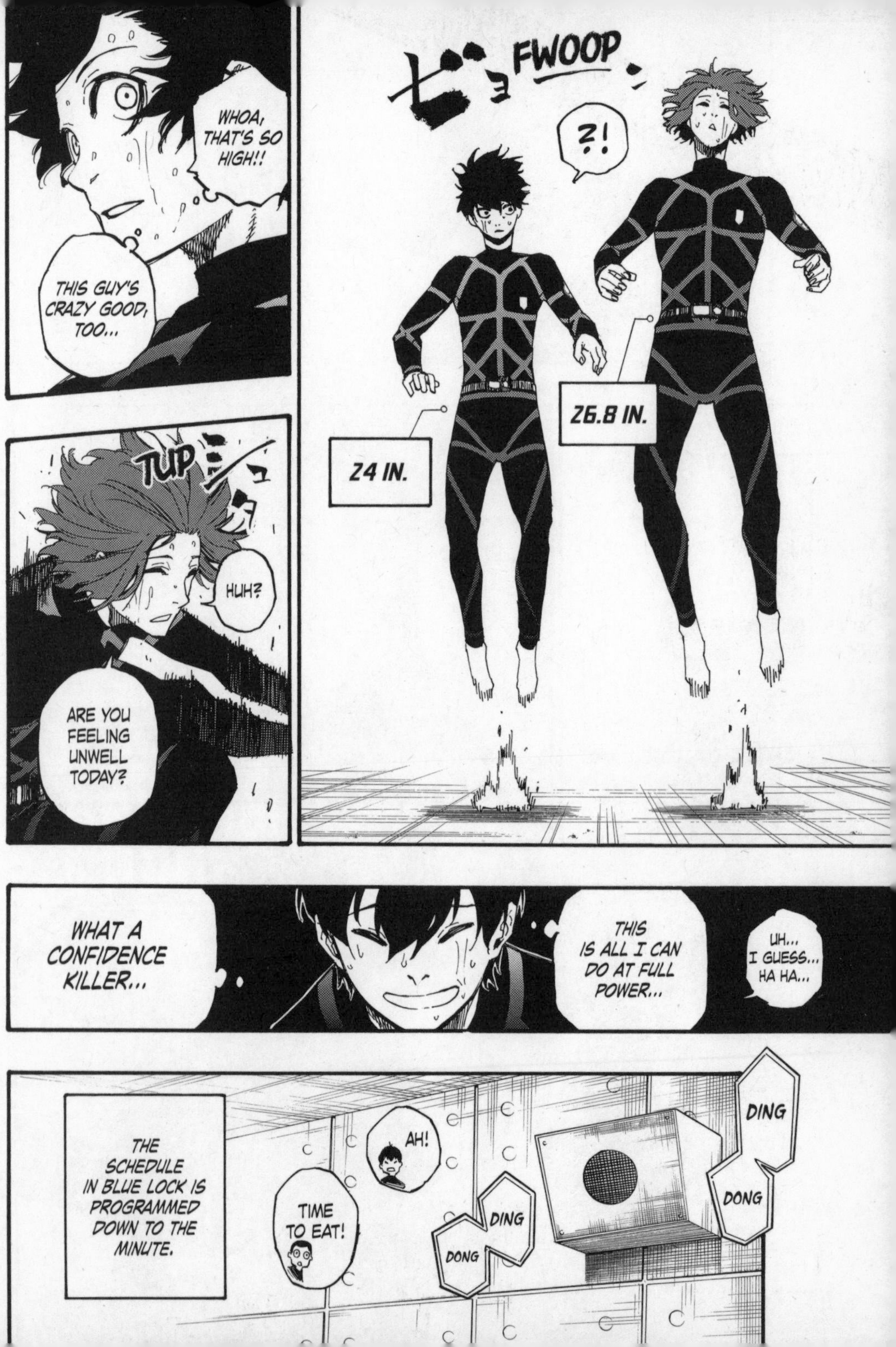
FWOOP
?!
26.8 IN.
24 IN.
WHOA, THAT'S SO HIGH!!
THIS GUY'S CRAZY GOOD, TOO...
TUP
HUH?
ARE YOU FEELING UNWELL TODAY?
UH... I GUESS... HA HA...
THIS IS ALL I CAN DO AT FULL POWER...
WHAT A CONFIDENCE KILLER...
DING
DONG
AH!
DING
DONG
TIME TO EAT!
THE SCHEDULE IN BLUE LOCK IS PROGRAMMED DOWN TO THE MINUTE.

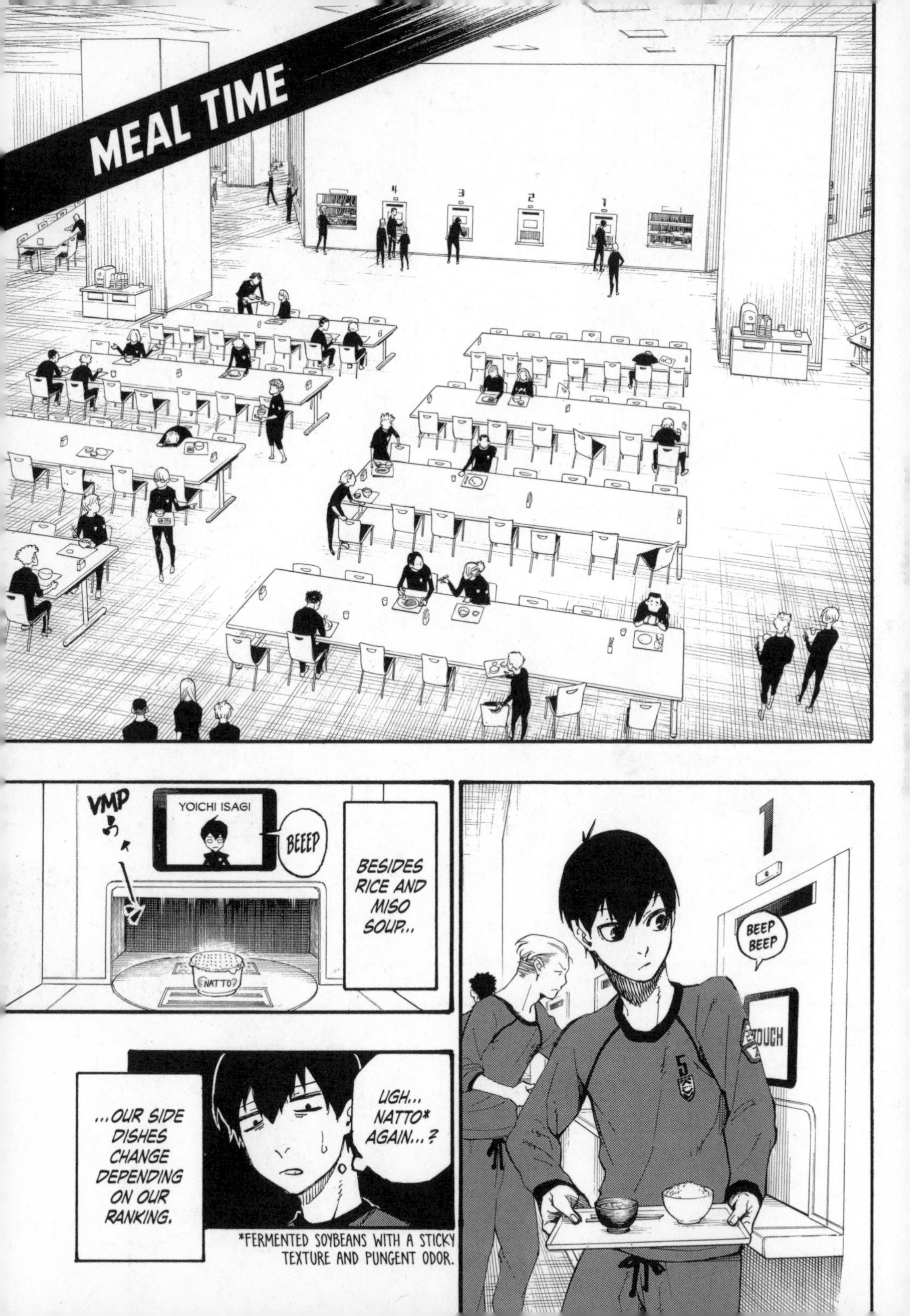
MEAL TIME
1
BEEP BEEP
TOUCH
BESIDES RICE AND MISO SOUP...
BEEEP
YOICHI ISAGI
VMP
NATTO
UGH... NATTO* AGAIN...?
...OUR SIDE DISHES CHANGE DEPENDING ON OUR RANKING.
*FERMENTED SOYBEANS WITH A STICKY TEXTURE AND PUNGENT ODOR.

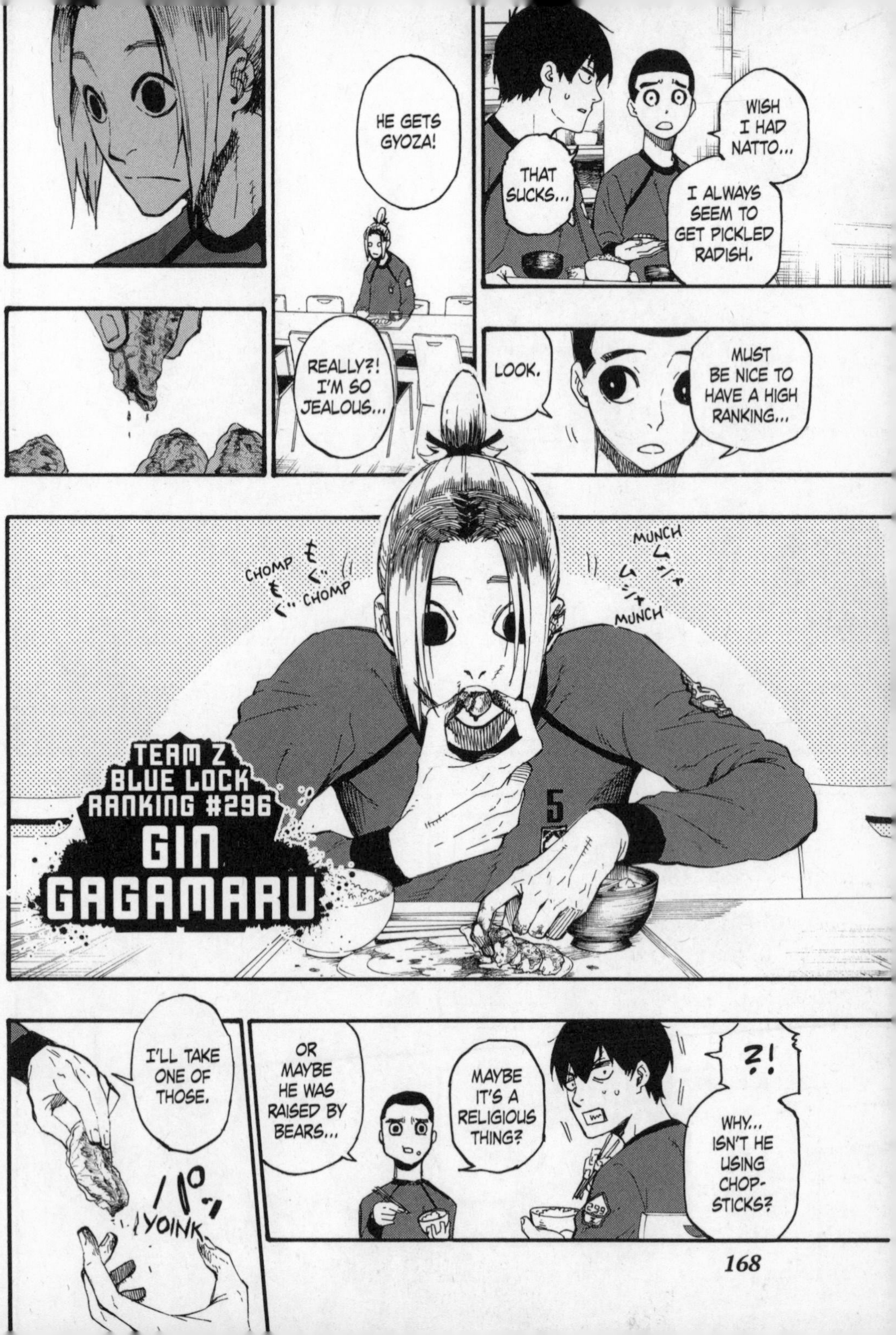
WISH I HAD NATTO...
I ALWAYS SEEM TO GET PICKLED RADISH.
THAT SUCKS...
MUST BE NICE TO HAVE A HIGH RANKING...
LOOK.
HE GETS GYOZA!
REALLY?! I'M SO JEALOUS...
MUNCH
MUNCH
CHOMP
CHOMP
TEAM Z
BLUE LOCK
RANKING #296
GIN
GAGAMARU
?!
WHY... ISN'T HE USING CHOP-STICKS?
MAYBE IT'S A RELIGIOUS THING?
OR MAYBE HE WAS RAISED BY BEARS...
I'LL TAKE ONE OF THOSE.
YOINK

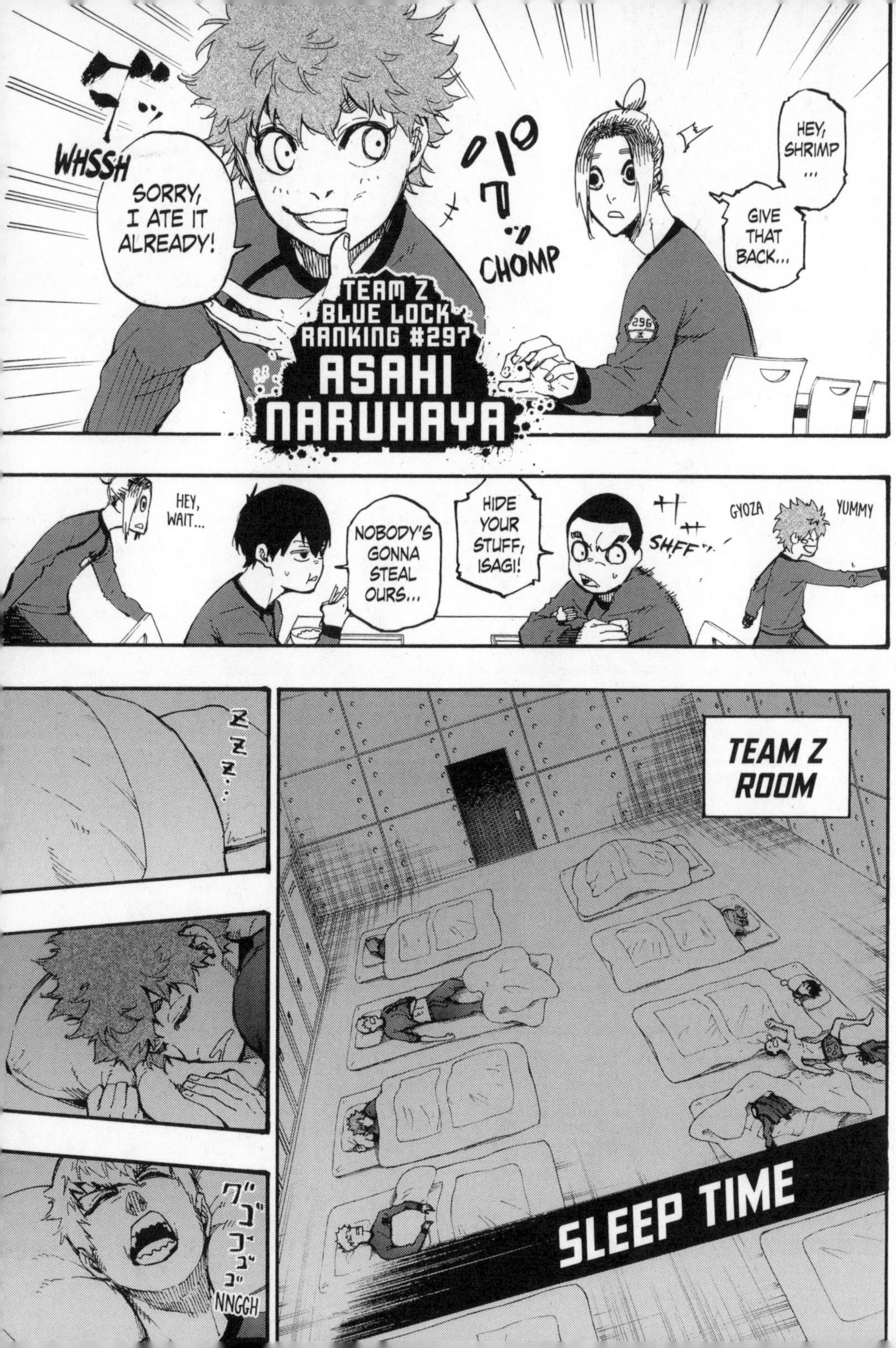
HEY, SHRIMP ...
GIVE THAT BACK...
CHOMP
TEAM Z
BLUE LOCK
RANKING #297
ASAHI NARUHAYA
SORRY, I ATE IT ALREADY!
WHSSH
YUMMY
GYOZA
SHFF
HIDE YOUR STUFF, ISAGI!
NOBODY'S GONNA STEAL OURS...
HEY, WAIT...
TEAM Z ROOM
SLEEP TIME
Z Z Z...
NNGGH

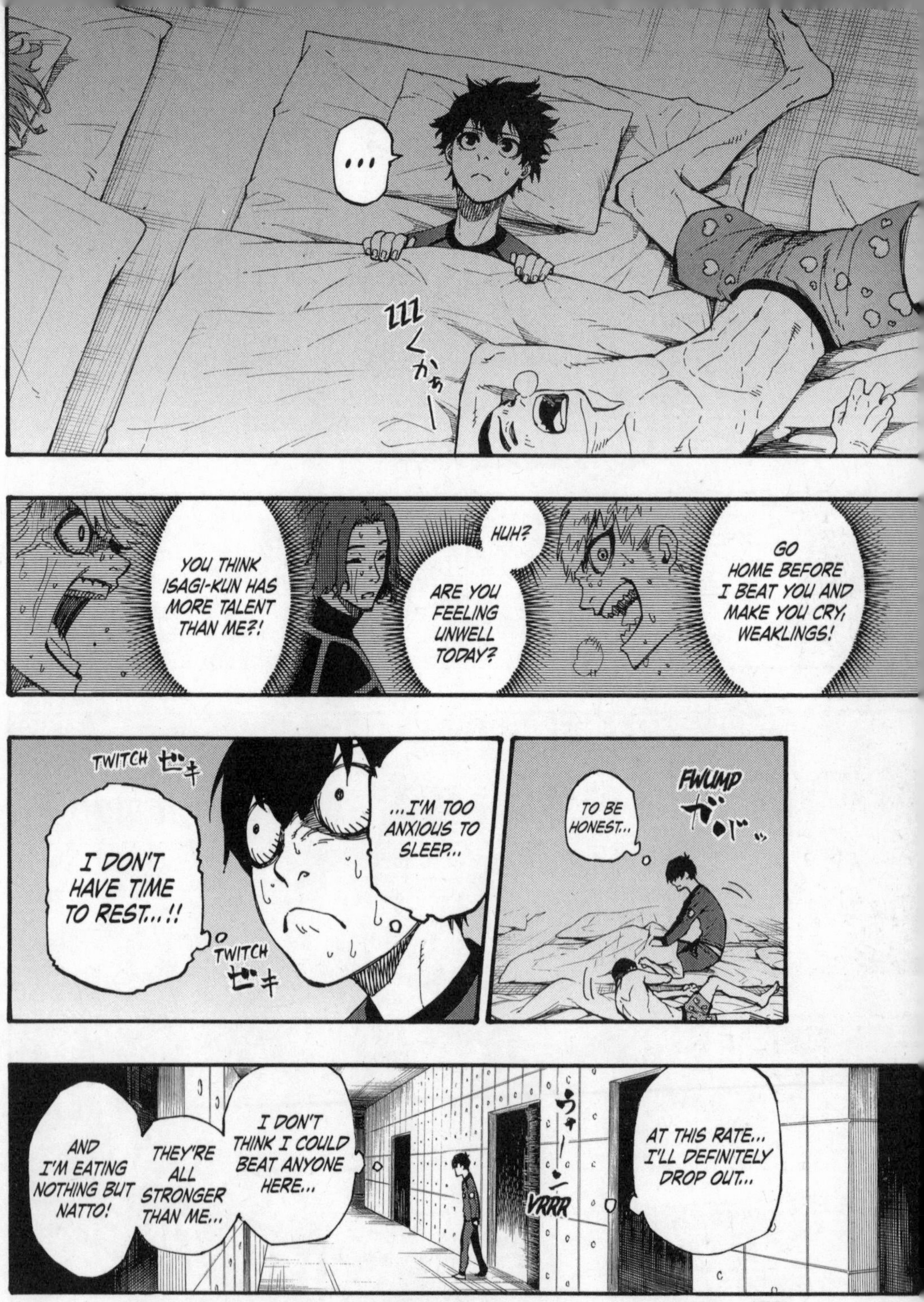
...
ZZZ
くかぁー
GO HOME BEFORE I BEAT YOU AND MAKE YOU CRY, WEAKLINGS!
HUH?
ARE YOU FEELING UNWELL TODAY?
YOU THINK ISAGI-KUN HAS MORE TALENT THAN ME?!
FWUMP
TO BE HONEST...
TWITCH
...I'M TOO ANXIOUS TO SLEEP...
I DON'T HAVE TIME TO REST...!!
TWITCH
AT THIS RATE... I'LL DEFINITELY DROP OUT...
VRRR
I DON'T THINK I COULD BEAT ANYONE HERE...
THEY'RE ALL STRONGER THAN ME...
AND I'M EATING NOTHING BUT NATTO!

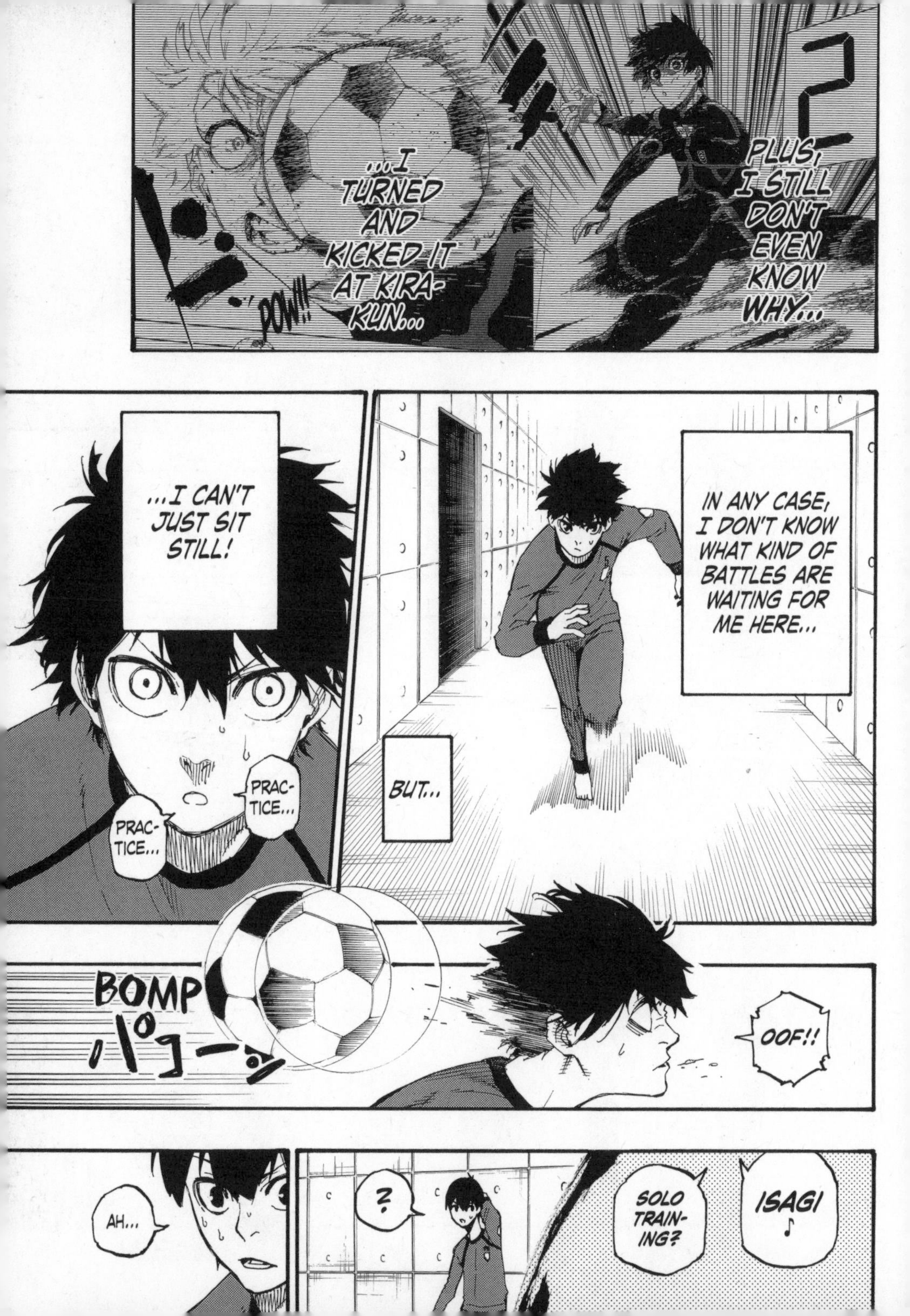

PLUS, I STILL DON'T EVEN KNOW WHY...
...I TURNED AND KICKED IT AT KIRA-KUN...
POW!!
IN ANY CASE, I DON'T KNOW WHAT KIND OF BATTLES ARE WAITING FOR ME HERE...
BUT...
...I CAN'T JUST SIT STILL!
PRAC-TICE...
PRAC-TICE...
OOF!!
BOMP
パコーン
ISAGI ♪
SOLO TRAIN-ING?
?
AH...

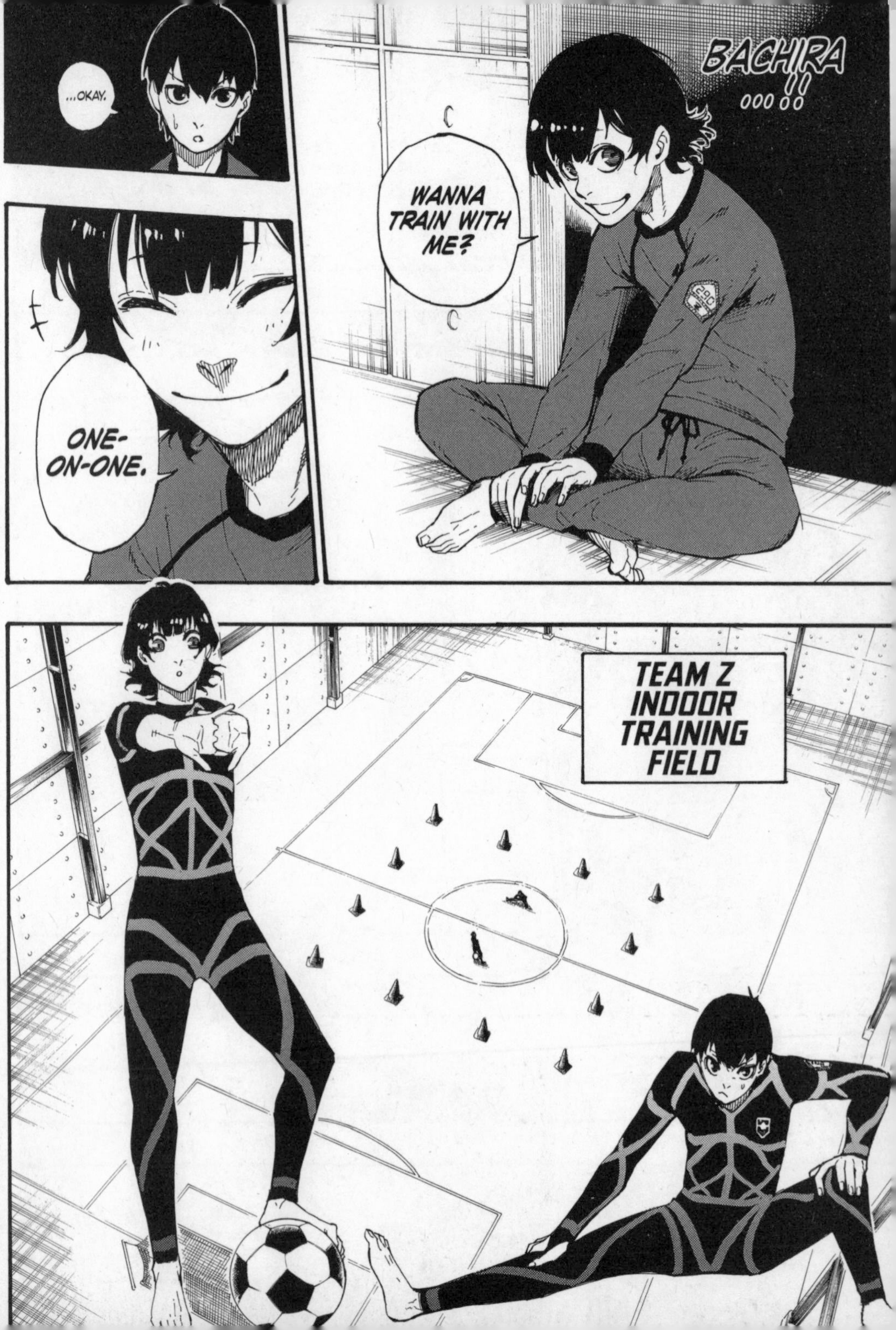
BACHIRA
ooo!!
WANNA TRAIN WITH ME?
...OKAY.
ONE-ON-ONE.
TEAM Z INDOOR TRAINING FIELD

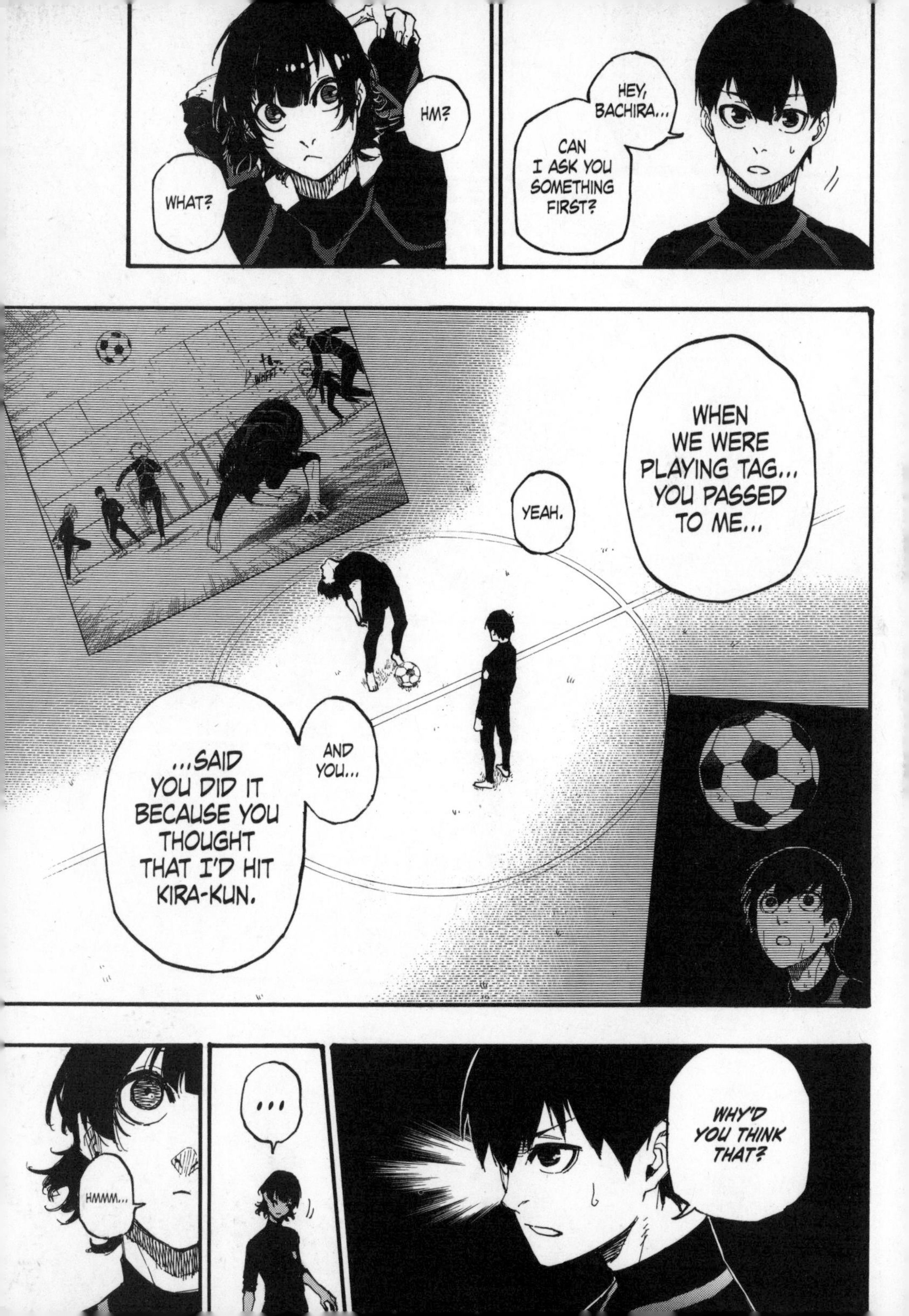
HEY, BACHIRA...
CAN I ASK YOU SOMETHING FIRST?
HM?
WHAT?
WHEN WE WERE PLAYING TAG... YOU PASSED TO ME...
YEAH.
AND YOU...
...SAID YOU DID IT BECAUSE YOU THOUGHT THAT I'D HIT KIRA-KUN.
WHY'D YOU THINK THAT?
...
HMMM...

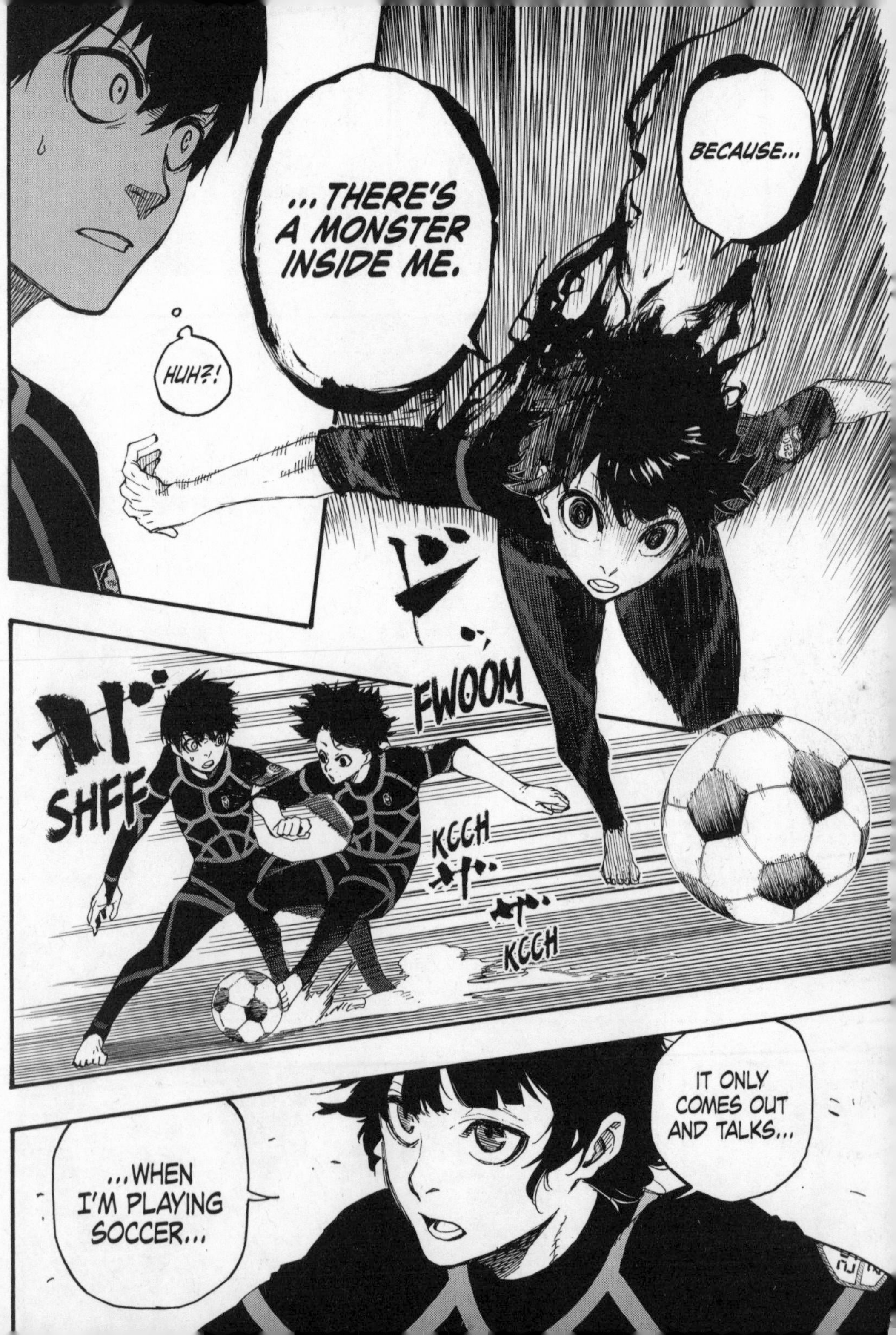
BECAUSE...
...THERE'S A MONSTER INSIDE ME.
HUH?!
FWOOM
KCCH
KCCH
SHFF
IT ONLY COMES OUT AND TALKS...
...WHEN I'M PLAYING SOCCER...

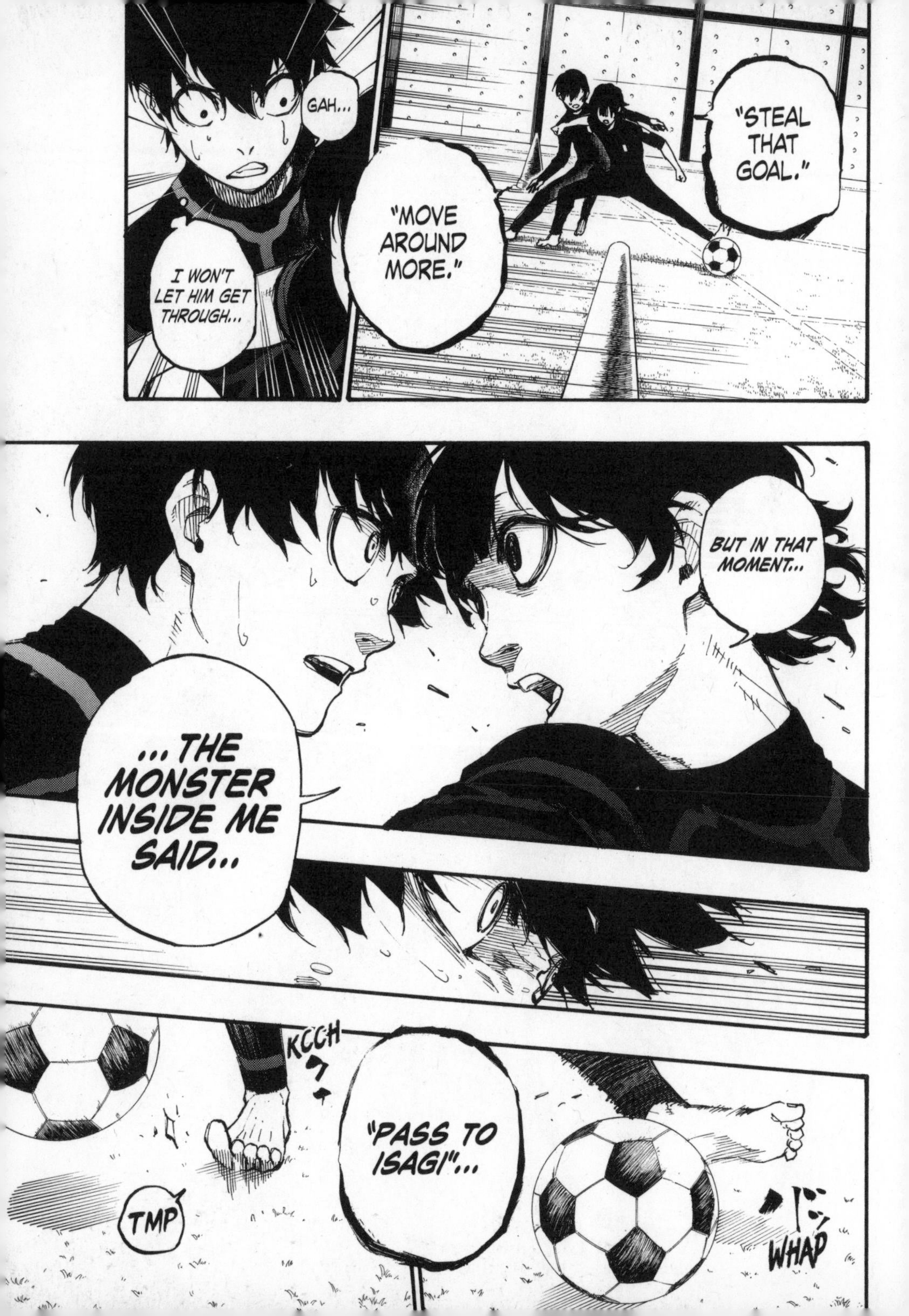
"STEAL THAT GOAL."
"MOVE AROUND MORE."
GAH...
I WON'T LET HIM GET THROUGH...
BUT IN THAT MOMENT...
...THE MONSTER INSIDE ME SAID...
"PASS TO ISAGI"...
WHAP
KCCH
TMP

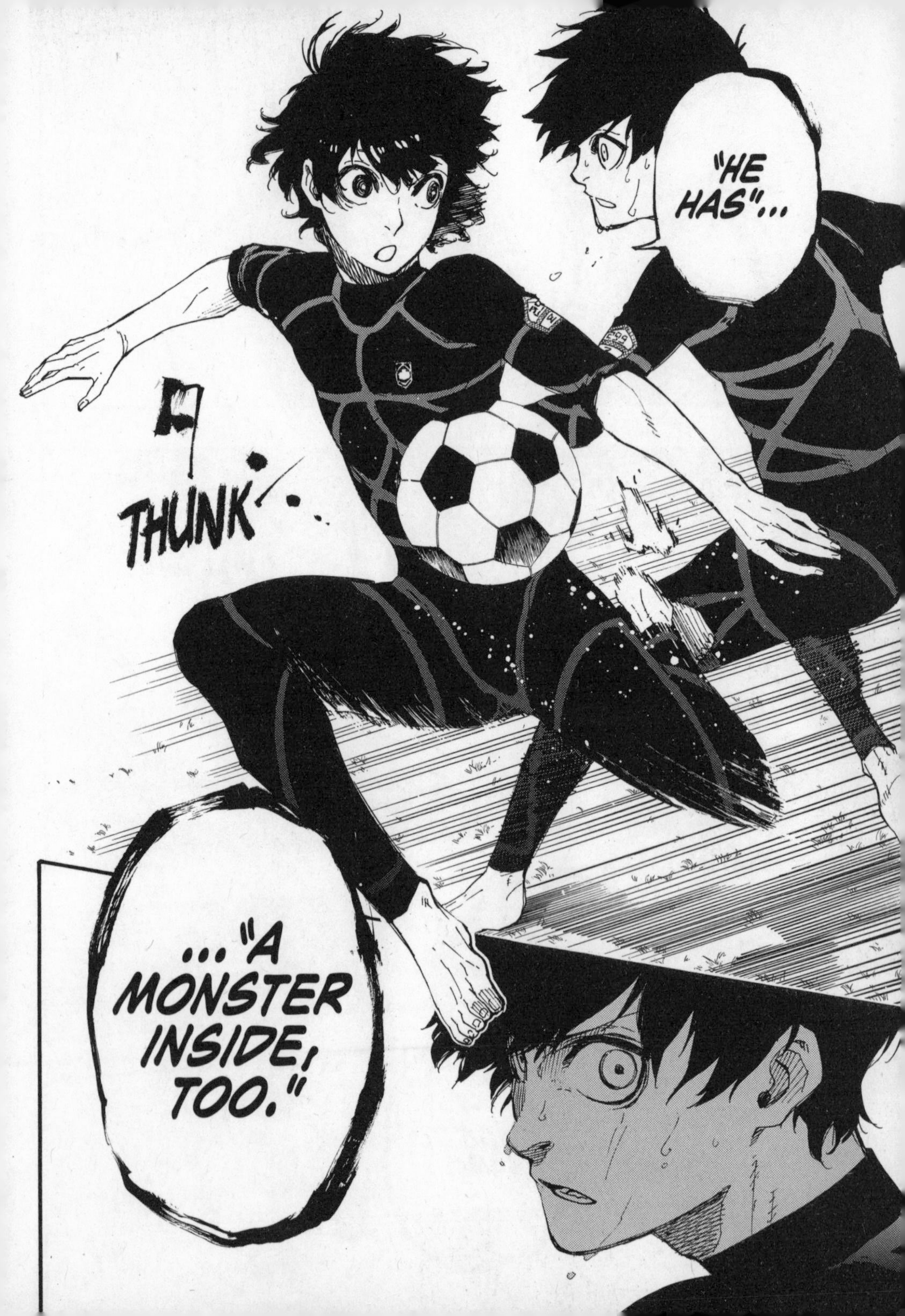
"HE HAS"...
THUNK
..."A MONSTER INSIDE, TOO."

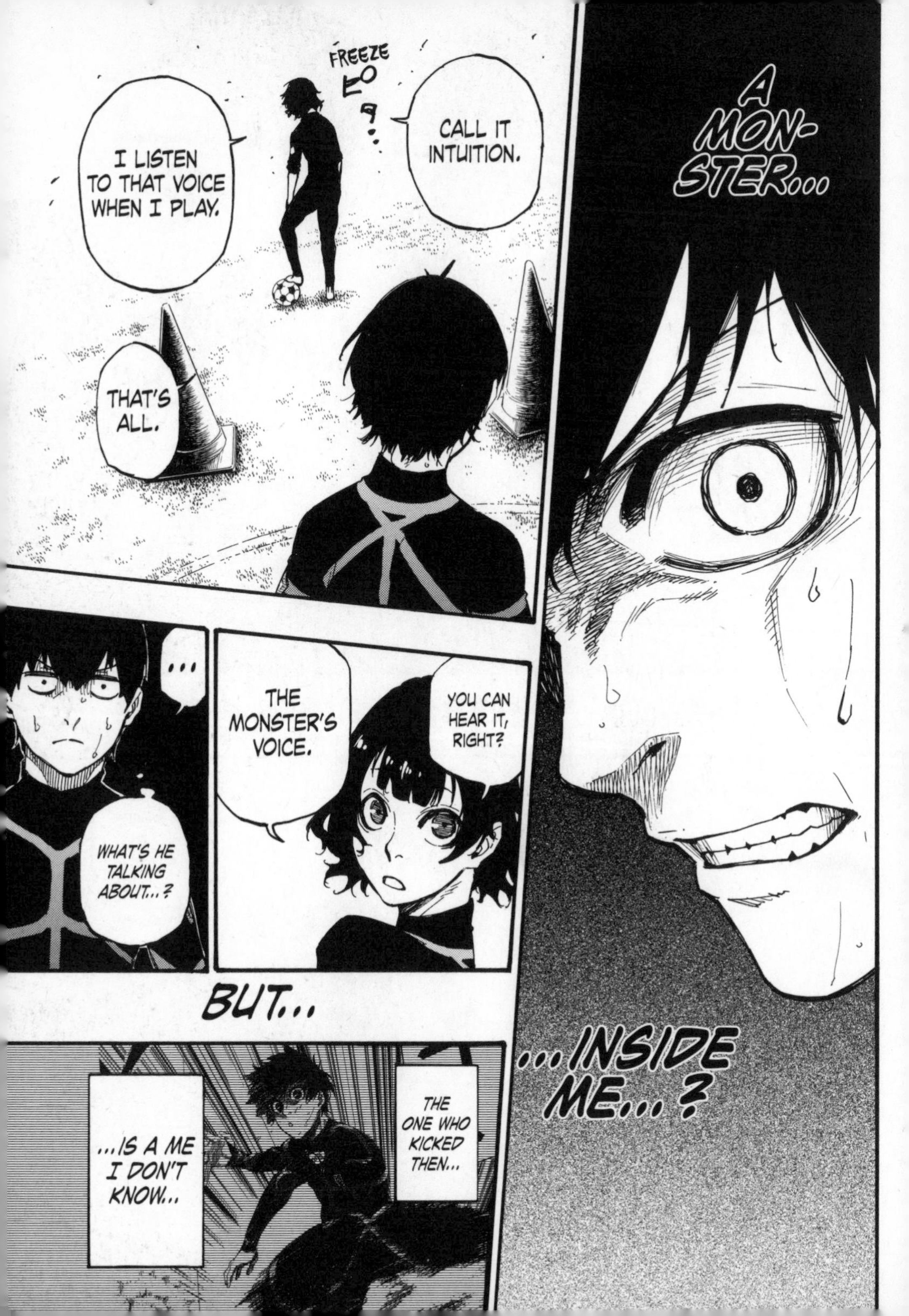

A MON-STER...
...INSIDE ME...?
FREEZE
CALL IT INTUITION.
I LISTEN TO THAT VOICE WHEN I PLAY.
THAT'S ALL.
YOU CAN HEAR IT, RIGHT?
THE MONSTER'S VOICE.
...
WHAT'S HE TALKING ABOUT...?
BUT...
THE ONE WHO KICKED THEN...
...IS A ME I DON'T KNOW...

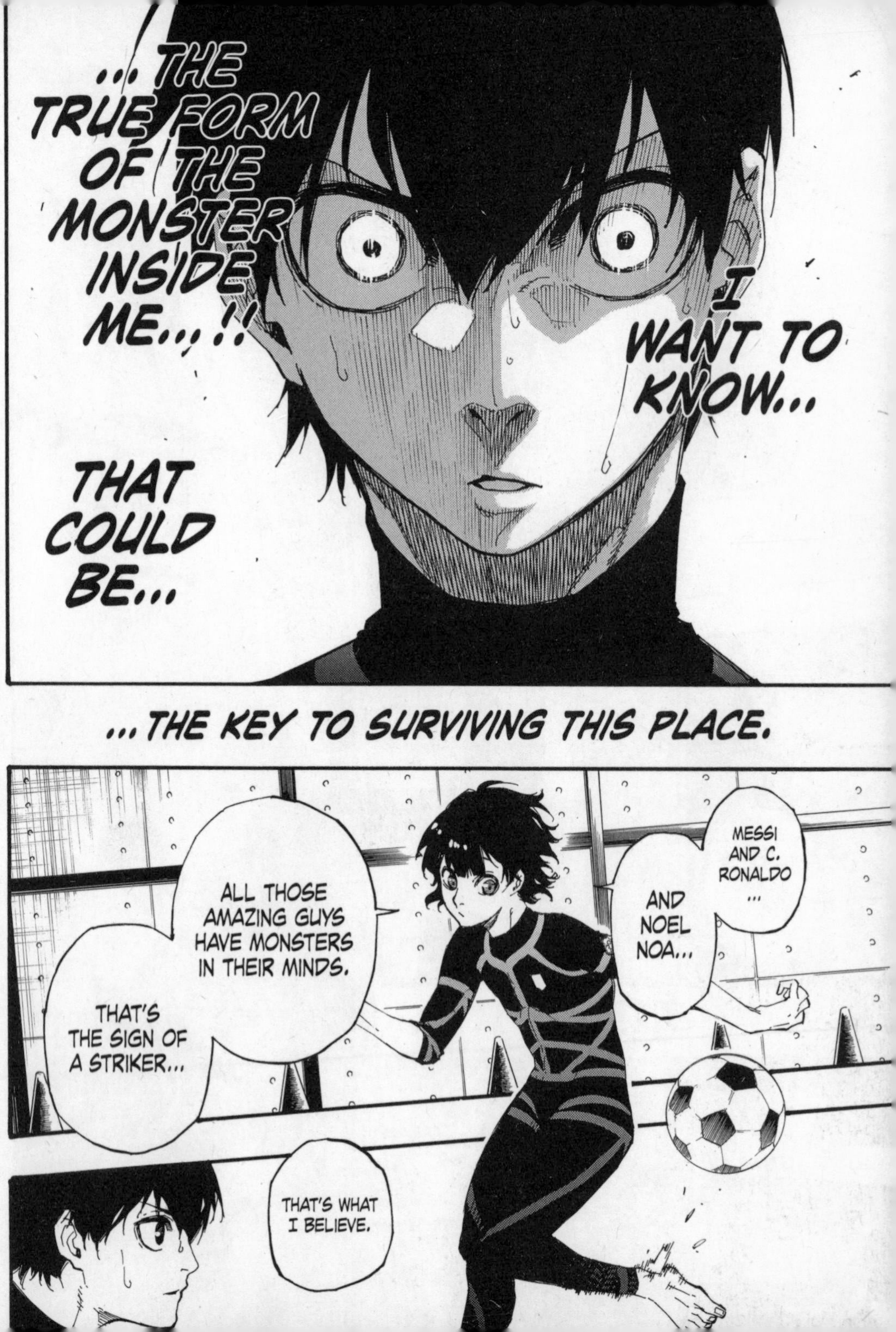
I WANT TO KNOW...
...THE TRUE FORM OF THE MONSTER INSIDE ME...!!
THAT COULD BE...
...THE KEY TO SURVIVING THIS PLACE.
MESSI AND C. RONALDO ...
AND NOEL NOA...
ALL THOSE AMAZING GUYS HAVE MONSTERS IN THEIR MINDS.
THAT'S THE SIGN OF A STRIKER...
THAT'S WHAT I BELIEVE.

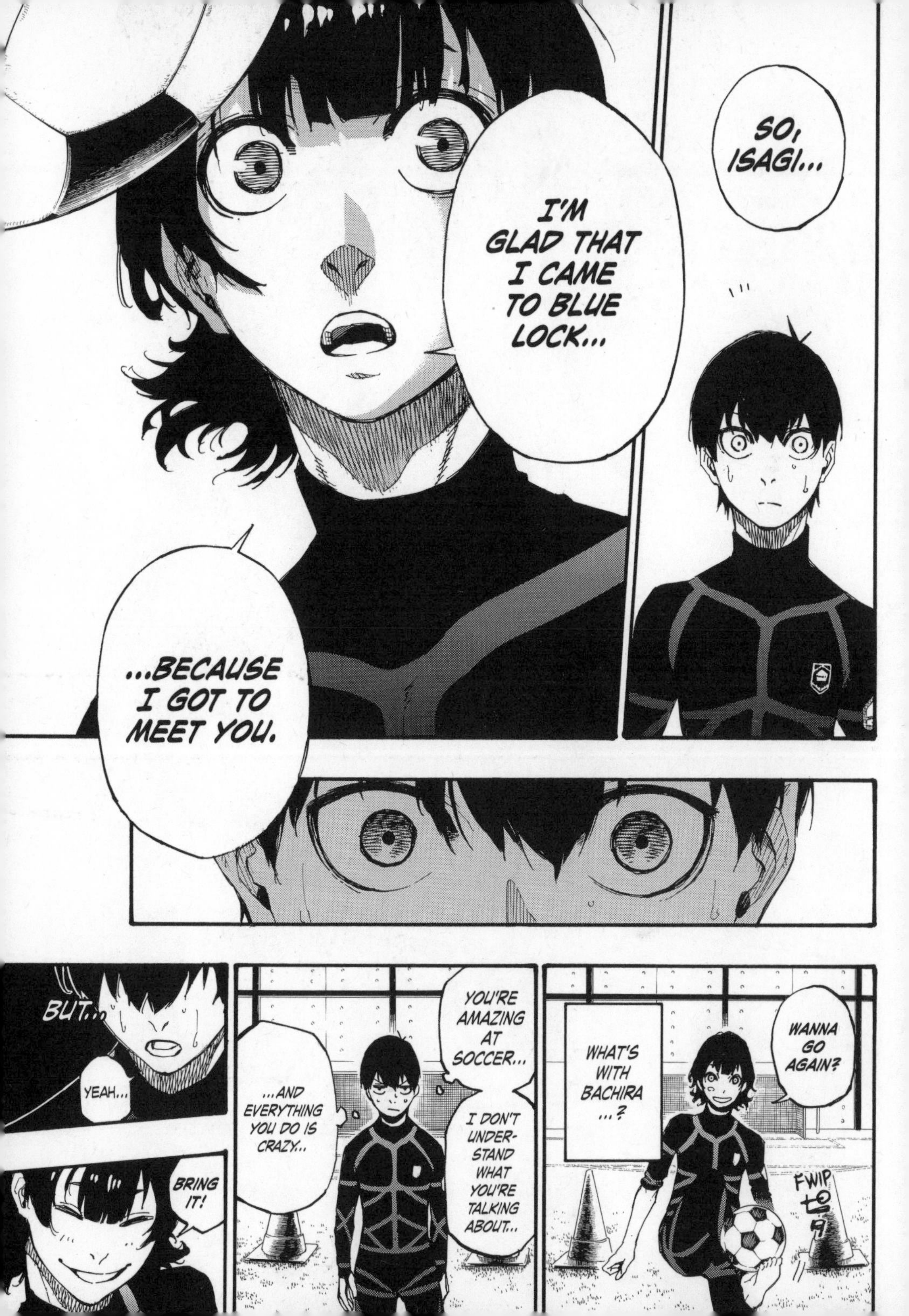
SO, ISAGI...
!!!
I'M GLAD THAT I CAME TO BLUE LOCK...
...BECAUSE I GOT TO MEET YOU.
WANNA GO AGAIN?
WHAT'S WITH BACHIRA...?
FWIP
YOU'RE AMAZING AT SOCCER...
I DON'T UNDER-STAND WHAT YOU'RE TALKING ABOUT...
...AND EVERYTHING YOU DO IS CRAZY...
BUT...
YEAH...
BRING IT!

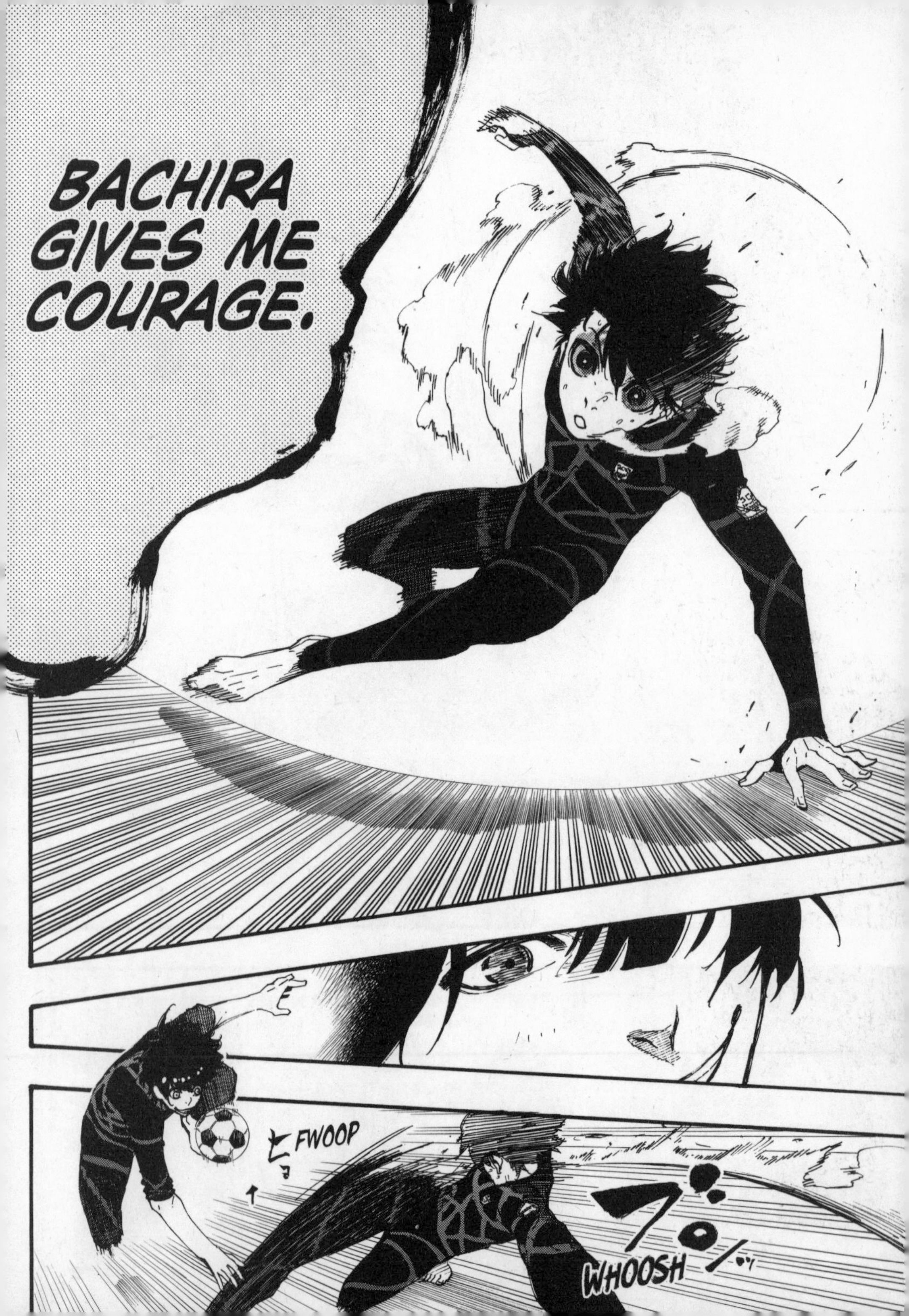
BACHIRA GIVES ME COURAGE.
WHOOSH
FWOOP

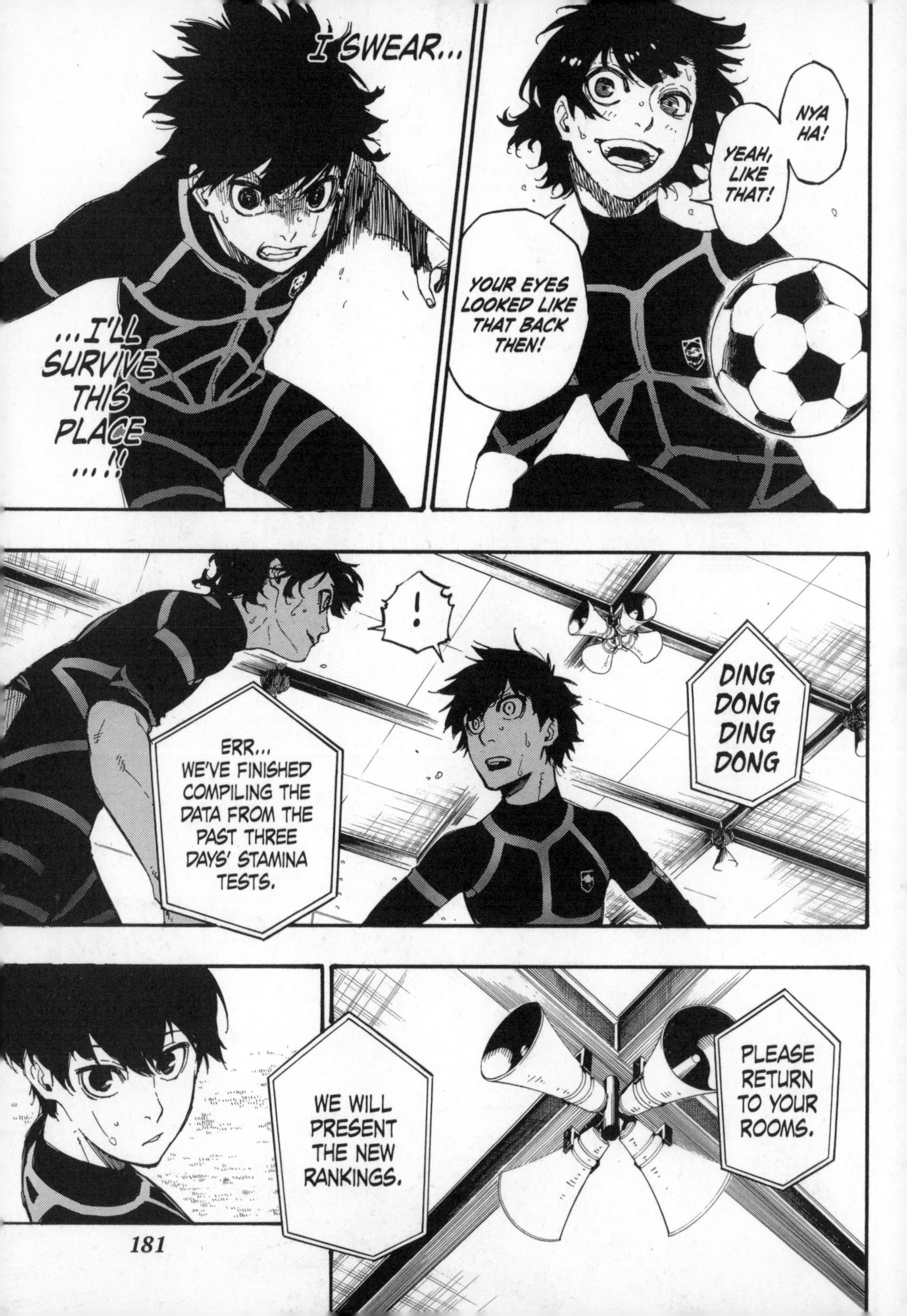
NYA HA!
YEAH, LIKE THAT!
YOUR EYES LOOKED LIKE THAT BACK THEN!
I SWEAR...
...I'LL SURVIVE THIS PLACE ...!!
DING DONG DING DONG
!
ERR... WE'VE FINISHED COMPILING THE DATA FROM THE PAST THREE DAYS' STAMINA TESTS.
PLEASE RETURN TO YOUR ROOMS.
WE WILL PRESENT THE NEW RANKINGS.

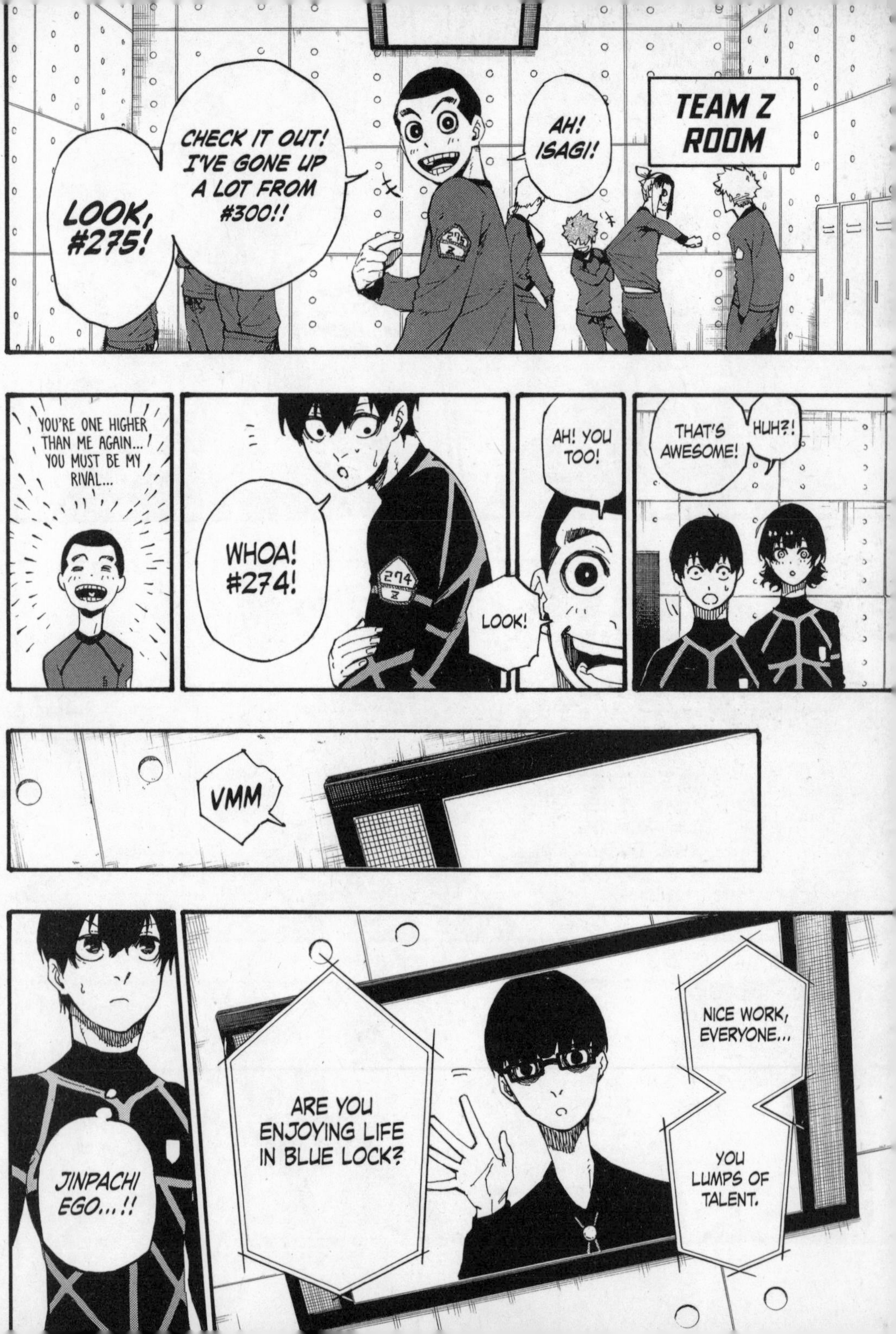
TEAM Z ROOM
AH! ISAGI!
CHECK IT OUT! I'VE GONE UP A LOT FROM #300!!
LOOK, #275!
HUH?!
THAT'S AWESOME!
AH! YOU TOO!
LOOK!
WHOA! #274!
YOU'RE ONE HIGHER THAN ME AGAIN... YOU MUST BE MY RIVAL...
VMM
NICE WORK, EVERYONE...
YOU LUMPS OF TALENT.
ARE YOU ENJOYING LIFE IN BLUE LOCK?
JINPACHI EGO...!!

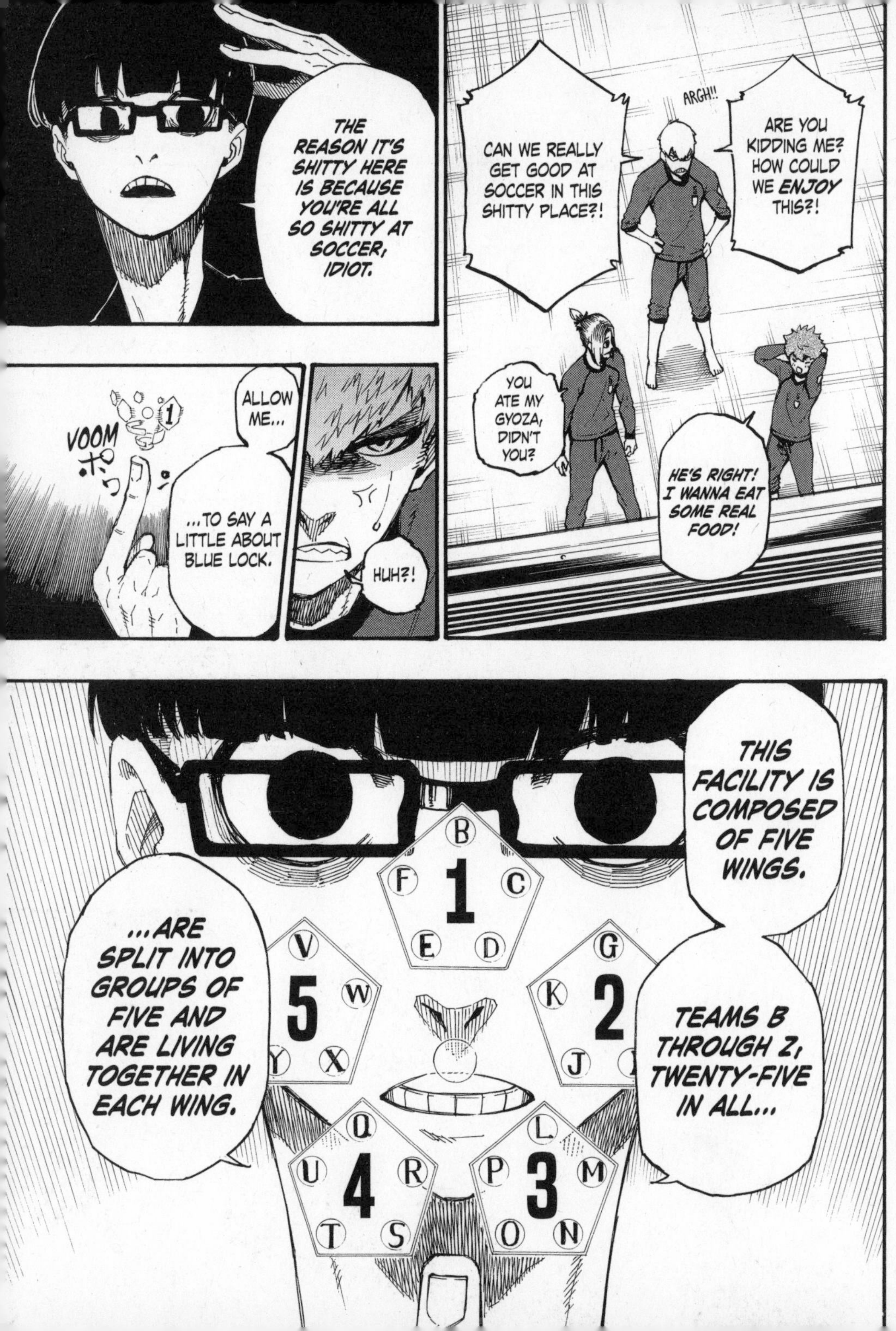

ARE YOU KIDDING ME? HOW COULD WE ENJOY THIS?!
ARGH!!
CAN WE REALLY GET GOOD AT SOCCER IN THIS SHITTY PLACE?!
HE'S RIGHT! I WANNA EAT SOME REAL FOOD!
YOU ATE MY GYOZA, DIDN'T YOU?
THE REASON IT'S SHITTY HERE IS BECAUSE YOU'RE ALL SO SHITTY AT SOCCER, IDIOT.
HUH?!
ALLOW ME...
...TO SAY A LITTLE ABOUT BLUE LOCK.
VOOM
THIS FACILITY IS COMPOSED OF FIVE WINGS.
TEAMS B THROUGH Z, TWENTY-FIVE IN ALL...
...ARE SPLIT INTO GROUPS OF FIVE AND ARE LIVING TOGETHER IN EACH WING.

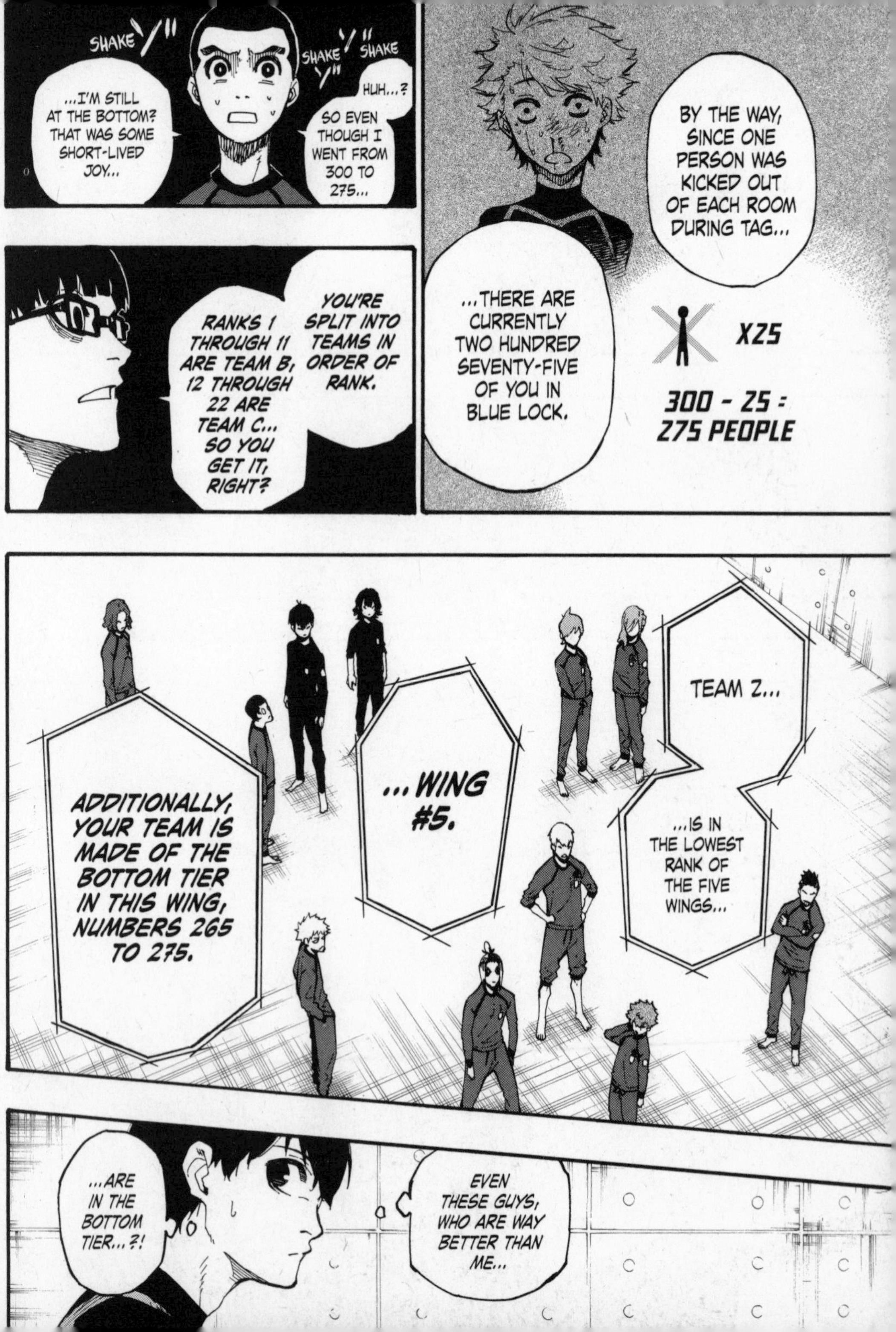
BY THE WAY, SINCE ONE PERSON WAS KICKED OUT OF EACH ROOM DURING TAG...
...THERE ARE CURRENTLY TWO HUNDRED SEVENTY-FIVE OF YOU IN BLUE LOCK.
X25
300 - 25 : 275 PEOPLE
SHAKE
SHAKE
SHAKE
HUH...?
SO EVEN THOUGH I WENT FROM 300 TO 275...
...I'M STILL AT THE BOTTOM? THAT WAS SOME SHORT-LIVED JOY...
YOU'RE SPLIT INTO TEAMS IN ORDER OF RANK.
RANKS 1 THROUGH 11 ARE TEAM B, 12 THROUGH 22 ARE TEAM C... SO YOU GET IT, RIGHT?
TEAM Z...
...IS IN THE LOWEST RANK OF THE FIVE WINGS...
...WING #5.
ADDITIONALLY, YOUR TEAM IS MADE OF THE BOTTOM TIER IN THIS WING, NUMBERS 265 TO 275.
EVEN THESE GUYS, WHO ARE WAY BETTER THAN ME...
...ARE IN THE BOTTOM TIER...?!

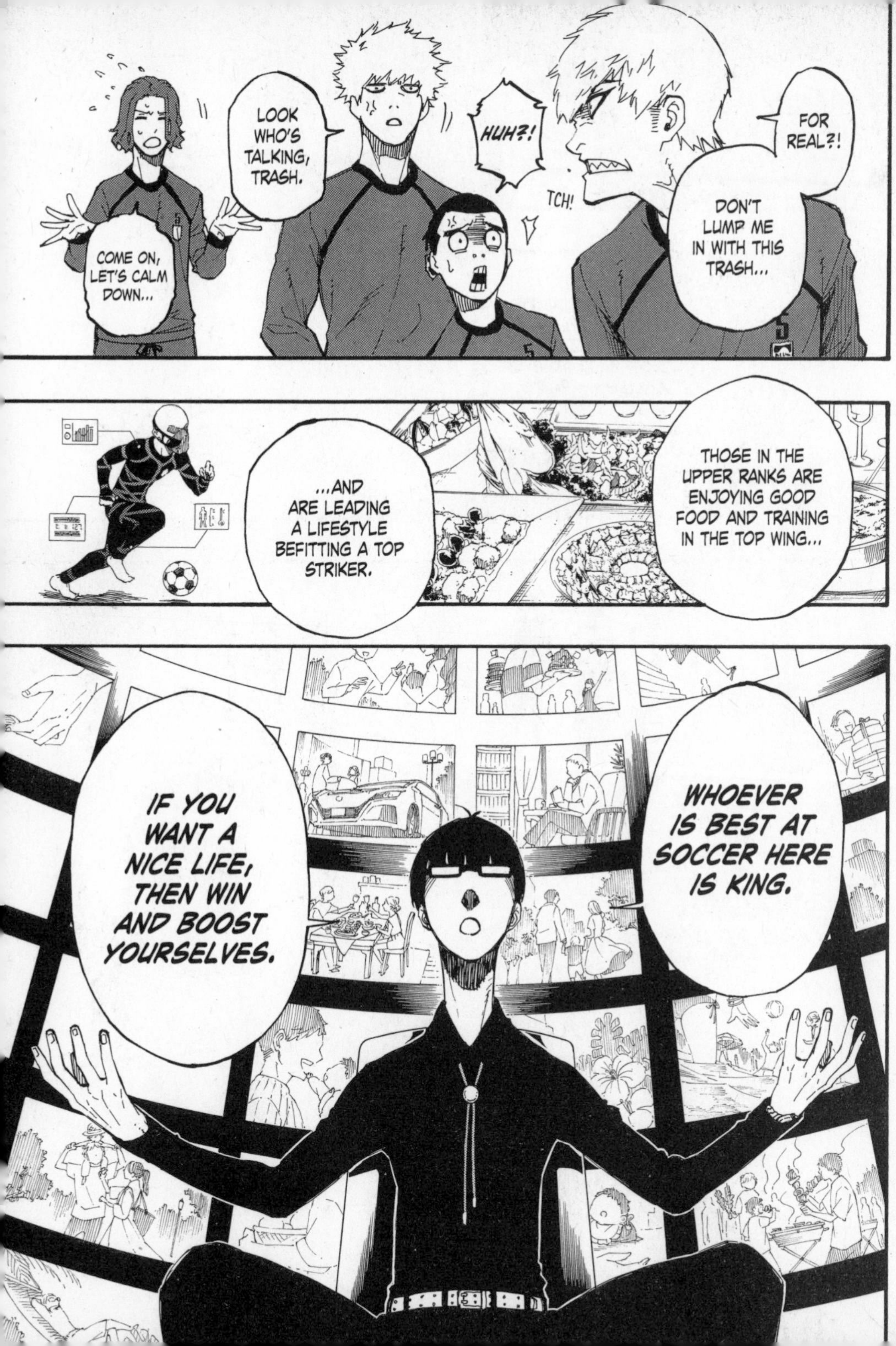
FOR REAL?!
DON'T LUMP ME IN WITH THIS TRASH...
TCH!
HUH?!
LOOK WHO'S TALKING, TRASH.
COME ON, LET'S CALM DOWN...
THOSE IN THE UPPER RANKS ARE ENJOYING GOOD FOOD AND TRAINING IN THE TOP WING...
...AND ARE LEADING A LIFESTYLE BEFITTING A TOP STRIKER.
WHOEVER IS BEST AT SOCCER HERE IS KING.
IF YOU WANT A NICE LIFE, THEN WIN AND BOOST YOURSELVES.

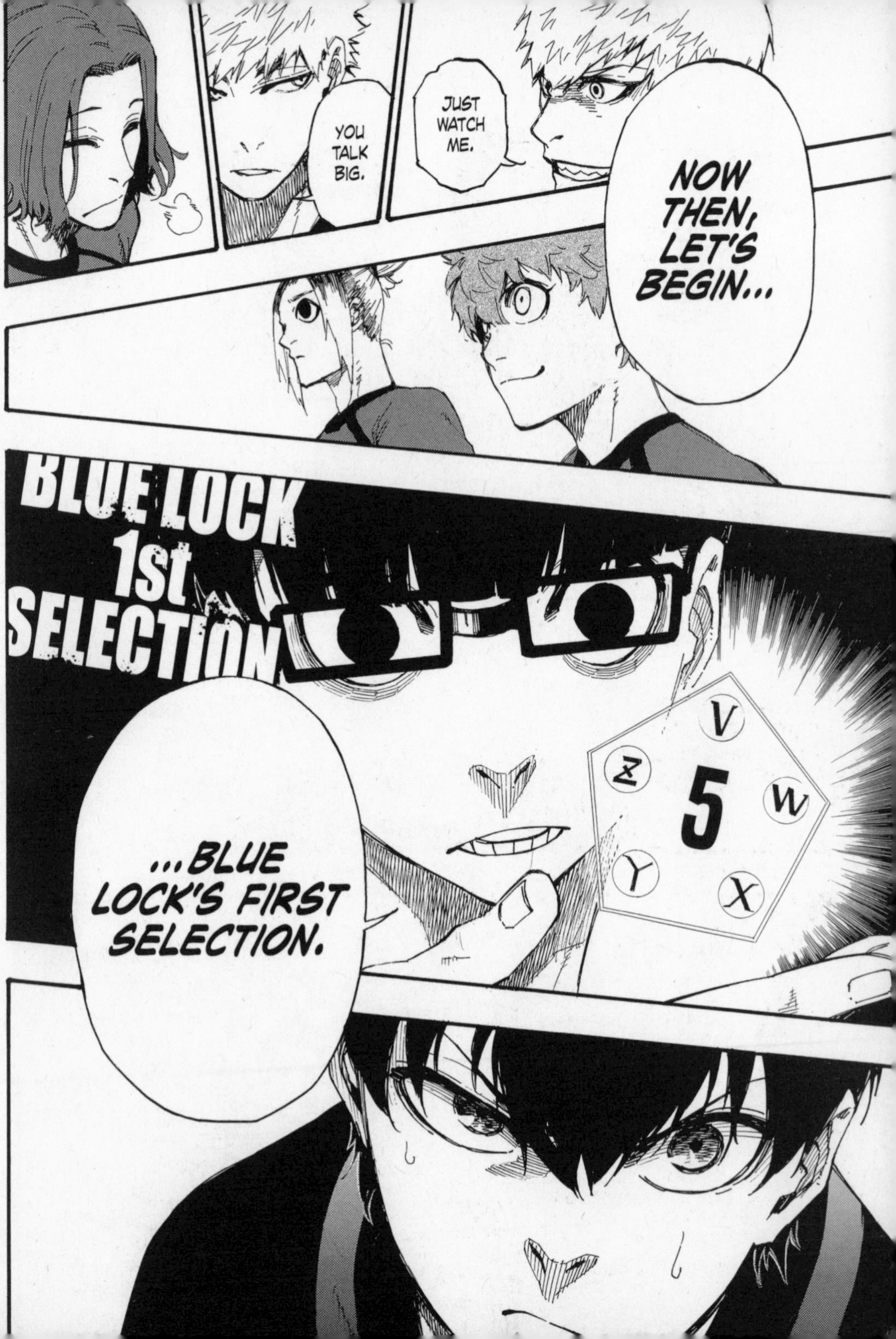
JUST WATCH ME.
YOU TALK BIG.
NOW THEN, LET'S BEGIN...
BLUE LOCK 1st SELECTION
V
W
X
Y
Z
5
...BLUE LOCK'S FIRST SELECTION.

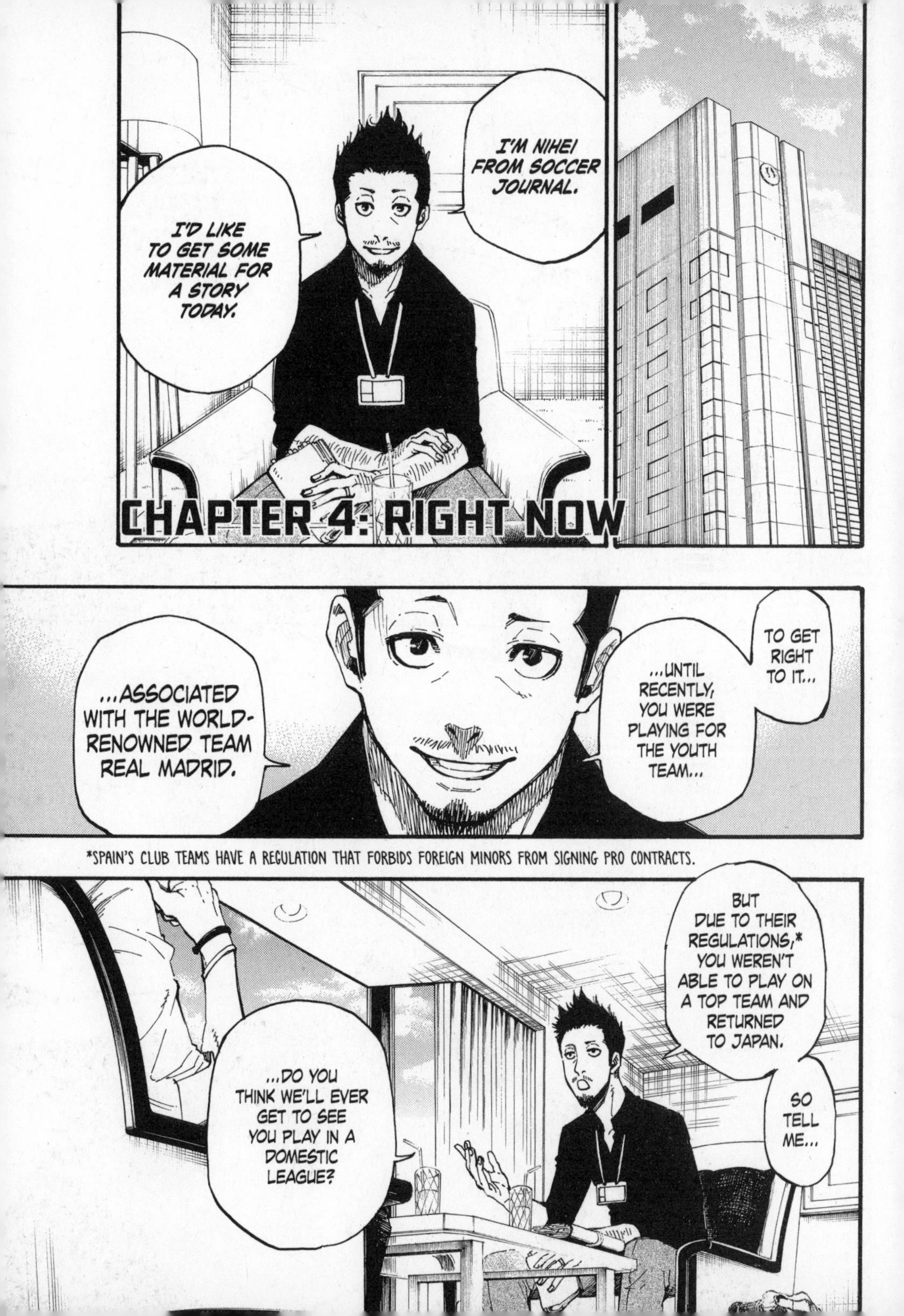
I'M NIHEI FROM SOCCER JOURNAL.
I'D LIKE TO GET SOME MATERIAL FOR A STORY TODAY.
CHAPTER 4: RIGHT NOW
TO GET RIGHT TO IT...
...UNTIL RECENTLY, YOU WERE PLAYING FOR THE YOUTH TEAM...
...ASSOCIATED WITH THE WORLD-RENOWNED TEAM REAL MADRID.
BUT DUE TO THEIR REGULATIONS,* YOU WEREN'T ABLE TO PLAY ON A TOP TEAM AND RETURNED TO JAPAN.
SO TELL ME...
...DO YOU THINK WE'LL EVER GET TO SEE YOU PLAY IN A DOMESTIC LEAGUE?

*SPAIN'S CLUB TEAMS HAVE A REGULATION THAT FORBIDS FOREIGN MINORS FROM SIGNING PRO CONTRACTS.

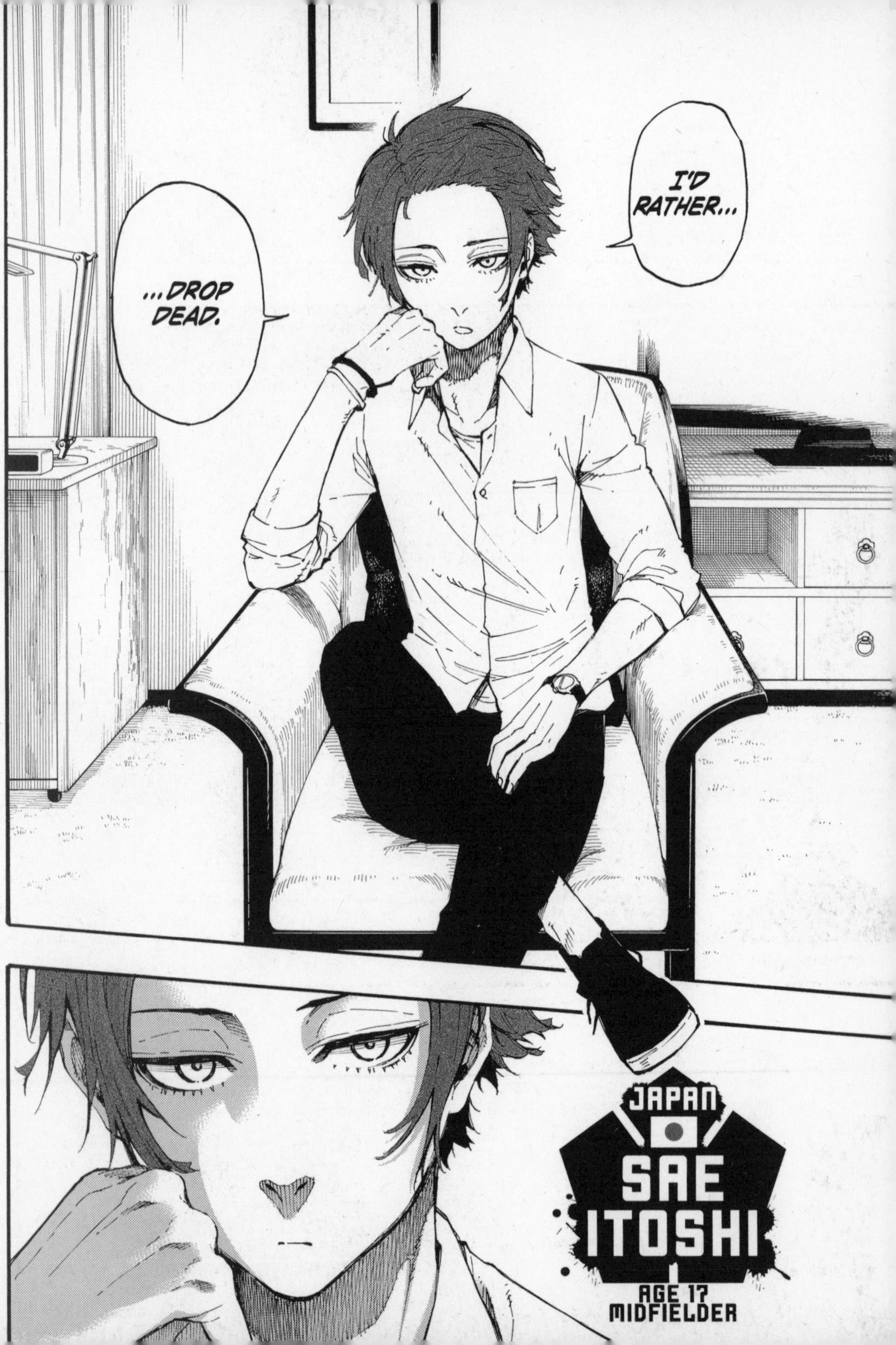
I'D RATHER...
...DROP DEAD.
JAPAN
SAE ITOSHI
AGE 17
MIDFIELDER

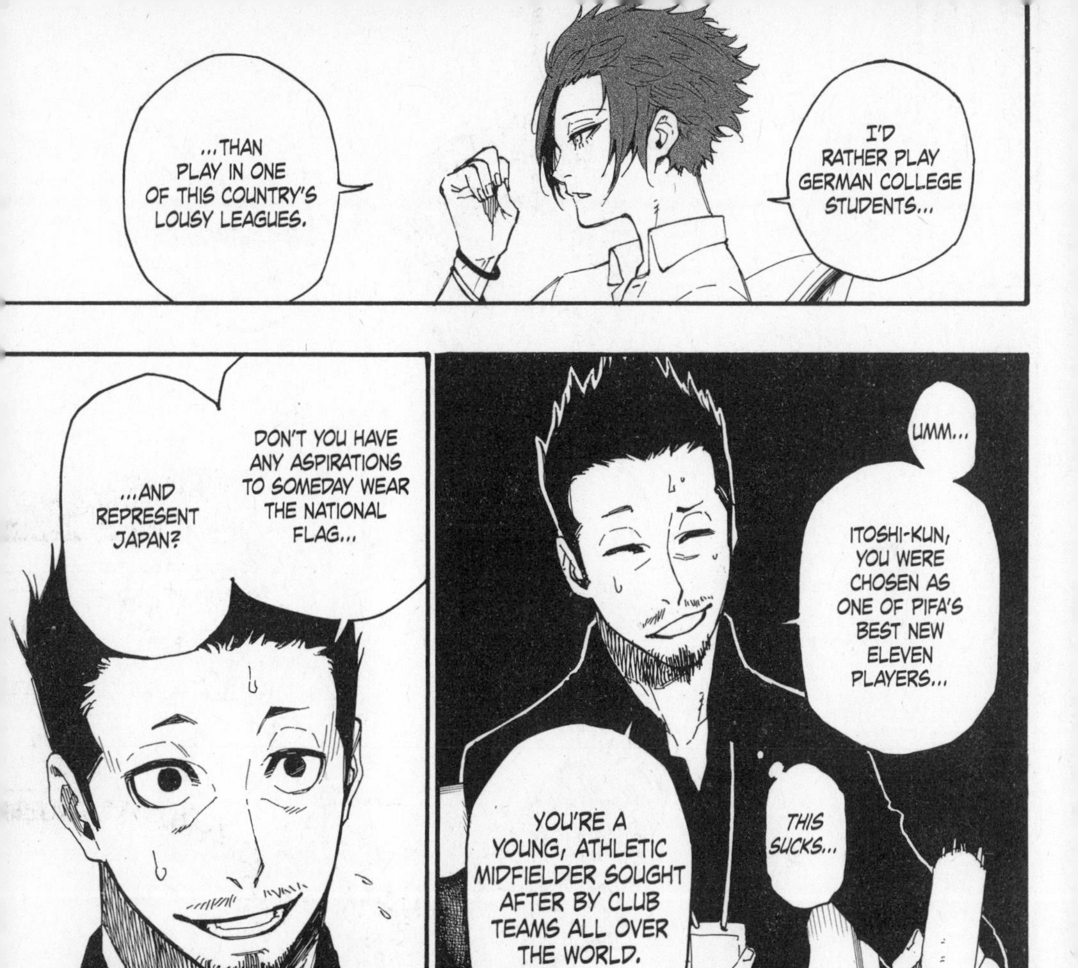
I'D RATHER PLAY GERMAN COLLEGE STUDENTS...
...THAN PLAY IN ONE OF THIS COUNTRY'S LOUSY LEAGUES.
UMM...
ITOSHI-KUN, YOU WERE CHOSEN AS ONE OF PIFA'S BEST NEW ELEVEN PLAYERS...
THIS SUCKS...
YOU'RE A YOUNG, ATHLETIC MIDFIELDER SOUGHT AFTER BY CLUB TEAMS ALL OVER THE WORLD.
DON'T YOU HAVE ANY ASPIRATIONS TO SOMEDAY WEAR THE NATIONAL FLAG...
...AND REPRESENT JAPAN?

*CHAMPIONS LEAGUE – THE PINNACLE OF SOCCER TOURNAMENTS, IN WHICH EUROPE'S CLUB TEAMS BATTLE EACH OTHER.

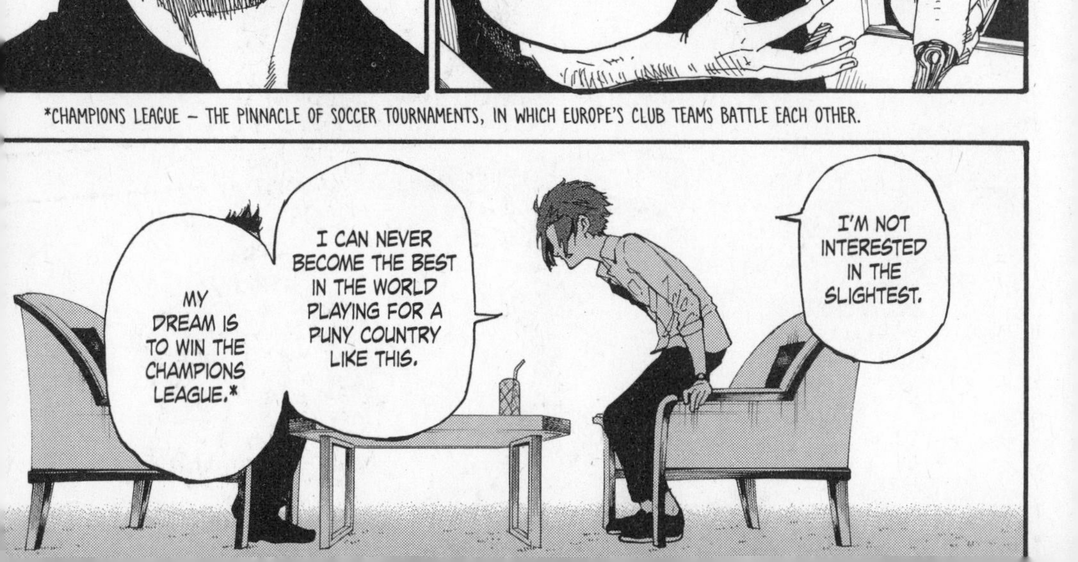
I'M NOT INTERESTED IN THE SLIGHTEST.
I CAN NEVER BECOME THE BEST IN THE WORLD PLAYING FOR A PUNY COUNTRY LIKE THIS.
MY DREAM IS TO WIN THE CHAMPIONS LEAGUE.*

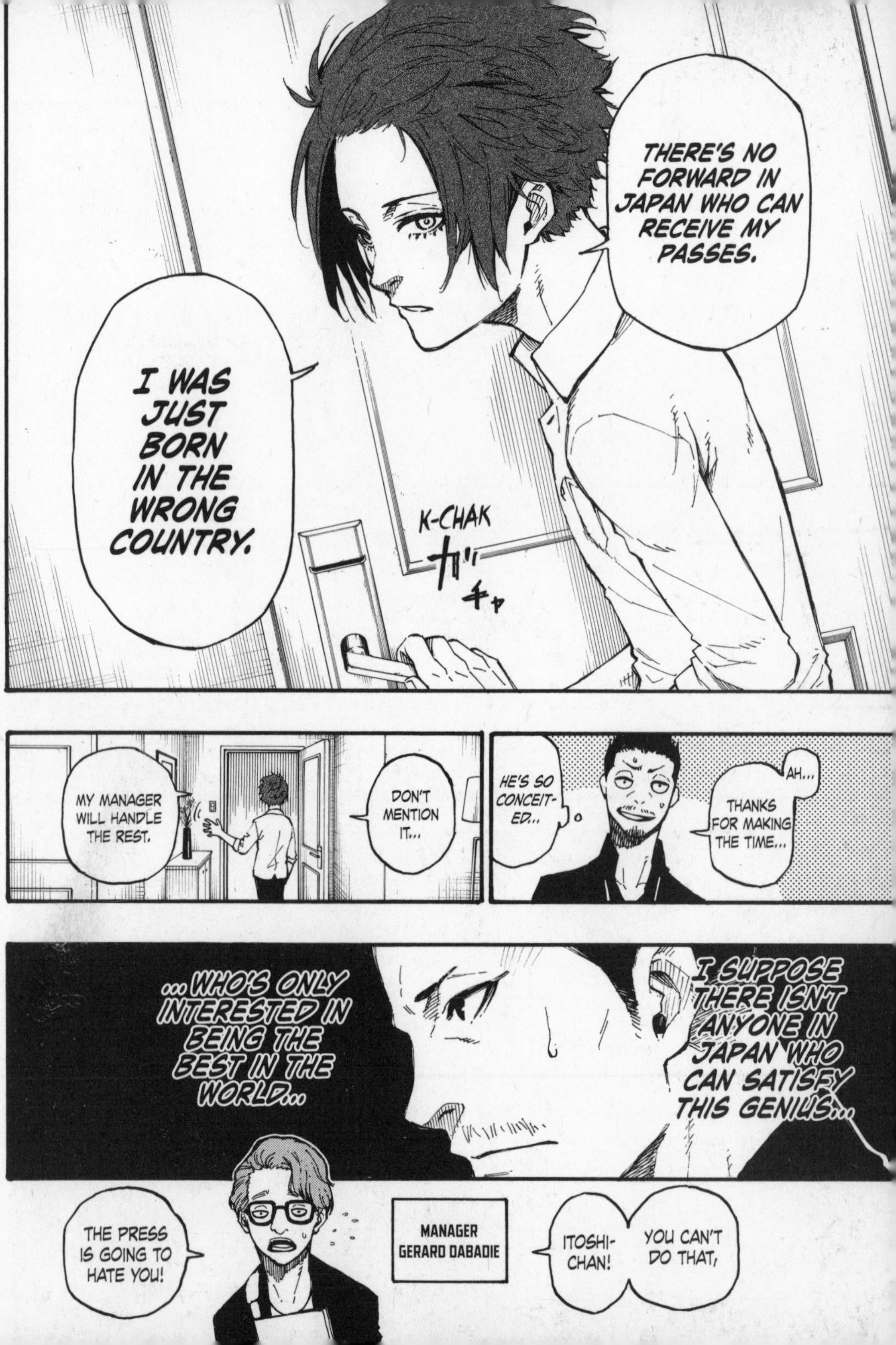
THERE'S NO FORWARD IN JAPAN WHO CAN RECEIVE MY PASSES.
I WAS JUST BORN IN THE WRONG COUNTRY.
K-CHAK
ガチャ
AH... THANKS FOR MAKING THE TIME...
HE'S SO CONCEIT-ED...
DON'T MENTION IT...
MY MANAGER WILL HANDLE THE REST.
I SUPPOSE THERE ISN'T ANYONE IN JAPAN WHO CAN SATISFY THIS GENIUS...
...WHO'S ONLY INTERESTED IN BEING THE BEST IN THE WORLD...
YOU CAN'T DO THAT,
ITOSHI-CHAN!
MANAGER GERARD DABADIE
THE PRESS IS GOING TO HATE YOU!

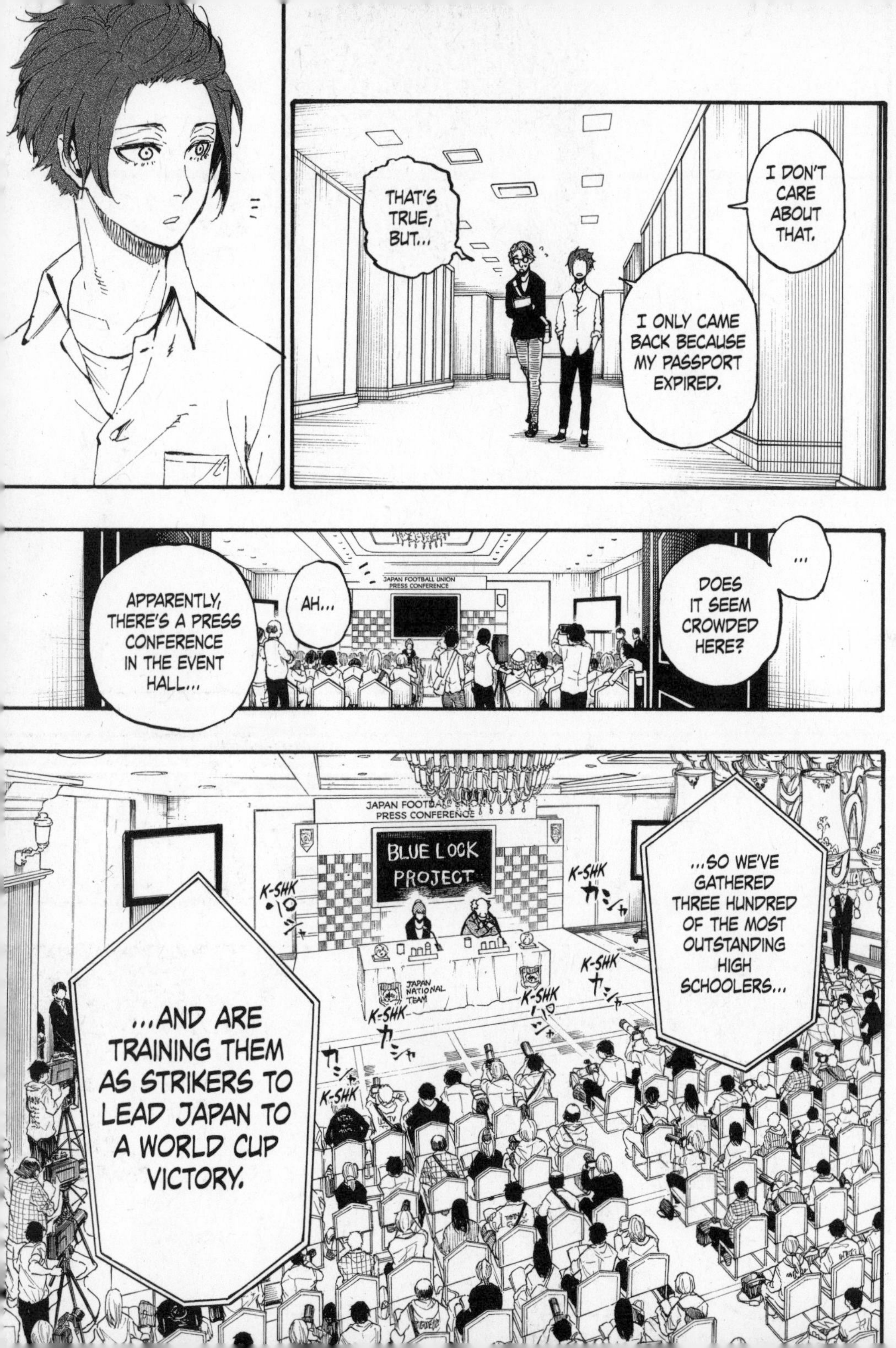
I DON'T CARE ABOUT THAT.
I ONLY CAME BACK BECAUSE MY PASSPORT EXPIRED.
THAT'S TRUE, BUT...
...
DOES IT SEEM CROWDED HERE?
JAPAN FOOTBALL UNION PRESS CONFERENCE
AH...
APPARENTLY, THERE'S A PRESS CONFERENCE IN THE EVENT HALL...
PRESS CONFERENCE
BLUE LOCK PROJECT
...SO WE'VE GATHERED THREE HUNDRED OF THE MOST OUTSTANDING HIGH SCHOOLERS...
K-SHK
K-SHK
K-SHK
JAPAN NATIONAL TEAM
K-SHK
K-SHK
K-SHK
...AND ARE TRAINING THEM AS STRIKERS TO LEAD JAPAN TO A WORLD CUP VICTORY.

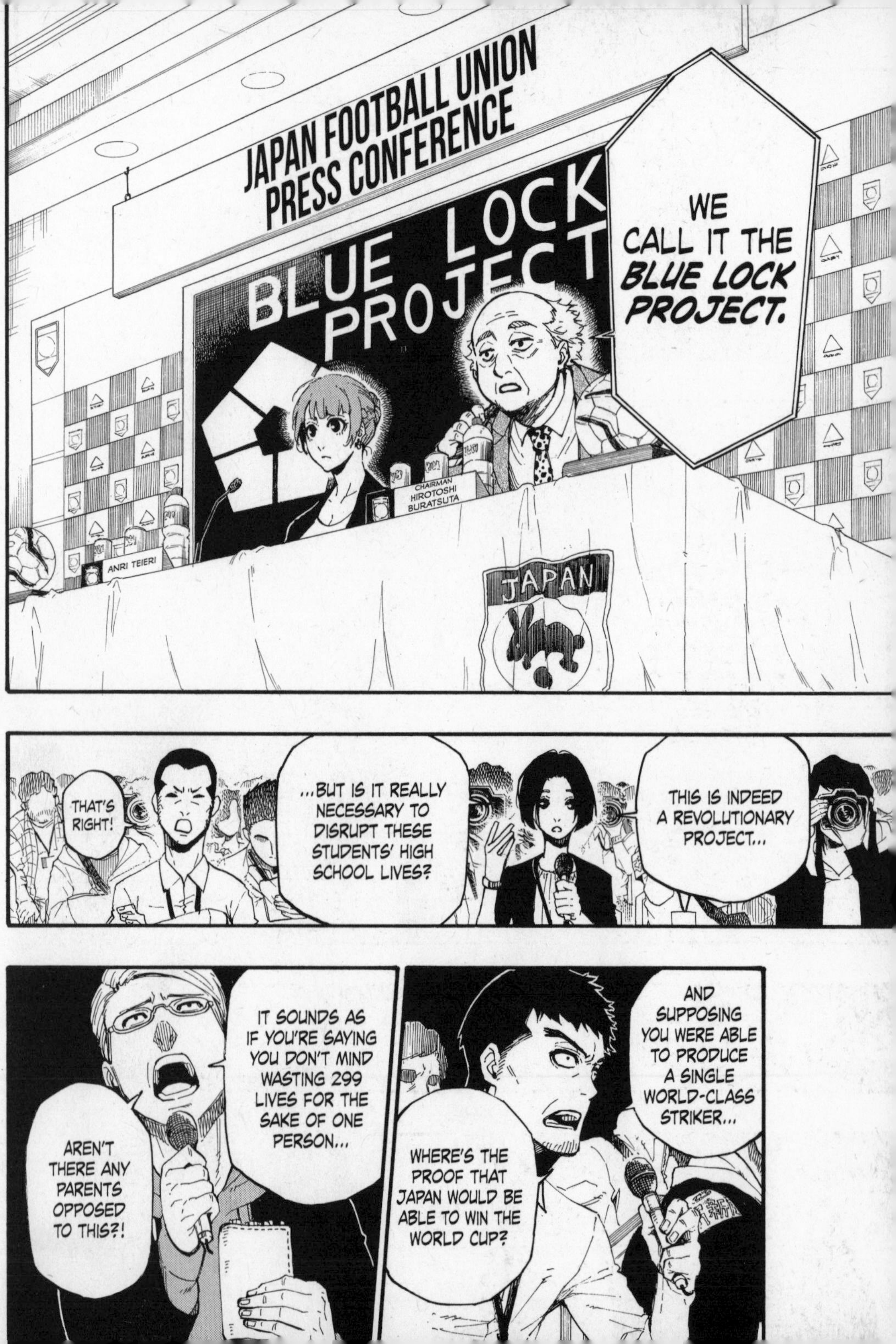
JAPAN FOOTBALL UNION PRESS CONFERENCE
BLUE LOCK PROJECT
WE CALL IT THE *BLUE LOCK PROJECT.*
CHAIRMAN HIROTOSHI BURATSUTA
ANRI TEIERI
JAPAN
THIS IS INDEED A REVOLUTIONARY PROJECT...
...BUT IS IT REALLY NECESSARY TO DISRUPT THESE STUDENTS' HIGH SCHOOL LIVES?
THAT'S RIGHT!
AND SUPPOSING YOU WERE ABLE TO PRODUCE A SINGLE WORLD-CLASS STRIKER...
WHERE'S THE PROOF THAT JAPAN WOULD BE ABLE TO WIN THE WORLD CUP?
IT SOUNDS AS IF YOU'RE SAYING YOU DON'T MIND WASTING 299 LIVES FOR THE SAKE OF ONE PERSON...
AREN'T THERE ANY PARENTS OPPOSED TO THIS?!

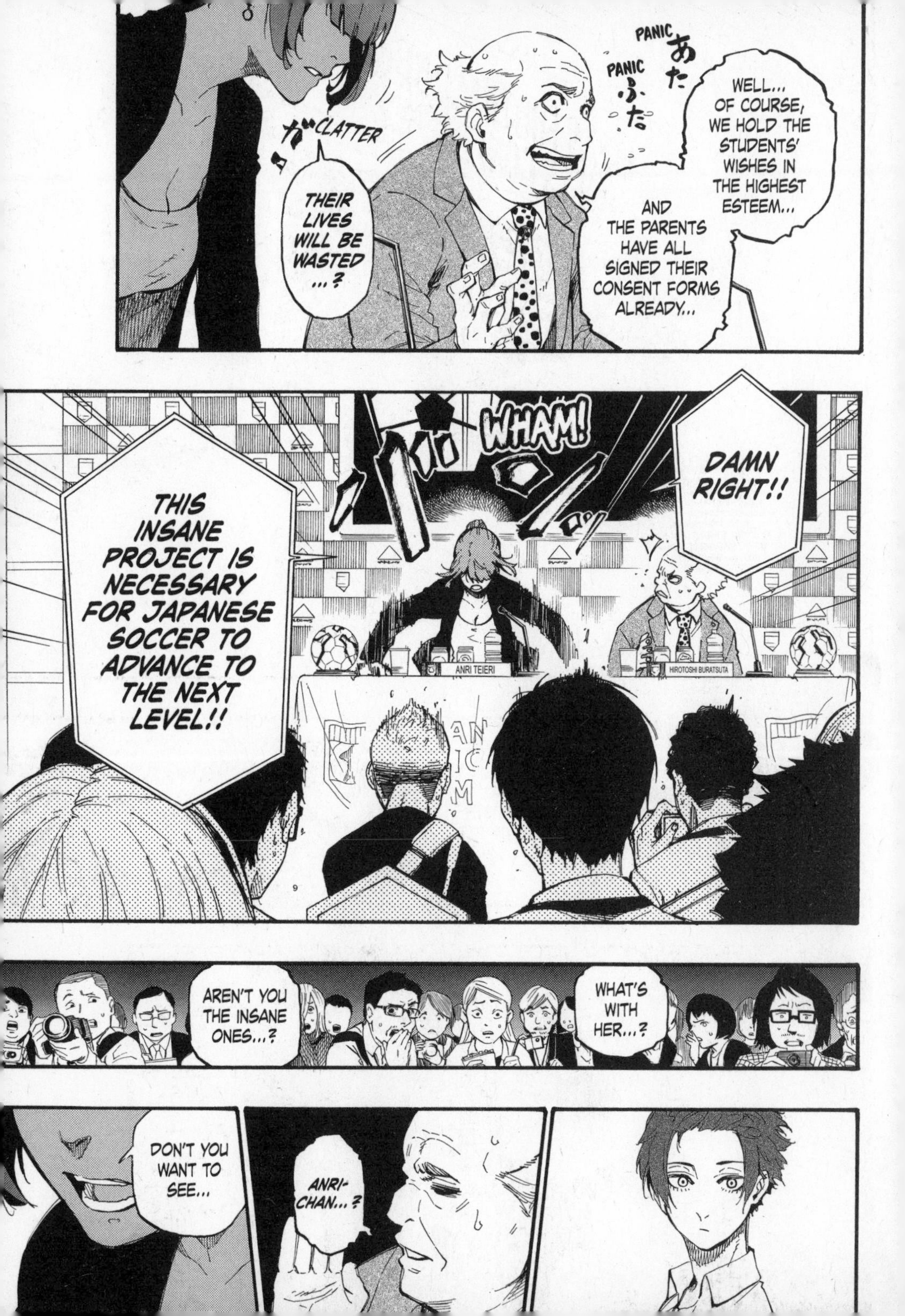
PANIC あた
PANIC ふた
WELL... OF COURSE, WE HOLD THE STUDENTS' WISHES IN THE HIGHEST ESTEEM...
AND THE PARENTS HAVE ALL SIGNED THEIR CONSENT FORMS ALREADY...
THEIR LIVES WILL BE WASTED ...?
ガ CLATTER
DAMN RIGHT!!
WHAM!
THIS INSANE PROJECT IS NECESSARY FOR JAPANESE SOCCER TO ADVANCE TO THE NEXT LEVEL!!
HIROTOSHI BURATSUTA
ANRI TEIERI
WHAT'S WITH HER...?
AREN'T YOU THE INSANE ONES...?
ANRI-CHAN...?
DON'T YOU WANT TO SEE...

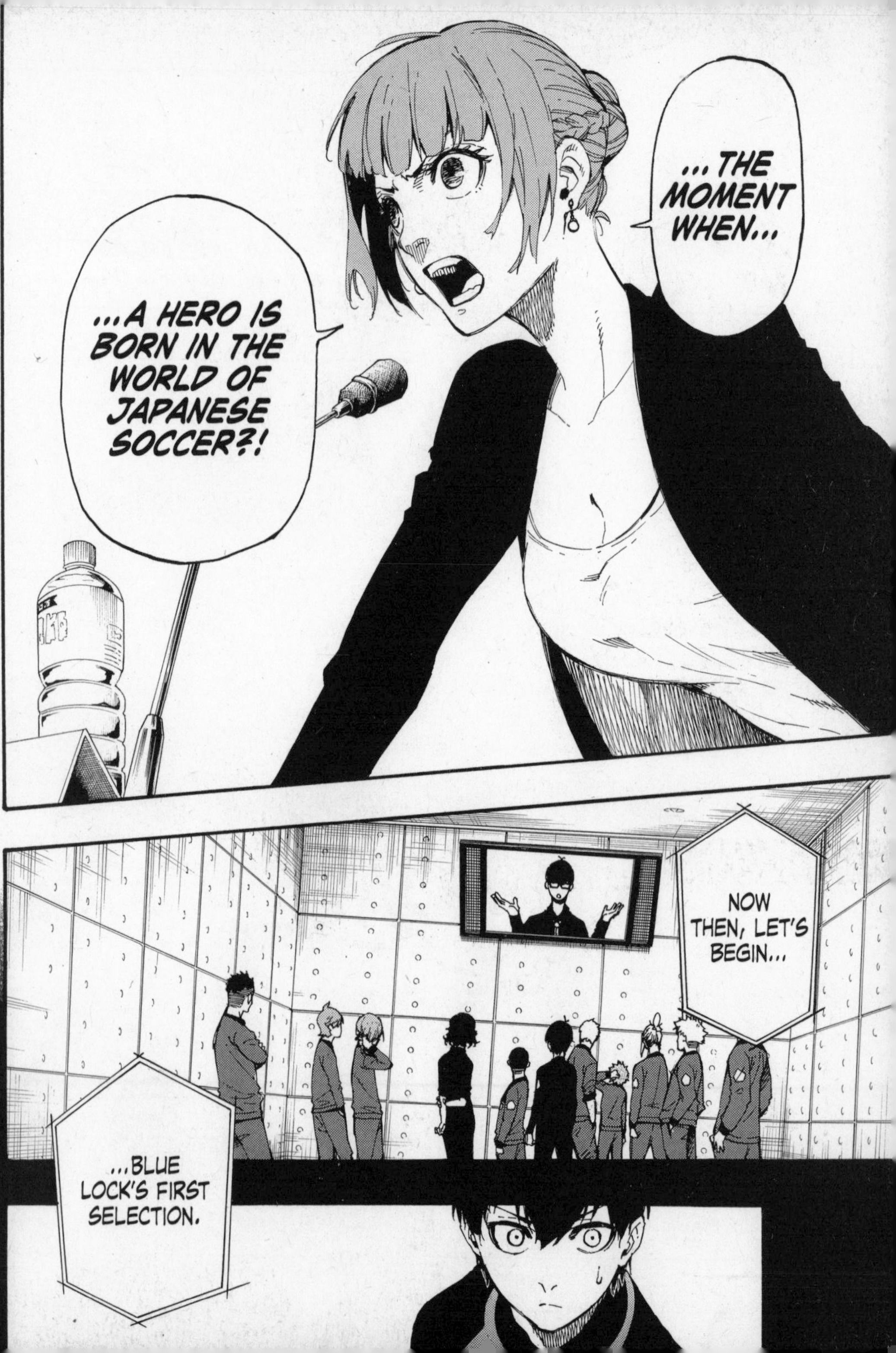
...THE MOMENT WHEN...
...A HERO IS BORN IN THE WORLD OF JAPANESE SOCCER?!
NOW THEN, LET'S BEGIN...
...BLUE LOCK'S FIRST SELECTION.

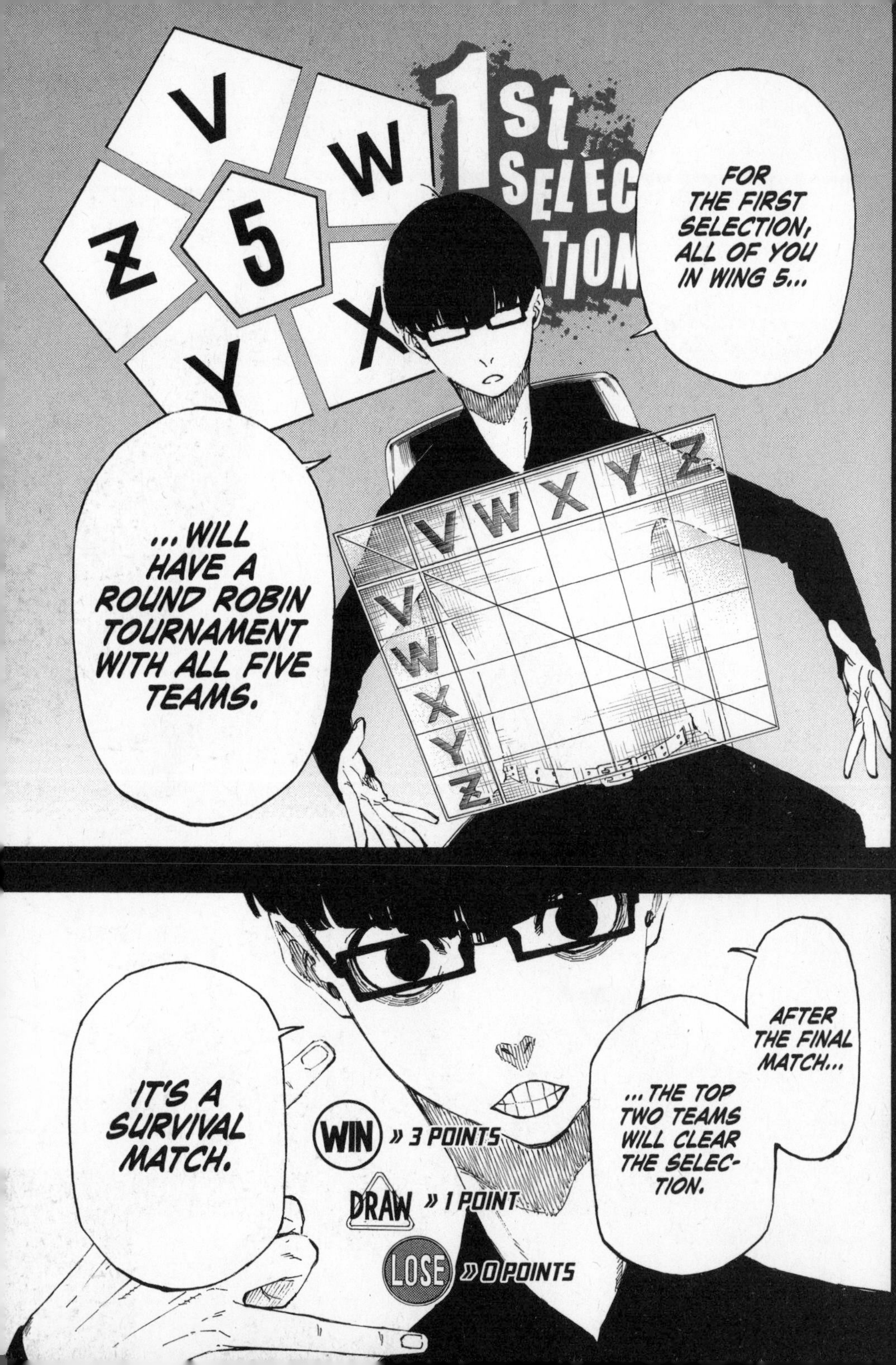
1st SELECTION
FOR THE FIRST SELECTION, ALL OF YOU IN WING 5...
...WILL HAVE A ROUND ROBIN TOURNAMENT WITH ALL FIVE TEAMS.
V W X Y Z
AFTER THE FINAL MATCH...
...THE TOP TWO TEAMS WILL CLEAR THE SELECTION.
IT'S A SURVIVAL MATCH.
WIN » 3 POINTS
DRAW » 1 POINT
LOSE » 0 POINTS

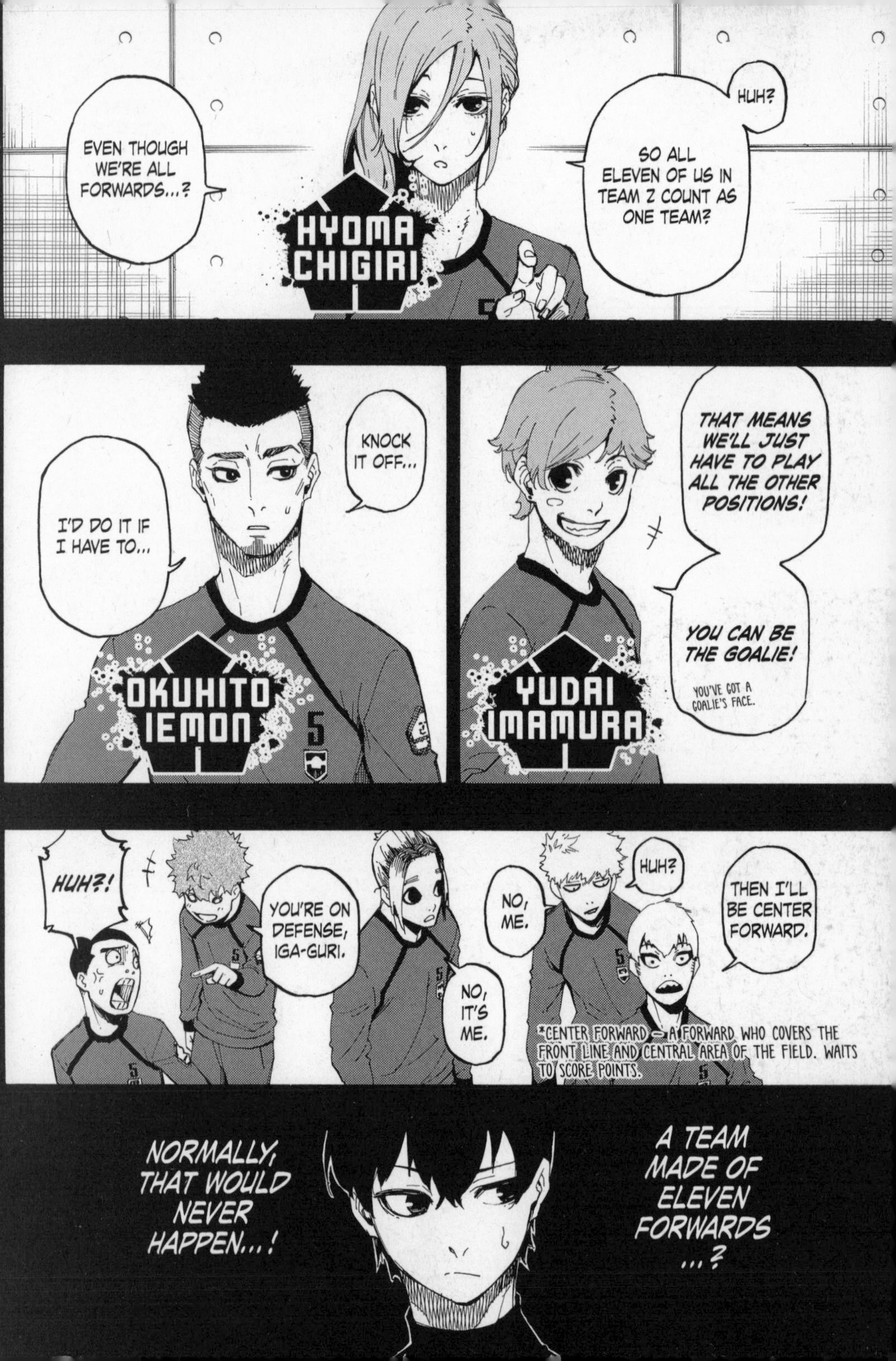
HUH?
SO ALL ELEVEN OF US IN TEAM Z COUNT AS ONE TEAM?
EVEN THOUGH WE'RE ALL FORWARDS...?
HYOMA CHIGIRI
THAT MEANS WE'LL JUST HAVE TO PLAY ALL THE OTHER POSITIONS!
YOU CAN BE THE GOALIE!
YOU'VE GOT A GOALIE'S FACE.
YUDAI IMAMURA
KNOCK IT OFF...
I'D DO IT IF I HAVE TO...
OKUHITO IEMON
THEN I'LL BE CENTER FORWARD.
HUH?
NO, ME.
NO, IT'S ME.
YOU'RE ON DEFENSE, IGA-GURI.
HUH?!
*CENTER FORWARD – A FORWARD WHO COVERS THE FRONT LINE AND CENTRAL AREA OF THE FIELD. WAITS TO SCORE POINTS.
A TEAM MADE OF ELEVEN FORWARDS ...?
NORMALLY, THAT WOULD NEVER HAPPEN...!

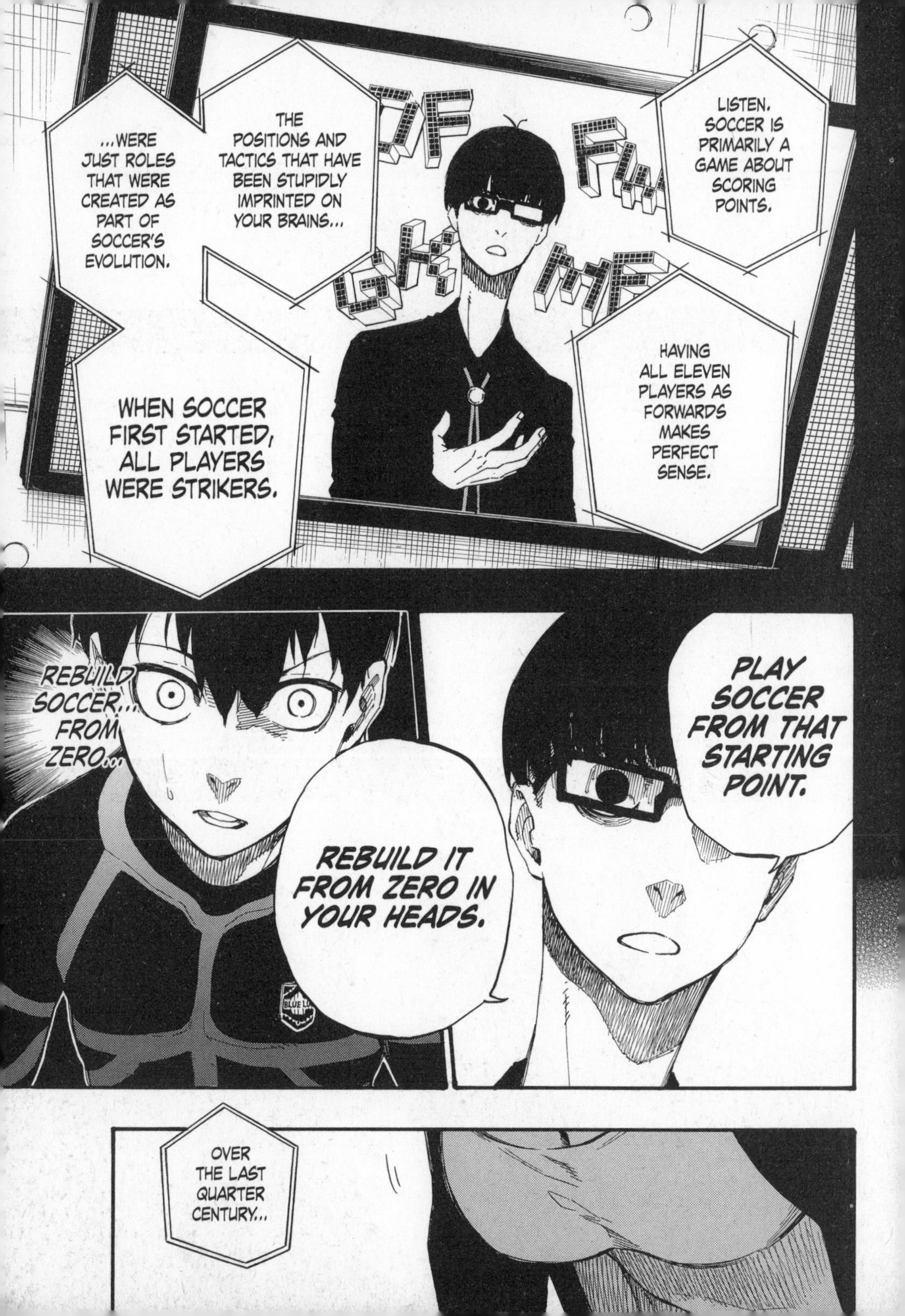
LISTEN. SOCCER IS PRIMARILY A GAME ABOUT SCORING POINTS.
HAVING ALL ELEVEN PLAYERS AS FORWARDS MAKES PERFECT SENSE.
DF
FW
GK
MF
THE POSITIONS AND TACTICS THAT HAVE BEEN STUPIDLY IMPRINTED ON YOUR BRAINS...
...WERE JUST ROLES THAT WERE CREATED AS PART OF SOCCER'S EVOLUTION.
WHEN SOCCER FIRST STARTED, ALL PLAYERS WERE STRIKERS.
PLAY SOCCER FROM THAT STARTING POINT.
REBUILD IT FROM ZERO IN YOUR HEADS.
REBUILD SOCCER... FROM ZERO...
OVER THE LAST QUARTER CENTURY...

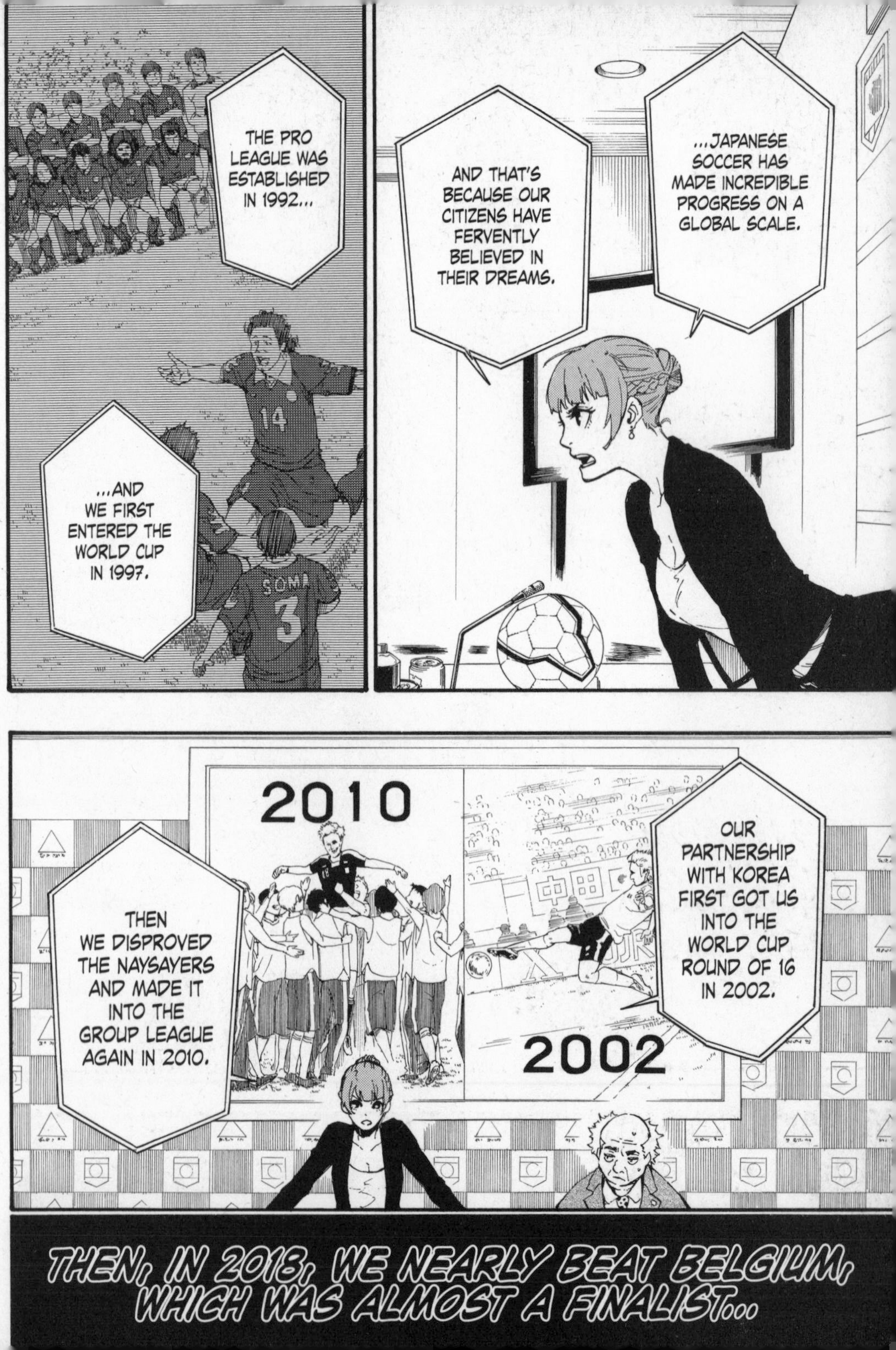
...JAPANESE SOCCER HAS MADE INCREDIBLE PROGRESS ON A GLOBAL SCALE.
AND THAT'S BECAUSE OUR CITIZENS HAVE FERVENTLY BELIEVED IN THEIR DREAMS.
THE PRO LEAGUE WAS ESTABLISHED IN 1992...
...AND WE FIRST ENTERED THE WORLD CUP IN 1997.
OUR PARTNERSHIP WITH KOREA FIRST GOT US INTO THE WORLD CUP ROUND OF 16 IN 2002.
2002
2010
THEN WE DISPROVED THE NAYSAYERS AND MADE IT INTO THE GROUP LEAGUE AGAIN IN 2010.
THEN, IN 2018, WE NEARLY BEAT BELGIUM, WHICH WAS ALMOST A FINALIST...

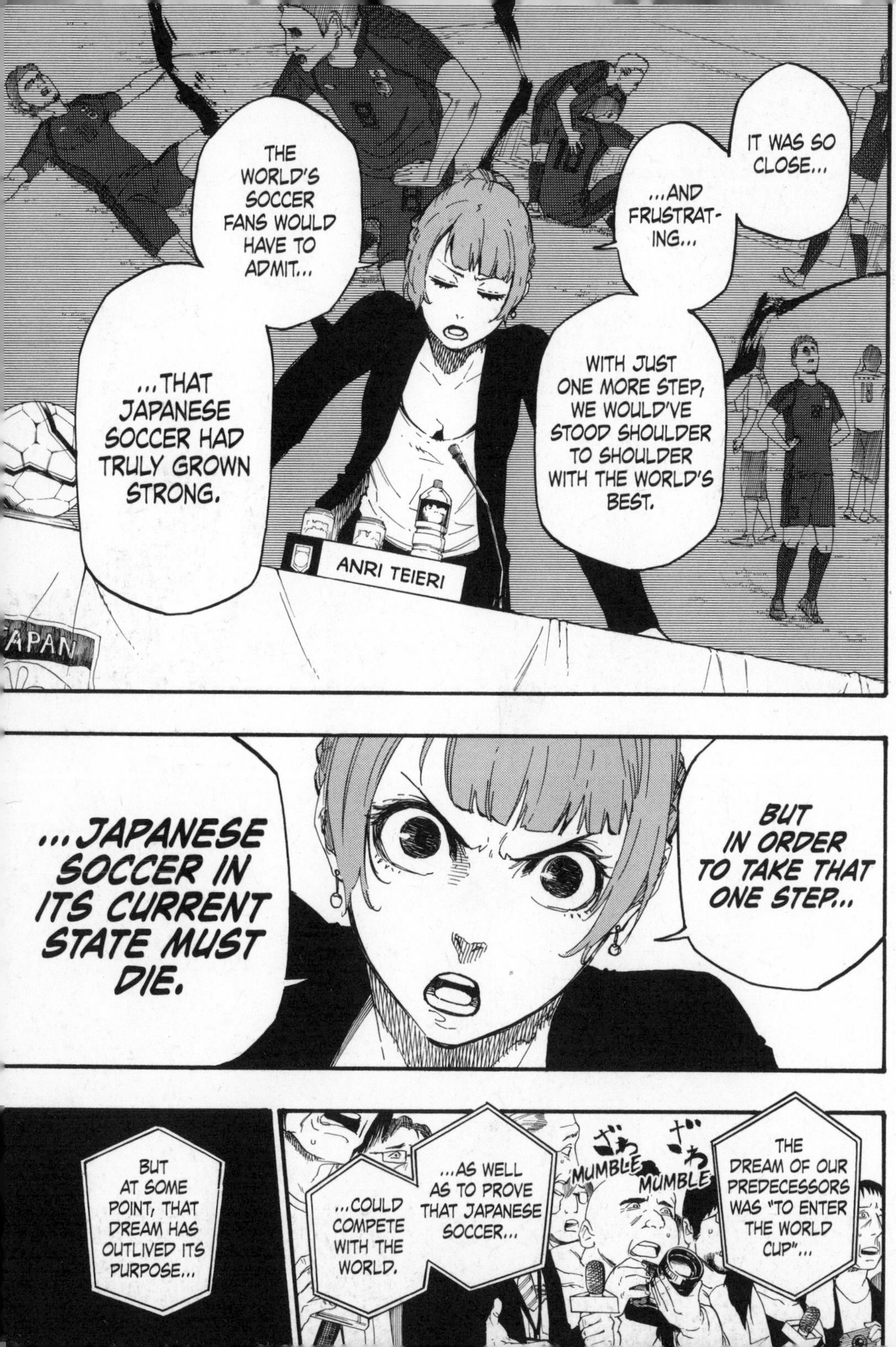
IT WAS SO CLOSE...
...AND FRUSTRATING...
WITH JUST ONE MORE STEP, WE WOULD'VE STOOD SHOULDER TO SHOULDER WITH THE WORLD'S BEST.
THE WORLD'S SOCCER FANS WOULD HAVE TO ADMIT...
...THAT JAPANESE SOCCER HAD TRULY GROWN STRONG.
ANRI TEIERI
APAN
BUT IN ORDER TO TAKE THAT ONE STEP...
...JAPANESE SOCCER IN ITS CURRENT STATE MUST DIE.
THE DREAM OF OUR PREDECESSORS WAS "TO ENTER THE WORLD CUP"...
ざわ MUMBLE
ざわ MUMBLE
...AS WELL AS TO PROVE THAT JAPANESE SOCCER...
...COULD COMPETE WITH THE WORLD.
BUT AT SOME POINT, THAT DREAM HAS OUTLIVED ITS PURPOSE...

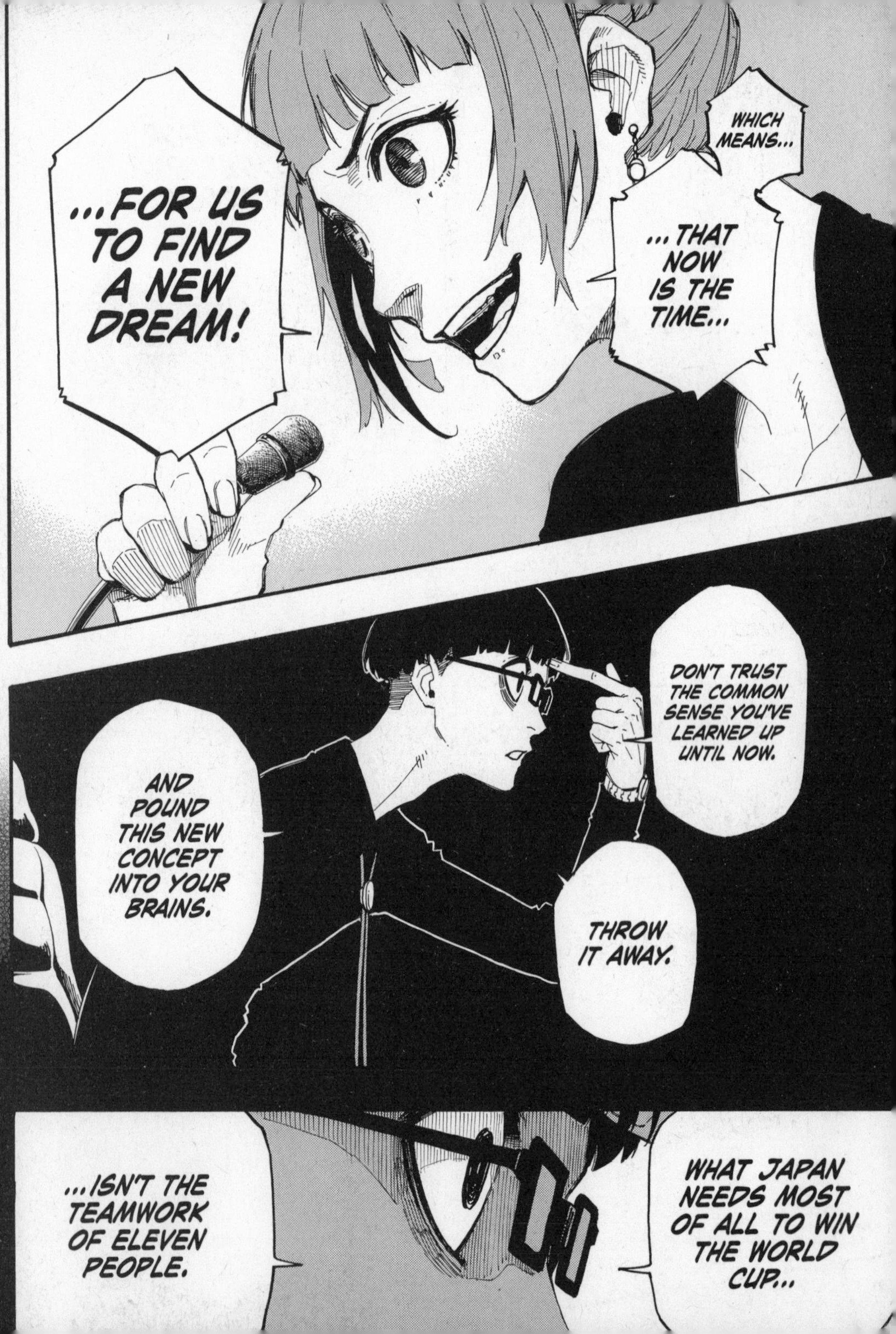
WHICH MEANS...
...THAT NOW IS THE TIME...
...FOR US TO FIND A NEW DREAM!
DON'T TRUST THE COMMON SENSE YOU'VE LEARNED UP UNTIL NOW.
THROW IT AWAY.
AND POUND THIS NEW CONCEPT INTO YOUR BRAINS.
WHAT JAPAN NEEDS MOST OF ALL TO WIN THE WORLD CUP...
...ISN'T THE TEAMWORK OF ELEVEN PEOPLE.

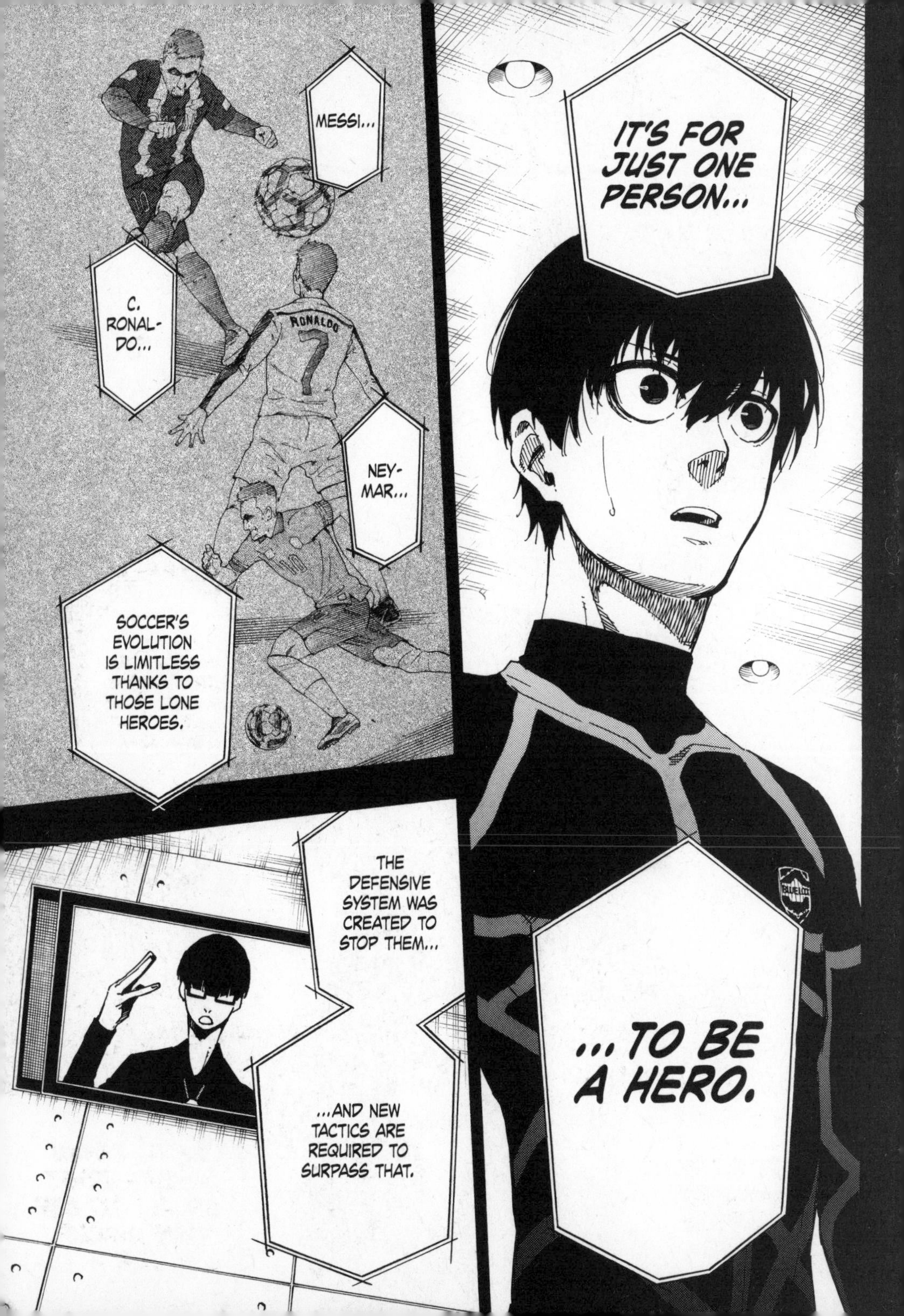
IT'S FOR JUST ONE PERSON...
...TO BE A HERO.
MESSI...
C. RONAL-DO...
RONALDO 7
NEY-MAR...
SOCCER'S EVOLUTION IS LIMITLESS THANKS TO THOSE LONE HEROES.
THE DEFENSIVE SYSTEM WAS CREATED TO STOP THEM...
...AND NEW TACTICS ARE REQUIRED TO SURPASS THAT.

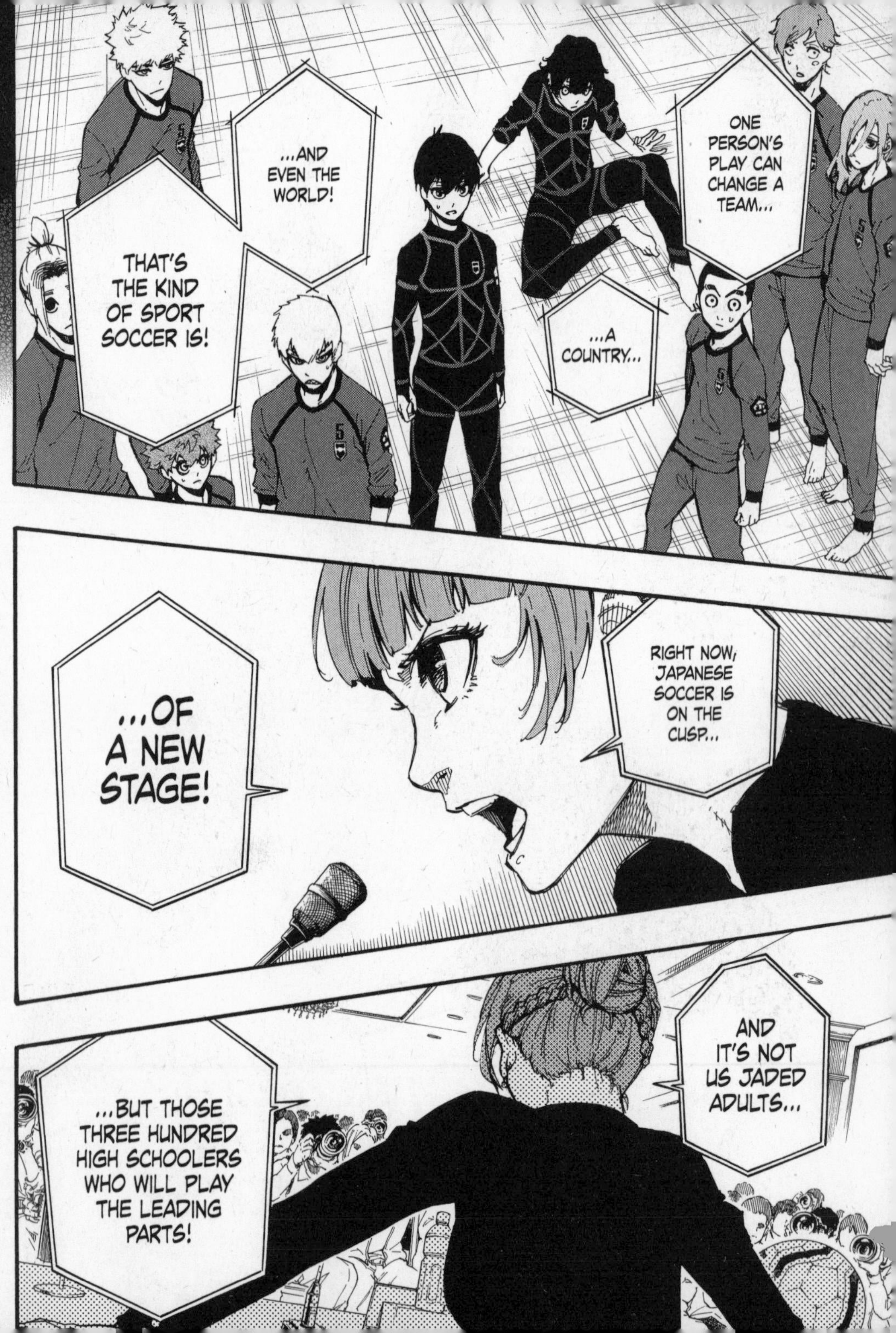
ONE PERSON'S PLAY CAN CHANGE A TEAM...
...A COUNTRY...
...AND EVEN THE WORLD!
THAT'S THE KIND OF SPORT SOCCER IS!
RIGHT NOW, JAPANESE SOCCER IS ON THE CUSP...
...OF A NEW STAGE!
AND IT'S NOT US JADED ADULTS...
...BUT THOSE THREE HUNDRED HIGH SCHOOLERS WHO WILL PLAY THE LEADING PARTS!

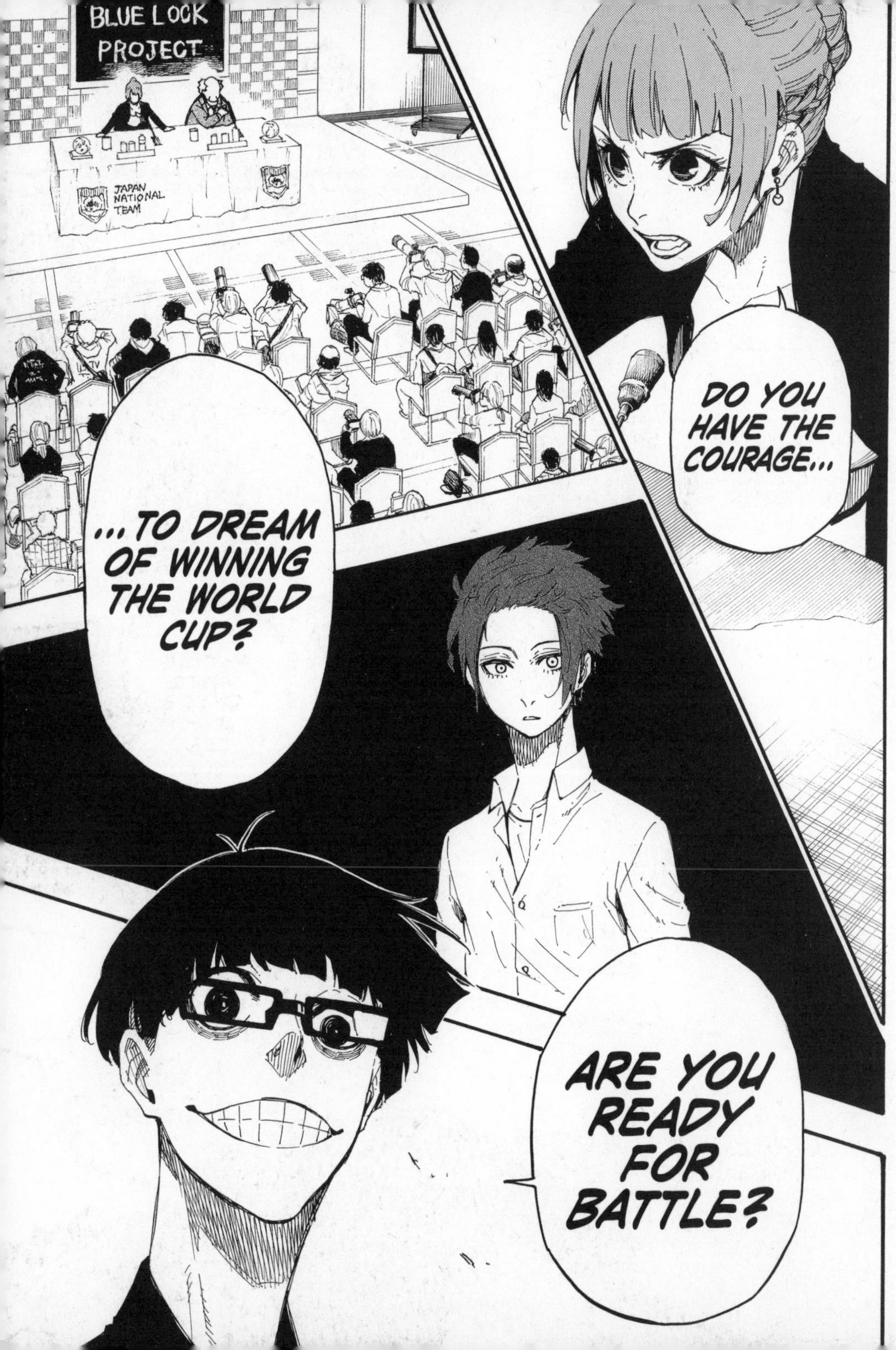
DO YOU HAVE THE COURAGE...
BLUE LOCK PROJECT
JAPAN NATIONAL TEAM
...TO DREAM OF WINNING THE WORLD CUP?
ARE YOU READY FOR BATTLE?

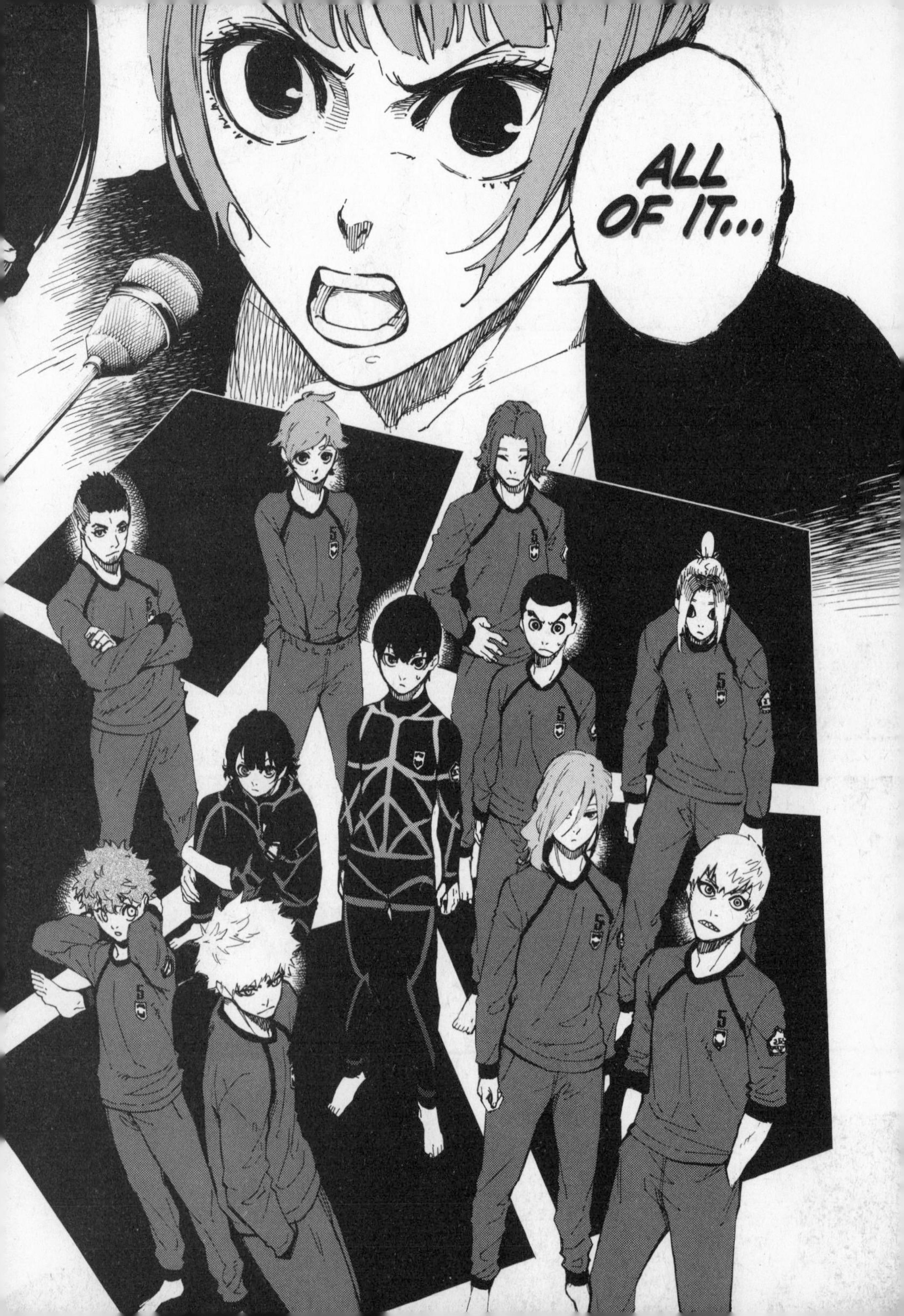
ALL OF IT...

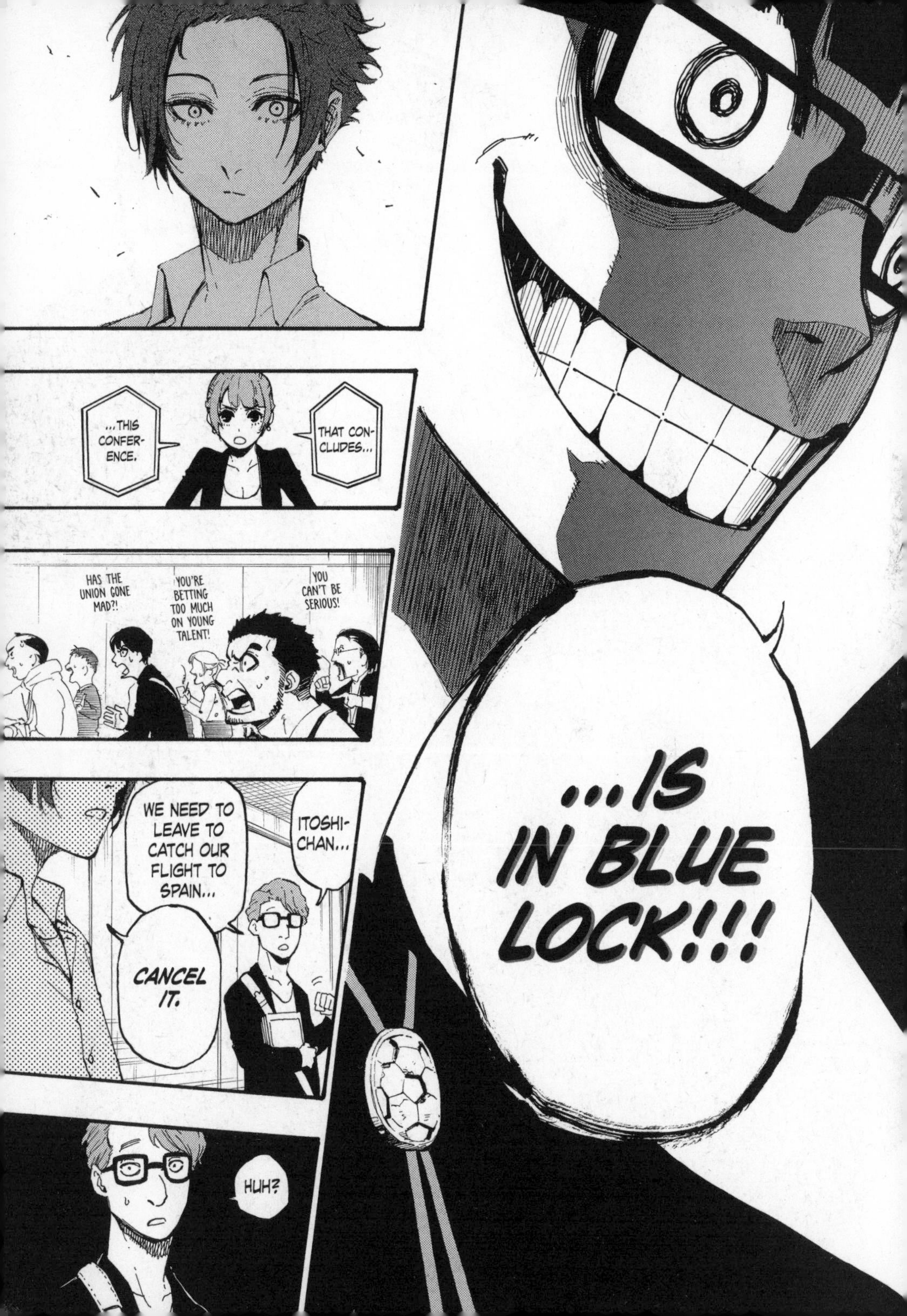
...IS IN BLUE LOCK!!!
THAT CONCLUDES...
...THIS CONFERENCE.
YOU CAN'T BE SERIOUS!
YOU'RE BETTING TOO MUCH ON YOUNG TALENT!
HAS THE UNION GONE MAD?!
ITOSHI-CHAN...
WE NEED TO LEAVE TO CATCH OUR FLIGHT TO SPAIN...
CANCEL IT.
HUH?

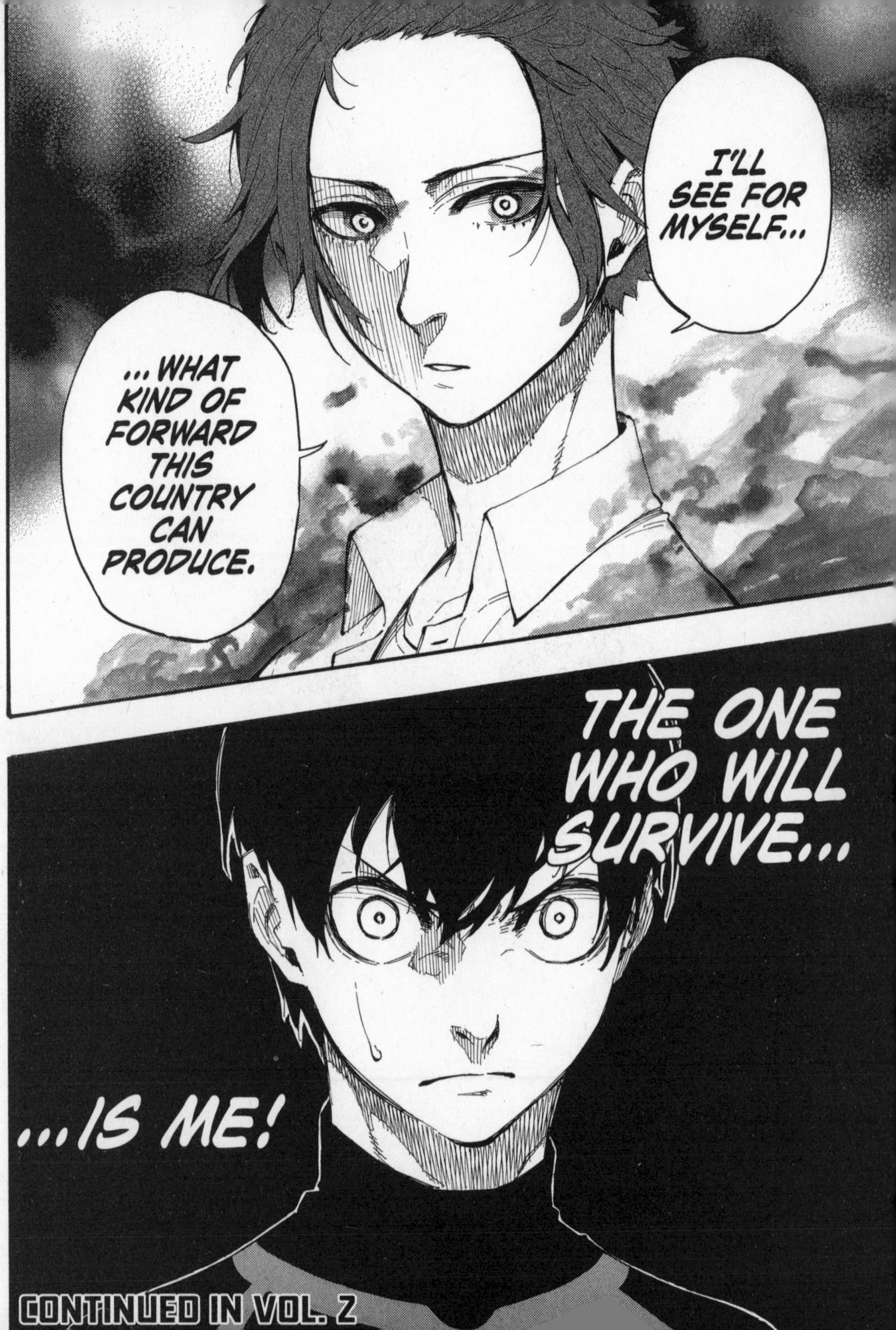
I'LL SEE FOR MYSELF...
...WHAT KIND OF FORWARD THIS COUNTRY CAN PRODUCE.
THE ONE WHO WILL SURVIVE...
...IS ME!
CONTINUED IN VOL. 2

Yusuke Nomura

"The first volume! For those who love soccer and for those who don't get it, I'll work hard so that everyone can enjoy it!"

Yusuke Nomura debuted in 2014 with the grotesquely cute cult hit alien invasion story *Dolly Kill Kill*, which was released digitally in English by Kodansha. Nomura is the illustrator behind *Blue Lock*.

Muneyuki Kaneshiro

"I love soccer. And I love manga. So, I dreamt up this story. I hope you enjoy it!"

Muneyuki Kaneshiro broke out as the creator of 2011's *As the Gods Will*, a death game story that spawned two sequels and a film adaptation directed by the legendary Takashi Miike. Kaneshiro writes the story of *Blue Lock*.

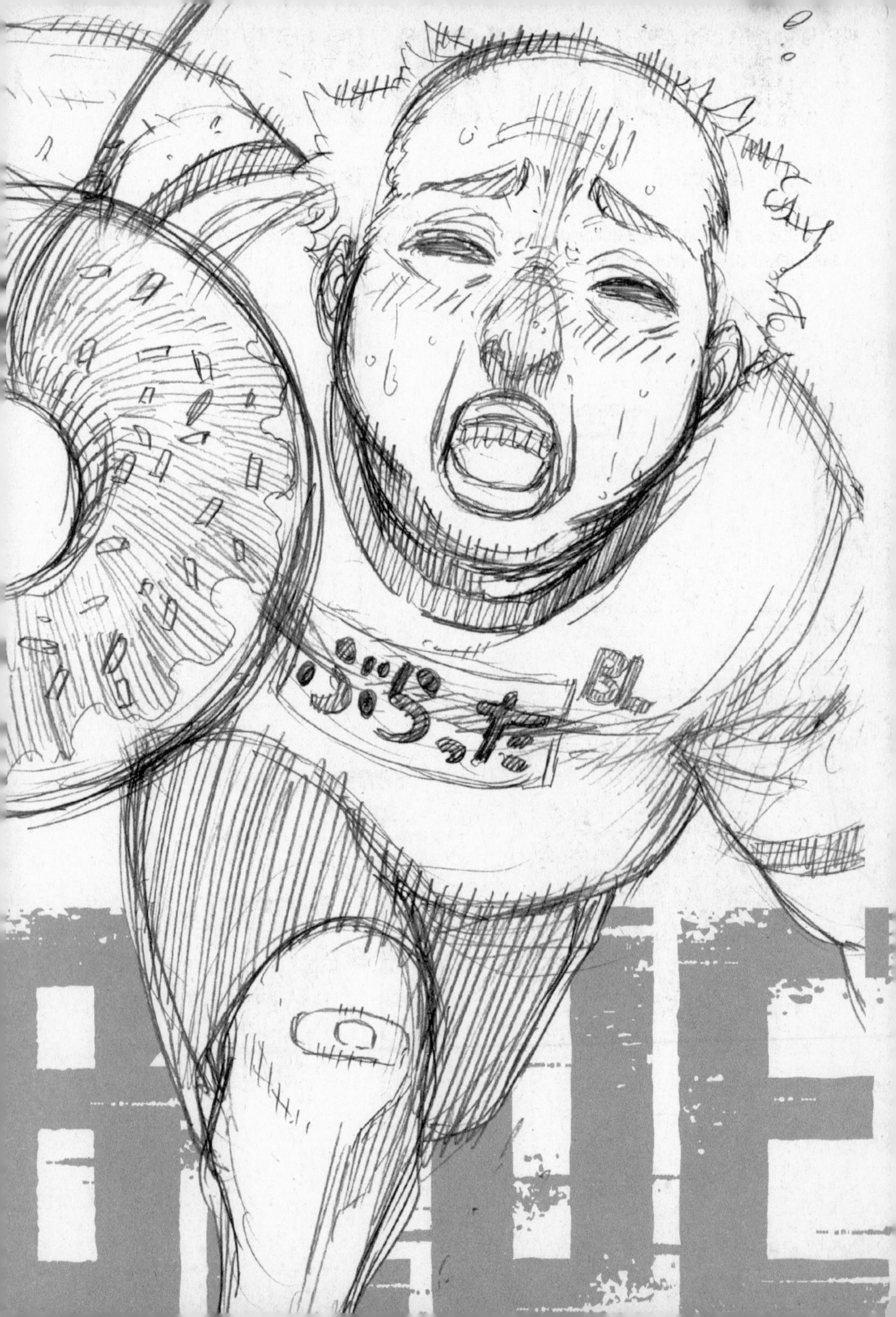

TRANSLATION NOTES

Maya Yoshida
page 9

Maya Yoshida is a famous Japanese player and Captain of the Japan National Team.

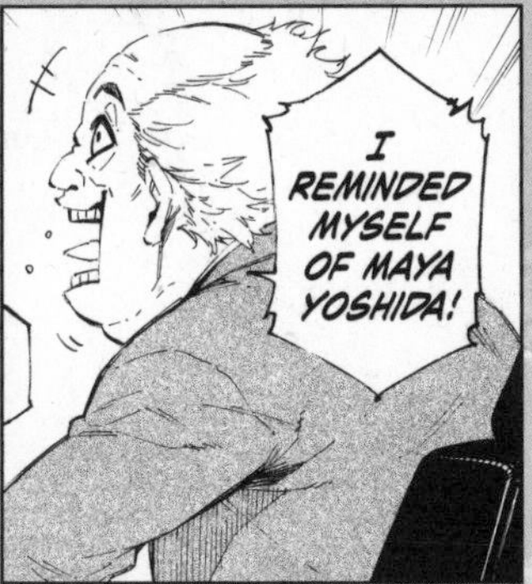
I REMINDED MYSELF OF MAYA YOSHIDA!

Tanuki
page 11

In the original Japanese, she calls the chairman a "tanuki", which is a raccoon dog. This can be an insult directed towards those with round faces who act childish.

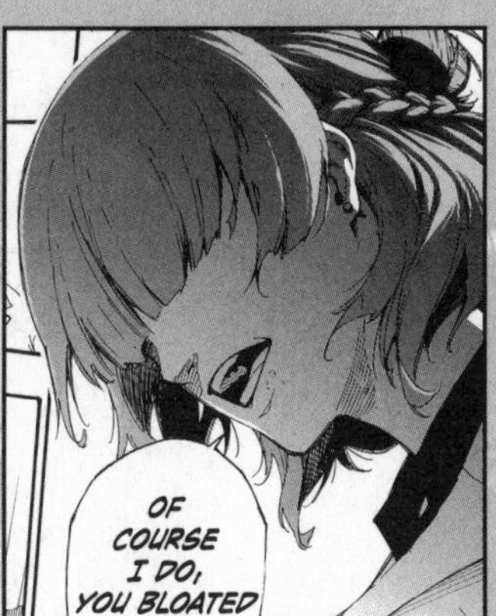
OF COURSE I DO, YOU BLOATED RODENT.

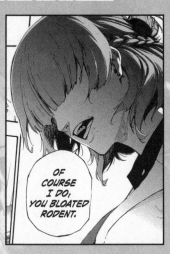

Third-years
page 27

Japanese high school have three grade levels, so a third-year student would be in their final year of high school.

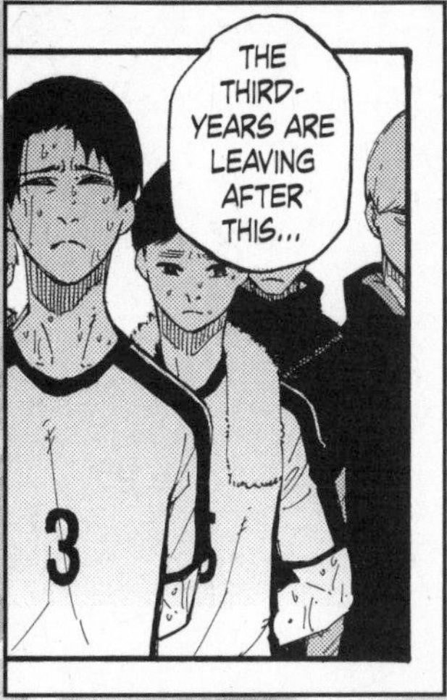
THE THIRD-YEARS ARE LEAVING AFTER THIS...
3

-sama
page 29

The suffix -sama to a name denotes high respect.

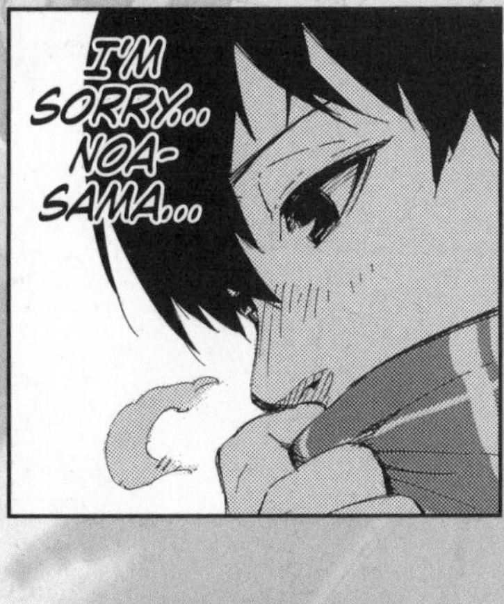
I'M SORRY... NOA-SAMA...

Goku and Krillin
page 32
Characters from the Dragon Ball series.

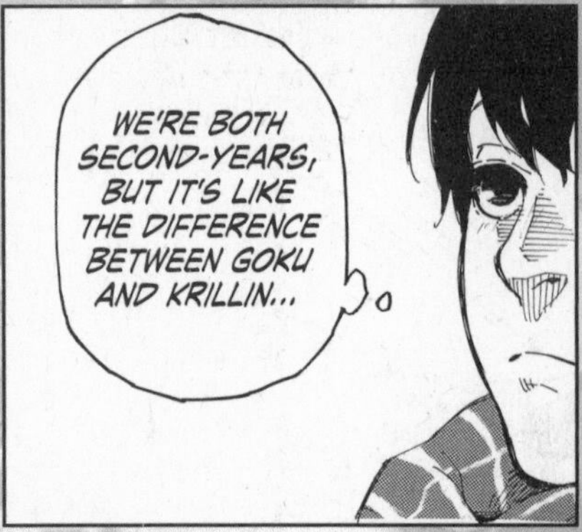
WE'RE BOTH SECOND-YEARS, BUT IT'S LIKE THE DIFFERENCE BETWEEN GOKU AND KRILLIN...

Pork cutlets
page 38
Eating pork cutlets, or tonkatsu in Japanese, ahead of a test or a sports match is a modern tradition for Japanese students. This is because "katsu" is a homophone of the verb "katsu", meaning "to win." Unfortunately, Yoichi's mother did not make this meal the day before the match.

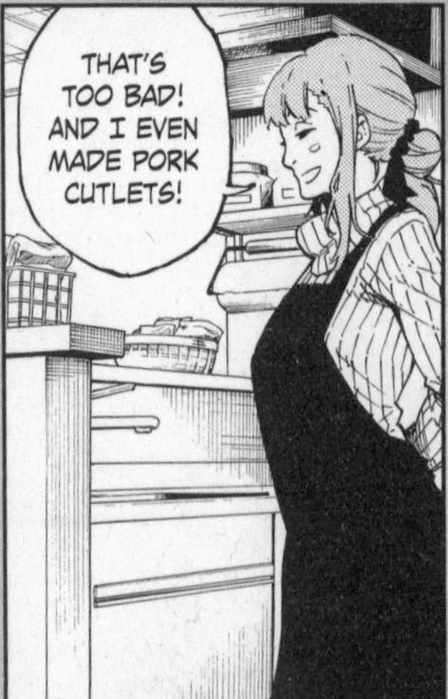
THAT'S TOO BAD! AND I EVEN MADE PORK CUTLETS!

"Messi of Aomori"
page 45
Argentinian soccer player Lionel Messi is considered one of the best soccer players in history. Aomori is a northern Japanese prefecture.

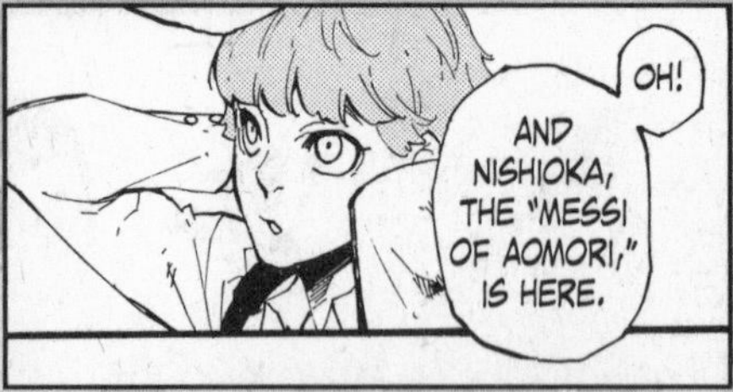
OH!
AND NISHIOKA, THE "MESSI OF AOMORI," IS HERE.

Kagawa, Honda
page 60
Ego lists the names of famous Japanese soccer players Keisuke Honda and Shinji Kagawa, who both play for the Japan National Team. They were both on teams that made it to the World Cup in the 2010s but did not win the championship.

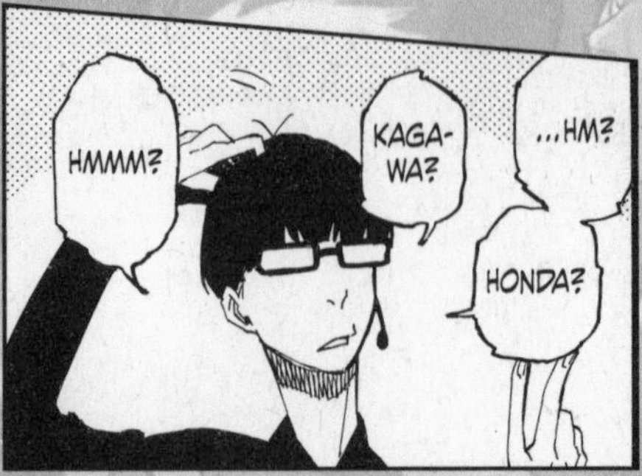
...HM?
HONDA?
KAGA-WA?
HMMM?

Zico
page 93
Zico is the nickname for Arthur Coimbra, a Brazilian soccer coach and former midfielder. He is widely regarded as the greatest Brazilian player to never win the World Cup.

Homage to the Three Treasures

page 105

A translation of the Japanese "Namusan" [南無三], this term is used as a call for refuge in Buddhism and is a prayer performed at the beginning of the day or before a practice session. The Three Treasures [or Three Jewels] are Buddha, the Dharma, and the Sangha. It's also a phrase that can be used when the person is surprised or fails, similar to "Jesus Christ!"

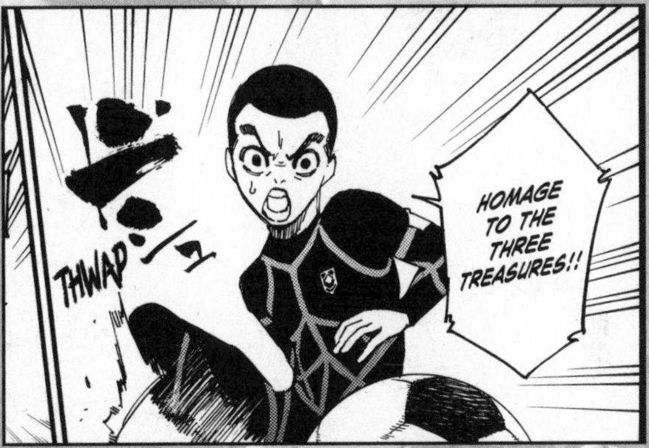
HOMAGE TO THE THREE TREASURES!!
THWAP

A Kodansha Trade Paperback Original

Blue Lock 1 copyright © 2018 Muneyuki Kaneshiro/Yusuke Nomura
English translation copyright © 2022 Muneyuki Kaneshiro/Yusuke Nomura

Published in the United States by
Kodansha USA Publishing, LLC, New York.

Publication rights for this English edition arranged through
Kodansha Ltd., Tokyo.

First published in Japan in 2018 by Kodansha Ltd., Tokyo
as *Buruu rokku*, volume 1.

ISBN 978-1-64651-654-4

Printed in the United States of America.

9 8 7 6 5 4

Translation: Nate Derr
Lettering: Chris Burgener
Additional lettering and layout: Scott O. Brown
Editing: Thalia Sutton, Maggie Le
YKS Services LLC/SKY JAPAN, Inc.
Kodansha USA Publishing edition cover design by Matthew Akuginow

Publisher: Kiichiro Sugawara

Director of Publishing Services: Ben Applegate
Director of Publishing Operations: Dave Barrett
Associate Director of Publishing Operations: Stephen Pakula
Publishing Services Managing Editors: Alanna Ruse, Madison Salters
Production Managers: Emi Lotto, Angela Zurlo

KODANSHA.US

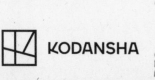

KODANSHA

DEC -- 2022